Sunday Morning, Shamwana

For Margaret,
Enjoy the Adventure!
Linda Disi Robinson

Sunday Morning, Shamwana

A Midwife's Letters from the Field

Linda Orsi Robinson

Pine Knoll Press

Pine Knoll Press
PO Box 418
Hulls Cove, Maine 04644

ISBN 978-0-9859350-0-9
Library of Congress   2012915365

Published in the USA by Pine Knoll Press 2012

Cover photo by Linda Robinson, Shamwana, February 2008
Author photo by Alexa Bonsey

Adinkra Symbol AYA "fern" symbol of endurance and
resourcefulness

For Beatrice and Gerardine

Shamwana means "land of the children." I had never heard of this place, a village in the center of The Congo, a mysterious and tortured country. I have always been drawn to Africa, possibly from watching Wild Kingdom as a child, but never imagined a village like this existed. I ended up there because I told Doctors Without Borders I was willing to go anywhere my skills were needed. A feeling of hopelessness had engulfed me stemming in part from the overwhelming tragedies of the world so readily displayed in our daily life and partly from my frustration with my own country's democracy–which didn't seem democratic to me anymore. I was also completely disgusted with our own medical system and wanted to get away. I wanted adventure and a feeling that what I was doing actually mattered. I wanted to take care of people who truly needed what I could give.

I had skills to offer. I had thirty years of experience as a nurse and a nurse-midwife, I had worked abroad in the Peace Corps in Malawi, Africa then in American Samoa. I felt I was a good candidate. My five children were grown, I was single, having gone through a painful period of abandonment and divorce, and the tiny hospital in rural Maine where I had been employed for fifteen years was willing to give me a year leave of absence. The stars all lined up. I was meant to do this.

Doctors Without Borders (*Medecins Sans Frontiers [MSF]*) is an organization I always admired. They started in France by a group of French journalists and doctors who were frustrated with the political decisions made by international aide agencies. The more I looked into their philosophy, both financially and politically, the more I thought this was the organization I wanted to work with. Because of their neutrality on political issues, they go into areas other non-governmental organizations (NGOs) don't. Often these are areas of conflict. The screening process is rigorous and their standards are high. I loved it.

My leave of absence was the deciding factor for the location I would be sent. I had one year, September 2007 until September 2008. I needed an assignment that would fit within those dates. I was willing to go anywhere, no matter what the danger. The Congo in the village of Shamwana was the fit. I needed to speak French since it was the national language there. My French, learned in school and used only while traveling in France and Quebec, was very basic. The assignment confirmation came in July and I had until the first of September to prepare. I worked hard to improve my skills in those two months. I also tried to learn as much about The Congo as I could, but trying to get my house and job ready to leave and focusing on the language, didn't leave me much time for studying. I learned a lot when I got there.

I left behind my five children and elderly mother. They were not thrilled about me taking off like this, but I assured them I would write every Sunday and somehow get the letters to them. I was so focused and intent on this experience that I met their concerns with the following rationale: "If you were hiding and being hunted in the bush, if your entire family had been killed in front of you, if you had nothing to eat, wouldn't you be hoping someone was coming to help? I'm not asking you to come; I'm only asking that you take care of yourselves while I'm gone. That's your contribution. Let me do this."

The letters were originally sent to reassure family and friends that I was OK. They went by e-mail and over the year they took on a life of their own. They became an outlet for me to express some frustration and use my native language. They became a survival tool for me. I tried to give a realistic picture of what life was like there without terrifying my mother. I kept a journal and wrote things I felt I couldn't include in the weekly letter. Some of those passages are included in this book and give an idea of what was going on in my head. I've let the letters give the reader the history I learned about how this poor country and its wonderful people have existed despite what seems to be the world's intent on eliminating them. I have included the stories about living on the team with its many frustrations and hopefully show the trials and triumphs of such an experience. I have changed the names and minor details in order to protect their privacy.

These letters were written in real time. Each time I go over them and prepare them for publication I think I sound insensitive and downright mean sometimes. I have not eliminated these passages (though was tempted) because they were a product of intense frustration and fatigue. That is a very real part of the experience.

Linda Robinson, August 2012

I know the exact moment I decided to do this. It was a Tuesday evening, mid-winter, and freezing cold. It was the last showing of *Hotel Rwanda* at Reel Pizza. I had wanted to see it and couldn't find anyone to go with. I was the only one in the theater and that oddity reinforced the loneliness I had been feeling for some time. I kept my coat on, still chilled from the walk from my office, and pondered the irony of the scene. Depressing movie ahead, depressed woman finding herself alone after twenty-five years of an enviable marriage ending suddenly *sans* explanation. The thought crossed my mind that it might have been a mistake to come. Everyone who had seen the movie told me they cried through the whole last half. I wasn't even sure if the theater would show it to only one person. I watched the previews and indulged in a bout of self-pity. "My life sucks," I thought. How on earth did I end up like this? I couldn't find a date. I was alone, lonely, and freezing cold. (Do they not turn the heat on for only one person?) Why do I do this to myself?

The movie started and I forgot where I was. Not long into it I thought, "No, Linda, your life does not suck. Their lives suck."

When the Red Cross worker jumped out of the Land Rover, unloaded shocked, terrified, hunted human beings, turned to me from her place on the screen, and said desperately, "I'll be right back with more," I looked at her and said, "I want to be you."

I left the theater a different woman. There was no decision left to be made. I had been thinking about this for a while now and this was it. I was going somewhere—I didn't care where—where my skills were acutely and desperately needed. There was something bigger I was supposed to be doing, and it was time to get on with it.

SUNDAY MORNING, SHAMWANA

PROLOGUE

Sunday morning
September 9

I am sitting on the back steps of guest house 3 (maison trois), having arrived in Lubumbashi yesterday sans baggage. I had no expectations really, though I was hoping luggage would arrive. Luggage. Baggage. I was hoping all my baggage would arrive. Hmm, I've spent several years trying to get my baggage to go away. Leave me in peace. What's in our baggage that we need so desperately? Clean underwear? We must be joking! Who really needs underwear? Why are we so attached to it? What do people have in their luggage anyway? What was in mine? I'm fine in these cotton pants and T-shirt for now. I'm not that upset about it. I'm surprising myself already.

The arrival at the airport was an adventure. The acclaimed Milan was not there, it being Saturday, but a feisty little driver whose name escapes me, was. Thank God he was identifiable by an MSF vest. My project coordinator, Therese, was also there returning from holiday in Holland. I was exhausted, and she seemed annoyed that my French wasn't better. I stupidly tried to reassure her in English that it was adequate, but anxiety was getting the better of me. After filling out the lost baggage forms and elbowing our way to the front of the throngs, we departed in an MSF Toyota Land Cruiser to the office where I started "briefings."

The first was from the financial coordinator where I got per diem cash in Congolese francs and $200 US in case of a hold-up. I was a little confused about this, and not wanting to appear overly anxiety-prone, didn't ask too many questions. They give us $200 in cash to carry at all times, so if someone wants to rob us, we have something to give them. Apparently the robbers don't believe you when you say you don't have any money, and then they kill you and discover you weren't lying. I asked how often this happens

- 5 -

(getting robbed), and the answer was, "Not often." I'm not sure what that vague answer meant in terms of actual statistics, but I'll carry the $200 and hope for the best, I guess. I wonder if we get to keep it if we don't get robbed.

So far the expats I've met are friendly enough, but seem burned out, frustrated, and a bit cynical. Mia, who takes care of the human resources, is bright and cheery but she has only been here two days. This guy Mark, from England, is very sour. He's drilling wells near Shamwana. I am not sure if he is here on R&R or just to complain, but he and Therese get on quite well. She seems to complain a bit herself. There is a logistician here who is quite nice. She is from France, on her way home after a three-month measles campaign. She is a bit cynical, but not as sour. I met the midwife from Kilwa. She is done with her contract and is apparently staying in Congo with the guy who was silently having breakfast with us this morning, but I am not sure of that either.

I feel a bit awkward. I sense that the expats don't want to have to deal with ANOTHER new person. But geez, this is how this is set up, so what am I supposed to do? Is this an orientation strategy? Weed out the weaklings? See how you can survive with hardly any information and barely a welcoming word?

The house is very basic—but fine. I have my own room with two twin beds, each with a mosquito net and room for nothing else. Guess it's a good thing my bags aren't here. My room is off the kitchen, so it's a tad noisy when the group makes late-night snacks. It's an odd place to come for R&R, not very restful. The field workers say it's more restful at their sites.

If I am to explore at all I will have to become more comfortable with the radio. I can't go anywhere without letting the base know. Walking is permitted during the day but not allowed at night. I am getting the feeling it is like living with parents that are too strict. Rather strange at this age.

Monday
September 10

Lubumbashi—Ah dear. There are lots and lots of people coming in and out here today. My luggage arrived though—very good thing. It's been more briefings today. Program. Information Technology. Health. In the morning meeting I was expected to say something. I wish I had known and could have prepared something nice to say in French. You'd have thought Therese would have given me a heads-up. I am really looking forward to getting to Shamwana. I don't know what to expect, but I need to get away from all the English speakers to have a prayer of getting better in French. I have tried a little here, but it is awkward. Everyone is nice enough, I guess. I am getting more comfortable with Mark and Therese. We went to lunch yesterday, then out for drinks and dinner together, and that was good. (In the restaurant they had to bring a box with the check to put all the cash into. It's 500 Congolese francs to a dollar, and a 500-note is their largest note. It would be comical if it weren't so pathetic.) It's going to be fine but I've got to get going with the French. In a way, it makes it easier for me to do the briefings in English, but if they were in French, I'd be forced to think in French already. I am a tad nervous about that. I hate looking like an idiot. I have a hard time remembering everyone's names. I've met a thousand new people today and they all know each other. I'm consumed with that awful left-out feeling.

I've heard many, many times how much work it is. How hard everyone works. I am starting to wonder what that means. So far it looks like people aren't wasting away. I am starting to regret that extra five pounds I put on before I left. That may have been bogus advice. From what I hear, the women gain weight and the men lose. Just like college, just like Peace Corps. I am really glad to be here, though. (I realize I keep telling myself that.) It is not going to be the drama it was made out to be. I think it will be more comfortable than I was expecting. Plane once a week, plenty of food, bucket showers, river water to drink (a little leery about that), my own room. But someone on the team snores, I hear. Badly. That's not good.

We are not allowed to take photos in Lubumbashi but I wish I could. The streets are a chaotic mass of dilapidated vehicles with travelers hanging out of open doors. These are punctuated with pristine, oversized SUVs from various Non-Governmental Organizations (NGOs) with solitary occupants. Crazy!

September 13–Thursday

Lubumbashi–I am still here. No flight until tomorrow. I feel a little lonely and bored and nervous about ever being good enough in French. And here I sit for two more days. I haven't ventured out, even to take a walk. It's not because I am afraid to go out and walk, but because I don't want to have to explain in French on that damn radio where I am going.

This makes two days sitting in this enclosed place watching the Congolese work around me. It's very odd. The house has a small yard surrounded by a twelve-foot wall with coils of barbed wire along the top. Actually, now that I look closer, it's razor wire, very prison-like, seriously unwelcoming. Today one guy has whitewashed the entire surrounding wall, but stopped short of polishing the razor wire. Philip sits guard. Venice has cleaned the house and done all the laundry and laid it out on the grass to dry. Someone else has washed all the walks and driveway. I am not sure what else they are all doing. I feel lazy and unproductive. I collected basil seeds off the dried plant out back. Maybe I can grow basil and make pesto in Shamwana. The sky is a very pale blue. It's hot. But nice hot, I think. Summer hot. Pleasant-in-the-shade kind of hot.

Someone now washes the drips of the whitewash off the green metal door that allows cars to enter. His rag gets caught in the metal barbs. He has splatters of whitewash on his head. They stand out against his black, black skull. I wonder if he thinks I am supervising him when I am just watching.

I hardly ever have days like this where I sit and do nothing but read and write. Two are enough back to back. I wish I had the guts to go out and explore a little. I can't wait to get to Shamwana.

September 14–Shamwana

Finally I am here. It's amazing. Remote beyond belief. My own tukul. Wood oven. Kerosene fridge. Dead battery in the camera. Confusing computer. Strange juxtapositions. Food is pretty bad. Chain smokers. Cute pilot. Grassy runway. Clean sheets and mosquito nets. New pit-latrine. Rainy season coming. Night sounds.

September 15–Shamwana

I am starting to worry that I didn't bring enough pens. I can't remember where I packed them. My first night in Shamwana left me considering all the things I should have brought and the things I should have left at home. I didn't need this many skirts. I wish I had brought witch hazel and some pictures from home. I should have brought running shoes and a small clock. Maybe I can get that in Lubumbashi. I should have brought a memory stick—with instructions.

I discovered a small garden this morning. It made me very happy and hopeful. It's cool now in the very early morning. I sip tea with powdered milk. I think about what to write home. I can think of so many stories. I have limited time on the computer. I'll need time to write, and then time to figure out how to send a group e-mail. I WILL LEARN TO DO THIS!

I sit under the mango tree, happy to be alone for a bit and collect my wits. I slept great last night. I can do this. I can live here for a year and do some good, I think. I hope. It feels very right to be here, very right. I am definitely where I am supposed to be, I am sure of that.

Village sounds are all around me. The team is still asleep—Dutch, English, French, Italian, Canadian, German, and me. American. That's the team. Babies are crying. There is a rhythmic drumbeat, but as I listen I think it's more likely a woman pounding cassava into flour. Roosters are crowing. There is a cool breeze. Earlier there was a radio playing music. I don't have a clock, but it wasn't light yet.

I need to learn to greet in the local language. Two Congolese, one man, one woman, walk by me. We greet in French. She takes a broom and starts sweeping the clay earth that has produced all these bricks for the house, the office, the tukuls. The roofs are thatched. The man is the cook. He starts cleaning up the mess left from the Europeans the night before. I am watching him collect water to wash the dishes. There are beer bottles on the table. I have forgotten his name. I met him yesterday. He is so respectful. I need another cup of tea. I'll write like this each morning—I think—then write on the computer once a week. I can do this. I need to capture this.

Bienvenu. His name is Bienvenu. She is Nasila. He has just told me this.

I can't find more tea. I'm drinking milky weak instant coffee now.

CHAPTER 1 ~ SEPTEMBER

September 16, 2007
Sunday Morning~Shamwana

Dear Friends,

It's been two weeks since I left home, and I feel like I've been dropped into a void between several different worlds, none of which I fit into very well. I sit in front of one of our five laptop-computers, the only one capable of sending e-mails. Since all the other ex-patriots on my team seem to have been born with a laptop in their diaper bag, they want to be on it all the time and can, at lightning speed, do all sorts of fancy things; it's a bit of a competition. I have discovered that early Sunday morning is unclaimed, so I guess that will be my time to write a long letter. When my flagging confidence is a little stronger, maybe I'll elbow my way in at other times, but until then I'll take advantage of the age difference between me and my teammates and get up early on our only day off.

It took me ten days to get to Shamwana. After the marathon-moving weekend over Labor Day, I had my New York briefing where I got my visa, signed contracts, checked insurance information, and left that night for Amsterdam. There, it was a day and a half of more briefings, more specifics for the organization and, finally, for the Congo, but only one of the people I spoke to had actually been here. The medical director for my section visited here for planning purposes and painted a pretty bleak picture for me. It was a bit surreal, though. I was jet-lagged, still exhausted from getting out of Bar Harbor, too nervous about finding my way around Amsterdam to even find the office from my hotel, which (due to some international conference in the city) was miles from downtown.

I went from office to office collecting papers, identification, and instructions for travel. Then I was handed a bunch of mail to carry and two small packages. They gave me a voucher for a shuttle to the airport, thank God, because shlepping all this stuff was ridiculous. Then it was overnight (the same night as the briefings) to Nairobi, one hour there to catch a flight to Harere, then on to Lubumbashi. I had a moment of anxiety in Amsterdam checking my luggage when the airport person weighing and checking my bags said, "Lubumbashi?

Hmmmm, I've never heard of it. Oh well, I'll check them through."
At that point I was sure I'd never see them again.

Oh my God, the airport in Lubumbashi. Think basement of some inner-city school built in the forties. No upkeep. Crowded. People pushing and shoving, languages I couldn't recognize, being funneled toward the immigration window, which looked like the token booth in some dark corner of the Boston subway back when I was in college. I had been told not to go through immigration until someone from MSF met me there, so tried to get out of this crowd when I noticed two other *mzungus* (white people) trying to do the same thing. We gravitated toward each other, and all said, "Are you with MSF?" possibly realizing simultaneously that that would be the ONLY reason we would be there.

We huddled together, trying to keep our carry-on bags from getting swept away in the crowd, when two Congolese men with MSF vests found us. One was with the Spain office and swept away the young doctor from Germany. The other was from the Holland office and Therese, a Dutch project coordinator, and I went off with him. Turns out Therese and I are on the same team. He took our passports, visa, mission letter, and some money and went–I don't know where. Meanwhile, we waited for our luggage, which never came. Well, one of Therese's came; neither of mine did.

While we were waiting, she lit up a cigarette, took a big drag and blew the smoke out of the corner of her mouth, a gesture of courtesy, since the alternative was blowing it right in my face. Then she said in the tone of an eighth-grade bully, "So, you are the new midwife. How's your French? Most Americans can't speak it very well." And I thought, "Everything I brought with me for a year is lost, I've been up for six nights in a row, the awful realization is sinking in that I am going to be living with a smoker, and now all my insecurities about the language are going to be made public."

She was Pontius Pilate. I wondered how I could get back on that plane before it went back to Nairobi. I managed a weak lie in a timid voice, "It's fine."

Well, it's not "fine" and it didn't take long for that to be obvious. I'm having a really hard time understanding the Congolese accent. At first I couldn't even recognize it as French. I thought they were speaking Swahili. Every time the driver said something, Therese would look at me and ask, "Did you understand that?" It was an obvious test, and I was obviously failing. I understood nothing. Not the language, not the reason for her being so cruel, not why I had chosen to put myself in this position. I started to panic.

I'm not allowed to take pictures in Lubumbashi for security reasons, but it's a pity. I'm not sure I can adequately describe it. First, the dust–it's what I pictured the dust bowl to be like. It is the dry season, so I guess this will change next month when the rains come, but one sees the whole city through a terra cotta screen of dust hovering above the buildings (which are mostly one-story, and all have broken windows). It has a Wild West feeling. Or would if the cars, which are going every which way, were stagecoaches. It took me a while to figure out which side of the road they drive on, because it doesn't seem to matter.

I spent six uncomfortable nights in Lubumbashi at the house designated for field workers passing through. It is called the *maison de passage*. It was filled with unfriendly and inconsiderate field workers from various European countries. I seemed to be an annoyance to them. (And for all of you who were worried about stray gunfire or malaria, my biggest health risk is lung cancer from all the second-hand smoke. Jesus. Chain smokers? What year is this?) To quell my rising panic I tried to focus on the positive. There were no mosquitoes. There were no cockroaches, either. It seems like the war has killed everything here.

I then had three days of briefings. Information about security, the computers, the set-up in Shamwana and the goals here (finally!), do's and don'ts while on R&R in Lubumbashi, all delivered by differently accented people with varying degrees of English proficiency. Every French word I had ever learned exited my brain. There is so much technology I have to learn and I hate it. I hate having to use this radio (which is all crackly) in French, so found myself glommed on to Therese and Mark like a barnacle. I kept apologizing, but tagged along with them anyway. They must get so sick of new people coming and going all the time. I felt trapped in that house with the surrounding wall topped with coils of barbed wire, being unable to go anywhere without a driver and a radio I couldn't use because I couldn't remember any French. Overwhelming anxiety consumed me.

The briefing with the information technology person at the office scared the crap out of me. He showed me a laptop, how to dust it carefully, and warned me never, ever to change the screensaver (he said this as you would tell someone never, ever to drink battery acid). I wanted to tell him I couldn't change a screensaver if my life depended on it, but wasn't sure if this would reassure him or terrify him, so I just nodded obediently and said, "No, of course, I'll never do that." Drugged-out Mai Mai soldiers and poisonous snakes don't come close to provoking this kind of fear in me.

It's been twenty-six years since I've been in Africa and, though it was a different country, and this one is very fresh post-war, not much has changed. People in the city with cell phones, that's new. But the villages are startlingly the same. I'm finding it both reassuring and tragic. When I stop worrying about what I'll be doing for work, and about living up to everyone's expectations, I find myself glad to be back. It feels comfortable and familiar. The people of Malawi (despite all their suffering and hardships when I was in Peace Corps there) were warm, effusive, welcoming people. So happy you were there. But their country was not at war. Here, the sadness of the people is palpable. Everything has been destroyed. The roads are destroyed, the economy, the health care system, mail system . . . all gone. And I'm not with Peace Corps; I have to get used to that.

With them, we lived in a village, ate with our counterparts, visited their houses. This is very different. I sense an us-and-them mentality. I'm in Shamwana now, hard to imagine a more remote place on this earth, and the Europeans are living very separately. There is a grass fence around our compound. It's called a "base." There is a village just on the other side of the grass fence. I can hear the babies crying at night, the radio in the morning, women pounding cassava root into flour, chanting and singing, and I woke my first morning here feeling like I was on the wrong side of the fence.

I have a lot to adjust to (uh oh, the first of the computer snatchers has arrived. I'm standing my ground for the time being.) My team is young. Therese (Dutch) is Project Coordinator. She is thirty-eight and has been in Liberia before this. The doctor, Carila, originates from Indonesia but grew up in Canada. She's twenty-nine, speaks fluent French, English, computer, statistics, and is probably a concert pianist, too–smart ,smart, smart. Stefano is Italian, I don't know his age, but looks late twenties. He is a water-sanitation person, doesn't speak very good French or English (and I'm not sure about his Italian—he doesn't speak much at all). Perrin is the logistician; he's French but speaks excellent English. He looks about sixteen. Nina is the midwife I will be replacing. She's German, twenty-eight, and absolutely lovely. She speaks great French, but has reassured me that for the first three months here she was "lost" so "not to worry." I am still worried.

Agna, also German, is the nurse, thirty-four, and is leaving this week. Her replacement hasn't arrived yet, which everyone is upset about. Man, I feel sorry for that new nurse; I can't imagine coming in here without someone to orient me. And she'd better not depend on me. Angelien, whom I haven't met yet, is the psychologist. She's currently on vacation in Kenya. She's also Dutch. They tell me she's my age, and that I'll get along great with her (they also tell me she snores). Everything I tell them about myself they say, "You and Angelien are going to get along great." I can't wait until she returns.

Congo is huge. Just my district, Katanga, is the size of Spain. I am nowhere near the current fighting in the Kivus. It's as if I were in Madrid and the fighting was happening in Norway. This district was the site of the bizarre Mai Mai rebel chief Gideon who, without apparent ideology, just wiped out entire villages. It really wasn't a part of the civil war (another horror story) but a madman with a gang just raping and pillaging. Entire villages were burned: cattle, fields, just everything destroyed. He (Gideon) was caught last year and I don't know exactly what they did with him, but there is rebuilding going on here from the ground up. The small buildings are made from local bricks made in the village. Cement has been brought in seventy miles from the nearest source by bicycle. Really! People brought the cement by bicycle seventy miles!

The one functioning building at the hospital is split between delivery room (about ten feet by fifteen feet) and the operating room (just a little bigger). The delivery room has two small windows with wooden shutters that close and lock from the inside. The operating room has two small windows that are nailed shut. They now have a battery-powered light above the operating table, but initially they were doing surgery by flashlight. There is a series of tents set up for intensive care, internal medicine, and postpartum. There is also an open area with a thatched roof for patients' families to sleep. There is a lot of building going on now over there: a lab and pharmacy are going up, and they are building a new operating room. The hospital complex is about a hundred yards from our "base" and the new buildings consist of a brick shell with corrugated tin roof and cement floor. Delineated spaces out of the rain for sure, but no more than that.

The initial response to the crisis here has moved to the next stage. It will be to prepare the Ministry of Health to start delivering health care again and then MSF will leave. That won't be before next year though, so I will be here for the whole year. I'm told I'll be doing more training and less emergency response. Right now there are two *accoucheuses* at the hospital who have had two weeks of training doing deliveries. They are different from TBAs (traditional birth attendants, or *matrons* as they are called here) because they have had some formal training. In French, a delivery is an *accouchement*, so literally the *accoucheuses* are "deliverers." This is different from a *sage femme* (midwife or literally wise woman, with more formal training) and *matron* (no formal training).

I'm told that people here don't trust western medicine. It's very different from when I was in Malawi. Here, they've all been so traumatized, running and living in hiding for years, all really thin, and with a hollowness about them that a blind man could see. It's heartbreaking. At the medical meeting yesterday (in French) they said that the hospital had a fifty percent cesarean rate, which I found shocking. But I was told that women don't come to the hospital until they have been pushing for two days in the village and are completely obstructed. They arrive here by bicycle, which has bamboo sticks laid across as a stretcher, and the situation is already critical. So there is an effort to get everyone to come to the hospital to deliver, but how to go about that is being debated.

There are four outpost clinics with health centers many miles from here. Given what the hospital is like, I can't wait to see the outposts. Nina said she tried to get to each of them twice a month, but it was hard with the transportation problems and lack of roads. *Mon Dieu.*

This is way too long, and I have left so much out. I wish I could just write to you with pen and paper and have some way to get it to you, but lacking an actual mail delivery system, that isn't an option. I'll get better at this, and faster, I hope.

Thank you everyone for all the good wishes and help and gifts as I was leaving. You have buoyed me, and I don't want to let you down. Write to me. Oh! But don't send any attachments or pictures. That was another dire warning I got in Lubumbashi. You cannot send pictures or attachments to this computer, only text. It has something to do with the satellite connection. I think we have to pay for the amount sent or something. Ugh! More to learn!

Love you all! Linda

Je suis celibataire. Je suis la mere de cinq enfants. Je suis heureux etre ici. *(I am single. I am the mother of five children. I am happy to be here.)* I am practicing for the morning meeting tomorrow where all the new people have to present themselves. This thing about marital status is supposedly very important to announce. I am dreading that. I feel like such an idiot. What if I have to explain why I have five kids and am single? I don't know how to explain it in French!

I am such a stranger here–stranger to the village, stranger to the languages, stranger to the cultures (African and generation Xers), stranger to the technology. I am too anxious to look good and to fit in.

Stefano is drumming on a small djembe. It is probably seventy-four degrees. The guard has just brought the lanterns. Therese passes behind me wrapped in a towel heading for the shower. Mark left today for one of his drilling projects and I am glad not to have his frenetic negative energy around. He doesn't like Stefano's drumming. I love it. It is soothing. I like Stefano. He is very quiet, but sweet and thoughtful. I met the chef du village today. Therese presented me to him, a formality. We all walked together afterward to see the foundation of the school that is being built. I did rounds at the hospital today. Almost fainted. Couldn't stop gagging.

It's hot. I am drinking warm sweet tea with lime. Clouds were covering the sky this morning, and for a while it seemed like it might rain. It is two more weeks before the rains are expected. This would be early. Nina is mad. She had a spat with Therese. Tempers seem short, and everyone seems burned out. Therese seems to hate her job. If I don't get some exercise I feel like I will splatter. I feel pudgy and my pants are too tight.

I have been questioning whether this was the right thing for me to do. Did I come here just for my own ego? Am I making things worse? I wonder if I will ever be fluent enough in French to be effective. When I start down that path of doubt I get panicky. If other people can learn a language, then so can I! Why am I so stuck? There is a roadblock *between my brain and my mouth. In my head I can speak just fine. Why won't it come out my mouth?*

September 23, 2007
Sunday morning, Shamwana

Hi Everyone,

    Culture shock hit this week and I spent two days wanting to go home. *Really* wanting to go home. I'm having some ethical struggles, and I am desperately missing people I love. If I could talk it out, it would be so much easier to adjust, but I can't do that here. Maybe that's why I feel the need to write so much. It's my only outlet.

    I had originally been told (by outdated written information) that the only way in to Shamwana was by motorcycle. Well, things have changed a bit since that was written. MSF cleared a spot in the bush for a crude airstrip and the plane comes in once or twice a week. MSF hires the plane (it's not like it's on a regular flight pattern) so they decide who needs to get where and how often they feel it's necessary to pay for the plane to come in. It's an NGO airline that flies for other NGOs. So when MSF-Spain needed the plane to fly a group into the place where the Ebola outbreak occurred, I had to wait two days in Lubumbashi. Don't worry, I'm miles away from that outbreak; I don't want to add to anyone's anxieties. The worst that happened to me was a little boredom. Waiting, as I now well recall, is so much a part of African life.

    The plane is used to transport cargo as well as people, and depending on the weight of the cargo, it can carry eleven people. On this flight there were three of us, including the pilot, and a lot of cargo. I'm not nervous in planes, even small ones, but this flight was not for the queasy passenger. The pilot's name was Jason and he didn't even look old enough to have his learner's permit. He told me he's from Halifax and used to fly for Colgan Air, and he's apparently old enough to be on his second job. The day I flew was complicated logistically as we had a lot of cargo that had to go to another site first (where they were dealing with the remnants of a cholera outbreak). Then the plane had to go pick up more supplies at a different site for the cholera site which were too heavy to have in the plane along with me and Mark, who was heading to Shamwana to finish up the wells he was drilling. I didn't care where I flew or where I waited, I was just so happy to finally be getting out of that city. I climbed into the co-pilot's seat and Jason told me to put the earphones on so we could talk during the flight. Then he said with all seriousness, "Try not to use the controls when we are landing." I cracked up! As if I would try and land the plane in the African bush! (Though the chances of me doing that are far greater than me trying to change the screen saver on this laptop.) We left Lubumbashi on a real runway (paved and everything!), flew for an hour and a half, landed quite nicely, I thought, on a dirt runway, which we had to "sweep" first because there were so many people on it. I kid you not: we had to buzz the landing strip so all the people carrying wood on their heads would scatter like antelope to the side of the runway. Then we circled back and landed.

We got off the plane, unloaded the supplies for that site and got into the waiting Land Cruiser. The cargo for Shamwana was left sitting on the airstrip, while Jason flew alone to the other location to collect more. Bruno, a guy from Spain, was dealing with the cholera and took us to see the little village where he was staying. He was a one-man team there, as the outbreak was controlled and he was just closing the project. There was a little shell of a clinic there. I looked around and saw IV fluids and some medications, a box with bananas, and a water filter. Talk about bare bones. We went back to the airstrip, and the Land Cruiser swept it of people so Jason could land the second time. We unloaded, reloaded, rearranged supplies, which took a while (and was the most exercise I'd gotten since changing gates at Heathrow), and left for Shamwana, another hour away.

This place is REMOTE. It is like being in exile. The landing strip—Oh MY God. I couldn't even see it until we were almost on it. It's not even dirt, it's grass and stones. There is a cute little windsock, though, and they have put whitewashed bricks along the edges, which is a sweet touch. Jason told me he hates landing here, which I thought was a tad unprofessional, but then the others told me he used to bless himself before landing and was told to cut that out. But it was OK. He did fine. We didn't hit anyone, no flat tire. I thought it was a successful flight.

Now I'm here, and the team is changing. Nina, whom I am replacing, is leaving, and Margaret, the new nurse, will be here tomorrow (pleasebeoverfortypleasebeoverforty).

As I said last week, the role of the project is changing as well, and I am very confused. I've been tagging along with Nina all week trying to learn what she does, but now I find out that's not what I'll be doing. Apart from supervising (or doing) the complicated deliveries here, my role will be more administrative and then we'll ease out. At least that's what I think it's supposed to be. My French is nowhere near as good as it needs to be. I was kidding myself. I feel like I faked them out in New York, and somehow they thought my language skills were good enough to take this on. And the more I panic about it, the harder it is for me to communicate. I've got to get a grip on this. I've been relying on Nina to translate (her French is really good) and that's been part of the problem. I just stand aside and let her say it for me. I am starting to understand the accent better, though, so I'm trying to be optimistic, but even that has been hard.

I have been so tired. I don't know why, there is no reason. I am certainly not working that hard, though I guess being overwhelmed with learning all I need to learn is tiring. French, centigrade, the political system, the European medical system, the chief system, the pecking order, who is sleeping with whom–it is a lot to learn.

I sit at morning report and can catch most of it now, but it's really hard. I've been overwhelmed. I feel like everyone thinks I'm an idiot. And then . . . my first delivery here was my worst nightmare.

I described a bit last week what the facility (ha, ha) is like. Well, Monday night, not long after we'd gone to bed, Nina came to my *tukul* saying we had someone in labor at the hospital. There was a woman there who'd been laboring all day (it was nine p.m.) and had been pushing, but the baby wasn't coming. Nina and I walked the 100 meters to the hospital accompanied by a guard with a kerosene lantern. It's hot here. The labor room, being a brick structure with a tin roof and two tiny windows, is like a brick oven. The laboring woman was twenty-three years old, having her second baby. Her first baby died at three months of age when they were being chased by the Mai Mai. Beatrice and Gerardine are the two *accoucheuses* and they were with her. This should have been easy. She was fully dilated, the baby's heart rate was fine, but she wouldn't push anymore. I figured she was exhausted, malnourished, scared, and who knows what else. She spoke Kiluba, which Gerardine and Beatrice speak fluently.

Nina got in there and tried to get this woman to push and I watched trying to get a sense of how things work here culturally. At first it was kinda neat. Nina and me, from the west, Gerardine and

Beatrice from here, all together supporting this woman who we really thought would deliver as soon as we could convince her to push. We were patient for a while trying different things, but this woman was so traumatized that she was almost trancelike. There is no vacuum extractor here. I think I could have gotten the baby out with that, but it wasn't an option. We tried fundal pressure with Nina standing on the bed, each foot aside this woman's head, and me giving rectal pressure. Didn't work. Nothing worked. We gave her some IV Pitocin, hoping that would help. Nothing. The baby was fine this whole time, just stuck in the pelvis.

After four hours of this Nina said, "It's not coming out," and I knew that, but having seen that operating room, did not want to believe that was where we were heading.

We sent a guard to get Benson, the Congolese doctor here. He arrived, and agreed we had to go to surgery. He said not one word to the laboring woman and brought her husband in to explain it to him and ask his permission. Benson and the husband sat behind a curtain having this conversation in Kiluba. Gerardine was shaking her head sadly and Nina asked her, in French, what they were saying. Gerardine told us that the husband was refusing to let her have surgery. He was saying to kill the baby instead.

The laboring woman, who had been nearly comatose she was so exhausted, opened her eyes for the first time in two hours and started trying to get up off the bed. At first I thought it was a good thing for her to get up, but then I saw what she was doing. Naked, she tried to wrap a cloth around herself, fell down during a contraction, got up, and tried to run away. She had to get by the four midwives (in this tiny dark room) and her husband who, as she was literally crawling by, grabbed her arm and pulled her back, dragging her across the floor to him.

Benson at this point had gone out to send a guard to get the other men in her family so they could convince the husband to let her have surgery. She was curled upon the floor in a pool of blood and shit. Every time the door opened she frantically tried to crawl out, and each time her husband dragged her back by the arm. It was like she was trying to crawl into the bush and die rather than have surgery. It was hideous.

The men arrived from the village. Another hour passed; it was two a.m. There was a big meeting outside that went on and on. She was still trying to escape, still being dragged back by the arm, writhing in pain when she got a contraction. I watched this horror show, totally useless. Gerardine was talking to the husband trying to convince him to change his mind. He was shaking his head no and crying. Somehow Benson (who is wonderful) convinced the rest of the men in the family (who apparently trump the husband) to let her have surgery, and she was dragged like an animal off the floor outside into the pitch black night, and into the door adjacent, which is the operating room. Though, that night, a more apt description would have been torture chamber.

She was tied down, kicking and screaming, onto the narrow flat table with a bare piece of plywood laid across for her arms. The male nurse used a roll of gauze to tie her down, arms on the plywood, feet together at the foot of the table. When Nina asked them to untie her feet so she could put a catheter in, the woman sat up struggling, with her arms still tied to the plywood, and nearly made it off the table, when she was tackled back down and Benson said, "Forget the catheter!" She thought we were going to kill her. It was so horrible. I wanted to comfort her somehow, but didn't know what to do. I didn't know if she thought we (whites) caused this; I couldn't ask anything in French; I was just a deer in the lights. There is no anesthesia here. They use ketamine, which is conscious sedation, so (please God) she won't remember the actual surgery, but I tell you, those screams I will not soon forget. It was like doing surgery in someone's garage. I thought I was going to faint, but was afraid to go outside into the pitch dark with practically the whole village of men sitting there. But when I looked down at the floor and considered lying on it, a voice inside me said that fainting was not an option. The whole thing was surreal. Even Carila's veneer was cracked.

The surgical kit was smaller than what I use for a delivery at home. I have no idea how they did this with so few instruments, with a small battery-powered bulb dangling down from a nail in the ceiling. The IV was hanging from a different nail. The baby was out quickly, and then I had something to do besides watch the grisliest scene imaginable. On a tiny table in the corner with a small hand towel covering it, Nina and I did a very nice resuscitation on a very depressed baby with nothing but an ambu-bag and foot-powered suction. No oxygen. She steadily came back to life and, relieved, we took her next door, groping in the darkness, to weigh her and wrap her in a cloth. Gerardine said, "We should name her Linda, for the first baby with you here," and I said, "That would be nice, because it's my birthday today." (Or the grammatically incorrect French equivalent.) Nina sat with her face in her hands and said, "I just want to go home." And I looked at her and thought, "I can't believe she's touching her face!"

We walked back to our *tukuls* at four a.m. by lantern light, accompanied by a guard. I was wondering what I was in for if this was just my first delivery. All seemed OK. I think. But it all makes me ponder. By our standards we did the right thing, but what do they believe and will we ever know? Did they ask us to be here? What if a giant space ship landed on the green in Bar Harbor and Martians got off and said, "We can't believe so many of you die of cancer!" and went around tying people down and administering Martian drugs. Which worked! I don't know. I just don't know.

Let me describe where we live. I told you we are in a fenced-off area (so weird) about the size of a football field. We each have our own brick room called a *tukul* with a thatched roof, which is not too different from what's on the other side of the fence in the village, the major difference being that the wolf can't huff and puff and blow my *tukul* down because it's brick, not straw. Literally, the villagers' houses are made of straw. Inside my *tukul* are a small bed and a metal trunk. I'm going to try and figure out some shelves to put a few things on. I'm sick of digging into my duffel bag for clothes. There are two very nice pit latrines, squat style with a lid, one for men, one for women. There is a common eating area, open with a thatched roof and a solar-powered light at night. About ten meters from there is the kitchen, a round, open area with a thatched roof, kerosene fridge, and charcoal fireplace. Near there is a brick wood-burning oven that I think is really cool. It is a metal oil drum on its side built into a brick structure with a fire chamber on the bottom. There is rebar piercing the drum as a rack. It's brilliant. The cook makes great bread in there.

We have a shower, which is a fifty-gallon plastic barrel sitting on top of a wood frame with a shower head coming out of the bottom. Every morning we pay eight women to walk to the river, fill jerry cans with water, carry them back here on their heads, walk to the top of this brick structure, and pour the water into the barrel so that we can take showers. This is also how we get our drinking water, but that gets boiled and filtered first. It's yellow water. There is a little voice in my head every time I take a drink saying, "You shouldn't drink yellow water." Since I don't want to look like a wimp, I have been ignoring that voice. I've found if I only drink out of the tin cups I can't see the color of the water and the voice stops.

We have two huge mango trees (loaded with mangoes that are almost ripe), ten papaya trees, and a nice little lime tree. It's really beautiful here. There are beautiful hills in the distance, adding a soft contour to the landscape, lots of trees, most of which I can't identify but many, many mangoes, bananas, and papayas. There's plenty of fruit to eat. Our meals are consisting of mostly rice and something canned, like peas or those horrid little hot dogs. Whatever—I'm eating it. There's plenty of fruit, lots of oranges that are sour, but good, so no scurvy yet.

Stefano and Perrin play soccer every Sunday with the locals out on a field nearby. I am envious. I am getting NO exercise and it feels awful. I've considered jogging. I'd have to run in long pants or a skirt, which would be OK, but the thought of running to get exercise past women who are walking God-knows-how-far to a river to collect water so that I can shower after my run, is just too ridiculous to contemplate. I'd rather jog in place in my *tukul*.

One last thing before I end this. I am starting to really see why they emphasize how hard it is to live with a team. Strong personalities (one might say know-it-alls) all making decisions together are making for some interesting dynamics.

I learned to play poker and it's fun! And I delivered a compound breech that went really well, so they actually got to see that I can do SOMETHING. I'm feeling a little better.

Write to me! Oh, another thing. They now send and receive e-mails every day but I've hardly gotten any, so I'm afraid people haven't received mine. Did I already write that? Yes?

Love you!
Linda

Poussez! Reposez. *(Push! Rest.)* I'm getting to know these words very well.

We are on a level three security because there are rumors of Mai Mai returning. I've got a bag packed to evacuate, but I hope I won't need it. As miserably as I feel I am failing, I don't want to leave. On the other hand,

I don't want to be killed or raped. I could probably survive a rape, but I promised my kids I wouldn't be killed. That would not be good.

It is morning, but I don't know what time. I hear chopping, kids, pounding, singing, roosters, crowing, sweeping, chirping. It all sounds musical and soothing, fitting in with the landscape.

Somehow it got to be Friday again. Two full weeks in Shamwana. I am not going to do a check-in of how I am doing. I'd given myself goals marked by number of days or weeks and thought somehow I should be understanding or speaking a certain way by then. Forget that. I was just driving myself crazy. I have new goals. Sleeping. Preserving the tea that's left. I feel so much more than two weeks older.

September 30, 2007
Sunday morning, Shamwana

Hi Everyone,

I'm really looking forward to these early Sunday mornings. During the week when I try to use this computer there is always someone standing around watching me, saying, "How long are you going to be?" and that always makes me feel pressured to hurry. I find that behavior rather rude. When I want to check my e-mail, if someone is already on the computer I just come back later. I don't hover. So far, no one is learning by example. I may have to be more direct.

I've had ups and downs this week, a little heavier in the down column, but if you look at culture-shock graphs, the timing was right, so I'm hoping I come out of it. My first sentence in this letter was going to be *WHAT WAS I THINKING?* But I woke up this morning with a sense of calm so it was way down to the eighth sentence. See how well I'm doing? My major problem with adjustment is the frigging French. It seems all I learned before I came is gone, and I'm at my eighth-grade level. It is so frustrating. The more anxious I get about it the worse it is, then I don't sleep, then it spirals into panic. I have got to get a grip on this.

This past week there was a vehicle going way out to an outer clinic, then further to a village called Mpiana, which is not in our health zone, but has a Ministry of Health clinic where we collect our vaccines. There was really no need for me to go on this trip, but I begged Therese to let me go for a couple of reasons. First, it's really hard for me to understand what the outer clinics are like until I see them, and to see how poor the roads are, so I can plan for the rainy season and for whatever outreach I'm supposed to be doing.

Second, I needed to spend a day with people who don't speak any English and it was only national staff going. Also, I needed to learn to use that radio which I've been dreading. The alternative was to finish the pharmacy inventory with Nina, which to me is the ninth circle of hell. So I went. It was exactly what I needed.

On the way out the vehicle was full with mental health workers, the Congolese outreach nurse, and a guy from Kiambi, a town seventy miles away, who works for the government, and who had come to Shamwana to inspect our "facility." He came by motorcycle, which broke down in Shamwana, and he'd been here for a week waiting for transportation home.

On these trips, the expat always has to sit in the front and be the one to use the radio. I'd been avoiding that. The radio is how they track us. So, in front of all these people, I made myself do it, them laughing at me the whole time, me looking at the driver to know what to say. MSF always has to know where everyone is at all times, so when a transport is out we have to report where we are every hour to our radio operator, Oscar, at the base. He then relays it to Lubumbashi.

All of this, for all the movements of everyone, can be heard over the radio that we must carry at all times. In my case, heard but not understood. I have to do this even when I am only going over to the hospital, 100 meters away. It's so crackly and in French with an assortment of accents, that I can't tell who's talking to whom. We have to use that international alphabet, which I never learned and assumed that if you were never in the military, you didn't either. But nooooo, everyone knows it but me!

Anyway, on this trip, I sucked it up, looked like a fool, and did it, and by the end of the day I was getting the hang of it. And it was so good for me to be on my own. If there had been another European there, I would have let him or her explain it in English and been more and more frustrated. Now I'm sure poor Choco, the driver, had a ridiculously frustrating day having to explain to me over and over and over in French how to do it, as well as try to drive over a track that would be difficult for two people walking side-by-side, but I apologized the best I could and gave them all a laugh at my ignorance, so hopefully it was a wash.

The land is so beautiful. I mean so beautiful. I'm amazed at how green it is at the end of the dry season. It was so good to get out of this compound and see some of it. It took three hours to get to Mpiana (a distance of thirty miles, to give you a little idea of what the "roads" are like) and I can see it will be impossible to get there when it rains.

We passed villages where people are literally not much past the stone-age, with huge mango trees surrounding them. I'm wondering if that's what made them decide to have their village there, or if they planted those trees many generations ago. When my French is better, I'll ask. They are hunter/gatherers living in inaccessible areas, watching a huge white Land Cruiser drive through to collect vaccines to protect them from diseases that we imported. Everyone smiles and waves as we drive through like a single-float Fourth of July parade.

It's overwhelming to take this all in. The beauty of the land, the strength of these people who are surviving despite unbelievable violence, the natural resources this country has, the distribution of its wealth, the languages, the expats like me who are here–for what? An exotic extended camping trip? Are we really helping anyone? Or just making ourselves feel better? I honestly don't know.

Last weekend Carila asked me, "So, what were you running away from?"

I said, "Excuse me?"

She said, "Well, most people who do this sort of thing are running away from something back home. Haven't you heard about the four M's of humanitarian workers? Missionaries, Mercenaries, Martyrs, and Misfits?"

Well, THERE was some food for thought. I worked hard making the decision to come here. I wanted to make sure it was not because I was running away. I waited until my broken heart had healed and was secure in my career and my responsibilities getting the kids through school were fulfilled. I didn't think I was running away. I felt more like I was running toward something I couldn't identify. I couldn't explain it, and stopped trying, but it was pulling me with a tremendous force.

That intro started us on a good conversation, though, about the personalities on the team—strong ones—and what this means for our time here. Margaret (nurse) arrived; she's thirty, has worked in Darfur, and will be here for six months. Carila and I had thought we'd wait until she got here to talk about our roles and figure out how we could accomplish something using all our strengths most efficiently.

Well, Margaret showed up with a whip-us-into-shape attitude that, frankly, didn't sit well with me. Carila, who hates conflict (she grew up in Canada, not to cast stereotypes), became quite passive and I got sarcastic and bitchy. After all, I'd been here for two entire WEEKS. Who was she to tell me what to do? Nina felt like she'd been a total failure and got depressed and withdrew. There ensued three days of jockeying for control and some feeling of self-worth, until it all shook down into, I think, decent working relationships. Actually, I quite like Margaret, but at first my only thought was, "This is going to be a very long six months." Oh, and Margaret's French sucks, too. The reason we had three days to sit around and have this exercise was that we weren't allowed to leave the compound for three days. It turned out to be a blessing in disguise.

Last Saturday night, with the kerosene lanterns casting their romantic glow, Therese and I were sitting at the table chatting when we saw Perrin approaching with his headlamp lit, and he asked to talk with Therese privately. I didn't like the way he said it, mostly because I felt left out. I mean, what could be private, for God's sake? She went off with him and came back about fifteen minutes later saying that one of our guards heard in the village that Mai Mai soldiers had returned to Kabala, which is a few hours walk from here. This was bush telegraph rumor, but all of a sudden that romantic glow became sort of an eerie glow. So we all gathered and said, "Uh, what do we do?"

We obviously weren't going anywhere. It was dark, so leaving was out of the question. Therese was calm and sensible, but cautious. We went over the plan for emergency, checked the first-aid kit (which is so huge we could open an emergency room with it), and checked out the "safe room" where we could hide if there is an all-out crazy emergency. We were hoping it wouldn't come to that, but if hiding became necessary, that's where we go.

It's a room with enough food and water for a month, but it's not in some secret tunnel, so it seems like we wouldn't be the ones eating that food for long. I must say I felt safe enough, but like a stupid, spoiled brat. I have all these resources, and the people on the other side of that grass fence have to fend for themselves. I'm having a hard time taking this all in. After a few hours of this weird kind of scary thrill, sort of campfire-ghost-story-meets-existential-crisis, we watched a stupid movie on Carila's laptop. A curious denial feeling was in the air.

The next morning (I had decided not to include this in last week's letter) I got up and wrote to you, and Therese called Lubumbashi; the team there then called Amsterdam to get some guidelines on how to proceed. The locals didn't seem too worried, so I wasn't either. Amsterdam said we had to stay holed up here until we had more information. We were allowed to go to the hospital, but that was it. We also had to have our small bag packed in case the decision was made to evacuate. Over the next three days bits and pieces of information trickled in via local staff–a man who had a brother who had a cousin who used to be Mai Mai who killed the chief's wife who then married his cousin's wife–shit like this! Bush telegraph, which is crazy by our standards, but was where the info was coming from. MSF-Spain, which has an office in Pweto, another city in the district, was also getting these reports, so it took a while to find out what actually was going on.

It turns out it was not Mai Mai, but government soldiers (who, Therese said, can be just as bad to the locals, but won't hurt expats) who were looking for the weapons that Gideon, the Mai Mai leader, had his followers hide in the bush. The big problem is that the government does not pay the soldiers, just like they don't pay the health care workers, and they are hungry! So they raid villages for food and anything else they can get to sell for money. Terrible. So these villagers, who have nothing but a few pots and a little stash of cassava, end up losing that, too.

After three days, Therese and Angelien (whom I LOVE) and a few local staff went out to Kabala to find out for themselves what was going on. The soldiers had been there, but had found the weapons and left. The men of the village had been tied up but not hurt, and they had been robbed of what little they had. And still they are resilient. It's mind-boggling.

The following day, we took a mobile clinic out there to offer some basic and mental health care. That pretty much means we hand out some antibiotics to people with nonspecific complaints and listen to their stories of abuse and despair. It's so depressing. Yesterday we went to a different village for information gathering. I was just an observer, but it was neat to go along. The group consisted of Therese,

Angelien, Willy (a *mobilateur sociale* or community liaison), me, and the driver. We arrived in this village, which was chosen because it had been rumored that the soldiers passed through there, and swarms of people came running toward the vehicle. The chief put wooden blocks down for us to sit on and within a few minutes there were at least 100 people there. We had passed a guy thatching the roof of a structure that was going to be a crude school a half a mile back, and within minutes he was under that tree as well. It was fascinating. The kids were all chanting, "*Muzungu! Mzungu!*" and I heard one kid say, in French, "I touched one!"

We stayed there for an hour or so with the villagers listening to their stories. The chief made sure everyone who wanted got a chance to speak. Willy translated from Kiluba into French, and what I couldn't catch Angelien then translated for me into English. God, this is confusing. I have GOT to be fluent in French.

The soldiers had been there, took some food and money and three villagers to carry stuff for them, and left. No one was hurt, just three forced into slavery of sorts, but the impression was that those three would be returning after they had gotten to the next place where the soldiers could take other porters. Everyone seemed really happy that we stopped in on this Saturday morning. Whether it was because they thought we'd improve their lives, protect them, or just because we gave them something to talk about, I don't know. The kids all appeared nourished. I heard one nasty cough in the crowd that could have been TB, two kids had conjunctivitis (judging from looking at them), but in general the people of this particular village seemed healthy by current Congo standards. There was cassava growing; there were mango and banana trees and little plots of land that looked cultivated, awaiting the rains. What more could anyone want?

So, I'm safe. Don't worry. I wouldn't have written all this to you if I were worried. We are allowed to travel again (obviously) and it was really erring on the cautious side. It was a bit of a drama, but we were never at risk. I pondered deeply about whether to tell you all this now or when I got home, but now that it is all played out, it seems lame, so I didn't want to wait. And you know me, even when I think, "I'm not going to say anything, I'm not going to say anything," I always do. My life is an open book. So at least you know I'm not hiding anything.

Let's see, what else? Well, there is my daily struggle trying to figure out how this hospital functions, since I'm supposed to be supervisor of the place. I did spend one of the two inventory days counting pills in the pharmacy, apparently because the pharmacist isn't trusted to do it himself. It was good for me to learn what's in there, but I am not going to do that every month. I might check the stock cards, but I am not counting every pill again. That's ridiculous. Frankly, I don't give a shit if they are stealing a few Tylenol.

Angelien is wonderful and we do have a lot in common. Her husband left her, after twenty-five years, for one of her friends. That was three years ago. She's from Holland, has three adult children, and is four years older than me. She's a psychologist and has done an amazing job here setting up a mental health program for these victims of unspeakable violence. One of these weeks I'll write some of the stories. She's frustrated as well, feeling like she hasn't done enough, but I am in awe of her. She has reassured me over and over that her French was just like mine when she arrived, but having to interview local staff and set up this program forced her to learn quickly. She's such a great people person. She's funny and insightful and energetic, and she grabbed me late one afternoon and said, "C'mon, we're going to walk through the village to the river." It was great, stopping to chat with the chief and with kids and women, further and further out of the village where the ground turns from sand to dried marsh with tall grasses. We could look back at the village and hear the drums and singing, and I just felt so happy and fortunate to be here. I'm sure I sound schizophrenic to you but, even with all my frustrations, I still feel like this is where I'm supposed to be right now. That walk to the river with this amazing woman, with rain clouds forming in the late afternoon light, beautiful hills all around us, and hearing those village sounds, talking about how life brought us to where we were, was just so unbelievably satisfying. This feels really right.

Then we got to the river and I looked with horror and said, "Holy shit! That's what we're drinking?"

It's been four hours and I have to share the laptop, so more next Sunday, and a little in between.

Love to all, and DON'T WORRY!

Linda

CHAPTER 2 ~ OCTOBER

October 7, 2007
Sunday morning, Shamwana

Hi Everyone,

OK, this food situation isn't funny anymore. The all-time low was the canned corned beef mixed with tomato paste over rice. I'm pretty sure my dog would have rolled her eyes at it. Last week the plane did not come because of a hemorrhagic fever outbreak, so there was no food delivery. Two weeks ago we received a box of potatoes and one of onions. That was it. The flour is gone, so we haven't had any bread for two weeks, and the only vegetables we have are those friggin' canned peas, and I am getting really sick of those. We do still have rice, pasta, canned corned beef, and canned sausages. We had sardines for lunch yesterday; that was a treat.

The mangoes are ripening so I've been eating tons of those, but my lips are starting to get itchy, and I think that might be why. We are getting dangerously low on tea and if that doesn't come this week, I am going to be very cranky. Beer is gone. We do have a bottle of gin that I brought, but nothing to mix it with. I picked some limes from our tree and thought I'd make some lime juice for the gin but after picking the two I could reach, some huge bug fell into my hair, so I decided not to climb up to get more. I'm not sure who is cohabitating with those bugs. Possibly small snakes. We do have lots of wine in cartons, which I actually think is pretty good, though the rest of the team made fun of me for drinking it. I noticed they all joined in, though, when I appeared to be enjoying it. So I'm guessing that will be gone soon too.

It is incredibly hot and humid now. I remember in Malawi the build-up to the rainy season. There would be huge dark clouds that would gather on the horizon for a few weeks as a teaser, and I'd be thinking, "C'mon, c'mon, a little closer, c'mon, rain already!" I was pregnant then and sick and miserable, which certainly isn't the case now, but I am recalling that longing for a break from the heat. There is a thermometer in our dining area and it was 39° Celsius in the shade and really humid. The OB room is like an oven; God it's miserable in there.

Speaking of that, I've formulated a few new goals for my year here, after spending eighteen hours in that cell on Tuesday. Let me describe the conditions. (Warning: You might want to put that snack away for later.) As I mentioned before, it's a brick structure with a tin roof and two small windows. It's about ten feet by fifteen feet. I swear it is 115 degrees in there. There is a metal frame bed with a mattress covered in plastic, and there is a rubber sheet over that. That's it. Women come in, labor and deliver on that rubber sheet. No cloth sheet, no pads, no pillow. The walls are mud with wasp nests near the roof. Oh, did I mention that there is only ONE rubber sheet? Yes, and no lubricant to use for examining women, so when I looked for something to wet my glove before an exam, Beatrice poured some diluted disinfectant over it. This is also what they use to clean the rubber sheet. When the amniotic fluid/blood/shit/ urine comes out, we scoop it up with our gloved hands and put it in one of the three buckets designated for "body parts and placentas." It is revolting. Add this to the fact that the women will not push, so we've had several four-hour pushing stages, and gee, it's no wonder the local staff keeps quitting. It's also not surprising to me that the women don't want to come to the hospital, though I must say, I haven't seen a home delivery so don't know what they do there. Nina told me they use a hot coal to burn the cord to crudely cauterize it because they have nothing to tie it with, whereas we have two small pieces of string, some gauze, and a pair of scissors. I am surprised the incidence of tetanus is as low as it is.

Nina left last Monday, so I'm on my own. I had an hour of total panic when she left because I was relying on her so much to translate. And I mean PANIC. I very nearly ran into Therese's office to throw myself on the floor and say, "Someone in New York made a big mistake. I cannot speak French well enough to do this job. You need to find someone else." As if she hadn't noticed I wasn't speaking French very well.

As I was walking with Nina to the airfield to say good-bye (and if the truth be known, I went because I wanted to get on the plane with her; I could have said good-bye at the base), they called for me on the radio, and I COULD NOT UNDERSTAND ONE WORD THEY SAID. Nina said, "They are telling you there is an urgent case coming in for you." I just stared at her with an expression that I was hoping would make her change her plans and stay. This was like first day of kindergarten, first day of summer camp, first day of prison all rolled into one. Utter, sheer, abject terror consumed me, and I had to concentrate to stand up. I think my vision even got a little blurry. An urgent case was coming, I was supposed to deal with it, and I could not even understand that they were coming? Without saying good-bye, I turned and walked back to the hospital murmuring, "Dear God, please help me. Mary, please help me. I am begging. Please."

After nearly fainting from fear, I had a moment of Zen (or divine intervention) and went over and dealt with it. It ended up being someone who had delivered in one of our vehicles. Everything was all right, but I have never been so full of anxiety in my life. Oh, let me interject here: please people, be kind to your foreign chain store pharmacist. My heart really goes out to them.

Monday night I was very depressed, really thinking I could not do this. It would be a challenge in English, but in French, it's ridiculous. Yes, I can let people know I care. I can smile and technically cope with the mechanics of it. But c'mon, ordering supplies for the hospital? Supervising nurses? Reviewing charts? Teaching? I am in way over my head. OK, I had a second cup of boxed wine that night. Then at four a.m. the guards were at my *tukul* window: "Mama Leendah, Mama Leendah," and I responded without thinking, *"Oui, je suis ici, je vien"* (Yes, I am here. I'm coming). And that was the first time since I've been here that I spoke French without thinking. I was a little surprised, like it came out of someone else's mouth. Then ensued a long, hot day, with two women delivering after long, difficult labors, and the French was coming easier and easier. I have a long way to go, but I got a glimpse of being able to do it. By the time I was trying to get the *accoucheuse* to NOT give up on the vaginal delivery (not eager to repeat that operating room experience) the French was coming out of my mouth easier and faster. Gradually it didn't matter so much to me what tense I was in, or how I sounded. Lord, I hope that vacuum extractor arrives soon.

I found some *torchons* (rags) to place under women during birth to sop up some of the glop, and went to the market where they actually had a bulb syringe for 1,500 Congolese francs ($3), so bought one as a gift for maternity. The only thing that's over there now is a foot-pumped suction that doesn't work very well. The rags are just cut-up blankets, but we have them in the storeroom, and they'll have to do for now. Stefano is in charge of water and sanitation, and I want him to designate an area at the hospital for laundry, as—get this—right now all the hospital laundry is washed together with ours (by hand) over here at the base. Yeah. Just found that out. Hospital blankets with our clothes. Not pretty. He agreed to get right on it and we'll have to hire another person to wash the hospital laundry. We now have a place to wash our hands at the hospital that wasn't there three weeks ago when I arrived, so improvements are popping up all over the place. It is a fifty-gallon barrel filled with brown river water, but still better than nothing.

Yesterday morning a man arrived here, having run ten kilometers, with a message written on a scrap of paper. The message said there was a woman who delivered the night before and had a retained placenta. She was bleeding and was being transported by bicycle. He asked us to take a vehicle and go meet them. Carila and I got into one of the Land Cruisers and started out, not sure what we'd have to deal with on the road, or if she'd already bled to death. We met them walking toward Shamwana about five kilometers from their village. I wish I'd grabbed my camera. The bleeding woman was balanced on a chair, which was tilted backward atop a bicycle. Four men were guiding it along the road. Her feet were resting on the bolts on the back wheel. Her mother walked beside, carrying the baby. She looked alive and in fairly good shape considering, so we got her into the Land Cruiser and brought her back here. Once here, we started an IV, gave her some Valium, and I manually removed the placenta, which was not easy, let me tell you. I slowly milked the placenta through the closed cervix with my fingers cramping, and eased it out little by little. The sweat was literally pouring off my face and dripping onto the woman during the procedure. Beatrice was sympathetically murmuring, "*Oh Mama Linda*," and wiping my face off with gauze. I had to keep blinking my eyes to see. Got it, though, and after a bunch of antibiotics and Methergine, she's doing fine. I'm quite happy about that. So I'm feeling more and more useful, and less like an incompetent burden (you should see me with that radio now), and I'll stick it out.

Oh, I've got to tell you this to illustrate the generational discrepancy here. As we pulled out of the base, on our way to collect this woman, in God knows what condition, Carila plugged her iPod into the cigarette lighter so we'd have some tunes on the way. I couldn't believe it. That was the last thing on my mind.

No more Mai Mai threats, but some people have been beaten by the military, and Therese and Carila have been taking their stories when they show up here for treatment. Then they write it up and send it to Amsterdam, part of the *témoinage* aspect of our role here. I love that word. It doesn't translate well into English, but means "bearing witness," and that is one of the three missions of this organization. Considering we go into areas where others don't, often we are the only ones to see abuses, and we have a responsibility to report them. Honorable, I think.

Last night two old men were here with whip marks and broken fingers after being sent by their village chief with the military to look for hidden weapons in the bush. When they couldn't find any, they were beaten, the military suspecting they'd been taken on a wild goose chase. It is just so sad. We went out twice this past week to one of the most traumatized villages and did mobile clinics, just to have a presence and let the people know someone is watching. The first day I was pretty much just handing out the medications that Deo, the nurse, was prescribing, and cleaning and dressing foot wounds. One poor old guy had an infected wound on his foot wrapped in a filthy piece of old tarp. I cleaned it with Betadine, wrapped it in gauze, tied a latex glove around it, and then put the piece of tarp back on because he didn't have any shoes. One little girl had a mangled foot that had been caught in the spokes of a bicycle, another had fallen into a fire.

On Friday when we went back there, I was doing all that, plus para-checks to diagnose malaria, which involves a finger-stick and a rapid diagnostic test (similar to a pregnancy test). There were so many people crowding around, shoving and pushing that Margaret had all she could do just keeping the crowd controlled. It was a long day and it was hot and I was so hungry, but there was no way I was going to eat the banana I had brought in front of all those people. Plus there was nowhere to wash my hands.

En route back to the base, feeling quite satisfied with the day, I actually had a conversation in French with national staff about which is harder to learn, French or English. It was a good day. After dropping two very sick patients at the hospital, we went back to the base. Just as we got there, thunder and lightning started and an amazing storm blew in. Torrential rain. The heavens just opened up; it was wild and incredible, and a huge relief. I took a shower in it behind my *tukul*—I never really feel clean with that river-water shower—and then Angelien and I sat in her *tukul* and drank whisky out of a little plastic pouch. You know how salad dressing is packaged at the cafeteria, or shampoo in cheap motels? Well, Angelien found some little plastic packets of whisky in Lubumbashi, and we opened them with little scissors. They cost 200cf (about forty cents) and I thought, given the setting, they weren't too bad. I may buy a few to have on hand. Never know when friends will pop in for a visit.

Yesterday afternoon, I made some shelves in my *tukul* with bricks and some wood I took from behind the office. Then I strung up some cloth in the corners, as little hammocks to put stuff in, and I'm quite pleased. I feel more settled, and it's rather cute if I do say so myself. There were some seeds lying around in the kitchen area, so I planted some vegetables and some sunflowers around the *tukuls*. The basil seeds I took from Lubumbashi are coming up, so hopefully we'll have something green to eat soon. I also think I'm going to look into getting chickens. There must be some around here someplace. I'd pay twenty bucks for an egg about now.

More soon. Stay in touch please. . . . .

Love to all,
Linda

Hier soir Angelien a coupé mes cheveux. C'est si bonne. *(Angelien cut my hair last night. This is very good.)* I love the simplicity here. The single-mindedness. Life will be much simpler for me when I get home. This is just what I needed. It's so right. I can hear a kid crying. Sounds like one of Oscar's. Their house is just behind my tukul on the other side of the fence. I hear his wife Nicole yelling sometimes, though I have no idea what she's saying. I can't even tell if it is Kiluba or Swahili she's speaking. I heard drums early this morning. Some days they are there, others, not. I wonder what the significance is. They were so prevalent when I first arrived.

October 14, 2007
Sunday morning, Shamwana

Hi Everyone,

I can't believe I've been in Shamwana a month already. At the beginning of each week, I think I won't have much to write about for the following Sunday, and have been saving lots of little stories for one of those Sundays. However, this is not one of those Sundays.

On Friday afternoons we plan the movements for the following week. The team has many different functions and we try to coordinate the movements as much as possible to make it more efficient. For instance, Stefano has been working on building refuse pits at the health centers, and when he has to travel to one, we might try to bring medications there at the same time. Stuff like that.

We've got this very confusing relationship with the Ministry of Health (MoH) here—we can't stay here without their consent— regarding vaccines. MSF is not supposed to launch vaccination campaigns here; that is strictly an MoH role; and politically it's a line that can't be crossed. However, MoH has no refrigerators, so they've asked MSF to collect the vaccines and store them until they get around to distributing them. Which, to me, seems like they are waiting for some cold day in this hell.

I am very passionate about vaccination. It's the only thing here that does any lasting good. So we have this refrigerator here at the base, full of vaccines that are not being distributed. They are going to expire, or go bad, and since my arrival here, I've been saying we should do something about it. For the past ten years kids have not been vaccinated. They've been hiding in the bush, dying of measles and tetanus and TB (loads of TB here), and there still is no plan for distribution. The vaccines themselves have come from UNICEF. So, currently, the only kids being immunized are the ones who are born at the hospital here, but even they are only getting their BCG (the vaccine for TB), and often nothing else because they don't come back. Oh, and for some reason, MoH has said that if we do distribute them, we can't give them to any child over eleven months. This might be because there is only enough for those numbers when you do a crude census, but there is no way to keep track, and an epidemic is not going to be prevented if all these older un-immunized kids are living together.

So, I've taken this on as a project, and plan to take the vaccines to each of our outreach centers once a month and start immunizing at least the under-one-year-olds. It's a start, anyway. I would rather just go village to village and immunize every kid up to age fifteen, but I'm told we can't step on MoH toes or we may be asked to leave. Then no one gets immunized, so I guess this is better than nothing. It's very frustrating. Margaret, the outreach nurse, agrees with me but she doesn't have any experience with it, so wants me to be in charge of it. Since it's what I did in Malawi, I'm happy to do it. I can't stand to see these expensive vaccines just sitting there. And now we have disposable needles and real cold boxes. It's so much better than when we had one needle to immunize 200 kids back in my Peace Corps days. It is going to take a while to explain the benefits and have anyone see the result. If the vaccines aren't kept cold, they are no good and the kids aren't protected, but the mothers can't understand this. It's going to take a while to set up an efficient system, but I am going to try to get something going and started this week.

Tuesday morning we set out for an overnight at one of the health centers with cold boxes full of vaccines to do some immunizations in the villages that are so remote they make Shamwana look like a thriving metropolis. We had two *mosos* (community liaisons); three nurses–Margaret, Deo (who is Margaret's Congolese counterpart), and me; and Choco, the driver. The plan was to get to the health center (three hours away), vaccinate whichever kids were there, and then if there was time, to go out to some of the further villages. There are four health centers in our health zone and getting to them from Shamwana is a feat. That is, a feat with our state-of-the-art Toyota Land Cruiser and experienced driver. Sick patients are expected to walk or be carried, unless we happen to be going in their direction. Then they can ride with us. If we have room. So we were on our way and Willy, who is one of the *mosos,* asked me if the roads were similar in the United States. This asked, as the Land Cruiser was almost on its side, so much of the road was washed away. The literal translation of my response was something like, "No, in the United States we have many roads, very different. More hard. Sometimes there are roads like this where people drive for fun. Or for, I don't know the word in French, men who kill animals in the forest, hunters, yes, hunters use a road of this sort sometimes." Big smiles all around. I'm so proud of my progress. And even though I have no idea if hunters in the states actually drive on roads this bad, it was almost a complete sentence, and these people are never leaving Shamwana district, let alone traveling to the US so I don't think it does any harm to embellish. Especially if I can do it in French.

We arrived in Kishale, and there were no kids at the clinic. So we immediately left again to set up a mobile clinic further out. That day we ended up doing three villages. We'd arrive, speak with the village chief, then send the *mosos*, each in a different direction, to ask mothers to bring their kids for their immunizations. We set up under a tree. Someone would go get chairs for us and someone else would take a table out of a house for us. Mothers would start to arrive with their children and line up for their shots. It was community organization at its purest. We immunized a lot of kids and we were pleased.

We went back to Kishale to spend the night in a mud house next to the health center, planning to do three more villages on Wednesday. It's too far away to make it back here to the base on the same day. We can't be on the roads after six p.m. as it's dark soon after that, and the roads are dangerous enough in the daylight. It's not an option to drive after dark. Some of the bridges we cross are exactly the width of the vehicle and they are just logs lain across a ditch or small river. It's crazy.

When we got back to Kishale I was STARVING. I had had nothing but a bowl of stale cornflakes with powdered milk that morning. All I could think of was getting something to eat. We were told that someone in the village would cook for us, but didn't really know when or how it all worked. This was Margaret's and my first outreach overnight and it was the blind leading the blind. Neither of us can speak French fluently though we did discover that combined we could have a conversation. Her sentence structure is better than mine, and my vocabulary is bigger. She and I were sharing a small, dark, room of mud, with camp cots and mosquito nets strung from the branches that support the thatched roof. There was a metal trunk between the cots, and we sat discussing who was going to go ask about some food when in came Choco, Willy, and Joseph with a big bowl of cassava "bread," called *fufu*, and a bowl of what looked, in the very dim light, like sautéed onions. Then Deo brought in a big bowl of water for us all to wash our hands in, and a big handful of beautiful tomatoes. Fresh food!!! Yeah!!!!

I was so happy to see this food. I was so happy to be the first to wash my hands, since the same bowl got passed for all to wash with, and then we ate with our hands. If you could have seen where all these hands had been. Ugh. So I was thinking "Yum, yum, yum, really this is all looking good." I broke off a piece of the cassava *fufu*, which has the consistency of uncooked bread dough, and scooped up what I thought were onions, and saw hundreds of little eyes looking back at me. Oh my God, these were not onions. They were little teeny fish that were mostly eyes. I already had a bunch on my plate, and was so hungry I didn't care what they were, but Margaret wouldn't eat them. I buried them in my cassava with my thumb and tried to ignore the gritty crunch and just swallow, hoping they'd been cooked well enough to kill whatever parasites had been living in their water.

And then . . . Deo took these beautiful tomatoes . . . and washed them . . . IN THE FILTHY WATER WE HAD JUST WASHED OUR HANDS IN!!!! Mind you, this was water I would have thought twice before using to water my plants. I almost started crying. Sorry. Fish eyes: OK. Pass on the tomatoes. Margaret only ate the cassava. After this lovely repast, Deo, Willy, Choco, and Joseph retired to their room next to ours, and Margaret and I talked for a couple of hours. We were trying to stay up late enough to not have to go to that pit latrine during the night. It was a challenge, but we were motivated. So, we chatted, we peed, we tucked ourselves in under our nets and started to drift off, when chunks of dirt started falling on my net as I heard some scurrying in the thatched roof.

Me: "Margaret. Something is living in the roof."
Margaret: "I heard."
Me: "What do you think it is?"
Margaret: "Don't know."
Me: "Do rats climb like that?"
Margaret: "Do snakes?"
Me: "Fuck."

Yeah, didn't sleep much. Little chunks of dirt kept falling on my net sifting through to sprinkle me all night. I tried keeping the cover over me, but it was so hot I finally just gave up and got sprinkled on all night. The thought of a rat falling on the net made the sifted dirt seem rather harmless, though I am covered with bites in the pattern of my tank top, so I don't know if there were bugs in the dirt or in the bed.

Next morning (I was amazed that I actually slept at all) we got up, brushed the dirt off, put on the same grubby clothes, brushed our teeth, had some tea and bananas, and off we went. There were three villages we wanted to get to, so, as we passed through the first, we left the message with the chief that we'd be back to immunize kids in a few hours and to pass the word to the mothers. We did this in the first two villages, and the plan was to get to the third and set up there, wait for the mothers, immunize the kids there, then backtrack having already informed the first two villages so they'd be ready. Following me? We got to the third village, and as we pulled in, a guy came frantically running toward us, telling Deo that someone was very, very sick and begging us to help them. Deo went to the house to investigate, came back to the Land Cruiser and told us he thinks its cholera. The guy was nearly dead from dehydration from the constant watery stools. Deo asked Margaret if we could take him back to Kishale, his only chance of surviving. Margaret looked at me. Well, what? I guess, of course, but how do we do this? The three of us went over to the house where this guy was. He had arrived there three days earlier from Pweto, where they had just had a cholera outbreak. Oh my God, it was so pathetic. The family had already isolated him in a makeshift tent outside the one-room mud house. He was unresponsive, his head in his wife's lap, their two-year-old sitting in the dirt next to them.

We unloaded everything out of the Land Cruiser, and put it in the house of the chief–vaccines, knapsacks, water containers, etc. We left the two *mosos* in the village, and Deo, Margaret, and I took apart the tent he was in, and used the tarp to cover the floor of the Land Cruiser. Then we used the disgusting soaking-wet blanket underneath him to lift him into the vehicle. He groaned when we did that, so that was a good sign: he was still alive. His wife and baby got in and we headed back to Kishale, an hour and a half ride, where they have a tent set up for cholera patients. Inside the tent there are cots with a hole in them where you place the patient's buttocks and put a bucket underneath to contain the constant watery stools. The diarrhea just pours out and there's no other way to do it. This man was in such bad shape, I wasn't sure he was going to live until we got there.

I was squished in the front between Choco and Margaret, all of us sweating profusely, and I kept glancing in the back thinking, "Oh my God, there is a man in the back about to die of cholera. Please don't die. Please don't die." He survived the trip, and amazingly, Deo got an IV in him. There was not much left to his veins. There is a rapid test for cholera, which we did, and it was positive.

So our day of doing immunizations was shot. We went back to pick up Willy and Joseph (while we were dealing with the patient, Choco had bleached the entire Land Cruiser), and drove out to Mpiana to try to get more vaccines (they had none). Then we collected three MoH nurses and headed back to Shamwana, which, from that village, was four and a half hours away. It was a long day. On the way back here I kept thinking of how resolved those people were to just accept their fate. That young wife was just sitting there with her husband dying in her lap. If we hadn't just happened to be driving through.

Thursday we decided that someone had to go back to that village to see if there were any more cases, to see if it was an isolated case or an epidemic. Margaret and Carila were leaving for the weekend on the Friday flight, so I was the only one here to do it. Friday morning, after checking on a laboring woman, I got packed up with IV supplies and got ready to go with Choco and Willy back to that village. Before we left, I stuck my head in the office door and said, "Uh, I'd like everyone on their knees praying that we don't find any more cases, please." Carila looked confused and asked, "What's the matter?" I stopped short. WHAT'S THE MATTER? OK. Now am I missing something? Am I being a wimp to NOT want to find more CHOLERA? By myself with a *moso* and driver? Excuse me? Maybe I just misunderstood her question and didn't have time to get into it. This isn't really a praying crowd, and maybe I offended her. Don't know.

I started praying really hard, though, the closer we got. "Please, please, please don't let me find a village full of dying people please, please, please . . . " After a long, bumpy (bumpy is nowhere near the right word) ride, during which Choco had to actually build some bridges for us to continue, we arrived in the village and asked the chief if anyone else had gotten sick. He said that a child had gotten sick that morning and the mother was taking her to Mpiana to the health center there. By foot. Twelve miles. 104 degree heat. Wrong health center; they don't have a cholera tent there.

We jumped in the vehicle and headed off to try to find them and it didn't take long. They had only made it as far as the next village where we had stopped to ask if they had passed through. They were there; the mother had stopped to get some water. The child was in bad shape, but still responsive, so we got them into the vehicle, headed back through their village, stopping at their house to collect some pots and food for them. The child's father, who only has one leg, scrambled with incredible agility using a stick, to collect a few pots and a bundle with food in it. He then hopped into the vehicle. Willy and Choco looked at me. It's MSF policy that we only take one *garde de malade* (caretaker) for each sick person and I was supposed to say the father couldn't come. I said in French, "If he wants to be with his family, this is good with me." Then I told Willy, "Explain," pointing to the crowd of people outside the house, "Someone must wash the things in the house of this child." Then pointing to the chief, "Explain, if someone becomes with this sickness they must go very quickly to Kishale, not Mpiana. Kishale is better for this sickness. This is very important. This is a sickness very serious." And that, I am embarrassed to say, was the extent of my health teaching to a village with a friggin' cholera outbreak.

We got them to Kishale, got an IV into this poor little thing who was vomiting all over the place. She didn't even flinch when the IV was started, that's how bad she was, and we got her onto the cot with the bucket underneath. The mother was just sitting unspeaking in the dirt outside the tent. Everyone was dazed and hollow. Watch your kid die, watch your husband die. It's mind-boggling. Happy note though, the guy we brought in two days earlier was doing great. Eyes open, speaking, alive! We didn't wait to see if this child actually had confirmed cholera, as the time limit for us getting back to Shamwana before dark was fast approaching, and I was not eager to spend another night there. I had the satellite phone with me and called Therese and asked what she thought I should do. She said to get on the road back.

Oh dear, I am afraid that I am making these letters so long that no one will want to read them.

We've had two heavy rainstorms a week apart. Apparently it is November before the rain comes consistently every night. This, I am told, lasts until April. The seeds I planted last week are coming up, and the zucchini even has its second leaves!

Yesterday a UN helicopter landed on the airstrip looking for information about the military activity that has been going on the past few weeks. The two guys in the helicopter only talked to the people who happened to go running to the airstrip when they saw the helicopter coming. I did see some UN peacekeeping troops when I was in Lubumbashi, but really don't know how they function. If this was their idea of information gathering . . . uh, that's pretty scary.

Thank you for writing! It was like Christmas when I got back from my little overnight trip. I took a shower, happily ate those disgusting little canned sausages and peas, and sat in here with my wine reading all your letters. I was very happy.
Till next week . . .

Love,
Linda

⚜

Je suis plus confortable ici. Le français vien plus facilement. *(I am more comfortable here. French is coming easier.)* I now have cotton sheets. I can use a memory stick. I can write a situation report. I am planning—with difficulty, and shooting in the dark—an African vacation. Solo. Go to Kilimanjaro, I guess. Meet up with a group, I hope. I'll figure something out. It's cloudy this morning. No rain last night. My seedlings are thirsty. Sitting in my doorway with a pot of mint tea, watching the lightning get closer and closer. It's sprinkling, feeling like it's about to pour but still deciding. Friday morning—another week. They are going fast. Someone has been in labor since two a.m. Twins, at least—she's huge. Or her belly is. Her limbs are twigs. It's amazing to see so much bulk held up on such a small frame. It's as if the babies have taken all her flesh.

⚜

October 21, 2007
Sunday morning, Shamwana

Hi Everybody,

Well, with my newfound compassion for two-year-olds and stroke victims, I am now communicating a little more effectively. I still have a long way to go, but the French is coming easier. I now have to think less before I speak, and actually say things in the past and future tenses. I'm still shy about speaking at our meetings, and when I have to speak during the meeting, I do it in French then confirm it in English, but it's coming along. I'm starting to get the accent, at least from the people I'm working with the most, so I understand them better. I still have to keep asking them to speak slowly, but I'm learning that about half of what they say isn't necessary. You know when you talk to someone who doesn't speak your language you say it in a simple way? The Congolese don't do that. They use these huge, long complicated sentences, and that's why I thought they were saying so much more than they were. I'm starting to be able to root out the message, and then confirm that I understand. It's tiring, but I can see the progress, so I am encouraged. I am also spending more time sitting around and chatting at the hospital during the down time, and that's helped my confidence and makes me feel less isolated.

Let me give you an update on the cholera situation. The original guy we picked up is fully recovered. So is the little girl. Yeah! That's so great. What's not so great is that two men have died as they were walking to the health center for treatment, both from different directions. But two women who contracted it made it to the health center and are doing well. The two who died have not been confirmed cholera (it's not possible to do the test after they've died, and they bury them right away) but it sounds like that's what they had– previously healthy men, acute diarrhea and vomiting, and dead within twenty-four hours. Classic cholera.

And there are two more children in the tent now just hanging on. The kids are harder to hydrate, because you can't do it quickly like you can with adults. Margaret went out there overnight, and over the SAT phone told us about the additional cases, but all seem to be contacts of the original one, so it might not be from a water source. But now we don't know how many people were contacts of the contacts. She said the two nurses out there are exhausted, and the Ministry of Health is supposed to be getting them some relief, but I don't know how or when that happens. If the number of cases are one percent of the population, then it's an official epidemic and we'd get additional MSF workers to come and set camp there until it's all contained. This week will be critical.

Margaret and Stefano got back last night, and said it was exhausting, but they've got a system set up now to keep everyone contained. There is a whole cholera protocol, with flow into the tent through one flap and out through the other. As you exit, you are supposed to step into a bleach solution, and have another bucket of bleach solution to wash your hands with. Last week after we brought in the first two cases, all the solution was mixed and the staff was well aware of contamination prevention, but apparently the caretakers of the sick were just walking in and out, and then into the village, so there may be more cases this week. If that happens, I am going to feel really horrible for not staying there last week and making sure everyone stayed right there in the fenced-off area. So far, all the cases have been contacts prior to arriving at Kishale, but I am preparing myself to feel really guilty.

Stefano dug a shallow hole in the ground at the exit of the tent, lined it with plastic, and poured the bleach solution for feet in it, so now there's no way to get out of the tent without stepping in it. And he set up the big plastic barrels with the spout on the bottom and filled them with the solution for hands and for washing the floor and buckets in the tent, so the nurses don't have to keep mixing up small buckets of solution. The *Comité de Santé* (CODESA), a local health committee, has been educating the local people about transmission and getting to the health center at the first symptom, and they are doing a great job. They've also been staying at the health center making sure the *gardes des malades* don't leave the confined area without washing.

We had planned to go out there every day or two with supplies and monitor the situation, but now we are out of diesel for the vehicles. The truck containing it is stuck somewhere near Dubie, and no one knows when it will arrive. Perrin thinks within a few days. We have motorcycles, which use petrol, not diesel, and we have petrol, so it's possible to take a small amount of supplies that way. If they run out of IV fluid we have to get it there somehow. There is a path over the hills, which cuts off twenty miles travel, but the Land Cruisers can't go that way. A bike or motorcycle can, apparently. I'd be willing to ride a bike there. In fact, I would love to ride a bike there, but I'm not allowed to. I can't imagine they would let people die rather than let us take bikes, but we'll see what happens if it comes to that. I'm sure we'll send national staff instead. I'll keep you posted.

New information came in yesterday. A guy arrived here on a bike from a village somewhere in our district with a report of a child with acute paralysis. He was sent here by an MoH doctor to get one of our cool boxes and ice packs so they can collect stool samples from this kid and bring them to the nearest lab in Kiambi (miles from here and across a big river) to see if it's polio. Polio! Well, this might help spark some interest in my vaccination bandwagon, but my God, polio. I have never seen a polio outbreak, but supposedly it's just as terribly contagious as cholera. It's a virus, not bacteria, but passed fecal-orally, same as cholera. There IS a very effective vaccine for it, though (sitting unused in our fridge), whereas there isn't one for cholera. *Mon dieu.*

It's been interesting and sad in maternity this week. Last Sunday, just after I finished writing to you, I was called with the report that there were triplets in maternity. I ran over and there were indeed triplets there, born prematurely at home in a village an hour's walk from here. After delivering these three tiny babies, this woman walked an hour with her sister carrying the babies until another woman joined them and helped them along. When I got there, the mother was lying in the maternity bed and the two other women were sitting on the floor holding the babies, who were wrapped in filthy cloths and slowly dying–two boys and a girl. They looked about twenty-five weeks gestation and there was no chance for them to survive. Even at home it would have been touch and go, but it was very sad.

Then Monday a young girl delivered after a long, long labor and long pushing stage (God, I can't wait until that vacuum extractor arrives), and the baby was born alive but in terrible shape with meconium aspiration, and we couldn't resuscitate him. It is so frustrating. We have no oxygen and no suction that works, so after going through all that labor, this mother lost her baby also.

Friday we did have twin girls, though, and they are both alive and healthy and doing well. That's happy news, though the mother is in the bed next to the girl who lost the triplets, so I felt awful for her when we walked the mother with the twins into that tent. But I have yet to see a woman who hasn't had at least one baby die. The twins were born on Friday morning during the time when loads of people were waiting to be seen for either a *maladie* (illness) or for antenatal care. As we walked this woman out of the delivery room to the maternity tent, all the waiting people started whooping and cheering for her, and I saw her smile for the first time as she walked by. She was skin and bones; I could count every rib on her. As she was gingerly sitting down on the edge of the bed, some guy came in and threw flour in her face. I looked at Gerardine and said, "*Qu'est que c'est?*" (What is this?) She said very matter-of-factly, "*Pour félicitations avec les jemeaux.*" (For congratulations for the twins) Apparently, that's how you congratulate people with twins around here: you throw flour in their face. The father walked in and he was covered in it, too.

Then last night, as we were sitting around the table listening to Margaret and Stefano tell us about the cholera situation, the guards came over to get me to go to maternity again. It is so pitch dark here at night that all we could see were the lanterns swinging as they walked toward us, and Carila and I sat still and said, "Hmmm, you or

- 49 -

me this time?" So last night it was me they had come for, and as we walked the 100 meters over to the hospital they reminded me to watch for *serpents* (snakes), as I walk a little too quickly for their comfort. The guards are so sweet. I love them. They are so serious about protecting us. They don't want me to walk fast because they don't want me to trip or step on a snake, and even though it's their job and they are paid to protect us, I find it charming.

When I got into the maternity (cell, I call it), Gerardine was frantic, babbling very fast that this was one of our TB patients, who had been admitted into the TB tent for treatment, and not due until January, and she was fully dilated and about to deliver. This was going to be another baby who had no chance of surviving. Gerardine ran out to fill two rubber gloves from the pot of hot water kept on the fire that the guards were huddled around. These were to put around the baby after birth to keep it warm. I wasn't sure it was going to be premature, because no one even knows how old they are here (really: next to "age" on the chart is written "adult" in most cases), never mind when their last period was. Gestational age is determined by just measuring the woman's belly, and they are often so malnourished that they measure small when they are really full term. And this woman had TB! She was a skeleton! So, when we were all ready, I broke her water, and the full-term tiny baby boy just slid out, vigorous and squalling. It was a wonderful, happy little scene. Gerardine opened the door to ask the husband for a clean cloth for his wife, and his first question was, "Is it alive?"

Side note here to describe what happens when a woman comes in labor: I told you before that there is one metal frame bed with a vinyl covered, two-piece mattress on it. Over this is a rubber sheet, and now, (new acquisition) we have a rag to place under her buttocks. She removes whatever clothes she is wearing and rolls them up to put under her head as a pillow. Then those same clothes are used after the delivery to sop up the fluids she is lying in and placed, dripping, into a bucket. Sometimes there is an extra one to wipe her. If not we use a piece of gauze and another rag, if there is one. Then Gerardine calls out the door for someone–husband, mother, or sister–to bring a clean cloth to wrap around the mother. The baby gets wrapped in an old towel. We have three old towels that get washed every day, so if we have more than three deliveries a day, it's a problem. We tie a strip of gauze around the mother's waist, if she doesn't already have a string tied there, to attach another rag that goes between her legs. Then she gets up and we walk with her over to the maternity tent, which at night is lit by lanterns hanging from rope from the tent pole. The beds are filled with women propped up on one elbow waiting for the new arrival. (Last night when we walked in there I thought, "Geez, this is like having a baby at Girl Scout camp.") Then we tuck her under a mosquito net, put the baby next to her, and she's pretty much on her own. When they come to the hospital people must have someone with them (the *gardes des malades*) to cook for them and wash their clothes, which are often just rags. Most of the time when it is a maternity case it's a female relative who comes, but I see lots of husbands here as well. Though, I must say, I've never seen a husband wash her clothes.

When the young girl whose baby died was in labor, I had asked Beatrice, "Who sits with the women when they deliver at home?" She told me the mothers and grandmothers are with them. I said it was too bad that this poor girl was here alone, as she was so young and seemed scared. Beatrice looked at me very quizzically and said, "She's not alone! You are here, I am here, Gerardine is here." Like she had no idea what I was talking about. She reiterated, "*Seul?*" (alone?) making sure she understood me and laughing, shook her head, pointing to all of us again, "*Elle n'est pas seul*" (She is not alone). Like women are women, it doesn't matter who's related to whom. She and Gerardine do mother the women in a really tender way. I love watching them. They'll whip off their *pagnes* (sarongs), revealing gym shorts underneath, and hop up on the bed to cradle the woman's head in their laps if it helps her to push. They also scold like a parent would. It's very touching. There really isn't any room for other people anyway, and it's already unbearably hot in there. A couple of times Gerardine has taken off her blouse, and continued giving fundal pressure in her gym shorts and black, lacy bra. All of us are usually dripping with sweat. There are many times when I've wondered why this is supposed to be better than delivering on the ground at home.

The rain is coming a little more frequently, three times this week. I'm getting more used to the heat, but the afternoons are still ghastly. I just want to go to sleep, and actually have done that twice this week. I sat in the hammock after lunch and felt drugged. I didn't feel much better when I woke up. The nights when it rains are so much more comfortable. It'll be unbearably hot from about two p.m. until the clouds start forming about four thirty. Then the wind picks up until it starts to look like the scene in *The Wizard of Oz* when Dorothy is trying to get back to the farm. Thunder starts rumbling and the clouds get darker and darker coming from, let me see . . . the east, yes, it's definitely the east because I've seen the sun come up over there. It always comes in the same way (at least for the two weeks that I've seen it). Dark blue clouds that come at us like a wall, and then lightning and pouring, pouring rain. I just love it; it's very exciting. It's an incredible relief from the heat of the afternoon, and it's so furious and wild and untamable. The heavy rain lasts for about half an hour, then steady rain for an hour, and then it stops. Then as darkness falls, there's a beautiful pink lighting to the dusk and the air is cool. I love it.

Friday night it was only Carila, Angelien, and me here, as Margaret and Stefano were out dealing with the cholera, and Therese and Perrin were in Lubumbashi. We had taken a walk to the market when the storm started coming in and, being outside the base, the oncoming storm was even more dramatic: people running for cover everywhere, mangoes falling off the trees by the bushel, goats and chickens scattering, and I was looking at these grass huts and was in awe that they don't blow down. Literally, their houses are made of grass. I guess the wind blows through them. They do have fires inside these dry grass houses and you can see the smoke coming out through the walls and roof. You have to see it to believe it. I suppose if the whole thing catches on fire it's not too hard to get out; you could run right through the walls.

I went to church today. I have no idea what denomination it was. They had Bibles, so I guess it was some type of Christian something. Oscar, our radio operator, took Angelien and me with him and it was quite the spectacle. First of all, the church is a woven grass structure with a thatched roof, about twenty feet by maybe eighty feet. Sticks were protruding from the ground where planks of wood were laid for seats. Men were on one side, women on the other. We sat with the men, as Angelien wanted Oscar to translate for her. I personally didn't care what they were saying, and found the low murmur of the translating annoying, but it seemed rude to get up and go sit with the women. There was a mud altar and four men were sitting behind it, getting up once in a while to stimulate the congregation to yet another energetic song and dance. Whoa, it was intense. The drums were amazing. A group of six boys were in a corner with different sized hollowed-out logs (four of them), using mallets made from sticks and chunks of old tire rubber. Then there was a big steel wheel on the ground, I guess from an old truck, and two kids were playing that with big bolts. One guy was singing through an old thermos that had been hollowed out with the bottom removed, so it was just the plastic shell he was using like a megaphone. He was also hitting the side of the thermos with a stick. And two kids were using a piece of PVC pipe as a horn! It was fantastic! The singing and dancing were nearly non-stop. I felt like I was in a life-sized fairy house like the ones we used to build in the woods. I was utterly transfixed by the scene. It was not only the stunning music created with such basic materials, but also the frenetic energy with which it was performed. I was filled with awe to be in the center of it. We left after two hours, and it didn't seem that a service had started yet (unless the "Amen" in-between songs was the service). It's now five hours later and I can still hear the drums. I don't think I'll go every Sunday, but it was neat to see, and I don't think I'd have a problem going alone and sitting with the women if I felt like it. There's no Catholic church here. I think the closest one is in Dubie, eight hours away. I heard that the missionary priest there had to hide in his water tank for two days during a Mai Mai attack a couple of years ago. Everyone talks really fondly about him; I hope I meet him someday.

For everyone who thinks I'm wasting away here, don't worry. There is enough to eat; it's just crappy food. I actually think I have gained weight from all the starch I eat and how little exercise I get. I don't think I've been this inactive since I was pregnant with the twins. A shipment of food arrived last week and, though I was happy to see the beer, it was more canned crap. One day I asked, "Who decides what we order for food?" and Angelien told me that Therese had been placing the order. I asked why she is in charge of food? She eats like this at home, for God's sake! If I have to do all the tedious inventory and ordering for the hospital, then I want to do it for us, too. I'm going to work on that one. I mean, really, canned corned beef? Canned carrots? Please.

I should be wrapping this up; there's some toe tapping going on. With only one laptop able to send e-mails, I write frantically until everyone gets up. If had a memory stick, like everyone else does, I could use the other laptop and just transfer it here to send. But I don't, so I do it all on this one. Margaret was writing home on the other laptop and started chuckling and said, "I just wrote about the three scorpions, listen to this . . . " And she read what she wrote which was really funny, and I said, "The scorpions! I forgot all about those. I didn't write about that." She looked at me incredulously and said, "You FORGOT about the SCORPIONS? Jesus, you *are* adjusting well."

More next week . . .

Love you all,
Linda

J'assist le tour de salle chaque jour. *(I attend morning rounds each day.)* *Yesterday, all of a sudden, during the tour de salle, all the death hit me. Everyone is dying. It's so hard. I couldn't stand seeing it. The twins (preemies) are dying. One is already dead. The other looks like she has congenital syphilis. She's got sores on her head, bruises on her arm and belly. I thought she looked like she'd been burned. She's not going to make it. I'll be surprised if she's still alive this morning.*

The e-mail crashed yesterday. That was upsetting too. Supposedly the stuff can all be retrieved and the e-mail switched to another computer. I don't know how long that will take. Perrin has to go to Kishale today. More cholera. Ten cases now. I'm not quite sure what has to happen before more help comes. There are a lot of egos at stake here. I can see that. They need another tent there, so we take one. They need another bucket, thermos, raincoat—whatever—they want us to give it to them. Some people don't like that. They don't have a hammer. They don't have anything.

I have got to be more aggressive about planning my trip. I'm seeing the need to get away.

I spent a lot of time in my bed last night. I didn't feel like being around everyone. I read and slept, thought and slept, slept and slept—much more than I thought I could. It was cool and rainy. Thought a lot about how useless I feel and feel guilty that everyone at home thinks I am saving all these lives. I don't feel like I am.

Friday morning, very early—still dark. I'm sitting at the dining table by lantern light with Sylvester the cat poking and fidgeting and putting his face in the journal and trying to paw at the pen. I'm waiting for Papa Abel to bring water for tea. It's lovely and peaceful. I've wanted to avoid everyone for the past couple of days. I feel sluggish and depressed.

It's just starting to get light, just the first hint. I'd love to be out walking—not around here though. What a strange existence. Still, I'm glad I'm doing it. How strange.

Sylvester is sitting on the front step watching Papa Abel collect the lanterns. He left this one, didn't even ask for it. He knew I was using it. He seems so wise. I wonder what his story is. How many people he has lost during the war. How he ended up as a guard for us and seems so content to have that job. Up every night, pleasant every time he opens the gate. Asks me how it went, gently encouraging the French, always a gentle smile. What am I doing here? Angelien will be gone in five weeks. What then? Who will replace her? Therese and Stefano leave the week after that. Then I will go on holiday for two weeks and then what? I wonder what the team will be like. I start French classes this afternoon. Thank God—I need some improvement. It would help my mood immensely. What will it be like when I go home? Sometimes I can see myself slipping right back into the same life, but with more stories to tell, more patience for little annoyances, more appreciation for the food and freedom. Maybe somehow I believe I could be more helpful in changing some of the problems in our system. I'd love to travel around speaking. If I wrote a book what would I call it? Will I ever have another lover? I'm starting to be able to see myself alone forever and be OK with it.

October 29, 2007
Monday

Hi Everyone,

I'm a day late, having spent most of Sunday in bed. Saturday night something microscopic hit me in the stomach, and I spent most of the night heaving, and all day yesterday sleeping. Today I have sore stomach muscles from retching, and my head is a little fuzzy, but otherwise OK. I must have eaten something a little off. Can't imagine which gastronomic delight it was, but my body was very intent on making sure it was removed. Since no one else got sick, good chance it was one of the eight mangoes I ate on Saturday. I think I'll be more careful about peeling.

I'm not sure when this is going to be sent. We've had computer problems and Perrin hasn't been able to get it to work. First it sent the e-mails but wouldn't receive them, and now it won't send, either. I'm very frustrated by this; I was getting addicted to reading mail every day. Hopefully, it will be fixed this week. I'm trying not to be whiny about it, but it's my little lifeline to a big world I left behind. When I get to Lubumbashi for R&R I will be able to use the Internet but that won't be for another couple of weeks. My R&R has been put off twice now because of plane schedules and maintenance.

I didn't think I would look forward to going to Lubumbashi again. I didn't really enjoy my time there, but I am starting to feel like a break from the constant death-in-your-face will be a good thing. It's getting to me. This past week it was seemingly constant. We had four more sets of twins born here, one set with congenital syphilis. Both of those babies died; one was covered in open sores.

The next twins were premature; one of those died, the other is hanging on currently. Another set, one of the twins had a rectal occlusion and after three days had a huge distended abdomen. They had been born at one of the health centers and brought in when Stefano went out there to check on his water project. The babies arrived in a cardboard box surrounded by rubber gloves filled with warm water covered with a towel. The babies were snuggled in between, perfectly warm, like a litter of puppies. It was remarkably efficient. We took the babies out of the box and the guy who had transported them was standing there, not leaving. I looked at him, and he pointed and said, "*la boîte.*" He didn't want to leave without the cardboard box. One baby was in bad shape, jaundiced with a huge abdomen. Benson tried to open the occlusion and succeeded first with an IV catheter and then with a pair of scissors (amazing), and it worked! The meconium passed, the abdomen went down, and we were so excited. But she only lived for three more hours, and that was really sad.

The last set of twins was also premature. The first was vertex (head first), delivered easily in the amniotic sac with the placenta attached. (I have never seen that before.) His twin sister then stuck one leg through the cervix, which clamped down around it. Unfortunately the cord came down too, and even though I kept trying to push the cord back up, by the time the cervix opened up enough to allow for the birth, that baby was compromised as well. She did rally valiantly with the resuscitation attempts and even gave a few good squalls. We were encouraged, and they were all—mother and babies— stable when we tucked them into the tent. But a few hours later Carila got a call asking her to come because that baby was dying, and she couldn't do anything to save her. Carila didn't tell me until the next day. She thought I was getting too fragile for one more death. By the time I learned about it, I was resolved, but I really think if the baby hadn't responded initially I would have lost it. Don't ask me why, it's not rational at all, but for some reason I am happy she lived for three hours.

It seems like we are taking turns being overwhelmed by the suffering here. Angelien, who is a psychologist, hears story after story of unbelievable horror, and she has a hard time letting it go. She repeated these stories over and over to us, until we finally had to ask her not to repeat them at dinner. I feel badly for her because she says over and over, "I can't do anything to help these people! I was depressed when I had to sell my farm after my divorce, and these people have watched their siblings be decapitated!" And after a few days of watching babies die, I just couldn't listen to her anymore. I spent the time when I wasn't at the hospital pretty much hiding in my *tukul*. I've been writing a lot and reading some, but I am dying (oops, poor choice of words) to go for a long, long walk–like hours and hours– but that's not allowed. Angelien picked up on the fact that I'm not lending my usual sympathetic ear, and tried really hard to sympathize with me this week, though I can tell she doesn't think my stories are as sad as hers. Very competitive group we've got here.

Let's see, cholera update. More death. Two children have died and there are ten more cases. An additional ten and we'll qualify for the emergency team coming from Amsterdam! We don't know if we should hope for that or not. I have not been out there since last I wrote about it, but there have been improvements in the system. Perrin went out with the logistics team and set up another tent, and built some new beds with smaller holes in them (the kids were falling through the standard size cots). Apparently, the health education has been wonderful and the new cases are coming in right away. The early treatment means that people are recovering more quickly. Two additional nurses have been sent out there; both have experience with cholera, so that's good. A young girl from Kishale arrived here at our hospital with malaria and is being treated for that, but we're hoping she hasn't brought the cholera here. We are already planning to move all the TB patients in together if we need a cholera tent. Right now the TB patients are separated into two tents, one for patients who are coughing and one for those who aren't (it seems to me, because they don't have the energy).

OK, let's see, maybe some lighter stories. Get this: I actually enjoyed doing the hospital inventory this month. Well, *enjoyed* might be a strong word. I didn't mind it. No one died while I was counting pills and catheters and syringes. I am developing a fondness for Portefeille, our pharmacist. He is taking his job very seriously, having been promoted from night guard, and we understand each other. Yes! And boy, can I count in French now. My vocabulary has expanded dramatically. Nothing I would use when ordering a meal in Paris, but I am feeling quite superior. This weekend we move the pharmacy to a larger room that is almost finished and we can get out of that dark, stifling closet. The new room has windows! And by the way, for all the building that is going on here (and it is constant—I can't believe the changes that have been made just since I've been here), the villagers make the bricks. They mold the clay soil into bricks, stack them, cover them with dried grass, and then light it on fire to fire them, like a crude kiln. It's really neat. So the only thing that has to be brought in is cement. Some of that is by bicycle, but MSF is trying to get a truck here with cement to finish the hospital building.

Margaret, Angelien, and I, are now taking French lessons and I love it. Emmanuel, our teacher, is an unemployed nurse and formerly taught secondary school. We all liked him and wanted to give him some kind of job, and Angelien thought of French teacher. It's great; he is taking it really seriously. So every evening now from six to seven, we sit by lantern light and make up sentences using new *adverbes de lieu, et adverbes de temps.* Stuff like that. I love it. It's like being an adult in seventh grade. And no one dies! He gets paid $1.50 an hour, which is more than he was making as a nurse. This is just what I needed. Between the language and the computer skills, I'm shooting for some kind of recognition in the "Most Improved" category.

The team. Every week I think I'll write about that, and every week it gets upstaged. The dynamics change a bit from week to week,

I've noticed, depending on who's had the least sleep and who's recently had R&R. For the most part, I find people generally respectful. At least I don't think anyone is deliberately inconsiderate. However, maturity level must be taken into account, as well as cultural differences. For instance, some Europeans may come across to North Americans as rude, but I don't think they really mean to be. It's just a cultural difference. Like when Therese snidely says to me "Maybe MSF should test people's computer skills before they accept them." She's not trying to be rude or hurtful, or trying to push me over an edge. And if I hadn't heard her say to Margaret, "If I'd known your French was so bad, and you were only staying for six months, I never would have agreed to take you, ha, ha, ha," I might have taken it personally. Instead I said to Margaret, "She's leaving in four weeks. Ignore her." Most of us have a hard time with Therese. Fortunately, she's easy to ignore. I think so, anyway, though others don't. We just heard today that her replacement is a Swiss guy with lots of MSF experience, (pleasebeoverfortypleasebeoverforty) but that probably means he's twenty-eight, not twenty-six.

I initially had a hard time with Margaret but now we get along fairly well. She dropped the know-it-all shit when it wasn't getting her anywhere, and now I find her entertaining. And she was very nice to me when she heard me throwing up. She brought me a bucket because she didn't want me running outside barefoot. She has not recovered from the scorpion incident.

Carila is sweet. She really is. I really do like her but she is so clueless about what she says to people. She's smart and thrives on emergencies like a lot of people working for this organization. She thinks this cholera outbreak is fun. She actually said that. Giggling. I mean, I crave excitement too, but it's a bit over the line for me. Like she's confused when I'm upset if a baby dies. She'll say, "What? You're still upset about that?" in the manner that you would say, "What? You've never seen Star Wars?" Maybe it's just me. In a way I feel sorry for her. I feel like she's keeping up such a front. She knows how to rapidly run a code, but doesn't know how to comfort a grieving mother. She's really young; it's not like she's been doing this for forty years and is burned out. Not that I am perfect by any means, but I am taken aback by the scarcity of compassion around here.

OK, speaking of really young, I have never felt so old. Honestly, I don't feel this old around my kids. Angelien and I have talked about this so much. Everyone keeps making not-so-subtle comments about how old we are. Not in a mean way at all. In fact, I think they are meant to be compliments. Possibly we are being too sensitive about it, and it may be cultural too, but here are a few of them:

"I would always defer to you in that situation; you have a lifetime of experience."

"You thought he was handsome? But he was so much younger than you!"

"Benson was so glad to see you were an older woman when you first arrived."

"I think maybe more women are coming to the hospital now because you are so much older than Nina."

"You remind me so much of my grandmother; she always had a garden."

"You were in Sudan before the war? Wow! You must be really old."

And my very favorite:

"You must have been very attractive when you were young."

The last comment was said to Angelien at dinner one night. Really, I had to get up and run out because I was blowing tea out my nose. Angelien looked like she'd been shot.

Hoping we can send and receive e-mails today!!!! Pleeeeeze.

Love,
Linda

CHAPTER 3 ~ NOVEMBER

November 2, 2007–Je suis fatigué. Je suis triste. Je suis frustré. *(I am tired. I am sad. I am frustrated.) I've been wondering how much detail I should write to everyone back home. It's starting to make me look insane to have come here. And then I wonder why I am worried about how insane I look. How can Gerardine and Benson keep working night and day like this? I am disgusted. My frustration is mounting. The computer is available for less and less time. The team is irritating the hell out of me. Dirty dishes and cigarette butts on the table, hogging the computer, irrational decision making—I can't stand it anymore. I need to make more time for myself this weekend: do my nails, do my hair, run out at the airstrip—I don't care what I look like. Buy a new pagne, shower before French class. Breathe. Breathe.*

❖

November 4, 2007
Sunday morning, Shamwana

Bonjour tout le monde!

Sorry I worried everyone last week. It was so frustrating trying to send that e-mail. First of all, not writing on Sunday morning was a big problem as it's the only time without fierce competition for the computer. Then the laptop that had the e-mail program on it died. Just up and died (seems to be the thing to do around here), so off it went on the plane to Lubumbashi with my list of everyone's addresses on it. I didn't realize that until I tried to send the e-mail on Monday. I panicked, then realized I had a hard copy of all the addresses, but had to type them all again. I did that by elbowing my way in, sneaking onto the computer when someone stepped out to go to the latrine, and pretending to be working frantically. I must have typed something wrong, because I couldn't send it. Or maybe the transfer of the program wouldn't allow so many addresses, I don't know. Whatever, I was getting very upset, and people were getting very impatient with me, which made me more frantic. I was running between the office and the hospital, where a woman was in labor. She had taken some traditional medicines and was writhing in pain, contracting non-stop. This was her ninth baby, no progress, and we were wondering if she was going to rupture her uterus (which she eventually did). I kept saying, irrationally and emphatically, "I have to send that e-mail. You don't understand, I have to send that e-mail, I have to send that e-mail." And I was starting to get looks from the team that said "Jesus, no wonder her husband left her." (I know that look.) I was biting everyone's head off. I finally thought of sending it all to one person and have it forwarded to the others from there. Thankfully for the team, that worked.

Adding to the stress around here, the solar battery is broken, so the only time the computer gets charged is during the time the generator is going, five hours a day, and now we have very limited time before the computer hibernates. This has exacerbated the competition for computer time. In addition, various behaviors are pissing various people off—leaving dirty dishes on the table from the night before (my peeve), feeding the cat in the dining area (Perrin's), leaving the cornflakes box open (Margaret's), leaving an ashtray on the table where we eat (mine), leaving the lid on the serving container ajar so the "food" is cold for the next person (Therese's)–it's all coming to a head. I suggested a team meeting to work it out. Too bad there's no beer or wine left; I'm sure that would help. No plane this week or next, so no food either. This is not a bad thing in my opinion (except for the beer). Yesterday our cook prepared cassava leaves and they were delicious. I think I said that one too many times at dinner, and the canned peas crowd was getting annoyed. I would happily live on mangoes and cassava leaves, but apparently that's beneath what we are expected to endure.

I have some intense stories this week. I'm not sure how many of them I'll have time to write about, but I'll try. I want to tell you about the woman with the ruptured uterus. I think I mentioned before that there are many people here who do not believe in western medicine. There are traditional healers here and many people use them for health problems. We've had a few women who have come in to the hospital in terrible pain because they've taken some kind of herb to induce labor. I have no idea what it is and neither does Gerardine or Beatrice. They told me it's a root and it's found in the bush, but they don't know what it's called or where to find it. I've got eleven months to learn what it is because I'm very curious. It induces tremendous contractions that don't do anything to dilate the cervix. It's terrible to see these women. God knows why they do this to themselves. Up until this last one, we've just waited until the effects have worn off, and then they start going into labor. This takes about eight hours of screaming pain, and then labor, which seems like nothing after that.

But on Tuesday of this week there was a woman who was really scary. Even Benson was scared. Her uterus was rock hard and would not rest. A sustained contraction like that is very dangerous. It almost surely kills the baby, and eventually ruptures the uterus. The mother was wailing all over the place. She looked possessed. We don't have anything here that could be used to relax the uterus, but I did end up giving her a shot of morphine and that terrified the national staff. They never use pain medication here; they are afraid of it. I wanted to give her 15 mg, but they were so shocked that I was giving her any at all, that I didn't dare to open a second vial. So I gave her 10 mg and she did finally settle down and fell asleep, but eight hours later, after pushing for four hours without progress, it was clear something was very wrong. You'd think you could push out your ninth baby. So we took the dreaded walk to the operating room, which in the daylight was not nearly as horrifying. Still like operating in a garage, but more like a Saturday afternoon kick-around-in-the-garage, not a mad-scientist-at-work-in-the-garage, kind of feel. Hot as hell, but not as eerie. And God, the smell. I feel like I am never going to get these smells out of my nostrils. And sure enough, the uterus was ruptured. The opening in the uterus was so big that Benson didn't even have to make an incision. The baby was alive though, and though the mother lost her uterus and an exorbitant amount of blood, she lived too. They are both alive still, and here it is Sunday. So amazing.

Next one. It was nearly the end of me here. Around seven o'clock Thursday evening I finally had the computer to read my e-mails, but only read two of them when the guard came to get me. Perrin looked up from his work and said, "Beeper going off, huh?" That's what we call the guard walking toward you with the lantern, "Beeper going off." I love it. It's so eighteenth century. Back to maternity I go, my feet starting to remember where the rocks are on the path as I step over them automatically. A little tiny girl was in labor, not more than four foot seven inches tall, supposedly twenty years old, but if it hadn't been for her breasts and pregnant belly, you'd have thought she was nine or ten. She was fully dilated and started to push. And push, and push, and push. Four hours went by, she was pushing her heart out, and the baby was not coming. I couldn't say for sure that it would. Let me just say for those of you who haven't worked in obstetrics, that the decision-making process starts getting complicated after a while. I started thinking, "Was that really progress or am I just hoping it was progress? Do I really believe this kid will fit, or am I just saying that to keep the mother encouraged? Do I really think it won't fit, or am I just thinking it won't because I'm tired? Is there another position we haven't tried? Am I just torturing her to keep going or should we call a cesarean?" It's hard enough at home when it's such a bummer to have to call our very pleasant surgeons, go to our very clean, well-lit operating room, with very nice, skilled people whom I always look forward to working with. With anesthesia! With oxygen! Here, that decision making process takes on a whole other perspective. Is the baby going to die if we don't go? Is she going to die if we do? If she doesn't die this time, will she die next year when she tries to deliver in the bush and ruptures her uterus? Was that *really* progress? It's really, really hard. After four hours, it was starting to sink in that this was not going to work. I hated to go back into that OR at night, but this baby was not coming out. The woman had a child's body. She had starved, hiding in the bush for ten years of her growth period, and now she had a full-sized baby that wouldn't fit. I asked Gerardine, "*Q'est que tu pense?*" (What do you think?) I did not want to be the one making this decision. I really didn't. Her reply, "*C'est grave. C'est trés grave.*" (This is serious, very serious.) She always defers to me. I sent the guard to get Benson. He arrived moments later, wearing a winter jacket, as the temperature had dropped to a chilly eighty-five degrees. We both knew what needed to happen. The baby was alive and strong; the mother had pushed so hard for four hours. The decision was obvious. It would not fit. Benson said he'd go speak to the family sitting in the dirt outside the door. He was out there for a long time–a *long* time. An hour went by. I heard them talking, talking, talking. She was pushing, pushing, pushing and I had nothing to help her except my hands pressed into the small of her back. Benson came back in and told me the family was refusing to let her have surgery. He said, "I've told them that she and the baby could both die, and they say it's God's will." This was her mother and father! I was sick! I frantically asked, "What are we going to do?" The thought of going to that OR had been terrible to me, now the idea of *not* going was unthinkable. The girl was pushing and pushing, whimpering quietly between contractions, but never crying out. Benson went back to talk to them and Gerardine went too. Another hour went by. In came the brother of the father of the baby (they weren't married, that's why the parents got to make the decision); he was a nurse. Gerardine tossed a box of gloves in front of him in disgust, not saying a word, but meaning, "Go ahead and check for yourself." He shook his head no. The decision was made. She could not have surgery. Benson brought in the parents so they could hear her whimpering. They shook their heads no. He was speaking Kiluba, but I could understand when he told them that they would be responsible if there was death. They got up and started to walk out when this poor girl gave a horrendous scream and the baby's head started coming out. I caught this baby, but it was not a birth, it was an expulsion. The head was mush. The eyes were half open and fixed. It was awful. Benson took one look, ran over to the door, grabbed the mother's arm and dragged her over to the bed and made her look, saying "You did this! You did this! God did not do this!" Benson is a remarkable man. He is so rational, and diplomatic, and kind, and gentle, and to see him this distraught, to have seen him spend two HOURS in the middle of the night patiently trying to explain the need for surgery to this girl's PARENTS was as heart-wrenching as seeing this now brain-damaged baby. We spent twenty minutes trying to get her to breathe, which she finally did after we injected some glucose into the cord. The heart rate was always good, but she had no reflexes at all. Fixed pupils. But here she was. Alive. Sort of. I held her for a while, trying not to cry, while we waited for the nurses to get a bed ready in the big tent for them. Then Gerardine and I walked with baby and child-mother to the tent, helped her onto the bed, placed the baby in her arms, put the mosquito net around them, and left. As I was walking away with the guard, anxious to get into the shower where I could start crying, Benson called to me, "*Mama Linda!*" I turned around, startled because I thought he'd gone home. It was pitch dark. He was sitting with the family, but I didn't walk back there, just stood where I was and said "*Oui, Benson?*" (Yes, Benson?) And he just said sadly, "*Grand merci, Mama Linda.*" (Big thank you, Mama Linda) And then I didn't think I could wait to get to the shower to start crying, but did manage a "*Merci aussi, Benson.*" (Thank you too, Benson). I just couldn't walk back over there.

Isaac, the guard, walked me to my *tukul*, where I grabbed my towel and headlamp and went to the shower. I shone the light in to check for snakes and scorpions, showered with the murky river water, and thought, "Did I really need to send myself to an obstetrical hell just to avoid electronic medical records?" And as awful as the whole night was, as tragic as that preventable outcome was, at that moment the saddest thing to me was Benson saying thank you. I'm going home next September. He is home.

So I cried most of Friday, off and on. I kept trying to tell the story to everyone here, but couldn't get through it. I read the nice e-mails everyone sent, and that made me cry, too. I sent an e-mail to Milan at the office in Lubumbashi and asked him to buy my ticket to Dar es Salaam for next month. I don't care what it costs. I am going up Kilimanjaro; that will be the long walk I've been craving. That's where I'll spend New Year's Eve. Once I made that decision, I was able to go back to work on Friday. I helped get the pharmacy ready to move on Monday. I took a block of wood and put a big nail through it so Portefeille could take the prescriptions after he fills them and poke them onto the nail as a way of keeping track of what's been filled and what hasn't. The way it's set up now, they are just blowing around in the room, or shoved into an old cereal box. Everyone loved the nail. They thought it was brilliant. I made them smile.

Early yesterday I made a list of nice things I was going to do for myself, which included washing my face with hot water from the thermos for tea, filing my nails, buying a new piece of fabric, walking the length of the airstrip and deciding if it's a good place to go running, and washing my hair with rain water. I did them all and felt much better. We played cards last night and laughed, and that helped, too. Therese and I made martinis with the gin and some olive juice left in an old jar of olives. We decided that in the right glass, it could sell for $7.50 in some upscale bar.

The rain is coming more regularly, and the cloud patterns are spectacular. The landscape is so beautiful. It really is. And now, with the clouds in layers of deep blues as a backdrop, it is just so, so beautiful. On the main "road" toward the market there is a line of orange trees all in bloom. The airstrip has an open and magnificent feel to it, and I'm going to start jogging there.

Juan, a surgeon from Spain, is coming to Shamwana for ten days to do some elective surgery–fistulas and hernias mostly. He arrives tomorrow. I met him in Lubumbashi, and I am looking forward to his stay here. He has worked with MSF for twelve years, and—whoa, man—has he got stories. If all goes well with the plane, I'll go to

Lubumbashi on Friday for R&R so next week's e-mail will either be from my Hotmail address if I have time to write there at the office, or not until at least Monday or Tuesday.

Oh, the immunizations are going really well. We've now been to all four outer clinics and are starting to get the word out about when we'll be back each month. We had between thirty and forty kids at each clinic, and I am pleased with that. I met with one of the supervisors from the Ministry of Health (two of them came through here on motorcycles) and talked about our plan for immunizing kids. He was reasonable and seemed supportive. (I hope–my French is still not perfect.) He said he will get me more vaccines and cards for the mothers for documenting who's had what. (I hope that's what he said.) We have enough vaccine here for one more month with the current numbers, and now that we've started I want to make sure we keep it going every month. I am really committed to this. It's such a positive thing, and eventually I want to make the clinics more social and do health talks.

The cholera is under control in Kishale, but yesterday we got our first case here.

I'm not writing about the ruptured ectopic pregnancy, during which surgery Carila actually did faint. I am not writing about the woman who was fully dilated for six hours at home and who traveled through the night by bicycle thirteen miles to arrive early this morning, and (Oh, surprise!) was too exhausted to push, I am not writing about . . . no more time.

Love you all, and thank you so much for all the encouragement and beautiful messages. I really appreciate them. Thank you for being so supportive. I sometimes feel like I am running a race and want to quit. Then I hear all these people cheering for me and it makes me want to keep going.

More next week,
Linda

Wednesday morning—cool after the rain last night. Morning sounds— roosters crowing, chirpy birds singing, men arguing, someone pounding flour, drums further away, children's voices. The arguing male voices are dominant.

Pounding and chanting goes on. "Ndoma" something, something. An adult woman is chanting and little kids are chanting back to her.

I'm recovering psychologically from last week, and had more long, hard, drawn-out deliveries over the weekend. It's much cooler; the mornings are pleasant. Seven weeks until my trip. Yummy, yummy. I can't stop thinking romantic thoughts of my December vacation. I am so happy at the thought of being away alone at Christmas. I love the idea.

I've been here almost two months. I don't feel homesick, though I am tired of the team and look forward to some time away in Lubumbashi. Then I will be back for two weeks and will go again to Dubie for a midwives' meeting. I hope I can go by "kiss" rather than by air as I'd like to see the whole road to Dubie. I love that term "kiss" for when the vehicles leave from different directions and meet halfway. We use it a lot. It has almost lost its other meaning for me. Lord knows that's not happening here.

I had salty rice and milk for breakfast. The oats are gone. I put too much salt on the rice, and the margarine tasted fishy. There is a heavy mist in the air this morning. I am going to finish my French homework. Make more sentences. It is interesting learning grammar when I don't even know how to speak the language. But I trust that it still has time to come together. I've given myself three months. It will be two next week. No beatings until I am ready to leave for my vacation, which is going to be fabulous. I can't wait! A hotel! Clean sheets! Real meals! Walking out the door when I want to! I don't know how it will turn out, but I have a good feeling about it. I was happy to see so many faces smiling at me when I returned from Kishale.

November 8, 2007—I'm hungry. There's nothing for breakfast. For the second day in a row I've eaten leftover rice from yesterday's lunch. I heated it with hot water and sprinkled it with stale Parmesan cheese from a plastic pouch. It was watery and awful, but I was so hungry I ate it.

November 9, 2007—I supposedly go to Lubumashi today for R&R. I'm annoyed. Couldn't check my e-mail last night. Computer has a dead *battery. Inconsiderate people. I'm sick of them all. Dirty dishes always on the table. I'm hungry. There is no bloody food. Everyone annoys me.*

November 18, 2007
Sunday morning, Shamwana

Hi Everyone!

I'm back in Shamwana after my R&R and by far, the most dangerous thing I've done here is cross the street in Lubumbashi.

I was happy to get back here but that said, it was nice to get away. I am truly amazed at how therapeutic three days away can be, even though it wasn't in the lap of luxury by any means. R&R, I learned, was not intended to be a vacation (we are still expected to work at the office on the Friday we arrive) but is really just a change of scenery and an opportunity to take a clean shower and have a meal served in a restaurant.

Friday there was talk of the plane not coming again and I panicked. I had to get away. I had been up too many nights in a row, had too many tragic outcomes back to back, and I was barely functional. I was struggling to keep from crying all day. The latest plane problem was that the two experienced pilots were on vacation (poor planning, I thought), and the others couldn't land here. They were going to cancel, but no plane had been here for two weeks, and we literally had no food left–unless, like the Reagan administration, you call ketchup food. I have new empathy for hungry people. I know we all know what it's like to feel hungry, but knowing there is nothing to eat when you are already hungry is something else altogether. I never thought I could be sick of mangoes, but after a while I was craving something a little more substantial. We were all crabby and irritable, and we started watching how much everyone else was taking for a serving at each meal of rice and stewed greens. It's been very interesting. There was no breakfast food at all. There was a half tin of powdered milk left, and a few tea bags, and after a cup of rice and cassava greens for supper, I was starving in the morning. The powdered milk was enough to feel satisfied for an hour or so, but then it was, "Think about lunch, think about lunch, think about lunch." The sole conversation was how hungry we were. I'm not sure if this was the reason for the special arrival of the pilot from Kenya who's capable of landing a plane here, but it was deemed important enough for the company that runs the airplane to bring someone in.

I understand the need for R&R much better now. It wears on you to be with the same people all the time, especially when you're all hungry. Then because there is absolutely nothing here, everyone asks you to buy them stuff in Lubumbashi. This gets annoying when you are hot and hungry. Umbrellas, thermoses, chocolate, books, milk, cheese . . . on and on, and I realized I was going to spend most of my time there shopping for other people, and I hate shopping. But I can sympathize. Like I said, there is nothing in Shamwana, and the local people have little chance of going to Lubumbashi themselves. And when they do, it's several days by bicycle. (I must say if I had enough food, I would love to make the trip by bike.)

The plane finally arrived–nice landing. We unloaded everything, loaded everything, and off we went. I asked the pilot why it's harder landing here than Dubie or Kilwa (the two other projects in south Katanga), though I could speculate, because even running on the airstrip is hard to do. It's soft and uneven and strewn with rocks. He said that it's not so much how soft it is, but it's on a hill, and curves, so if you don't stop the plane exactly at the top of the hill, it's really hard to stop. For anyone afraid of flying, this would not be the place to be.

When we were seated on the plane the pilot reached behind his seat, opened a cooler, and passed back little packs of cookies, ones I wouldn't be caught dead eating at home, and I scoffed them down in about six seconds. We took off, flew the thirty minutes to Dubie, landed on hard pack dirt surface, flew another thirty minutes to Kilwa, and then the hour more to Lubumbashi (paved). We flew really low, so it was a little bumpy, but very pretty. Usually there is someone vomiting on the plane from motion sickness (so I hear), but not on my trip. The only unpleasant smell was the petrol from the broken generator we picked up in Kilwa. That smell, along with the bumpy ride and hunger, gave me a splitting headache.

There were several of us on R&R from the various projects and it was a madhouse at the office. Every time someone asked Angelien and me how things are in Shamwana, we said, "We're hungry. There is no food." This scenario was repeated about ten times, and it seemed like they didn't believe us. But it's hard to be rational when you are hungry, so maybe they did. They didn't have the reaction we wanted anyway, which was to say, "Oh my God! We will send an extra plane of food!" We got a driver to take us to the closest restaurant and we ate fried chicken and potatoes and I can't even tell you how it tasted. It was food that had to be chewed, that was all I cared about. After that, I had no desire to do anything but lie down, so went to the house to which I was assigned and I just lolled around talking to the other people there. It wasn't bad. Mia, a wonderful woman from Holland, was there; she's here for three months working on contracts for local staff. There was a woman from London, Sheila, who's on the emergency team and came for the cholera cases, of which there are pockets around the district, not only in Shamwana. We talked our brains out for several hours and went to bed. There was a group of people going out to a bar, but I didn't have the energy to rouse myself, and didn't feel like paying for beer when there was plenty at the house.

Saturday I got up early and walked to the office. We are allowed to walk around in certain areas of Lubumbashi between the hours of six a.m. and six p.m., but we have to call by radio and let them know where we are and where we are going. And we have to leave the radio on so they can contact us. It was six a.m., and I radioed to the base to tell them I was walking to the office, a distance of about a mile. I thought I was being rather clever to go use the Internet before anyone else got there, and I walked and walked and walked, and realized I was totally lost. I was hoping they didn't notice at the base that I should already have been there, and as soon as I started thinking of this, on the radio I heard *"Base pour Linda"* (Base for Linda), and I had to answer *"Linda écoute."* (Linda listens). *"Ou étes vous?"* (Where are you?). And I had to say *"Je suis perdu."* (I am lost). They noticed. I told them what corner I was on, and they told me which way to walk. It was rather handy. I could NEVER have done that in French when I was there in September. I realized how much progress I'd made. I found my way to the base, and then it all went downhill. The Internet wasn't working, a zillion people showed up all having the same idea as me, all looking for transportation to different locations in the city. I was a total bitch, miffed that now I had gotten nothing accomplished and was going to spend my entire day looking for stuff for other people and waiting. Waiting for rides, waiting for others to finish their errands, waiting for food. I was not having fun. The city is noisy and polluted and hot, and the traffic is like nothing I have ever seen before. Only the main roads are paved, the side roads are dirt (dusty in September, muddy in November). Cars are everywhere, minivans have their side doors open with at least twenty people crammed in there hanging out the door, honking and swerving all over the place. There are no sidewalks, just dirt (mud) paths covered with trash, and the cars are all over these too. The buildings are broken down, bombed-out brick structures, barely a single window left unbroken. I wish I could take pictures. I've never seen even a bad part of another city look like this, but I've never been to a post-war city before.

Now let me say, that, having learned my way around a bit, there is potential to be more efficient and savvy next time I go. This was a learning experience—an unpleasant one. The shops are small, crowded, dark, dingy, smelly hot places with a hodgepodge of different stuff in no particular order. Because of the money situation (a 500-franc note being the largest, and its worth being one US dollar), you have to go to a window in the shop (like a bank window) pay for what you want (which takes forever), then take your little slip of paper and collect the purchase. I had no bags, so I was carrying four thermoses and three umbrellas through crowded streets with beggars pulling at me everywhere, still looking for the other stuff I promised to buy, muttering, "I am never doing this again." Ugh. I was not a happy camper. Now that I know how it works, I will be more efficient next time, but this time was not fun. (Oh, did I already say that?) I should have walked to the city center early (before the lethal traffic), with a few of my own bags, done the shopping, then called for a car to come and pick me up with all the stuff. I had to wait for two hours in a hot photo shop waiting for Angelien because she had promised people she'd get their film developed. It was hard to leave and do something else because we thought we'd never find each other again. Plus, they kept telling us it would only be ten more minutes; twenty times they told us this.

Saturday was pretty much a bust. I tried later in the afternoon to get on the Internet again, trying to book a flight from Dar es Salaam to Kilimanjaro, but couldn't connect. Finally, Milan, who makes all the international travel arrangements, offered to do it for me this week. Technically, he's not supposed to do travel plans for our vacations, but he understood I wasn't going to be able to do it and took pity on me. That helped my mood. By this time it was nearly five p.m. and there wasn't much left to the day. I had planned to call home at six p.m., so made my way back to the house and used the cell phone there to call my mother's house where my family was gathered, helping her move to a first floor apartment. It's amazing how therapeutic that phone call was. Even though my chat with each person was short, it was so nice to hear their voices, and all the frustrations of the day seemed insignificant. It suddenly seemed silly that I had been so worked up about everything.

The group that was gathered at *Maison 2* started with a happy hour with laughter and good conversation, during which everyone noted the change in my demeanor. We met the others at a local restaurant where, after several beers, the food was edible. It was overpriced for grisly meat, but filling, and we had fun. Dennis is a new financial controller, from Dublin, and very funny. There was Rose, who is adorable, from France. She's working in Lubumbashi as a logistician coordinator at the capital level. Angelien and I spent a good deal of time complaining about the food situation to her. There was Philip, a nurse from Kenya, Mark, who's drilling wells, Mia, Sheila, Angelien, and me. It was fun to be in a crowded, outside restaurant with music and loud conversation. Good time all around.

Sunday morning I got up very early (the only time I'm alone), wrote in my journal, and gave up on the idea of trying to write my weekly e-mail from there. The Internet connection is too unreliable, and the keyboard is a French one so typing would have taken me forever. At six thirty I called a driver to come get me and take me to church. I had seen a big Catholic church in the center of the city the day before and wanted to check it out. It was so much more pleasant to drive in the city at that hour on a Sunday. There were hardly any other cars out and being a solitary traveler, I could chat with the driver more easily. He pointed out landmarks and I discovered I was learning how to get around. He left me at the church in time for seven o'clock mass. This was not to be missed. I am so glad I went.

The church itself is a very simple brick structure, but quite large. It was the largest building I saw in the city and the only one without broken windows. It was packed. The choir consisted of about thirty people, all with operatic voices. They were magnificent. The hilarious thing was the accompaniment. It was a tinny, electronic thing with canned music that was a hybrid of polka/folk/Polynesian-sounding music that was totally out of place. Someone must have donated that. As soon as people started singing, though, you couldn't hear the accompaniment anymore. The songs went on and on, but they were so beautiful I didn't care. The music was all-encompassing, like sitting in the center of an orchestra. On the altar, the twelve altar boys were standing in groups of three and they all started swaying and swiveling to the music in perfect unison. They looked like the Supremes behind Dianna Ross. Everyone in the whole church was swaying and clapping. I half expected Whoopie Goldberg to come dancing down the aisle in habit and wimple. God, it was great. Plus, I felt like I fit in. I didn't feel like an outsider, even though I was the only white-skinned person out of the 500 or so there. It was very comforting to be part of a familiar ritual, albeit with the local flair. I wish I could go every week. The mass was in Swahili, I'm not sure if there was a later mass in French. Probably. You know, come to think of it, this was the first Catholic Church I've seen anywhere without a sign on it and without the schedule of masses. The driver had to tell me it was the Catholic Church. It wasn't marked. I'll have to ask about that. Anyway, the mass went on for two and a half hours, and the time flew. Kneelers were a bit rough, though. Then, as we were walking out amid clouds and clouds of incense, there was a huge crowd fighting to get in to the next mass, as if it were a rock concert with unassigned seating.

I stood outside on the steps in the rain, used the radio to call a car, which was already on its way with Sheila, Angelien, and Rose. We all headed over to the outside market, which was a much more pleasant shopping experience. For me anyway, Angelien hated it. I wanted to wait until Sunday to buy fresh vegetables to bring back to Shamwana. The supermarkets are closed on Sunday, but the open-air market is so much better. Yes, it is dirty and there are beggars hounding you the whole way, but that didn't bother me. I just love open markets. It was inexpensive and we could just pay directly after haggling a little bit. I loved it and didn't want to leave. I bought mounds of eggplant, peppers, and avocados, flour to make bread, and more seeds to plant in Shamwana. I am determined to become self-sufficient here with the food. I mean, c'mon! What kind of example are we setting?

When we got back to *Maison 2*, our housemates were just getting up and we spent a pleasant morning with a big breakfast, reading, watching a movie, and relaxing. Later in the afternoon, Sheila and I went for a long walk, got lost again, tried in vain to figure out where we were before six p.m. when we had to be either back at the house or the base, so had to call for a car again and admit we were lost. Damn! I get lost a lot, and I hate having to call and admit it. But we needed a car anyway to get to the restaurant on the lake where we were all meeting to watch the sunset and have a few beers. (Detecting a pattern here?) It's a small bush restaurant with tables outside under thatched umbrellas, and the setting was beautiful. We were having so much fun there that we stayed for hours, through a fantastic thunderstorm, laughing hysterically while debating the important topic of which was worse, bad sex or no sex?

The next morning we returned to Shamwana with our head of mission (the one in charge of our whole project in Katanga district) and the president of the board from Amsterdam. The timing could not have been more perfect because, even though some food arrived on the Friday plane, it wasn't much, and was almost gone by the time we got back here on Monday. We had the food that we had bought, but it wasn't going to last long for nine people. I was so glad that these higher–ups got to see what it was like here. Well, don't you know there was an extra plane arriving on Wednesday loaded with enough staples for a month. Yeah! Still no beer, but I did find those little packets of whisky in Lubumbashi and bought ten of those which I'm hoarding for the rough days.

After all my bitching about shopping for everyone, it was so sweet to see the reactions when I handed out the purchases. They were like little kids on Christmas morning, and I felt bad for being such a sourpuss. The local staff only asked for stuff they really needed, and they gave me the money for it. It wasn't like they expected me to buy it for them. It was the expats who asked for the chocolate and cheese although they were like little kids on Christmas morning, too. And, really, to see someone smile here is so nice. I've often wondered, after all they've suffered, if they'll ever find any happiness in life again, but I can already see the difference in the short time I've been here. There's just more life here in general, more chickens, a few goats, I even saw some baby ducklings when I was walking to the airstrip yesterday.

Before I went away for the weekend, I was overwhelmed by the lack of incentive to live that I saw everywhere. It seemed like it'd all just been too much and everyone had given up. In labor for instance, the women just won't push. They just give up. I have never seen anything like it. There's no drive to get it over with. Their bodies just go limp, even with strong contractions, and there is not even a cellular biological response to bringing this baby out. I'm starting to wonder if it's a deep traumatic response in a post-war population. The women don't report rape because they are cast out of the family afterward, so I'm wondering if many of these babies are a product of rape, or if it is complete exhaustion from trying to survive. I am definitely seeing a pattern. Most of the women are having their fifth, six, seventh babies (and up from there), and it should not be taking three or four hours for these kids to come out after she's fully dilated, but that's what it's taking. They almost work to keep the babies in. Maybe, because most of them have lost several of their kids, it's an overwhelming fear or depression, I don't know. It would be an interesting research study. None of them look at their baby or reach out to hold it. None. The only woman I've seen yet who made any effort was the girl I wrote about last time whose parents refused the surgery. She saved herself by pushing that baby out (probably cracking her pelvis in the process), but her uterus didn't rupture. It was the first woman I've seen who showed a drive to live. I am glad I have a whole year here. It will be interesting to see if this observation changes over my stay, if the peace in the district holds out, and if the will to survive manifests itself differently over time.

It's quiet at the base this weekend now that our visitors are gone and Juan is on his way back to Spain. He'd been here for two weeks doing elective surgeries in our new, larger operating room. He has worked for MSF for twelve years (this was his fourteenth mission) and he said he's never been in a place as remote as Shamwana. He was fun to have here; I'll miss him. He did several hernia repairs and hydroceles, and a few hysterectomies in women with huge fibroids. There wasn't a need for any c–sections while he was here. It was good for him to operate with the team so he could do some teaching. For the most part, he thought the surgical team did a good job with what they have to work with. It's more difficult to teach the decision-making process, to decide if surgery is needed, so they reviewed that quite a bit. The local doctors rather like doing surgery and it's not always warranted. There is now a German surgeon in Dubie for two weeks who specializes in fistula repair, and the women with fistulas are being transported there for that surgery. I can see why they have so many fistulas with the horribly long second stages of labor and lord knows what kind of sexual abuse. They have to stay there for six weeks after the surgery with a catheter in the whole time. It's a big process, so they are all being done in one place. These poor women are continually leaking urine and stool and are often cast out of the family for it. Horrible.

Also gone this weekend are Carila and Margaret. Margaret left for her R&R and Carila is in Dubie for a medical meeting. So I am the only medical person here, which meant that when Deo (the outreach nurse who works with Margaret) arrived at the base on Friday afternoon telling us we had two suspected cases of measles in a village thirty kilometers from here, everyone looked at me to make the plan. Measles is a huge, huge crisis if it turns into an epidemic. It's worse than cholera. Measles is a lethal disease for children. So Friday afternoon was spent making the arrangements for transportation and personnel to go out and confirm this. Deo and the nurse from Monga (a clinic closer to the village) were coming, as well as Perrin (who was very excited since he hardly ever gets to leave the base) and Angelien, who didn't have anything to do on Saturday and could help with the immunizations. Therese was trying to get in touch with Sheila in Lubumbashi and also with the Ministry of Health here for some guidance, but the protocols are very clear. Confirm the cases, isolate the kids, and according to the World Health Organization (WHO), immunize all kids from six months to fifteen years. We have enough measles vaccine in the 'fridge here to do that, but for some unknown reason the Ministry of Health refuses to let kids over five be immunized. It is such bullshit. They don't even want us to immunize kids over twelve months! It's criminal. I really thought that once we got there and confirmed the cases they would say go ahead and give the vaccine but that's not what happened.

We got packed up here yesterday morning, with enough vaccine to immunize 400 kids, which was the number of children recorded in that village. A messenger had gone to the village the day before by bicycle to tell them that we were coming. We arrived, examined the sick kids, and confirmed it was definitely measles. One child had already died. Three were very sick, and eleven others have the symptoms. We told the chief that he had to arrange for all the sick kids to be put in one or two houses and be kept away from the other children. Then another elder took the megaphone we brought, and went around the village telling everyone to bring their children to the chief's house where we were set up under a tree. In the meantime, we called Therese by satellite (SAT) phone to tell her what we found, and she said that she had contacted the MoH and they wanted to talk to us directly before we did anything. So it was a complicated radio hitch-up that went through our base radio operator to theirs. Straight out of M.A.S.H. Thank God Perrin was there to do that. They started by telling us we can only immunized kids six to twelve months. I said to Perrin, "Tell them that all of the confirmed cases are in kids over two years old!" He relayed that message. They came back with an OK to do kids up to twenty-two months (no one even knows how old their kids are). My thought was, this is bullshit, let's just do everyone, they'll never know. But supposedly we'd be kicked out of the country for that. We got the nurse from Monga to talk to them. He's employed by MoH, and he reassured them that we were not making this up, that the confirmed cases were kids up to age five. We finally got their permission to immunize the kids up to that age when we told him there was already one death. Unbelievable. We immunized 134 kids and treated the ones who were sick. We will go back there on Wednesday to count for more cases and immunize any more we missed. Tomorrow we will go to the surrounding villages to look for more cases.

When we got back here, I had to write a report to Sheila in Lubumbashi. There was already an e-mail from her warning me not to rile up MoH, it was a politically sensitive issue, and they wanted more "rationale" before launching a major immunization campaign. I am going to do as I'm told, but Jesus! What more rationale do they need? Fourteen cases in an un-immunized population, one dead, and WHO guidelines all over the fucking place! My God. It killed me yesterday to have to say no to the older kids who were sticking their arms out for their shots. God.

As the sun was setting and the air was cooling off, I had just sat down with a cup of wine to talk to Angelien and Therese, and was looking forward to a shower. Isaac, the guard, came running over to ask Therese if we could take a car to collect his wife who was in labor and unable to make it by bike. He asked me to come with him. I got up, handed my wine to Therese, got in the Land Cruiser, and drove to the next village where I entered one of these houses for the first time. Sweet Jesus. It was like being in a hole in the ground. The laboring woman was lying on a crude bamboo cot. I helped her up (couldn't see a thing), helped her mother wrap her in a *pagne*, lifted her into the Land Cruiser and made it back to the hospital in time for the delivery. Long day yesterday.

OK, this really is getting too long. I'll be in Dubie next weekend, so might be late with my letter next week.

Happy Thanksgiving! (Is it this week?)

Love you all, Linda

Thursday Morning—November 22, 2007

Je donne remerciements. Je suis reconnaissant. *(I give thanks. I am thankful.)*

Thanksgiving—Up until this morning I'd barely thought about Thanksgiving. I didn't even know if it was this week or not. I heard from several people that it was today, and now I am thinking about the niceness of the day, how much I'll look forward to the holiday at home next year with all my kids there. Thanksgiving means it's close to Christmas. I wonder if the time will go fast. Dubie this weekend, then leave here on the 21st, which is less than a month away now. I'm going to take out my hiking boots and start wearing them. I also need to arrange transport to Kili. Might go by road. I'll plod through the day today and daydream about future Thanksgivings—happy that I am here for this one.

November 25, 2007
Sunday morning, Shamwana

Hi Everyone,

I am so discouraged. After our great start last Saturday trying to keep the measles epidemic contained, the Ministry of Health is refusing to let us immunize any other children. Zippo. Nada. It is utterly criminal. In August, when they received the vaccines from UNICEF, they supposedly did a campaign to immunize all the children in the country against measles. Well, they didn't quite do that, and now apparently if we do it, it makes them look like they didn't do their job. Which they didn't. But apparently it is preferable to have children die and be maimed from this disease than to have us show them up.

OK. That is bad enough. But the thing that I am even more frustrated about is our capital team going along with it. This worry about being kicked out of the country is, in my opinion, overblown. And why are we giving in to threats, anyway? I mean if MoH put a gun to a kid's head and told us to pull the trigger or they'd kick us out of the country, would we do it? Because that's what I feel is happening. And my angry e-mails to Lubumbashi are getting me nowhere. I get replies saying they can understand how frustrated I am, but we cannot go against MoH when it comes to measles. It's political. We need more rationale. Please. We have enough vaccine to immunize 1,000 kids sitting in the fridge creeping closer to its expiration date, and we can't use it.

I am also frustrated with the sheep-like behavior of the Shamwana team. I think we should just go do it. Who's going to know? It's not like we've got oodles of caregivers from MoH coming around checking on things. No one comes to this God-forsaken place, or gives a shit about the people here. We could've just played dumb and said we didn't understand what they meant. It's always easier to get forgiveness than permission; every kid learns that growing up, for God's sake. I don't care if we give MoH the credit! Let's just go immunize, and say that someone from MoH did it in August! We could have done that instead of waking up all these sleeping dogs and giving them some NGO meat to go after. So stupid. So self-serving.

In the meantime, the measles is spreading like wildfire. It's impossible to keep kids isolated in the village. So this week we brought a tent to the health center, herded all the infected kids into that, and stuck one nurse in there for the fifty kids that now have a fifty-fifty chance of surviving. We had a great open window of opportunity to protect the surrounding villages, but politics is winning once again. I want to scream. Or cry. Or give up. I don't know. I'm just not sure what I should do and how to live with myself. It's just so wrong to be going along with this. We've got our own MSF guidelines that clearly outline what we should be doing. The fact that we are not following our own guidelines (which are based on WHO) should be argument enough, you'd think. But that doesn't seem to be working. I'm switching to guilt. I told Therese that if she wants to go along with Lubumbashi, then she can go out to the village herself and explain to those mothers and fathers that, even though we have the vaccine, we are not going to give it to their children. I am not going to do it. I told her that maybe she should get out from behind her computer and see what kids with measles look like. Maybe then she might change her mind. This tactic might stimulate a little backbone in the other medical team members (Carila and Margaret) who agree with me but "don't want to get involved." Excuse me? Isn't this a bit of an extreme experience for someone who doesn't want to get involved? They *are* Canadian, though. I think I might get somewhere with this approach, though it's already late in the game. I'll keep you posted. (Uh, don't anyone publish this anywhere) I have just realized though, after my big soapbox scene, that we don't have enough dilutant for all the vaccine. It's just sterile water, though. I think I can just use the right amount of sterile water we've got for other uses. I'm certainly not going to go asking for any.

So that has occupied most of my week. I haven't slept well. I was supposed to go to Dubie this weekend for a meeting of the three midwives from the three projects, but that got cancelled because the plane didn't come again. I was bummed. I really wanted to talk with them about how they handle things, though all the projects are very different. The other two centers are much bigger than Shamwana. Dubie was the place to which all the people from Shamwana fled during the Mai Mai attacks. Now I don't know when we'll get together, probably not until the end of January. I again offered to go by motorcycle (it'd only be seven hours or so), but the project coordinator in Dubie cancelled the whole thing, which I thought was rather inappropriate since she was not even involved in the meeting. Everyone is on a fucking power trip.

Early this morning the guards came to ask me if we could go collect a pregnant woman who was bleeding, and on her way here by bicycle. So I woke up Perrin who is in charge of the transportation, but I also wanted to make sure I had the story straight, because if my French is just a little off, it changes the whole scenario. I had gotten it mostly right, so he sent for a driver, and the driver, the messenger, and I set out toward Mungumbu. I had been to this village before but, whoa, what a difference three weeks of rain makes. I couldn't even tell there was a road there. It looked like we were just driving through jungle. Everything has grown up like crazy. I can't imagine what it will be like in three months. You know, I was surprised, arriving at the end of the dry season, how green everything still was. Now I am realizing what a jungle this is. Quite spectacular. It's impossible to leave my arm out the window now when we're driving (by the way, I have a fabulous tan on my right forearm). The branches and vegetation were battering the vehicle the entire way.

We found the entourage, the bush-ambulance bicycle rigged with bamboo branches forming a reclining seat, and the pregnant woman (about twenty weeks along, I thought) balanced on top, writhing in pain with blood running down her legs. Got her into the Land Cruiser (you should see trying to turn that thing around now in this thick bush) and headed back to the hospital. She had been trying to deliver for two days at home, and the poor thing was in agony. The fetus was stuck halfway through the cervix, but I don't know how long it had been that way. She wasn't real chatty. I gave her some morphine and pitocin, and it wasn't too hard to deliver the baby who had died sometime before. I wrapped him up, thinking the family would come and do a burial. That's what has happened with all the other babies who've died. But the husband and mother came in, looked over the baby, then took him and threw him in the latrine. I found this so shocking that I gasped as they did it. Everyone else just shrugged and walked away. I don't know, some days a year seems a very long time. Beatrice found the look of shock on my face extremely funny. She was chuckling away *"Ah, Mama Linda!"*

I struggle with the gallows humor here sometimes but this is not to say that I don't find making people laugh here extremely satisfying. In fact, it is one of the activities I am thoroughly enjoying. True, most of the time they are laughing *at* me, but I don't care. I love to hear them laugh. I love to see them smile, too, but hearing them laugh is the best. I think it's happening more and more, which might be a sign that life is in a healing process here. I'd like to think that, anyway. Example: You know how I told you that we have to keep reporting back to the base via radio every single movement we make? For instance, when we leave the base, we have to name everyone in the vehicle and say where we are heading. Then we have to call and say we arrived. Then we have to call and say we're leaving that place, heading toward the base, and say if we picked up any sick people, etc. Well, we were leaving one of the outer clinics heading back here, and we had picked up one of the extra nurses who had been sent there to help with the cholera. His name is Moustique. There were eight of us in the vehicle, and I was on the radio listing everyone by name: Rigobert, Jean Çlaude, Gerardine, Choco, Linda, Stefano, Willy, and Moustiquaire. The Land Cruiser exploded with laughter. Choco had to stop driving he was laughing so hard. I'm going, *"Qua? Qu'est que j'ai dit ? "* (What? What did I say?) Choco, trying to collect himself, chokes out *"Moustique! Pas Moustiquaire!"* So, instead of calling this nurse "Mosquito," which is his name, I had called him "Mosquito net." It was the funniest thing they'd ever heard. I was telling this story at supper that night, and Margaret said, "Yeah, as if it's not funny enough that his mother named him Mosquito."

Emmanuel is my French teacher. I am having so much fun making him laugh. Did I tell you that I am the only one in the class now? Angelien disagreed with something he tried to tell us, so she stopped coming. Margaret didn't like that I had already learned the past imperfect tense, and she hadn't. I personally find this easier than the *passé compose*, but she was miffed that I showed her up a bit, so claimed that she had "too much work to do" and stopped coming, too. (Did I mention we're a tad competitive here?) Anyway, I'm still going and I think it's really fun. He gives me these lists of words and I'm supposed to put them in sentences for homework. So I write sentences like "The crazy man won't be happy until he finds a crazy woman." And "Today is a big feast in the United States. Everyone eats a fat turkey with a fatty meal. Afterward, everyone feels fat and doesn't want to eat anything fatty." He just falls all over himself laughing. It's fun. I've got a good one for tomorrow. I took all thirty of the words and put them into a crazy story instead of just writing sentences. I can't wait to read it to him. Which is a challenge by lantern light. You should see us reading with our faces one inch from the paper

We had a salad with the lettuce I grew today. That's big news. Mia is here for a few days from Lubumbashi and she brought some pickles and capers and made a tuna salad. I picked some lettuce and two teeny zucchini, which I had planned to cut up into the salad. I was bursting with pride. I showed them to everyone, and then left them on the table and came into the office to write. When I went back to the kitchen, Mia said casually, "Oh, I hope you're not upset, but I was talking to Therese and burned the zucchini. Sorry." She burned the zucchini. She. Burned. The. Zucchini. Burned...the... zucchini. And she thought that little apology was adequate? Good thing I like her.

The team is going to be very different in a few weeks. Angelien leaves next week, and her replacement is a thirty-one-year-old psychiatrist from Belgium. Stefano leaves two weeks after that, and his replacement is a twenty-six-year-old woman from France. (Did I already tell you that Stefano is deaf from measles? He wears very high-tech hearing devices, so can hear some things, but you have to be looking right at him to talk to him. You'd think he'd be on the measles tirade, but he's in his own little world.) And Therese's replacement is also a thirty-one-year-old from Switzerland. I've given up hoping for anyone my age. I'm now just hoping they don't smoke.

The team will be all francophones except for me and Margaret, so that will be different, but I'm glad. It's very hard to become fluent when we all speak English together.

Hope everyone had a great holiday . . . and now that I've written all this I'm not as down as I was when I started. So thanks for listening! Really, I don't think I could do this if I couldn't write to you every week.

Love you all,
Linda

December 2, 2007

Je le rêve de promenade. *(I dream of walking.)*

Wow, it's December. It's funny how I lose all track of time until I write the date. It seems timeless here. Everyone stuck in purgatory forever and ever, and time stands still. It is remarkable to me how the days seem so endless, but the weeks somehow pass. I don't miss being home though. I am sure of that, so I guess I am content to be here. I received very few e-mails this week. I remember that happening around the holidays when we were in the Peace Corps. Everyone stopped writing because they were too busy. In three weeks I'll be in Dar! Keep looking forward!

December 2, 2007
Sunday morning, Shamwana

Hi Everyone,

Ah, a nice, rainy Sunday morning, and after Angelien's going-away party last night, I'm sure I won't be bothered for hours. I'm settled in the office with my pot of tea and predict solitude for most of the morning.

Yesterday was World AIDS day, and the local CODESA planned a bunch of activities to raise awareness. There is no AIDS program here. We don't have a lab set up yet, and therefore no way to test for HIV status. The disease is here, but I don't know what the incidence is. I've seen people die at the hospital, probably of AIDS, but they were being treated for TB. They looked utterly wasted and didn't respond to the TB treatment, so I'd go with the other diagnosis myself, but nothing official. Anyway, it was supposed to be a day where village activities got people together and a message dispersed.

It started at eight a.m. with a parade. Let's see, for the line-up there was the *Croix-Rouge* (Red Cross) with their torn and tattered Eagle Scout uniforms. Attached somewhere to the outfit was a red cross, and a few had them painted onto their hard hats. There were maybe twelve of them, and they alternated between a strict military-like formation and chaotic dancing. Quite the combo. They were the most official looking group. There were a few groups of school kids, and MSF, and then the rest of the village. No one actually watched the parade, they all joined in. We walked down the main road, then through the village paths picking up everyone along the way, singing I don't know what, and bopping along to the drumbeats. It was incredibly hot, and everyone was soaked with sweat. We all ended up on the football field and formed a big circle (kept in very tidy formation by the scary looking *Croix-Rouge* who had ropes and knives dangling from their waists).

Then the entertainment began. First was the *Croix-Rouge* in the center doing a dance and song, I think it was some national Red Cross song. Then the school kids, who ranged in age from about nine to eighteen, did a song. The leader stood out in front of the group and sang, "What are you going to wear when you have sex?" and the group sang back in unison, "We are going to wear a condom!" Someone was playing a drum and a few of the kids had plastic whistles, and the same lyrics were repeated, oh I don't know, 150, maybe 200 times. This was all done in Kiluba. Gerardine was next to me translating into French while laughing her ass off. Then—this was great—the Catholic youth group moved into the center of the circle. I didn't know until yesterday that there was a Catholic group here, but there they were. One guy stood in the center with a flag with a peace symbol on it, and all the kids (aged about nine to eighteen again, but all boys) had on neckerchiefs with the same peace symbol. Like Cub Scouts wear at home. Their song was similar, in that one guy sang out a question and the group sang back the response. His question (sung while dancing incredibly erotically) was, "How many women are you going to have sex with?" and the group sang back, "Only one woman!" Repeat, and repeat, and repeat. It was the most erotic dancing I've ever seen; he actually appeared to be having sex with the flag. God, I was wishing my old Peace Corps friends were there. We weren't even allowed to say the word condom in Malawi. I couldn't believe my eyes. I was the only expat from MSF who stayed to watch. Everyone else was "too hot" or had "too much work to do." Then there was a skit (OK, this did go on too long) about men and women meeting up, in what I think was supposed to be a bar, and having sex with each other. This was implied by hugging; they stopped short of actually having sex on the ball field. Then there was a long drawn-out sequence of skits. A husband and wife are HIV positive, he blames her because a small child coughed in her face and she got it from that, she blames him for having sex with other women, and takes a big stick to beat him, when the police arrive with toy guns carved out of sticks, and drag them both away. There was a clinic scene in there somewhere, and I'm not sure what the whole message got summed up as. I was nearly dying from sunstroke.

In the afternoon there was a football game, but I didn't go watch that. I read my book, soaked my feet, and then went for a run. We were getting ready for Angelien's good-bye party. It's a strange set-up here. The one who's leaving has to plan and pay for the party. Well, there's not much planning, it's the same every time. The departee pays a local staff person to find and kill a goat. This is done on the day of the party. Weeks (preferably months) before the party, the departee is supposed to arrange to have enough beer here for local and expat staff to actually enjoy the goat. Angelien, as much as I love her, is very disorganized, and failed miserably in the arrangement of beer delivery. Panicked, she had to use the Christmas stash, hoping it will be replaced before then. I'm not worried about that because I won't be here for Christmas and, obviously, neither will she. So, none of the expats could drink the beer last night because there wasn't enough for everyone. Luckily, I had my private little stash of whisky packets, which I hadn't touched yet.

The evening started with some masked dancers from another village, which Angelien had requested and her mental health staff figured out how to hire. That was really cool; I took lots of pictures and a short video, which I finally figured out how to do on my camera. They were very creepy, covered in a chain mail-looking garment made of some kind of fiber, and all the local Congolese were afraid of them. Every little wisp of fiber that fell from their costumes was quickly picked up by a boy whose sole job that was. The village chief told us that it was very dangerous to leave anything from these dancers around. I got a little freaked when one of the dancers came over to me and danced really closely and then started making movements with his hands for me to either follow him or give him something. The fiber-collecting boy said something to me in Kiluba. The village chief was seated next to me and I looked to him to translate into French, and the chief said that the guy wanted cigarettes. Obviously this dancer's powers of perception were not too keen, as I'm the only one here who doesn't smoke. Or maybe that was his point. I was just glad I wasn't supposed to follow him. The drumming was fantastic, though.

After the dancers finished and danced off into the sunset, there was an awkward period of sitting in a circle, looking at each other, before the speeches started. I am so glad I have nine more months to prepare for this. There were several speeches about how wonderful Angelien was and then she had to say a speech, which she wrote and had had Gericose (our administrator) translate into Kiluba. But she lost the translation, so had to do it in French. They don't really care what you say; you just have to talk. Then came the food, which was goat and rice. The goat was so tough that I was hoping someone near me was skilled in the Heimlich maneuver, but there was nothing else to eat, so I gagged it down. It was unchewable. Then the beer was passed out to local staff, and Angelien and I hit the whisky.

Then the music started. It was the same repetitive music that the drivers play in their vehicles, which usually makes me want to claw my eyes out, but after a few shots of whisky—and not enough food— I could detect a good beat, and the dancing began. It was a total blast! We danced for two hours straight, a free-for-all, until nine o'clock when, for some reason, the party abruptly ended. After all the limbo contests, though, I was ready to stop. My quads haven't had a workout like that since skiing the moguls in Quebec. It was very fun, and we get to repeat it in two weeks when Stefano and Therese have their good-bye party. Something to look forward to!

I have now done my third pharmacy inventory and I'm getting the hang of it. We have a big stockroom at the base filled with medical supplies and medication. Weekly, the pharmacist makes an order and the supplies that are needed for the week are transported from the base over to the hospital. The inventory is so much easier to do in the new building, and I am starting to teach Portefeille how to think ahead for stuff that might be needed over a weekend. He doesn't look at the two remaining vials of ampicillin and think we maybe should order more if we have six people admitted who need it. That thought only strikes when there is no more, and it's Saturday afternoon and the guy with the keys to the stockroom is nowhere to be found. So we're coming along.

We're back to having very limited food. No plane this week or last, and since we've had lots of visitors, the supply that came in is almost gone. We're down to our last small bag of rice which, right

CHAPTER 4 ~ DECEMBER

now, on a full stomach, I can say I am really sick of. But give me a few days and I'll be upset that I can't have my breakfast of rice which was left over from supper, which was left over from lunch. I am picking one small zucchini per day now, and a good amount of lettuce. I think we're OK in the vitamin department. And we still have the flour I bought, so we've been getting fresh, brick-oven baked bread every day. Things aren't desperate yet. Still plenty of mangoes, and I saw some onions in the market a few days ago. Thank God the corned beef and sausages are finished. I can't even look at that anymore. I'll fry up these flying ants before I eat that shit again. I haven't built a chicken coop yet; the measles took up the last two weekends. Maybe this afternoon I can get going on that.

The garden is a challenge. I can't let the zucchini get very big or it gets wormy. The cukes are all leaves but no cukes. The tomatoes rot before they ripen and the carrots sent up a shoot of green and just sit there refusing to grow. The basil and cilantro, I must say, are looking very healthy. I might just start eating that in the salad. There's not a lot to mix it with. Oh, the sunflowers are awesome. They have huge buds, which hopefully will turn into huge flowers. The eggplant and peppers are growing nicely, but haven't produced anything yet. The peanuts are growing everywhere, and I am really looking forward to that harvest.

In three weeks I'll be in a nice hotel at the base of Kilimanjaro, ordering off a menu. So I am not going to complain too much right now. Vacation is just around the corner and I am going to live it up.

I think I've brought you up to date. I'm going to plant some beets and work on my French homework, and then have Angelien cut my hair before she leaves tomorrow for good. I'm going to miss her. I feel like she's leaving me alone with the children.

Love you all,
Linda

⋙⋘⋘Ɔᴑ⋙⋙⋘

Je pense trop et ne peux pas dormir. *(I think too much and can't sleep.)*

Monday— It's early morning and I've just eaten leftover eggs/tomato/onion mixture from last night, with grilled bread. Not bad. I didn't sleep well last night, and spent the last several hours waiting to eat. I was hungry and unable to turn my mind off. I've been thinking a lot about what's going on at home. Here's the flip side of getting the longed-for e-mails. Life and friends there are changing, and I wonder how I will fit in when I go home. Or will I ever fit in again? Financial worries and limited coping skills have been the headlines this week in news from home. That upsets me. E-mails have dropped off, holidays etc. I guess, or maybe people are just tired of writing, but it all got to me last night. I felt lonely, though I have no desire to go back home. Hopefully by September I will. Nine months is still a long time. With the vacation coming up and the change in the team, it may not seem so endless.

It's hot already. I'm sweating and it's still very early.

Sheila is here from Lubumbashi, and she is really great. It really points out all that's lacking in the other team members. I can't stand Therese, though I still am able to see her strong points. She's just very unpleasant to be around. Rude, negative, takes no responsibility, and let me add incompetent. She tries to blame everyone for all her inadequacies. Margaret has encroached upon my precious early morning solitude. Not bad enough she's got all the computer time and food, now she's taking my solitude, too.

There must be a funeral going on. I hear lots of wailing and chanting this morning.

December 9, 2007
Sunday morning, Shamwana

Hi Everyone,

You know, it's amazing what you can get used to. There are days when I get back after work, get undressed and wonder, "Hmmm, can I get another day out of these pants before leaving them to be washed?" If I were home, I would throw these clothes away. When I arrived here three months ago, I was so appalled at the conditions at the hospital I spent most of the time trying not to gag. I didn't realize how used to it I'd gotten until Sheila came here from Lubumbashi and did rounds with us at the hospital. She was asking the same things I was when I first arrived, "God, can't we get some ventilation in here? Do these kids have anything to write with or look at since they are here for months at a time? THAT's where they do the laundry? THAT's the only fetoscope?" It's been good, since I wanted the bureaucracy to see what it's like here. But it made me realize how accustomed I've become to conditions here.

Sheila is on the emergency team (it's a big deal). When there were both cholera and measles outbreaks, they sent an E-team person from Amsterdam to evaluate and coordinate. She's really good; she's been meeting with officials at the MoH trying to get permission to do vaccination, but we're still waiting for the final approval. It's a big step, though. She's skilled at navigating through the unbelievable red tape, and does it with good humor. She's also incredibly normal, which is a breath of fresh air, and she doesn't smoke. She told me that she's never seen a project (meaning all of the three sites and Lubumbashi staff) with as many misfits as this one. She's worked with MSF for a long time and has something to compare it to, which I don't. I found that comment reassuring since I am getting more and more frustrated with the team here, on all levels. Everyone has their quirks, but this measles thing has shown the true colors of people, their maturity (or lack thereof), and skills (or lack thereof). I don't want to use all my precious computer time complaining about the team again, but I certainly could.

Sheila is here for a week, and on Thursday I was going out to Kishale to deliver the medications for the month, pay the staff, collect several sick people whom I did not have room for in the vehicle when I went out to immunize the prior Tuesday, and check to verify a measles case in that health center. It's in a completely different area from the other measles outbreak. When I was there on Tuesday doing the routine immunizations, an eight year-old girl arrived on the back of a bike from Kiambi (a very long way away) and was very sick. She did have conjunctivitis, and her legs were covered with lesions, but they weren't measles lesions, they were large, open, oozing sores. But the nurse there was suspicious and isolated her, which was very smart. The cholera tent is still there, and there weren't any more cases of cholera, so she was placed in there. I told them we'd be back Thursday with the supplies for the month, etc, and would check on her then, and if it did declare itself to be measles, we'd take her to Monga where the measles tent was (a long way away). There were no other cases in this area, and she had come from visiting family in

Kiambi, so I was hoping she didn't stop and breathe on other kids along the way. At a very, very long meeting on Wednesday night we decided on the movements for Thursday. I thought it was an outreach (meaning, Margaret's) job, but she bailed, so I went. (I am angry and lacking perspective right now, so I'll not write about that until I can be more insightful.) But the good part was that Sheila decided to go with me, and that was great. It was one less seat in the vehicle for transporting a *malade* (sick person), but it was really helpful for her to see the situation there, how the cholera tent was set up, how far away it is, etc. Plus, it was finally like spending the day with a girlfriend. What a relief.

Kishale is three hours away. We usually leave here at six in the morning when we go, because we have to be back by five, and that gives us a few hours to spend at the center. That's if it's a day trip. If it's overnight, it's not so rushed, but overnighting there is not pleasant, especially now that it's raining. If I had my own little tent I wouldn't mind it at all, but I'm not anxious to be under that crawling, leaking thatched roof again unless it's really necessary. And Thursday I thought we could be very efficient: get out there, get everything done, and get back in the vehicle to come home. The vehicle can hold ten people, including the driver.

I had to find a TB patient who had been in the hospital here for months, and was at a stage where he could go back to the village with a month's worth of medication. Then he was supposed to come back to Shamwana for the next month's supply. Well, when I went on Tuesday, he told me he had taken all the month's worth in fifteen days and now needed more. So he was either sharing it, or not taking it correctly, so I had to take him back here and have him be supervised with his meds again. He looked great, though; it's amazing how TB patients recover with the treatment regime if you catch it in time. It's complicated and many times it's just not possible for them to do the six-month treatment in the village without medical supervision. So there was him. Then there was another woman who we suspected had TB, then there was a fourteen-year-old pregnant girl who was four foot, six inches tall with a breech, and there was a baby whose mother died a month ago, and the baby was now terribly malnourished. And then there was the eight-year-old girl who, we found, definitely had measles. She had a raging fever, pneumonia, and was covered with flies when we got there.

The ride out there is getting more and more lush and beautiful.

It's harder to see the mountains now and, with the clouds in different layers, they are often hidden completely. I can't see the huge anthills at all anymore; they are completely covered with vegetation. They used to stand out like monuments. I don't think the road is much worse, aside from being muddy in some spots. We do have to drive through some water, but we haven't gotten stuck yet, or slid off any of the bridges. It is hard to see people on the road now, so we do have to go slower, but so far it's been fine. Jean de Dieu, our driver, had his cassette player break this week, so without the cloying music we're usually forced to listen to, I thought the ride out there was quite pleasant. I've learned to enjoy the ride *to* the health centers, because the ride back is decidedly *un*enjoyable.

We didn't leave until late, because we had to load up all the supplies, and it took forever for Gericose to count out all the salaries for me to deliver. Imagine paying ten people their monthly wages in one-dollar bills. That's what it's like. I think it was almost nine a.m. when we left, so by the time we got there, unloaded everything, counted all the inventory for them to sign off on, lugged this huge wad of cash into a dark room, and had them come in one by one to receive their pay, count it in front of me, then sign off on it, sent a messenger out to the village to find the patients we were looking for, and collected the bundles they needed to take with them for their unknown length of stay at the hospital, we did not have enough time to take the measles case to Monga. We had to bring her back to Shamwana, and planned to transport her to Monga on Friday. I called on the radio to tell them the situation, and they set up an isolation spot for her. We've been trying really hard not to bring any measles to Shamwana, but I didn't know what else to do. We couldn't leave her there. This is why I was so glad that Sheila was with me. Besides the physical help, it was so nice to have someone confirm and collaborate on the decisions. It was two p.m. when we were ready to leave, and I still wanted to try and make it to Monga, but Therese said no when I called, so we headed back here. Once we got going, I was really glad we weren't adding another hour to the trip, but I was still uncomfortable about bringing the girl to Shamwana.

Just figuring out how to seat all these people in the vehicle was a challenge. The grandmother of the malnourished baby had never been in a vehicle before and she was terrified. She was also high risk for vomiting, especially if seated sideways in the back, so she sat facing front in the middle seat. We figured it would be easier to immunize the baby against measles than treat her for TB, so we put the measles case and her mother next to them (the mother between), and the others went in the back facing each other. On every trip like this, someone ends up vomiting out the windows as we go along, and this was no exception. Sheila and I were sharing the front seat, and the combined smells of urine, body odor, and vomit, wasn't too bad until it started pouring rain and we had to shut the window.

When we arrived back here, the staff at the hospital was waiting for us. They were all smiles and *"Bon retour's!"* (Welcome back) as if we had gotten back from a vacation and were bringing gifts instead of more work. They amaze me. The measles girl and her mother were guided to the partially finished room that will be the lab soon, and is a good distance away from the little hospital community, with children, goats, and chickens now scurrying around all over the place. I spoke briefly with Vindicien, the nursing supervisor, and said I'd bring some measles vaccine over in the morning for all the kids at the hospital now that we had taken this girl here. It was the right thing to do, we decided in hushed voices, and left it at that.

I leave in two weeks for my vacation. I am very excited about it, but very worried that I'm not going to get out of Shamwana to get my flight to Dar es Salaam. The plane cancels regularly now: either a pilot who can't land here, or clouds are too low. I want to leave a few days earlier by road and go to Dubie. I want to see that project anyway, and there is a better chance that the plane will get out of there. They have a proper landing strip and it eliminates the pilot issue. Chances would go up that I'd make it to Lubumbashi.

It's cooled off quite a bit, and last night was downright chilly. I had to put on a long sleeved T-shirt while we were playing cards. The days are still hot, but when the wind and rain start, the temperature drops and it's such a relief.

Our bitching about food has paid off, and we've got a large store of staples now. A big box of perishables came on the plane Friday so I have no complaints in that department. We've had gorgeous meals of eggplant, salad, and potatoes, and I've been making myself an egg every morning. It's wonderful.

Hope everyone's happy and healthy back home. Didn't hear from many this past week, so I'm assuming December has everyone busy. We finally got the inverter for the battery fixed, so I'll have more flexibility with computer time now and can answer more individual e-mails this week.

Love you all! Linda

Je ne peux pas comprendre la guerre. *(I can't understand war.)*

Tuesday—I am trying to learn more about this place. It's a strange (but maybe more real) way to go about it, living here in a destroyed community among confused and desperate people, and trying to grasp all the events that could have possibly brought them to this. I know I can never understand completely, or even relate. There are too many barriers. It's such a bizarre experience to be living with a team who I also don't understand and have very little in common with besides skin color, trying together to accomplish a monumental task. We disagree on so much. I chose this, I remind myself. Why don't I know more about this war? What do I occupy my time with at home? The Congolese are right when they say everyone has forgotten them, but it's more like no one ever knew they existed.

I wish I had more time to write. I find on Sundays I am summarizing the week, and I know there is so much more I should be including. I wonder if everyone stopped reading my letters. I wonder if that's why I don't hear from people now.

December 16, 2007
Sunday morning, Shamwana

Hi Everyone,

There was another party last night, this time for Therese and Stefano. Same format, though the dancers didn't show up, and since the two of them are not as loved as Angelien was, it didn't have quite the same zeal. Still fun—we danced for two straight hours—but it was more subdued. There was a woman in labor, and Gerardine and I had been up the entire night before (transverse lie, arm and cord in the vagina), so I couldn't drink anything. But it's so nice to dance and laugh with the national staff that I think we should do it once a week. Without the speeches or food we could dance for an hour on Friday nights. I think the national staff would love it. There's nothing else to do here. We show a movie for them on Fridays and Saturdays, but there's no reason why we couldn't do the dance before the movie. It's just a big boom box with incredibly poor quality cassette music in front of the office. Hmmm. Think I'll work on that. They dance so beautifully, and they love it, and I love it so… a good thought for the new year. It seems silly to wait until someone leaves to do something that we all love to do.

Beatrice hadn't been up with us the night before, so she was elected (more like instructed) to stay with the laboring women so Gerardine and I could go to the party, and call us if needed. At 9:15 when the party was winding down, we had to go over to maternity because Beatrice couldn't get the woman to push out her eleventh baby. This phenomenon is still occurring. She finally delivered two hours later, and I came back here and went into a coma, I was so tired. Too tired to take a shower, I just dumped disinfectant over my foot where the amniotic fluid had splashed, and collapsed into a dead sleep. I am getting a late start this morning. Hopefully everyone else will sleep late, too, and I'll still have my four hours to write without interruption.

The team is changing and so far I am very happy with the prospects. Lucile arrived from Belgium to take the place of Angelien. She's a bit overwhelmed like I was, though her French is much better, so she's not completely lost. She comes from the Flemish part of Belgium so she speaks Dutch as a first language, but her boyfriend speaks French, so she's pretty good. She is having a hard time with the accents too, though, so that made me feel less inadequate. She's a psychiatrist, not a psychologist. Angelien had been worried about that, but Lucile's really normal and easy to be with. I like her. It's nice not being the new kid on the block anymore, and I'm having a good time getting to know her and showing her around. She wants to run with me; that's nice. Finally, someone with a little sense of balance. On her first night here, I was called out at eleven o'clock. It's disturbing to everyone when this happens, because the guard stands outside the *tukul* and calls me, so everyone who isn't a sound sleeper wakes up, too. I went off to the hospital and came back about two hours later and was wide-awake. We had a visitor here from Lubumbashi: Edgardo, the capital logistician–a fat, chain-smoking Spaniard. He was in the *tukul* next to mine, snoring like a freight train. I went over to the dining area, made myself some warm powdered-milk, and was reading my book, when I heard Therese scream "Help!" in English, then horrible, blood-curdling screams, then a bunch of Dutch that sounded like she was speaking in tongues. It was terrifying, but I remembered when I first arrived Carila told me Therese had nightmares, though I had never heard anything like this before. I was about to go check on her when one of the guards came walking over quickly (no one runs here) to ask me if I was all right. I said, *"Je pense que Therese as eu un mauvais reve"* (I think Therese had a bad dream), circling my ears with my hands, like you do when you're trying to describe someone as crazy (like she is). He went over to her window to wake her; she was having a horrible nightmare, and smashed her hand against the wall. All was calm after that, but believe me, *everyone* heard it except for Stefano, who is deaf and takes his hearing aides out at night. In the morning I had another delivery early, and then left for Kampangwe for immunizations. I didn't see Lucile until I got back late in the afternoon, and asked her how her first day was. She said she was really tired because she hadn't slept at all. I said, "Did you hear Therese?" and she said that she had, and thought it was a Mai Mai attack, and laid in her *tukul* shaking in her bed for hours waiting for the next victim. She was too terrified to move. She said, "I lay there thinking, I can't believe this! My first night here, and we're being attacked and I spent so much time reassuring everyone at home that I'd be OK!" So that was her welcome to Shamwana. Traumatic, but now that we've all developed a black humor, pretty funny.

We just got the confirmation that Lucile's boyfriend, who is a doctor, is going to be Carila's replacement in February. That'll be interesting. He has worked for MSF for several years and, having gotten to know Lucile over the week, I have a good feeling about him, too. Anders is our new PC (project coordinator). What a breath of fresh air. He arrived on Thursday with Bridgitte (Stefano's replacement) on the plane in which Edgardo thankfully departed. Anders is Danish, and this is his fourth mission with MSF. His last project was in the Kivus, a much more unstable place than Shamwana, so we were expecting him to have a good head on him. Nothing could be worse than Therese, whom I think is an incompetent fake who drinks way more than her fair share. I had been trying to cut her some slack, thinking she was burned out, but this measles outbreak has shown how useless she is. Anders does smoke, but so far that's my only complaint, and he's been considerate. He's bright and full of life, and laughs a lot. His background is as a lab technician, so having someone with a medical background is good, especially since the lab here is almost finished and will hopefully be functioning soon. James, who will be our part-time lab tech, has worked with Anders before and was happy to hear he would be our new PC. That was also encouraging. He's thirty-one and engaged to a Kenyan woman, so don't anyone get any ideas.

Bridgitte is a little teeny bit of a thing, young, just graduated from engineering school in France. Whoa, was she shell-shocked. She's a vegetarian, and you should have seen the look on her face the first night when she opened that container of canned peas. She had had a kind of dazed look about her the whole day, but I thought the peas would push her over the edge. Didn't help that the other container held goat, but it was the peas that evoked that "Oh, *mon dieu*" expression. I was elated. Finally, someone who cared about food. I said, "Don't worry! I just did the four-month food order, and the food is going to be much better!" She looked at me with that get-me-out-of-here-I-want-to-go-home-I-don't-believe-you look, but I wasn't sure if it was because I said it in English or not. She's moved into the *tukul* next to mine and she doesn't snore. This is good. This is very good.

I think I've been a little unfair complaining about how young everyone is. I've realized it's not the age; I have nothing against young people. It's their maturity level that's a bit sub-par. Combine this with their utter lack of self-esteem, and attempts to compensate for that with competitiveness and control, and team-living has been a challenge for me. That's what was so refreshing about Sheila. She wasn't trying to impress anyone or compete. She was just doing a good job. Example: Margaret. We were sitting at supper one night, and I was talking about Choco and how hard he has to work when he's driving, often having to cut down trees, etc. and she pointed a fork at me, jabbed it in my direction, and said, "Hands off. He's mine." I was stunned! I said, "What the hell are you talking about? I am not interested in Choco! He's the age of my son!" She said, "Yeah, well, it didn't stop my mother." I said, "Well, this might be a good time to remind you that I am NOT your mother, so please start putting your own dirty dishes in the basin." Gimme a break! I mean, I think the drivers are great, and I am happy that they are a little heavy in the testosterone department. Driving here is hard, and it takes a certain amount of bravado, but I am not taking one home with me. Please.

Then this happened: This week we had to take two vehicles to

Kampangwe, and one was spending the night (the one with Margaret in it). So she asked me which driver I wanted, Choco or Jean de Dieu. A little test, as if I couldn't see right through that one. I said, "You choose, I couldn't care less. I like them both." She, frustrated that I didn't take the bait, said she'd let the drivers choose then. Another test. She came back annoyed, and said, "Choco wants to go with you. I am insulted." I said, "He probably just doesn't want to spend the night! C'mon! Let's take off our paranoid hat and stop being threatened by the old lady here, OK? Maybe Choco misses his mother or wants a haircut." She flirts with him shamelessly, and though I can see why she's attracted to him (he's great), we are not supposed to be getting involved with local staff. Anyway, want to know why he wanted to go with me? He told me that he thought I was very similar to Sheila. We are the same size and age, have short hair, and carry ourselves similarly. All the locals thought we were sisters. Well, Choco, who is motivated, strong, and intelligent, wants to be on the emergency team. It is another step in the nearly impossible process of getting out of here. So Choco's line of thinking was that because I look like Sheila, I will have more influence on whether she accepts him onto the emergency team. That would mean he'd get to move around for the measles, cholera, and Ebola outbreaks, and have more opportunity for any kind of advancement. It was both adorable and heartbreaking to me. He wanted to show me what a good job he does (which I assured him I already knew), but the desperation that he had—trying to use every morsel of opportunity to make his life better, knowing that his chances to ever live anywhere but here are so slim, seeing his look of expectation and hope that I could help him—just made me want to cry. He grew up in an Internally Displaced Persons (IDP) camp in the Kivu area. His mother fled with him at the height of the war. If you've ever seen pictures of these camps, you'd have an idea of how motivated this guy had to be to improve his life. To have even gotten to be a driver is our equivalent of becoming an astronaut. I told him I would put in a good word for him when I saw Sheila in Lubumbashi, and he smiled as if I told him I'd pay his way to the states.

The measles is spreading everywhere; all the resources are tapped to the limit trying to get each kid through the crisis phase alive, and still the fucking MoH is refusing to let us immunize. After all Sheila's work, all the time wasted writing proposals, figuring numbers, blah, blah, blah, we just got an e-mail from Sheila saying that they said no.

I have been doing a big fat "I told you so," just walking away at Therese's, Carila's, and Margaret's frustration because they now have to find nurses to staff all the extra places. (Actually, Therese doesn't give a shit.) I was of the belief that we shouldn't go looking for permission, we should just go ahead and do the right thing (which I secretly have been doing, but on a much smaller scale than I could have if everyone got behind this), and now Carila is saying that I was right. Small comfort now with this mess. And now that we've submitted all our inventory numbers, it's going to be hard to explain the missing vaccines. MoH did agree to get us three-months supply of other vaccines for our routine immunizations, though, as I was running out of those. So I'm being very nice and just going about my business and just doing the "routine." This week was the adventure of collecting those vaccines. They have to stay cold, yet they come from miles away, and it's 100 degrees out.

The vaccines come from the Ministry of Health, as I've said, and the nearest office is in Kiambi, which is 100 kilometers from here across a big river. On our side of the river is Mpiana where there is an MoH health center, which has a fridge and can store vaccines. Since we can't cross the big river (there is no bridge, they have to come by dugout canoe), the way of obtaining the vaccines has been for the MoH to get them to Mpiana, and then we drive to Mpiana to get them. There is a smaller river that we need to cross to get to Mpiana. This river has a bridge, but we had reports that the bridge had been broken for a while. Even though it's a smaller river, it's still too big to drive across. We need the bridge. After all the lobbying to get vaccines, a plan was made for the MoH staff to take the vaccines to the bridge and we'd cross by foot and collect them. The bridge is five kilometers from the health center.

I got packed up with cool boxes and cold packs, and was about to leave with just a driver, and then Therese decided we needed to take another person in case the Land Cruiser got stuck. Then there would be someone to help Horace, the driver, dig out. I will give her credit for that; it was a good idea. We took a *journalier* (a daily worker, an unskilled laborer who gets hired by the day) and, at the last minute, I thought to throw a bike on the roof, just in case they didn't arrive at the bridge, we could send the *journalier* by bike to go and get them. I was determined not to have this be a wasted trip and, being white, I'm not allowed to leave the vehicle and driver. Safety rules. Three-and-a-half hours out there, and three-and-a-half back; I wanted it to be productive. We got to the bridge, having had a gorgeous ride through thick rain forest, orchids blooming all over, and empty villages. Everyone was off working the fields. Even Horace's music was tolerable. The ride was wonderful.

The bridge is a steel frame with two steel beams lain across that were not long enough to traverse the whole bridge. Logs were strewn over it to fill in between the steel beams. It was about twenty-five meters across, and it was fairly high, like high enough that if the car fell, it would not be retrievable, about fifty feet. There was a big section that didn't have any logs on it at all, it was just the open frame. So Horace got out and started trying to move logs over the open spaces trying to fix the bridge, and I could see he thought we were going to drive across it. I told him we were not supposed to go over it. Unsurprisingly, MoH was not on the other side waiting for us and we had to send Kayunga (the *journalier*) by bike. Horace was all dejected like a little kid; he was all pumped up to fix the bridge. So I told him to wait and I'd call Therese by radio and see what she said. I told Therese that Horace thought he could fix the bridge well enough to safely drive over. She initially said no (like she always does) but then went to get Perrin to ask his opinion. Perrin said the driver is the one who should know if it's safe or not, so if he thinks it is, then let him do it. Yeah! So it took about half an hour for Horace and Kayunga to move these huge logs into place (they used a big crowbar that was in the Land Cruiser), then Horace, all hyped up, drove over. I was so proud of him! He was so happy. I walked across and took pictures of his triumph.

The Mpiana health center is an old Belgian structure that sits on a huge bluff overlooking the river. When we arrived I looked down at the river and could see the dugout canoe with the bright blue tops of the cool boxes containing the vaccines. The guy paddling the canoe was struggling in the current, but finally made it across. The staff ran down the trail, retrieved the cool boxes, and climbed back up, huffing and sweating and euphoric that it was a success. As I am writing this it doesn't seem like such a big deal, but standing there that day, I was blown away. The amount of effort and coordination and combination of different modalities, just to transport something that would arrive by Fedex at home, well, I was just overwhelmed. I just had to tell you about it. There were enough vaccines to get us through the rainy season, and they were all still cold. It was a fabulous success. I was thrilled. We switched them to our cool boxes and headed back home.

God, it was one of those days when I just love it here.

Oh, let's see. I have so many more things I want to tell you. The office is filling up, I've spent too much time complaining about the team, now I am under pressure, let me think. OK. I've got a bunch of delivery stories, but I'll tell you a quick one. It is the one that happened Lucile's first night here. I already told you I went over there about eleven p.m. but the delivery had already happened. This was a woman from Kishale who'd come to Shamwana a few weeks ago to wait for labor here, because out of her previous eight births, four had been born prematurely and died. So, at one of our visits there, we took her back here to stay in the maternity tent until she went into labor. Which she did on Monday night but, instead of calling the guard to go get Gerardine or Beatrice, she went out behind the tent and had the baby in the mud. The guard heard the baby cry and went and got Wilfried, the nurse, who cut the cord, wrapped the baby up, and stuck him in the labor room while the guard went and got Gerardine. Gerardine sent for me because the woman was squatting out behind the tent refusing to move, the placenta plopped on the ground under her. For some reason, when I coaxed her, she came with us into the labor room. Perhaps she was afraid to say no to me, or something, I don't know. But it was very surreal. I was thinking, "Wouldn't you know, the one woman who doesn't have to push for four hours, delivers in the mud, in the rain, in the middle of the night." Poor little baby was cold, but full term, and I got some hot water from the guards, who keep a pot on the fire all night, and made a warm bath to put him in. Gerardine was cleaning off the woman, and cackling at her, scolding. She reminded me of the crows in my backyard at home. The woman was silent, never explaining why she went and delivered her baby like that. When they were both cleaned of the mud and dirt and blood, we walked them back to the maternity tent, and started to tuck them under the mosquito net by lantern light, and one by one the other women in the tent called out softly, "*Mwafuko*" and the new mother replied to each one, "*Eyomwa*" in a soft sing-songy voice. "*Mwafuko*" is the word in Kiluba for "congratulations" or "thank you," and women respond every time, politely, respectfully, and kindly to each other with "*Eyomwa.*" It was one of the most beautiful expressions of sisterhood I've ever seen. We left the tent, Gerardine picked up a hoe, went over to the spot where the woman delivered the baby, and covered all the blood with dirt. She is amazing. We said our "*Grand mercies*" to each other, and both walked home. That was the night I couldn't go back to sleep.

All right, I've got to stop now. I won't be writing for a few weeks. I leave on Thursday by road to Dubie, then go by plane from there to Lubumbashi on Friday, then to Dar es Salaam on Saturday. I hope you all have a wonderful Christmas and New Year. I love you all. Thank you so much for all the support. I feel it every day. I feel so fortunate to be having this experience, especially at this time of year.

Christmas here feels much more like the original one.

Be safe and well, and I will too!

Love,
Linda

CHAPTER 5 ~ KILI

January 13, 2008
Sunday morning, Shamwana

Hi Everyone! Happy New Year!

Get comfy. This is going to take a while.

As I recall, I left you with the plan to leave here by road because it wasn't at all certain that the plane would land in Shamwana. Air Serv has a new pilot who is a nervous wreck and won't land here, and the other two pilots were on vacation. So, by road it was: Stefano, Deo, Willy, and me. Stefano was leaving for good, and Deo and Willy were leaving for their annual month of vacation. After long drawn out *au revoirs*, a last minute set of twins to deliver, and a barrage of shopping lists thrust in my face, we finally set off toward Dubie. That was on Thursday, December 20th. The small plane was to come to Dubie on Friday, and my flight to Nairobi, then Dar es Salaam, was on Saturday. It's a six-hour ride to Dubie, and the roads were pretty good for the first half. We had to stop half-way for Jean de Dieu, the driver, to have a half-hour rest in a village called Mutendeli. Just as we were getting back in the Land Cruiser, a guy came running at us, saying that a woman was in labor and there was no one there to help her. Everyone in the vehicle looked at me, and I am going to admit to you, as awful as this seems, that my first concern was getting my clothes dirty. I was so nice and clean! And I had to travel with these clothes! I thought maybe we could put her in the vehicle and take her with us to Dubie, which was a ridiculous thought, but I just wanted to be on vacation! I grabbed some gloves out of the medical box and was led to the hut where the messenger translated that it was her eighth baby. I got on my knees and checked her and she was fully dilated (we're talking grass walls, mud-floor hut here), and I went back to the vehicle to radio the base that we had to stay in this village until she delivered. Oscar, the radio operator, said I only have twenty-five minutes before we have to be back on the road, otherwise we wouldn't make it to Dubie before dark. If she wasn't delivered in twenty-five minutes I had to leave. I thought that was ridiculous: I couldn't leave before she delivered, and who knew how long it would take! I then remembered I wasn't in Shamwana anymore, and maybe she would actually push the baby out. I grabbed a pair of scissors and some gauze and went back to the hut. There was an older woman with her who spread a cloth over the ground for the woman to lie on, and the three of us, alone in this hut, witnessed the beginning of another life. I can say "push" very well in Swahili and Kiluba now, and that was all I needed to say! She pushed, the head crowned, amniotic fluid spilled onto the cloth (only splattering me a little bit), and the baby was born. I used the gauze to tie the cord, cut it, and the older woman handed me a cloth to wrap him in. I handed the swaddled baby to her, delivered the placenta, checked to make sure she wasn't bleeding too much, said, *"Mwafuko"* and left. They gave me some water to wash my hands, and I ran to the Land Cruiser with two minutes to spare, with all the villagers cheering and yelling *"Mzungu!* Photo!" I jumped in the Land Cruiser where everyone was already seated and waiting for me, and we took off. It was a hoot! There was some blood on my pants though; I wasn't happy about that. I was thinking how crazy the timing was, that we would show up in that village at exactly that time, and then I started thinking about how it must have been for the laboring woman. A white ghost shows up out of nowhere, delivers your baby and then runs away. Really. Think about that.

Oh my, I've already written two pages and I haven't even gotten to Dubie yet. Oh dear, I hope I don't run out of time.

I was laughing, and enjoying the ride, which at this point was a teenage boy's fantasy, driving through water more similar to ponds than puddles. The terrain had become quite flat, so not much of the road was washed away; it was just huge areas of standing water, which we plowed right through. Aside from the occasional worry that I might have to get out and get my nice hiking boots soaked on top of my bloody pants, I was quite enjoying it.

We got to within a few miles of Dubie and a huge tree was across the road. There was a group of men working away at it with homemade axes, but it looked to me like it would have taken all day with a chain saw. We had gotten out and were watching, when Jean de Dieu decided he could go around it, and, by God, he did it. I was sure we'd be stuck there forever, but he put it in whatever-drive, went up over the embankment, plowed through the surrounding jungle, and down the other side. It was impressive. My kids would have loved it. About two miles later, a bridge was completely washed away. Women, unconcerned with vehicular transportation, were doing wash in the river below. We were within walking distance of Dubie, but if we left the vehicle there, the driver would have had to stay with it, which Jean de Dieu did not want to do. He got out, threw some stones in the river to see how deep it was, dragged some logs over to toss in (he was running around like crazy), and then decided he could make it. Stefano and I had gotten out, fully intending to wade through the river and walk the remaining distance, so we were up on the embankment, which offered a great view of the passage. It was awesome. The Land Cruiser flew, bounced off the rocks, hit the water, and plowed through to the other side with spray shooting off in all directions. There was a guy running alongside cheering him on. Jean de Dieu emerged from the vehicle with his arms up like Rocky, and everyone was cheering. It was so much fun, I was having a blast. And, to boot, I thought I'd have twenty-four hours in Lubumbashi to wash my pants, call home, and do a little of the shopping. Life was good!

I was very happy to see the project in Dubie and get some ideas about where to be heading in Shamwana. Dubie has been around much longer, is very well established, and has a midwife who is also an American former Peace Corps volunteer. The MSF hospital there is a former Catholic mission hospital established over ninety years ago, and the sisters are still very involved (I detected some resentment from the MSF staff about that). There's a huge secondary school, a big village and market, and lots of food. It's where many people from Shamwana went when they fled the Mai Mai. I loved it there. I had a tour of the hospital (it's huge, maybe thirty structures, no tents), visited with Sarah, the midwife, and walked around the village and market.

Three expats from Dubie were also leaving for Christmas, so everyone was a little pre-occupied. I actually felt a bit in the way. Stefano and I watched a movie (they have electricity) and it was the most I've visited with him since I arrived. He was heading back to Italy and was extremely happy to be leaving.

The next day I went over to the hospital to watch their routine. The plane was coming at one p.m. so we had some time.

December 21, 2007 Dubie

J'arrive, je reste, je pars. *(I arrive, I stay, I leave.)*

Winter Solstice: hot and humid

All us travelers received good wishes from the national staff at the morning meeting. Someone counted and the wishes were clapped out at the count of seven and flew to our outstretched arms to be gathered and put in pockets to take along. The driver next to me told me to hurry and put them in my pocket before they flew away. It made me cry. They have nothing left, and still they give. I walked to the market with Stefano. It's so well established here, and feels safer. Kids were playing checkers with bottle caps and men were sitting in groups talking. Women were shopping; there was a huge selection of vegetables and fruit. There was freshly butchered pork hanging from a tree. I felt like I could live here. I wanted to go over and have a tour of the mission, and Stefano came along. It's now nearly deserted. The garden is sadly neglected, and the veranda needs repair. I could just imagine it in its heyday. Shame. One of the guards there showed us around, but he was listless and uninterested in us. I don't think he understood what we wanted there. The priest was away on his motorcycle visiting somewhere. We came back to the base and I watched Grease with Stefano while waiting for the plane. That felt strangely naughty. The team here is unwelcoming and I feel like I'm in the way. What the hell are they all doing in that office? How come they have so many more laptops than we do? Funny that our travels allowed me to get to know Stefano in a way I never did living with him in Shamwana. Two strangers here. It's a bonding experience. He's an interesting man, set apart from others by his deafness. He's the most subdued Italian I have ever met. Here we sit now—he reads and I write—waiting for the plane.

⚜

After lunch, we all went over to the airstrip, having gotten word that the plane was on its way. Five of us now, all with holiday plans and other flights to catch. We saw the plane coming. He flew down

low over the airstrip, we were waving happily, and then he circled …
and flew away. Decided not to land. Didn't like the way the puddles
looked on the airstrip. It would have been a great scene in a movie. I
could just picture it on the big screen: happy little travelers with their
backpacks leaning prettily against their legs ready to load onto the
small plane coming to take them away to fun adventures and loved
ones, then the smiles start to fade as reality starts sinking in, arms
slowly descend from the frantic greetings they were offering, then
confused glances at each other, and Philip (the Kenyan nurse in
Dubie) says flatly, "He's going back to Lubumbashi." And no one
speaks. Haven't decided on the music yet, maybe mournful violins,
maybe African drums. Fade out. So, that's the scene that flashed
through my head before I started freaking out saying "WHAT
NOW????!!!!!!! WHAT ARE WE GOING TO DO????????!!!!!"
OK, I was a little upset. No one else said anything, but I couldn't tell
if it was because they didn't care or if they were too stunned.
Everyone had big plans. Stefano couldn't wait to get back to Italy,
Sarah was on her way to Germany to visit her brother and Philip was
going back to Kenya. I wasn't the only one with a plane to catch. And
the only plane out of Lubumbashi was the next day. Suddenly the
bloody pants (which I was still wearing) didn't seem like such a
tragedy. We were three days away from Lubumbashi by car, so that
wasn't an option. We went back to the base (my lower lip quivering
the whole way), and Philip got on the radio trying to see if Francine
(our head of mission) could arrange another Air Serv flight for early
the next morning. These flights each have to be paid for, so they don't
casually send an unscheduled plane. I guess after doing the math,
though, she figured it would be cheaper to send another plane for us
than to reimburse us for the failed vacation plans (climbing Kili is not
cheap) and all the mental health counseling we'd require. So, the plan
was for Air Serv to try again Saturday morning early, and if it was not
raining, and if there were no puddles, and if the neurotic pilot felt safe
enough, we could still get to the airport in time for the flight to
Nairobi.

Je suis inquiété. *(I'm worried.)* Dubie–The plane came but didn't land
yesterday. I'm scared I won't get out of here. It's very early morning now—

foggy with very low clouds. Again, waiting for the plane. Hoping, hoping, hoping the clouds lift a bit. Please God, I need to get out of here.

⁕⁕⁕

Seven o'clock Saturday morning we were all back on the airstrip watching the plane approach, not waving this time, all saying a silent prayer that the low clouds were not deterrent enough for this guy . . . and he landed the plane. He opened his door, dropped the ladder, jumped down from his seat, and frantically started unloading stuff from underneath, telling us to hurry up and get on, we have to be out of here in ten minutes, like we were being attacked or something. He was worried it might start raining. He is at least six-foot-four and weighs less than I do. He has that emaciated look that is so popular here in the Congo. He started running up to each of us asking how much we weigh, writing it down on his clipboard with trembling wiry fingers, then running those fingers through his hair like this was the worst situation he's ever been in. I felt like slapping him. Jesus, don't they screen these guys? So after all this drama, we took off without incident, and throughout the one-and-a-half-hour flight he kept telling us he didn't know if he'd be able to land in Lubumbashi, we'd just have to wait and see. They have a paved runway there, for goodness sake! We flew the last half hour below the clouds, just above the treetops. Luckily there are no power lines for the wheels to get caught on. We landed fine, three hours before the Nairobi flight, but checking in there is an utter nightmare, and took two of those hours. We had just enough time after checking in to race to the office, get the stuff we needed out of the safe (like credit cards, bank card, money) and race back to the airport to leave. Ah, it was exciting, and I was so happy to have made it, even though I was still wearing those pants.

Everyone complains about the airport in Nairobi, but I don't think it's bad. It's fairly clean and the lines actually move. I had no problem getting onto the flight to Dar, which left on time! My friend (a woman who used to work at the Jackson Lab in Bar Harbor, and now lives in Dar es Salaam) met me at the airport and whisked me away in her nice air-conditioned car. I felt like a celebrity, and she certainly treated me like one. It was wonderful. I spent that evening meeting her family and driving through the city. We went to get local food for supper–spicy chicken cooked on open coals on a busy sidewalk corner, served with a 7-Up in a heavy green glass bottle, crammed at a table with dozens of other families, with most of the women wearing burkas. I loved it. It's really hot in Dar, probably about the same temperature as Shamwana, but seemed a bit worse because of the buildings and traffic. I stuffed myself with fabulous food. There was fresh fruit and hot spicy meats, and I couldn't get enough of it.

The next morning was Christmas Eve and I was taking the bus to Marangu where I had a hotel reservation and where the climb was organized. Actually, the bus was to Arusha, but the guy at the hotel told me to get off in Himo, and he'd send a car for me there, as Marangu is not on the route. It was an eight-hour bus ride, but quite comfortable; the road was paved, and I got to see a good piece of the country. It was an old Greyhound bus, and everyone had a seat. It wasn't like a local bus with hundreds of people hanging out the door and onto the bumper. And it was only nineteen dollars! Every couple of hours we'd pull into a village market and hoards of people would swarm the bus selling food and crafts. No one got off the bus; you can buy stuff right out the window. Just hand your money out and get handed up fresh pineapple, or bags of cashews, or greasy chicken in a little paper bag. Now THAT'S my idea of drive-through. And for your nineteen dollars you get a Coke, a real Coca-Cola in a glass bottle with a straw. Halfway through the trip a guy got on with two cases of Coca-Cola and Fanta, and walked down the aisle, opening them and handing them out, while the bus was moving. After a bit, he walked back down the aisle collecting the empty bottles, put them back in the case, the bus pulled over, and he got off. They've got it all worked out. I couldn't stop smiling.

We were going merrily along, the landscape looking more and more like the southwestern United States, and about three miles before Himo we were stopped by police. There was a huge crowd of people there and a big flatbed truck was off the road. The bus driver opened the door and two policemen got on and talked to him in Swahili. Then a group of people carried three wounded, bleeding, unconscious people onto the bus and laid them in the aisle. Next, they carried on a woman who was conscious, but obviously had two broken legs with her feet at awkward angles to her calves, and laid her near the driver. Then they brought a screaming child, who was not hurt, but terrified, and put her in one passenger's lap. Two of the policemen stayed on the bus and we took off again. Apparently the truck had hit people on a bicycle and ours was the next vehicle to come along that could transport them to the hospital in Moshi, a forty-five-minute ride away. It was horrifying looking at these people lying on the floor of the bus, listening to the screams of that child. I felt like I should be doing something for them, but I didn't know what. Then, three miles later, where the road turns to go to Moshi, the bus stopped so I could get off, and I was trying to get my backpack off the overhead rack without stepping on these wounded people, when a guy got on the bus with one of those little hotel signs on a stick with my name on it. Mind you, I was the only white person on this bus, and this was definitely spoiling my attempt to look like a local. The scene was surreal. I got off the bus shaking, imagining an ambulance full of wounded people at home heading to a hospital, stopping to drop off a tourist.

Another fifteen kilometers in a comfortable van, and I was at the hotel by five. Paradise. With the peak of Kilimanjaro in the distance, and beautiful but simple gardens around the individual bungalows, I was just in heaven. All my correspondence with this place had been by e-mail, but when I went to check in, they acted as if I was a long-lost relative. It was so nice. Everyone was so friendly and welcoming. It was how I remember Malawi, where the lifestyle is very simple and the people poor, but there is a sense of contentment and happiness that is utterly absent in Congo. Well, they have food for one thing, and some semblance of infrastructure, and tourism, for that matter. There you go. That helps. And it has been a while since they've had a war.

I checked in, went to the bar and bought a beer, then went to my room and turned on the faucets for the bath, and warm, clean water came out. It was a lovely sight. I took a nice, long bath, drank my beer in the tub, read my book, then got dressed for dinner and sat in the garden watching the sunset. There were several groups of people there, but I didn't meet anyone that night. I was quite content. I walked to a nearby Catholic church and spent a while trying to figure out when a Christmas mass was, but my Swahili is quite poor, consisting of about ten words (one of which is "push"), and I got six different answers from people around the church. Anyway, it was all closed up, and I deduced there wasn't a mass that evening, so I went back to the hotel and went to the dining room for dinner. This place was such a deal, fifty dollars a night, and that included a three-course breakfast and a five-course dinner. And the food was pretty good, not fabulous, but good. I was tired and happy and after eating, went to my room to read and sleep. It was cool enough to need a blanket. It was a lovely Christmas Eve.

Christmas morning I walked to the church, having no idea what time it was since I don't have a watch. It was early, anyway. The church was open and there were a few people inside, so I figured a mass was sometime in the near future, and went in and sat. After a while, people started coming in and it was becoming evident that I was sitting on the men's side. That was rather strange; all the men were on one side, all the women and children on the other. So I moved across the aisle and sat down again, and then into my pew filed ten nuns, all in white habits. Oops, nuns' pew. So I went to move again, but they pushed me back down into my seat. I sat there with them looking like a photographic negative–they with their black, black skin and white, white habits, and me with my white, white skin and black, black dress. Let's just say I didn't blend.

It was a simple little church, decorated for Christmas with chintzy silver garlands and blinking red lights that surrounded the nativity scene. And then, the guy with the keyboard came in. What, did the Vatican get a deal on these or something? The same tinny sounding keyboard they have in Lubumbashi, in Pago Pago, and apparently in every Catholic church in the third world. The Christmas carols sounded worse than at Wal-Mart. And, get this, at the end of each carol he ran his fingers down the keyboard from high to low, like they do on a talk show when the host tells a really bad joke. I couldn't even elbow one of the nuns and roll my eyes or snicker. And, because the keyboard was plugged into the same extension cord as the blinking lights, the lights kept going off, and he had to keep getting on the floor and fiddling with the plugs.

After the three-hour mass, I went back to the hotel for breakfast, and watched a huge group of hikers get ready to go off to the mountain. Their preparations were quite the production, and watching them made me anxious to get going up there myself. I had a whole day of waiting stretched out before me, so I hired a guide for six dollars and set off to explore the area. I had asked at reception if they had a map of the area, but they didn't and I didn't feel comfortable wandering around alone knowing how easily I get lost. The woman at reception told me that they usually send people off with a guide and I could either go to the waterfalls, the coffee plantation, the banana plantation, or the market. I asked, "Can't I go to them all?" I mean, I had nothing else to do that day, and it had been a long time since I could just walk and walk and walk. She said, "Yes, it's possible. The guide is six dollars for the whole day. You can take as long as you want." Perfect. She went off to the neighboring village, and came back moments later with Edward, who at that moment thought he was making a quick six bucks. OK, I won't go on and on about this day, but it was quite pleasant. Not sure if Edward thought so, but the coffee and banana plantations were really beautiful, and were on the way to one of the waterfalls, which was spectacular. I would never have found that without a guide. He was teaching me a little more Swahili along the way, and we stopped after a few hours and I bought him a beer at a local restaurant, where really horrible Christmas music was playing and it seemed all of the men in the village were spending a Christmas afternoon with each other and the local waitress. I met Edward's brother, who sat and chatted with me while Edward disappeared for a really long time. I knew he'd come back, though, because I hadn't paid him yet. He did, and was obviously disappointed when I said I wanted to go see the other waterfall. He was walking rather sullenly then, and the Swahili lessons weren't forthcoming. We got to the second waterfall, and I decided not to ask to go to the market. I was afraid he might start crying. We walked back to the hotel, and I paid him, along with a big tip, and he bolted.

I took my journal and went out to sit in the garden, and an older man asked if he could share my table. Then his girlfriend and another friend joined us. They were from Norway, and this was the man who engineered and built the huts on the Marangu trail on Kilimanjaro in 1973. He was there visiting for the first time since then. He was not in physical condition to climb the mountain again, but he and Desmond (the owner of the hotel) were friends, and had come to spend Christmas. He had a very bad limp and was missing several fingers. I asked him if that had happened while he was building the huts, and he told me no, that he sustained his injuries during an ambush in South Africa. Man, has he got stories. And he was happy to tell them. We had tea in the garden and they invited me to have dinner with them. I went back to my room, took another bath just because I could, dressed, and went over to the dining room for a very traditional Christmas meal. It was so civilized, with pleasant conversation, good food and drink, and an appreciation for personal experiences unique to those celebrating holidays with near strangers.

They were heading to Moshi the next day, where I wanted to go. I hopped a ride with them and checked out that city, then got on a local bus back to Marangu. It was a cheap ride, I'll say that much, but not the safest mode of transport. It was an old eleven-seat Toyota van in which I was one of thirty passengers. Being white, I was one of the five that got to sit in the front. For travelers on a budget the forty-five-minute ride was only $1.30. The taxi ride would have been fifty dollars.

Late that afternoon I had to have all my gear checked for the climb by a hotel staff person. I was instructed to put everything on the bed and wait for her to make sure it was all in order and of the right quality. After that I was to meet for a briefing with the four other women who were going to be doing the hike with me. Desmond had told me they were "from the English speaking world" and he hoped we would be well-matched.

I laid out all the warm stuff I'd brought, and was expecting some high-tech-mountaineering-type person to come in and check it out, when an old woman in a *pagne* and head wrap came in with a clipboard and started pawing through my stuff, shaking her head sadly at most of it. There was a long list of things we needed to have— warm socks, two hats, mittens, long underwear, etc. and I had brought all these things but they weren't passing inspection. She signaled for me to follow her to a room that was crammed full of winter jackets, mittens, hats, scarves, water bottles, gators, and boots. This was all stuff that other people had left there, and they offer it to climbers who don't have all they need. It was quite impressive. I picked out things to complement what I'd brought, and then headed over to the briefing room.

There sat Maureen and Ginny, two young American women who were Peace Corps volunteers in Zambia. Next to them were Stephanie and Margie from Victoria, British Colombia. Stephanie was a nurse working with her family near there for a year, and Margie and her family had come to visit. Their husbands and young kids were fending for themselves for six days so they could do the climb. It was a great group from the first minute on. I was so psyched. The briefing lasted two and a half hours, with Desmond going over every last detail of what to expect and how to take care of ourselves to maximize our chances of having a good experience and making it to the top. For the five of us we had four guides, six porters, and a cook. I was so lucky with this place. I had just taken a chance and went with the only name I had with an e-mail address, and they were fantastic. It's a family-run business that's been there for fifty years, and they are very involved with improving the lives of the local community, and ensuring that the guides and porters get paid fairly and that their equipment is adequate. (Though as we got closer to the top, I had my doubts about this last point).

✺✺✺✺✺

December 27, 2007 Marangu

Je suis rempli avec l'excitation! *(I am filled with excitement!)*

It's clear. I have a perfect view of the mountain. We start today. I am so excited. We had a two-and-a-half-hour briefing last night that was really interesting and good. There are five in our group now. All women, all good, I think. I'm waiting for breakfast. Feeling fat. I've eaten so much. I'm too distracted to write. I had no clock, I was twenty minutes late for breakfast, and now I am feeling rushed and jumpy.

✺✺✺✺✺

OK, next day (bear with me, I'm finally getting to the climb). After breakfast we got packed up (which was a project in itself), and piled into a huge bus/truck hybrid-type of vehicle. When I saw what these porters had to carry I was ashamed of my little daypack. It all had to be weighed; they are not allowed to carry more than twenty kilos each, but still, all on their heads, it looked like a lot. We got to the mountain gate, and there was a big process of signing in, paying the park fee (635 dollars per person), leaving our passport numbers, etc. before we started walking. And the first three days, it really is just a walk. It's a very gradual incline through thick tropical rain forest the first day, across moorland the second day, then alpine desert the third. After that it is exceedingly steep scree and polar ice cap. Quite the range, I must say, and it was unbearably beautiful. In the forest there was wild lobelia growing all along the trail, and wild impatiens! Wild! Looking completely comfortable and at-home and blooming away.

The key is to go really slowly to adjust to the altitude, and we heard that over and over and over again. Nelson, our lead guide, must have said *pole pole* (little by little) two million times over the six days. It was lovely going that slowly because you could take in the surroundings and appreciate the views along the way without stopping, just plodding along. It was very comfortable. We stopped for lunch and water breaks, but the stops weren't for fatigue. It wasn't hard at all to go at that pace. The first night we were at 2,700 meters, a sweet camping area with A-frame huts and a large dining room. It was an option to camp in tents, but we were staying in the huts. At first I was a little disappointed at that, but after the first night, I was really, really glad we were in the huts. We "oohed" and "ahhed" and sat in the late afternoon sun chatting with other hikers from all over the world, while our porters delivered our packs to our hut. Then they made us tea. Now, I am the first one to say that colonialism was an evil, evil thing. But at *least* the British instituted tea-time. God, is that sweet. We were sitting there on the grass, and one of the porters came over with bowls of warm water "for washing before tea," and Ginny turned to us and said, "I'm trying to figure out what I'm supposed to wash." And I cracked up, because I was thinking the same thing! I said, "I know, even after hiking all day, I still feel cleaner than I do after my shower in Shamwana." So we washed our hands and faces, then strolled to the tables where tea was laid out. We each had a few cups, and I was thinking that life just doesn't get better than this.

And the dinner! The meals they prepared for us were astonishing! Soup, then gorgeous fried chicken, with perfect French fries, and a beautiful salad. I couldn't believe it. Many people lose their appetite at high altitude, but that sure never happened to me. I'm probably the only person in the history of climbing that mountain who's gained weight during the climb. In fact, I felt great the whole time. I never even got a headache. I was so lucky.

Next morning, after they brought us tea in our sleeping bags at six thirty, we enjoyed a breakfast of toast, porridge (which Maureen taught me to mix with a scoop of fresh, local, peanut butter), eggs, and sausage, and more tea. We donned our little daypacks and set off across moorland with gorgeous blooming wildflowers, and stunning views of the peak. It was a heavenly day slowly walking in this beauty.

That night we were at 3,720 meters, a busy camping area, because this is where those ascending and descending all converge for the night. It was crowded, but I didn't think unpleasantly so. It was a rather festive atmosphere, I thought. We were spending two nights there, to do a day hike the next day to acclimatize. Oh my God, the views! Both sunset and sunrise were spectacular. At tea and dinner you could hear everyone talking and asking, "Are you going up or down?" and if the answer was "Down" it was always, "How was it? Did you make it? Any advice?" We were all ears, until we heard one woman say, "Make sure you take the Diamox. It'll keep you from throwing yourself over the edge." (Diamox is a medication that slows your respirations and helps keep you oxygenated. We were all taking it.) That was it. No more asking for advice. After that, every time we heard someone talking about it, Stephanie put her hands over her ears and did the "WAA waa waa waa waa." At this point Marge had a headache and was nauseated and didn't feel like eating much. Ginny, Maureen, and I divided her portions and shoveled it right in.

The big problem for me was I was so cold at night. My feet were freezing, and then I couldn't sleep. I kept putting on more layers the higher we got, but I started worrying that I had on almost all of my clothes and I still had the coldest part to do. It was making me nervous. I would lie in my sleeping bag at night wondering if I could possibly wear the bag to the top. We were all cold. Stephanie said, "And I'm Canadian! I'm a disgrace to my country!"

December 28, 2007

J'ai froid. (I'm cold.)

Horombo hut, late afternoon

Tea. I am in heaven. I am ecstatic. It's a little alpine village. We're above the clouds. We spent all day walking across moorland with wildflowers and incredible cloud formations and rock formations. It's magnificent. There are a lot of people here now, but it's rather festive. Some are going up and some are coming down. There are big groups and small groups. The hut is great, it has six bunks and we are all together. There are big windows facing east. Right now I am watching a guy bathing with the little bowl of warm water down by the river. I have a perfect view. I'm sitting here wrapped up in fleece and he's stark naked outside bathing. He must be from Finland. There isn't a single part of his body he's missed. I've just washed my hands and face and called it good. We have two nights here before the big push. This is so exciting.

Next day was a relaxing day hike for about five hours, which Marge didn't do. She just rested at the camp. I'm glad we had that extra day. It was beautiful, and we got to see another part of the landscape with spectacular rock formations.

Day four. We left around nine o'clock and started the climb up to Kibo hut, which is at 4,703 meters. It was another beautiful day, across alpine desert with gorgeous sweeping views. There was a low-lying anxiety among us, though, because it's the day when we had to get up at midnight to start the climb to the top, and there was something about knowing you were going to be up all night that left some anxiety hanging there. And Desmond had told us that Kibo hut, where we'd only sleep from six until eleven is really cold and uncomfortable. He did say this is the day when we would all question the wisdom of this, but assured us it would be worth it. A few people we passed coming down said things like, "Don't worry, it's worth the pain." Others, (mostly men, I must say) were ashen and not speaking. Then we got to Kibo, and the anxiety started growing when we saw the condition of many of the people there. Guys were puking their guts out, and a few were being taken down on carts that had a big wheel in the center. Porters surround the cart and literally run down the mountain with it. Rapid descent is the only treatment for altitude sickness. It was about four in the afternoon, and we were all sitting on warm rocks, watching the drama in front of us. I've got to say, most of the women we saw looked pretty good. Marge kept asking, "Doesn't anyone else have a headache?" but none of us did. Then she got more nervous. And so we all just stopped talking.

December 30, 2007

Je regarde et attends. *(I'm watching and waiting.)*

Kebo hut 15,520 feet. I'm sitting on sun-warmed rocks. Tents, stone hut, porters, guides, hikers all milling around, some like us just arriving, ready for the push to the summit at midnight. Others are coming down and are happy, but totally exhausted. We had our tea and are waiting for supper so we can go to bed. I hope I can get a little sleep. I feel tired enough. I feel great, though. I don't have a headache, no nausea, definitely no loss of appetite; I've been eating everything in sight. I love my group. I'm a little worried about Marge. She has a headache. I know she's concerned wondering how you know when it turns into real altitude sickness. I feel so good, that I don't want to tell her. We're all quiet now. I wonder if we give words to our anxiety, we'll chicken out. I'm cold. I am scared about that.

❦

About five o'clock we had a meal of pasta in that dungeon of a hut, and boy oh boy, was I glad I wasn't there alone. We got into our sleeping bags wearing all our gear except gaiters and boots. I refused to wear my two jackets to sleep, thinking I would freak out if I was still cold with my jackets on inside my sleeping bag, but the others did. I didn't think I'd sleep at all, but I did, and much better than I expected. Nelson woke us up at eleven o'clock and we were all pumped. I think our low point had been at dinner. I was wide-awake, drank the tea, went out to the latrine, and it was so stunningly beautiful I couldn't wait to get going. The moon wasn't up yet, but the stars were so bright, they actually gave light to the ground. It was magnificent.

We got in line with our guides, and started the slow zig-zagging up the scree. It's supposed to be timed so that we get to Gilman's point (the crater) just before sunrise. It's a five- to seven-hour climb, and Desmond told us that as we neared the top we'd have to stop after every third step to rest. That's how slow you have to go. It was such a gorgeous night. And it didn't seem overwhelmingly difficult. Yes, it was a slog, but going that slowly was tolerable, for sure. We just kept up that slow, steady pace, and really only stopped a few times to rest. Then the moon came up, and we didn't need headlamps anymore. I can't even describe how beautiful it was. It was a culmination of the beauty, the excitement of being there, the physical exertion, and the feeling of camaraderie that made me feel I would burst. The guides were so incredible. Every time they sensed that we were getting tired or discouraged, they started singing a beautiful song about the mountain, in harmony and then in rounds. It was magical. As we said afterward, it's a good thing you do this last part in the dark, first of all because it's easier when the scree is frozen and, second, because psychologically it's better if you can't see what's ahead of you. You just move Zen-like in your own world. We passed a few other groups who had started before us, because we didn't need to stop very often. One girl we passed was sitting on the ground, (Desmond had told us NOT to sit when we stopped to rest) and I heard her ask her guide how many more minutes to the top, and when he told her two-and-a-half more hours, I heard her say, "THAT's not what I wanted to hear." I was actually sorry I heard that, too, but then tried to forget about it and just keep plodding. Every so often Nelson told us we were doing really well, and making great progress. "You are strong Americans," he kept saying, and though I didn't want to waste any energy by talking, I knew the Canadians wouldn't like being lumped in with us, and after he said it a fourth time, I managed a "North. That's North Americans," for which Stephanie thanked me later.

It's been a couple of weeks since the climb, and I am still trying to figure out a way to describe that feeling when we got to Gilman's Point. It's where you come onto the ridge of the crater, and I'll just never get over it. We made it there in just five hours, so it was well before sunrise. It's so steep you are just seeing the boots of the person in front of you. And because I couldn't see where we were going, I wasn't expecting it. When we reached the level area, the guides all started cheering us and singing, and I came over the rise and this immense, snow-filled crater—it's two and a half kilometers across!—was moonlit in front of us, and if I had had enough energy I would have cried. Ever since I was a little kid I have wanted to climb that mountain, and it was just overwhelming.

The perfect scenario would have been to warmly hunker down between the rocks and wait for sunrise while sipping the hot tea they had brought, but that's not what happened. After a perfectly calm night, as soon as we got to the crater it started blowing and a cloud was coming toward us, and Nelson said, "OK, we keep going to Uruhu!" The summit of the mountain was still another 300-meter climb around the edge of the crater. 300 meters! I kept telling myself that's not even one time around the track. How hard can that be? Well, I'll tell you, it was hard. It was so frigging cold and the wind was blowing so hard I had to keep using my thumbs to scrape the ice off my glasses so I could see. (I didn't wear my contacts because Desmond said that some people have had them freeze to their eyeballs.) It was hard to stand up in the wind, but it's not a ridge with sharp drop offs. I wasn't worried about falling off or anything; I was more worried about freezing to death. I suddenly understood the woman in my room shaking her head at my thin little gloves. We could see the side of the huge ice cap just before the cloud obscured it completely, and then it was an hour-and-a-half of just trudging to the top in a white cloud. It wasn't a blizzard exactly, just a fine ice battering us and stinging my face. Clouds up there are cold! I was so bummed that we couldn't see the sunrise—or anything, for that matter—but it was still exhilarating. So it was one of those summits where you take a picture as fast as you can, then get the hell out of there. My camera froze solid after three shots, it's little eye-half-shut. But taking three pictures was all I could manage without losing a few fingers, anyway. We said we'd all share our photos, let's just go down! Stephanie scared me when she said, "I don't feel cold at all anymore, I just want to take a nap," and Marge scared me when she stopped answering questions altogether.

We started back down, and when we got to a sheltered area, we had the tea and biscuits. I am sure holding that warm tea is the only thing that kept my hands from getting frostbite. By the time we got back to Gilman's Point the wind had died down and the descent was slow but much warmer. Going down was much, much harder for me than going up. My toes were not happy crammed into the top of my boots. It was really steep. Before I got back to Kibo, I was completely spent. I had some chocolate in my pack, and if I hadn't had that to suck on I would have had to be carried.

We made it back to the hut by ten in the morning where we crawled into our sleeping bags and slept for an hour before they woke us, fed us some more pasta, and guided us down three more hours to Horombo, where we were spending New Year's Eve. Aside from the sore feet, it was great. In the dining room was a huge group of Japanese people, all having their oxygen concentration checked with a pulse oximeter, and then cheering wildly when it was New Year in Japan. So we toasted to that with our tea, did the same at breakfast when it was New Year on the east coast, then again at lunch when it was New Year in British Colombia. I was very happy.

December 31, 2007

Je suis monté la montagne. *(I climbed the mountain.)*

Horombo hut—We did it! We did it! All of us! I'm way too tired to write what I want, but it was fantastic. Starlit climb—hard, cold. Moonlit crater—huge, cold. Uhuru—blizzard, minus 70, wind to knock you over. Pictures (froze the camera), then headed down. Long, long day—but oh so happy, happy New Year.

We descended to the base on New Year's Day, peeling off layers as we entered different climatic zones. We were back to the gate by three o'clock and had a pickup truck waiting for us to go back to the hotel. There's a whole ritual that has to happen then, with giving back all the gear, showering, and celebrating with the guides and porters. It's traditional that the tips be given out in a little ceremony while we're all drinking beer and receiving our certificates. They all sang for us again, we took pictures, and relished our accomplishment. Stephanie's husband was at the hotel with all the kids when we got back. He had gone out the morning before to photograph the peak as we were reaching it. I thought that was so romantic. He had fantastic shots of the cloud moving in on us.

I had three days before I had to be back in hell, and figured I'd try to zip over to Zanzibar and check out Stonetown. From what I'd read, it sounded fascinating, and I didn't think I'd be coming back to Tanzania anytime soon. I tried to get a flight, but they were all full, so caught the Dar express bus early the next morning and made it to Dar just in time to grab a cab and get to the ferry terminal in time for the last boat over to Zanzibar. Since I was leaving the hotel before breakfast, they brought a thermos of tea to my room the night before, with two wrapped sandwiches, hard boiled eggs, sausage, and fruit, all wrapped for me to take along. God, I loved that place.

The boat ride across the Indian Ocean to Zanzibar (a three-hour ride) was not what I'd call pleasant. First of all, it was a fight to get by all the thieves trying to get to the ticket window, then the boat was packed and the ride rough, and everyone around me was barfing. I was actually amazed that I didn't get sick. I usually get seasick if someone says the word "ferry" too many times. But for some reason I didn't despite the fact that a pregnant woman in a burka six inches away from me was vomiting for the entire three hours. I knew it was going to be dark when I got there, and was a little uneasy about not having a place to stay. I had gotten the name of the hotel where

Stephanie and her family had stayed, and I figured I'd just take a cab there and if there was no room, at least I could have someone help me find a place. She had raved about this hotel, saying they took about twenty pictures of the room alone it was so gorgeous. Upon arrival, I asked at the immigration desk how much a cab should cost, and told him where I wanted to go. Oh, yes, yes, yes, he could get a cab for me for three thousand shillings, and told me that the driver should wait at the hotel in case he needed to take me to another one, all for the same price. Cool, I thought, I'll just have to find a place to change some money. I turned around and there was a cab driver right in my face, and I went off with him. He seemed to know what he was doing. We went through these teeny little roads and he stopped the car and got out indicating that I should follow him on foot. I was a little nervous because I didn't see any hotel around, and Stephanie made it sound like the hotel was on the beach. I said, "Uh, where are we going? I want to go to the Dhow Palace." And he said, "Yes, yes, yes, this way, the road is too small to drive." So what was I going to do? I had to trust him. The tiny streets were crowded with people; it wasn't like a deserted alley or anything, so I figured it was safe, sort of. I followed him through these little narrow walkways, and we ended up safely at the hotel and I was praying now they had a room. Yes, they did, and I was hugely relieved. I paid the cab driver, surprised that I actually had three thousand shillings in my pocket, and he tried to get me to sign up for a tour the next day (a bit pushy). I told him, "Yeah, maybe. I'll call." Oh, I was so glad to be there. I got shown to my room, which, yes, was very interesting, but I was thinking I wouldn't really take twenty pictures of it, Stephanie must be very easily impressed, when I dropped my bags and looked at the night stand that had a pamphlet on it with the name of the hotel, and I realized I was not at the Dhow Palace. Oh well.

January 2, 2008
Je suis sur une aventure. *(I am on an adventure.)*
Stonetown, Zanzibar

Whoa, funky day. I'm sitting in a rooftop restaurant of some seedy hotel, which I hadn't planned on being at—but here I am. Breeze blows through. The lights of this ancient city are on three sides of me. Most of the tables are empty, only a few people here. I'm drinking a Tusker (Tanzanian beer), putting my swollen feet up on the other chair. I caught the four p.m. boat over amid thieves and con-men. There's a route to navigate for sure. I didn't do too badly though, thank God Maureen warned me. I did ask the cab driver to take me to a certain hotel, and ended up at a different one, probably a relative's. Whatever—I'm here and it's fascinating. It is very hot here, though with the sun down, it's balmy. The bus was fine, caught that this morning just outside the hotel. They brought us a thermos of tea and a packed lunch last night to take along with us. Only two days into the New Year and I feel like I have accomplished a year's worth. Got up and down Kili, made my way to Zanzibar and found a hotel. Three thousand shilling appeared in my pocket to pay for the cab. I swear that Mary mother of God put it there. (There is chanting going on in the street below, call to prayer? Is that what it is as I sip my beer? Exotic.) Just ate my prawn and avocado salad. I would like to note here, that I did not get seasick. Very remarkable.

January 3, 2008
Early morning, Stonetown

I can open the shutters on the windows, look out to the alley, turn my head to the left and see a tiny patch of sky turning to daylight. I feel awake, that's how I know it's morning. I'm hungry. Breakfast is at seven thirty, but I know it's way earlier than that. I'll have breakfast on the rooftop. The swelling in my feet is down. They are still sore, but not as bad as yesterday. Today I want to go to the fish market and walk around. I might have to find a different hotel, not sure if they were lying when they said they were full tonight. Exotic place. The bed, the lock on the bathroom door, the door itself. Persian, strong, ornate, this ancient trading city, how incredibly exotic. The mosquito net is draped around this bed, like a sensuous curtain. The bed is huge, with ornate carving in the footboard and headboard. Glass panels are inserted, painted with flowers and tropical birds. I heard the call to prayer again this morning. What time do they do that? There's a clock in the lobby, and since I have NO idea where I am or what time it is, I'll shower, dress, and go down to look around before breakfast. Church bells are ringing now. Three at a time. What does that mean? Six a.m.? Where's a church? I'm going down.

January 4, 2008

Quite the fascinating city, and I haven't really gotten lost. I walked all over yesterday—hours and hours—fish market, small alleyways, beach, museum, shops, markets, schlock, lots of schlock. I ordered two fried eggs this morning, and the waiter brought me two orders of fried eggs. Four eggs. So I ate them; they were pretty bad. The fruit is good though. I didn't sleep well. I met a guy yesterday, Bruce, from California. He's insecure but a nice guy. We walked around, watched the sunset, ate some salty street food (a bit hard on his delicate alimentary system) then came to the rooftop for beer and dinner. We stayed late, talking and drinking beer—it was fun. He went off to his hotel, and we didn't even exchange names or e-mail addresses. We both knew we'd never stay in touch. It was refreshing. But then I slept poorly. I've been awake for a long time. I thought I'd go to six o'clock mass, but couldn't find my way to the church, so walked the beach waiting for breakfast. I'll go to the memorial to the slave trade called "the slave market" this morning, buy a ferry ticket, and head back to Dar on the noon ferry.

I am out of time and can't give details about my days in Zanzibar. I found as my vacation was coming to an end, I started having a sense of dread about coming back here. I was trying not to admit it, but it was definitely there. My return to Shamwana was touching. Everyone seemed happy to see me. I'm hanging onto that. I hate to end this, but I have to. Bye! Write soon!

Love,
Linda

Je suis retourné. Je suis de retour. *(I have returned. I'm back.)*

January 9, 2008–I'm back in Shamwana. I was dreading it, but it's not so bad. Carila is away, and Therese is gone, that helps a lot. We went out to Kampangwe yesterday and had a good day. The French is coming easier. I'm not as freaked out about it; in fact, I am feeling rather comfortable with it now. I like speaking French. The words that have been floating around in my brain seem to have found their way to my mouth in some sort of sensible order. The drama of living here, real and imagined, is in perspective for me a bit more. I'm more self-confident, and less likely to get sucked into others' unnecessary, self-induced stress.

This morning I've got reports to write and inventory to do, so I'll have priority with the office computer. That'll make me feel important. Ah dear, what to wear to the office?

It's cloudy, though we haven't had rain since I got back. It's only Thursday and I got back on Monday, but still, it IS the rainy season. Writing reports doesn't take that long. I am amazed at how long people can take to do that. At least Carila's not flopping around the office trying to look important. Oops, Margaret has finished her cereal and gone off to the office to do God-knows-what on the computer. Early morning and all afternoon she is draped over the desk intently looking at the computer screen. She leaves for R&R tomorrow, then six weeks later for good. Heavy, low clouds today. Wonder if it will rain.

Halfway through January. Almost halfway through my time here. Sometimes I think it is going fast, and sometimes it is standing still. I finally got some e-mails from home and that made me happy. I hadn't realized how much adrift I had been feeling. Word from home really anchors me. I'm feeling better about being back. It was harder than I thought it would be. I'll have to be mentally more careful about my next vacation.

January 16, 2008

It's Wednesday morning, a holiday here in Congo. Tomorrow is a holiday too, though no one seems to be able to say why. There isn't much food to eat, so this should be interesting. Let's see, on my list of holiday things to do: 1) make another skirt, 2) finish reading my book, 3) write a story in French about a factory, 4) run three miles, 5) avoid Margaret like the plague, 6) answer some e-mails, 7) check out things at the hospital, and 8) plant some more seeds.

January 17, 2008

Why am I so sad? I've gotten really lonely all of a sudden and I can't figure out why. I'm starting to slide into that worry pattern about being old and alone. That wouldn't be so bad, so I don't know why it is upsetting me so much. Why I should feel over-the-hill now I don't understand. Things have been going along quite well in the emotional department. I've been feeling like I have lots of friends out there in various walks of life. It may be that lately I haven't heard from many of them, so feel a bit abandoned. I can just picture myself next winter, all alone in that big house, cold, with crappy icy rain, just wandering around being cold. What will I do? I could write. I could see myself doing that on the nice new laptop I intend to buy myself. I can see Chloe and me in the study, or by the fire together—that's us, me and my dog. Once in a while going to the movies with a girlfriend. It wouldn't be a bad life; in fact it will be a fine life—especially when I compare it to life here. But for some reason, today it seems sad and lonely.

January 18, 2008

Seems everybody was down in the dumps yesterday. That's interesting. We were all affected by the death of Patrice Lumumba in 1961, I guess. That was the reason for the holiday, I discovered. January 17 was the day he was assassinated by our CIA. How despicable. Why didn't I ever learn that in *school? A democratically elected president, removed by a US- and Belgian-funded coup, because we didn't agree with his philosophy. This country and its people have been paying ever since. What kind of world is this? Back to work today, so we'll see if that lifts everyone's spirits. Also see if mail comes in—none last night—which was both a disappointment, and a relief, strangely. I'm wondering . . . it's five weeks until Margaret leaves. Could her replacement be more unpleasant? Are we in for a reward, or could it really get worse? I can't imagine anyone taking up more space than this with an attitude. It's Sunday. I'm in the hammock. This is my usual writing time but the computer is taken already and I'll have to squeeze in later today. Sunday morning is getting crowded. I'm still in this January funk. Hopefully I will come out of it. It's bad enough here when I'm feeling good.*

January 20, 2008
Sunday morning, Shamwana

Hi Everyone,

This week just doesn't have the same *je ne sais quoi*. I'm not bubbling over with stories. It has been really hard to be back here in Shamwana. After being in Lubumbashi it's nice to get back here, but being in Tanzania made it feel like coming back to prison. Yes, it was touching initially when everyone seemed so happy to see me. But then seeing how their faces fell when they discovered I hadn't brought each and every one of them a gift, well, that warm, fuzzy feeling headed south. Emmanuel was very happy with me, though, when I gave him the French/English Dictionary I got him in Dar. He is teaching English to the national staff, as well as continuing with my French lessons, so it seemed appropriate, but everyone got jealous. I tried to explain that it really was for everyone! Everyone was going to benefit from this gift! But no one seemed to catch on to that concept. He got the gift and they didn't. That's all they saw. As far as the French goes, it's funny what happened on my trip. I was a little worried about not speaking French for two weeks, because even on Mondays after speaking mostly English on the weekends, I feel rusty, so I thought I'd get back after two weeks and be lost again. But listening to the Tanzanians speaking English, I started wondering if this was the kind of French the Congolese were speaking, and realized I have been trying way too hard to be perfect. It's made me much more relaxed about it, and therefore it comes out a lot easier. OK, there's a little bright side to being back. Other than that I'm in a bit of a slump. The measles has spread everywhere, still no permission to vaccinate, and I'm disgusted with our capital team who keep congratulating themselves with their "progress" having set up one meeting after another with MoH officials to "discuss" the problem. These officials are power-mongering bureaucrats who, I think, must be laughing their asses off at how they keep stringing us along. But somewhere along the line it got decided that this was the game we were going to play. I did hear it mentioned that one option was to just get our own vaccines and then we can give them to whomever we want (which would be all children up to fifteen years), but I don't know where that idea is hovering. MoH makes money on the UNICEF vaccine, that's why they don't want us to use it. It seems now that, by the time we vaccinate, all the kids will be naturally immune from having the disease. Blind, deaf, and/or dead, but immune.

It's been an interesting and depressing couple of weeks. The day after I got back, we went out to Kampangwe for an immunization day and for Margaret to supervise the clinic staff. Well as soon as we got there, she was called in to the office to be present at an evaluation of a rape case. This was a thirteen-year-old girl, and the accused perpetrator was one of our drivers. That was sickening news, and I really was hoping it wasn't true. The MSF staff gets accused every once in a while of various transgressions, because it is well-known that they get paid and have money to pay local fines. I was really hoping this was one of those cases, but Margaret and I certainly weren't in any position to sort the whole thing out during an outreach visit. We decided to bring the girl back with us to Shamwana with her mother, who also happens to be an MSF employee. A big evaluation and treatment took place, and eventually Horace admitted that he had sex with her, though he claims it was consensual. A thirty-year-old having sex with a thirteen-year-old wouldn't necessarily be considered unusual in the local milieu (I've been at births of fourteen-year-olds, third wives of older men), but as it was explained to the entire staff, we are a western organization who maintain western standards, and all employees sign a code of conduct, etc. etc. etc., and Horace has been fired. Then it turns out that three of our other drivers have let their licenses expire. Now, it's not like we have speed traps or anything. The only thing stopping us when we are out on the road is, well, the road, or lack thereof. But, again, we have standards, and now they can't drive, and it's not like they can hop down to the local registry of motor vehicles and stand in line, impatient for the three people in front of them to be finished. So now Choco is our only driver, and he had just gotten a job with the Lubumbashi team, and now he can't go until we get other drivers. The atmosphere around here is tense.

And there have been a few other incidents where staff has been accused by other staff for "having women" during working hours, and being "disrespectful," but these have all been one's word against another's, and I am just so glad I am not the project coordinator. Poor Anders has fallen into a hornet's nest of human resources. I must say, though, he's handling it admirably. It's hard to figure out why now there is this undercurrent of mistrust and jealousy. I didn't sense it before, but maybe it was always there, and I just wasn't aware of it. Anyway, it's not pleasant.

We've got to find another midwife for Shamwana. Gerardine is pregnant, and due in early April, so she can't keep working day and night like she has been. I am panicked at the thought of not having her around; she is so good. She tells me she still wants to work after the baby, so her fourteen-week maternity leave will bring us until shortly before I leave. I can't quite figure out her family situation. She is married, but her husband lives somewhere else, and her two kids live with her mother in another place, and it doesn't seem like there is any plan to be reunited, but she doesn't seem upset about any of it. I'm not even going to try to figure out the timing of this pregnancy. I just want to find someone with some kind of formal training to take her place. She's had one year of training in Kilwa, and I totally depend on her, especially in the outer clinics where the *accoucheuses* don't speak French. Gerardine is amazing with languages. She speaks all the local dialects as well as Swahili and French, and now she's learning English.

Let's see. I'm feeling a bit scattered and unorganized this week with my thoughts, so this might be a little disjointed. I think the January blues hit me, even though you'd never know the season changed anywhere on the planet. It's still hot, the rains are not coming like they should and everyone is worried. It does rain, but not very hard, and often threatens but passes us by. Benson said the balance isn't right in the atmosphere and that is throwing everyone off. It certainly seems true. We get tiny snippets of news. There was a flood in Mozambique, riots in Kenya, more slaughter in the Kivu region of DRC, but life here, such as it is, just plods along, feeling now as if it's on tiptoes. Our team has all been down in the dumps, swinging through one of those phases where we all feel like we're not doing any good here. Well, I shouldn't speak for everyone, but Lucile, Bridgitte, and I are feeling that way. Lucile has been listening to people tell their stories of torture and loss and, like Angelien, just can't see people ever living normally after that. Several people, though, told her that when we are here it's the only time they feel safe, because they know that if the Mai Mai were coming back, we would leave. So as long as we are here, they know the Mai Mai aren't. That was even more depressing, thinking of how we know we would all turn tail and run if ever faced with the kind of violence they have endured. So when we feel useless, it has to be enough to just be here and be white, I guess.

I think I'll leave some of the labor and delivery stories for another week. We did have a run of about eight days with normal deliveries and no problems; I didn't even get called over there. But the last few days have been back to the same long, drawn-out births, and it's just exhausting. This is part of the reason I'm not so chipper as I write this today: I was up all night last night. Did avoid a C-section though, so that's always a triumph. It was a seventeen-year-old girl, skin and bones, transferred here because her pelvis was so small. But I figured the baby couldn't have been more than four pounds, so it should fit, and it did, after the usual four-and-a-half hours of her not pushing. God, what has happened to these poor women? Before that was a woman with a hemoglobin of 2.3–so anemic it was miraculous she was alive. And she was in labor. She actually pushed well and produced a full term 1,400-gram baby. That's pretty small.

On my agenda for the next few weeks is to get a *tukul* built at the hospital so we can have a place to do some health education and have a place out of the rain and sun for women to wait for their consultations. Two babies died this week from starvation because of the traditional belief that the initial breast milk (colostrum) is not good for the baby. It's too thin. So some of the women wait five days to feed their newborns, after a traditional ceremony where the traditional healers make cuts in their breasts and put ash and herbs in the wounds to help make thicker milk. In the meantime, the babies just quietly starve and die. These are mostly women who deliver at home, and then bring the babies in when they are nearly dead. But we've had a few at the hospital who refuse to feed their babies, and we've just got to get something set up to do some teaching. The brick building is almost done for the new ward, and soon we'll be moving patients out of the big tent and into that. Then we'll get a nicer tent for maternity, and an area where we can put the *tukul*. I'm thinking just a round, open structure with a thatched roof and bamboo seats around the perimeter. Then every morning we can give some little talk about how to have more than a snowball's chance in hell of having a better life if you just _____ (fill in the blank). I don't know. It's just an idea.

There were other things I wanted to write about this week, but now I'm brain-dead and can't remember any. I'll have to do better next week. There was even less computer time this week, because we had to do the six-month international order and that took all week on the computers. That's when we order all the medical supplies (for six months) that get shipped from Amsterdam, and it's very tedious and time consuming. It's almost done, though, so this week should be a little more flexible. I'm not the only early bird on Sundays anymore so . . . another challenge.

The team dynamics now are much more respectful and mature. Lucile and Bridgitte started running with me out at the airfield, and they are interested in learning to cook, so it's fun on Sundays now when we cook together. Not as know-it-all-y and more open to learning about what each of us has to offer. It's more what I thought it would be like. So that's good. Oh, and our cook Bienvenu is in love with Lucile. That's been a distraction. I thought he'd been hanging around a lot more than usual, clearing our plates when he never used to do that. This week, he asked Lucile if he could speak with her, and told her that he was in love with her, and would she mind bringing him back to Belgium with her? Or if it wasn't convenient for him to go with her right away, they could get married and he could stay in Lubumbashi while she supported him through nursing school, and then he could go to Belgium later. When she asked him how his current wife and four kids would manage, he replied that there was no problem leaving them here. Not to worry. She told him that she already has a boyfriend who will be coming here in March, but that didn't seem to matter to him. Minor obstacle. In the meantime, we are all benefiting from his attentions, as he is doing a wonderful job making meals out of nothing, and foraging for bananas and other fresh fruit. It's amusing to watch.

I've got to go to bed, and I missed the evening download, so this won't go until tomorrow.

Love to everyone, and please write soon.

Linda

Je suis déprimé. *(I'm depressed.)*

January 21, 2008– Everyone is an early bird these days. I can't even get a cup of tea in before the place is buzzing like flies. So I take my tea back to my tukul and sit in the darkish morning light, and try to figure out what time it is by the sounds I hear outside. There is a motor running, so it must be getting close to seven. Monday morning—order supplies for the week, Perrin's meeting, the whole week ahead, insecurity, building, tearing down, water flowing under the table—the year blurs together.

January 27, 2008
Sunday morning, Shamwana

Hi Everyone,

I am adjusting to being back here, and not quite so whiny this week. (I hope. Let's see how I am once I get writing.) Thanks for all the booster shots last week. It really helps. Every once in a while I get panicky that I won't hear from anyone anymore, and then I know I couldn't do this. Really. You should see us all at download time. I feel like a little kid waiting for a present from Santa. As the e-mails come in from the satellite (I have no idea how or where they get stored out there in cyberspace), there is a list with all our names on it and they pop into our inboxes and we can all see how many we are each getting. It used to be a competitive activity with a "Ha ha! I got more than you" feel to it, but now with the kinder, gentler, more mature team, it's more like a supportive, pat-on-the-back– "There, see, you do have friends" event. Much better. People are even considerate about sharing the computer time now. I am so much happier with this team.

At the hospital this week we moved from the tent into the building. Whoa, what a difference. It's only one of the tents that got to move into the nicer digs, but it is going to change everything. The main tent, or *tente principale*, started leaking this week after a huge deluge of rain on Monday. It was lovely to have the break in the weather, but it was heavy like when the rains first started, and two of the tents had water running through them. As soon as the building was ready, the patients went from a cramped, dark, stifling tent, to a large, open, airy brick room, with screens on the windows. It was quite a step up. Also the nurses now have a separate room, with a solar-powered light so they can actually see something at night. Very nice. Now we can move the maternity tent to a better spot, and (I'm hoping) put a concrete slab down for a floor, which will be luxury beyond compare. There will never be a maternity building (at least not in my lifetime here), so Anders agrees we have to make the tent more functional. A concrete floor will be so much easier to sweep out and keep dry. The canvas that is on the ground now is all ripped, there is dirt coming up through, and the ground is uneven. It will take eight bags of cement, which we don't have, and since our big truck is broken down I'm not sure when we'll get more from Dubie. Hey, I wonder if we can send someone on a bike, well, four bikes, to get some. I'll have to look into that. Once that is done, we can move our tent and then build the *tukul* for the waiting area. I'm very excited about this. It's really going to improve the current set-up. And we don't even need a permit! Love it. Just decide what we want to build, and build it. OK, so there's no wiring, plumbing, inside walls, or drainage. We don't have to deal with zoning regulations. Trying to look at the bright side here.

The water system is a marvel. There was a hand pump put in at the hospital last year, but the water from it wasn't potable because it had too much uranium and manganese in it. I wasn't aware that the uranium for the atomic bombs used in WWII was from the Congo! Apparently there are enormous quantities of uranium here, just no end to the resources to pilfer out of this country. Anyway, it was safe to be used for washing but not drinking. Stefano set up an intricate filtering system where the water comes up into a holding tank by solar pump, and then goes through a tank filled with sand, and then one filled with gravel, and then goes into a pipe that runs underground a little way, so people can get their water now from a tap. It's really remarkable. He took a water sample with him to Amsterdam to have it tested for potability, but we haven't heard back yet. Hopefully it works. It has been exciting to see all that has been accomplished in just the short time I have been here. We'll see where we are by the end of the year.

The market is growing, too. Still not much there for food except for dried fish, but some of the bamboo racks have been replaced with little mud buildings with thatched roofs, and there is just more activity there in general. We can now get candles and matches. I saw some toothbrushes there the other day, the selection of *pagnes* has grown considerably (I buy one each week just to give them some business), and there are some flip-flops and some used clothes now. On one of my market excursions I received a marriage proposal from one of the merchants who wants to go to the United States. I told him I'd be here until September, so there was no need to be hasty. I had bought a *pagne* from him two weeks in a row, and I guess that was a sign that I was interested in acquiring a husband to support. I have a few months to figure out how to break it to him that I've already been there and done that.

Gerardine and Beatrice started doing little talks to the women who come for prenatal care about how good colostrum is for babies and how dangerous it is to wait five days to feed them. This is apparently a local problem, not generalized around the entire country. I guess that means there is hope. Part of it is local tribal customs, and part, the isolation of this place. Anyway, it's a start. I want to set it up so there is a little health talk every day in our soon-to-be-built *tukul*, and we'll see if it has any effect. I'm not quite sure yet how we'll measure that, but it's something to try.

When I first arrived here in September, Nina did a talk to all the *accoucheures* about breastfeeding. Out of the six of them, only three speak French, and only Gerardine speaks it well. So Gerardine had to do a lot of translating into Kiluba. At one point, Nina was drawing a diagram of lactating breasts on a flip chart. She drew the outline of a woman's body, then the breasts, then put the nipples on them, then started drawing the milk ducts going out from the nipples, explaining the whole time what she was drawing. Everyone stopped talking and was watching her with looks of utter confusion on their faces. Then, all of a sudden, Mama Marie had a light go on in her head, and she exclaimed, "*Ndiyo! Sawa!*" (Yes! OK!), a huge smile on her face. She reached into her blouse and scooped out one of her large breasts and started pointing to her nipple, showing everyone else what was being portrayed on the paper. All the others got that same look of revelation and said, "*Ahhh! Sawa!*" in recognition, finally, that the picture on the paper was a woman's breasts! And that round dot in the middle was the nipple! And they were all congratulating Mama Marie for figuring it out, and she was shaking all their hands, and they were clapping her on the back. The absurdity of it all was hilarious. That someone would draw a picture of a breast, when we had sixteen of them right here!

Let's see, measles. We had another death this week from measles. Small child, I don't know how old, respiratory distress. I told Sheila that, to me, every one of those deaths from measles is a murder that we've been accomplices in. That's how I feel. She tried to be reassuring that our mortality rate is really quite low because we've been doing such a good job with the care of the sick kids, and I just exploded. I got up off the couch (this was when I was in Lubumbashi, fresh off vacation), pointed my finger at her and said, "Is it because you don't have children that you could make such an outrageous comment? Do you think those mothers of the ones who died are pleased with the care they've gotten? What the FUCK! And that vaccine is still fucking sitting in our fridge?" Oh, Oh, Oh, they are working on it, don't worry, they understand how hard it is in the field blah, blah, blah. Margaret thinks our medical coordinator hasn't visited Shamwana because she's afraid of me. Whatever. I'm way beyond worrying about what the capital team thinks of me. Incidentally, the Shamwana team has come around to my stance on vaccinating, and we are going to be very busy this coming week, as we were last week, visiting villages. Busy, busy, busy, yes, indeed.

The driver situation has calmed. Jean de Dieu quit, which I am really bummed about. He was a great driver, but he had a big attitude, and Perrin was always on his case. My feeling was, so what if he has a cocky way about him? He never gets stuck in the mud, and he's never argued about what we needed to do. He asks for favors, sure, like can we take his wife to Dubie with us? But when you say, "No," he says, "*Ça va*" (OK) with a smile, and that's the end of it. Perrin gets mad at him for even asking, because he knows it's against the rules. My feeling is, so he tries, so what? All you have to do is say no. He doesn't try to sneak anything. Anyway, he's gone. Five guys came this past week looking for the three available jobs, and, after testing their driving skills all week, Perrin hired two of them. I'm a little leery, because they don't have gobs of experience, but we'll see. Choco, who is fabulous, will be leaving soon for Lubumbashi, and then we'll just have these rookies. I hate being stuck in the mud. I really hate it.

Sunday is the day we cook for ourselves. And guess what we are having today? Fresh string beans! Yes, yes, yes, I am very excited. I've been watching them all week, and they are ready today. The others don't know yet; it's a surprise. Bienvenu, our cook, (don't you love that name?) found some dried beans at the market last month, and before he cooked them, I grabbed a handful to plant. I did that before I left on vacation, and they are the stars of the garden. Carila brought back a chicken from Lubumbashi ready to roast, and I'm going to cook that over the coals. I'm saving the beans for a dramatic entrance at the table. Too bad Lucile and Bridgitte are on R&R. They would really appreciate it.

OK, I'm going to wrap this up and try to get it to go with the next batch that gets sent. I have to laugh at how much I've learned about computers since I've been here. Who would have thought I would go to what has to be the most primitive place on this earth and learn how to download off the satellite (yes, I can do that myself now) and use a memory stick? Before I came here, I didn't even know what a memory stick was. Every day I say to someone, "My kids are not going to believe this."

Love you all! Write to me!!!
Linda

CHAPTER 7 ~ FEBRUARY

Je me demande. *(I wonder.)*

February 1, 2008–Another month. How can it seem that time is standing still, but the days keep going by? I wonder if that's what it's like in prison. You'll be there forever, but you can't believe how fast forever is passing. I only have seven more months here. Almost halfway done. It's starting to feel like a steady pace is all that's needed now, and I can stick it out.

Cool morning. I'm in my tukul drinking green tea with milk, listening to one of Oscar's children cry behind the fence. It's about seven a.m. Today will be a stock-day and collect-data day. Anders is getting ready to leave on Friday (for three weeks!), I have R&R coming in there somewhere (two weeks, I think), then Margaret leaves, then Carila. It all rolls along. No outreach this week, nothing to break it up. We'll go next week though, so I will stick to the base, write my French sentences, hope some food comes on the plane today. The Superbowl was last night, Super Tuesday tomorrow.

February 6, 2008
Sunday morning, Shamwana

Hi Everyone,

We spent a full day Monday in the village of Kabala immunizing every kid we could get our hands on. It was very satisfying. When we arrived there, we set up our station under the big mango tree near the village chief's house. As people saw our vehicle coming, they started making their way toward the center of the village, and when enough people were gathered, Joseph, the *moso*, did an explanation of how vaccines work and why this is so important with the measles that is spreading but, since he spoke in Kiluba, I have no idea what he said. The parents all seemed happy that we were there, and the kids were curious, but once they found out that they had to get a shot, many of them ran away and had to be dragged back, screaming, to our little set-up. I felt a little bad, but still happy we were there. It was the right thing to do.

These villages are so incredibly remote. I mean, Shamwana is remote, but I can't even find the right word to describe how isolated some of the outer villages are. Really, except for the fact that they have a metal blade on the hoe, they are not far past the Stone Age. OK, the synthetic-blend rags that they are wearing are another give-away, but that's it. And I look at the rags and think, why bother? The rags seem like more of a problem to wear than not, draped around one shoulder with just the ribbing holding up a piece of one sleeve. It seems like it would be annoying to wear, and it is not covering anything or keeping them warm. I look at the bright eyes of the kids, and the size of their heads, and I think, they have really big brains, and they have so much spirit in their eyes. They are incredibly intelligent people. And then I look around, and I know that most of them are never, ever leaving this village. They will never wear a pair of shoes. They don't even know there is anything else in the world aside from this grass hut, and manioc *fufu*, and mangoes for one month out of the year. Some of the villages have bananas, but others don't even have those. And the few who do leave and come back bring measles with them. How unfair is that?

We got back to the base and prepared to go out to Kishale on Tuesday where we were spending the night. We had the outreach and the water/sanitation teams together, and didn't have enough drivers to take two vehicles. So it was a little camping trip. We left at six in the morning and I had really wanted to get to sleep early the night before, but as soon as I went to bed, some guy started screaming right behind the fence behind my *tukul*. It was the most hair-raising screams I'd ever heard. Sometimes sounding like he was scared, sometimes like he was running and out of breath, and sometimes like a weird grunting. He was moving around the village behind us, and I could tell it was the same person the whole time. It went on for hours and hours and hours. I thought maybe someone was drunk, and then thought if that was the case, someone else would have stopped him from screaming, but it was very unsettling. I didn't sleep at all. I heard our guards walking around the *tukuls* all night. Very creepy. I think I fell asleep an hour before I had to get up. We got packed up to go, and once on our way, I asked if anyone else heard the screaming. Margaret and all the men slept through it—didn't hear a thing. Bridgitte said she heard it and lay awake like I did, and Gerardine said she heard it for a while before she fell asleep. It was just an exorcism. Apparently, every once in a while in Shamwana, there is someone possessed by demons, and the local exorcist takes care of it. No one in the vehicle turned a hair at this. La-dee-da, just a Monday night exorcism. It seemed awkward to ask for details, like, who exactly is the exorcist, and do I know him? And does anyone think this is unusual? And what, you think you are possessed so you call the exorcist? Or your family thinks you need a good exorcising so they call? What? This gives you a little idea of the population we are working with. I'm wondering what the possessed guy's symptoms were, and how much worse they were than what he sounded like that night, and if he's cured now. But I got the impression that people in the car didn't want to talk about it. They all looked out the windows when I started asking questions.

And this breastfeeding thing is right up there with the exorcism. Women, of course, all breastfeed their babies here, but there is superstition about the colostrum that is unique to this area of the Congo. Gerardine worked in Kilwa, still in Katanga district, about 100 miles from here, and she said the women there did not follow the custom of cutting their breasts to get rid of the evil spirits. It's kind of a local thing. I asked Benson if there was some way we could honor the custom of a ceremony for the baby (they call this breast-cutting ritual a "ceremony"), and maybe offer it at the hospital without the cutting of the breasts, but he didn't think it was something we could blend into the western-style medicine we are offering. I guess that was a bit of a stretch on my part.

The driver on our trip to Kishale was the guy who usually drives the big truck, the Unimog (that's what everyone calls it, I'm not sure how to spell it), but since that was broken down and we were short of drivers, he drove the Land Cruiser. This is a guy about my age, one of the oldest national staff working here. His name is Mario: he's from Burundi and has worked for MSF for thirty years. We got stuck once on the way there, but it wasn't too bad. We got out using shovels and a jack, with six of us pushing. I don't think we were stuck for more than a half-hour.

We got to Kishale and had another full day of immunizing kids and then, since we were staying overnight, were just sitting around. It was incredibly hot, and you could feel there was a storm hovering around out there. Late in the afternoon Bridgitte and I went for a walk. The landscape there is different from Shamwana and incredibly beautiful in a different way. It is much flatter and open, without the ring of mountains surrounding, and more plain than jungle. When we had walked about a half-mile, the dark clouds started coming toward us, and the wind started whipping up, and within seconds it was a fierce wind with the trees bent nearly sideways. We quickly headed back to the health center and ran for the little mud guesthouse where we were spending the night (the one with the living creatures in the thatched roof). We got into our little room just as the rain started pelting, and it started pouring in through the roof, soaking everything. They had thrown a tarp over the thatching a few weeks ago, but the wind blew it off, and all the beds and our packs were getting drenched. Bridgitte, Gerardine, and I were in there trying to find a spot that wasn't under a steady stream of water, but we were all getting wet. The lightning and thunder were magnificent, occurring nearly simultaneously. There was nothing to do but wait it out, and we sat on cool boxes in separate corners of the room hoping the entire roof didn't blow off. When it let up, we went out to sit in the guard's *tukul*, which is like a small gazebo, where Mario and the guard were sitting by a little charcoal fire.

Before the storm, Mario had gone and collected wild lemongrass and mint and was making a tea with it. It smelled so good, and the air was cool, and tea sounded perfect. He was a little surprised that I wanted to drink it: expats don't usually ask to share the national staff's food. But I was desperate for a cup of tea and was willing to trust he knew what he was picking. Bridgitte and I grabbed two empty cups from our camping gear and got comfy around the fire and sipped the tea. It was fabulous. I was telling him that I love finding local food and wanted to see where he found the herbs and asked if we could find any in Shamwana. The rain had stopped, and he showed me where he found it, and we picked a bunch to make another big pot of tea. Mario brings his own cooking pots with him on the overnights and cooks for himself because he's Muslim and can't eat from any pot that's ever had pork in it. The rest of us were waiting for the evening meal made by a woman in the village, who cooks it at her house and delivers it ready to eat. We went back to the *tukul* where Mario made another pot of tea, and then started making his supper, which was manioc *fufu* and smoked fish that he roasted on the coals. He cut a lime he picked off a nearby tree and squeezed it on the fish. He was urging us to taste it, but I felt bad taking his food; there wasn't much of it, and we had ours on its way. It seemed rude not to try a little, though, so I took a small piece of *fufu* and broke off a bit of the fish with my thumb and popped it in my mouth. It was the most delicious thing that had passed over my deprived taste buds since I don't know when. I had to restrain myself from eating the whole thing.

The eight of us who were waiting for our meal sat watching him eat. I was drooling. Remember? this was the place where we had the fish eyes and tomatoes washed in dirty water. Well, this time I was ready for anything. Or that's what I thought until she actually brought the food about eight o'clock. It was pitch dark, and we went into the little room with a candle and started spreading out the three pots. Let's see, *fufu* in the big pot, about one cup of stewed greens (for eight people) in the little pot, and two stewed rats in the medium pot. Oh yes, rat for supper tonight. I thought, "I didn't understand what they just said, they can't mean rat, like in English, rat." I asked Bridgitte, "Did they just say that was rat?" She nodded slowly. Oh yes, that's what they said. Rat. I was starving and I tried to forget that this was a rat, but after one teeny bite I couldn't eat it. The texture. Couldn't do it. Not like there was much more than one bite each anyway, so I just used the sauce from it to give the *fufu* a little flavor and called it enough. *Fufu* is filling, I will say that much about it. God, I wished I had eaten with Mario.

The rain had stopped and the evening was very pleasant, cool even, and after our lovely little repast we all sat in the guard's *tukul* and talked for a while. The conversation revolved around how the Congolese men will cook for themselves when they have to, but would never, ever cook for their wives. That would be a sign of weakness. And the three of us who were expats and women were trying to explain that in Europe and America a lot of men cook for their wives and it is not a sign of weakness at all. Women like it when men do that! Blank stares, then exclamations of shock and horror! But it was one of those really wonderful evenings where two cultures try to understand a little bit about each other. I loved it, rat and all.

The next morning there was nothing for breakfast, unless you call instant Nescafe something. Bridgitte and I said we would never make it through the morning without something more than that, and I told her I was going to ask Mario if he would make some more herbal tea for us. Then I said jokingly, "I think he likes me." A few weeks ago he had left a stalk of sugar cane in the office for me, and every time I shake his hand in greeting he holds onto it a little longer than necessary. But still, I was just kidding.

I asked him if he'd make us some more tea, and he obliged, and we were sipping away, and he said to me, "Mama Linda, would your children accept a black man?" I said, "Of course!" and wanted to say emphatically that my children are not racists, but didn't know how to say racist in French, so said, "My children believe that the color of skin is not important!" And he nodded, and I left and went over to the health center. As I was walking away, I started thinking that maybe there was more of that conversation yet to come.

Several hours later we were finished at the clinic and I didn't have anything to do until we left, so I sat down with my book to read while the vehicle was being loaded with our camping stuff. After he was done packing up, Mario came over to me and asked the guard there to leave us alone so we could talk. I'm like, Oh shit. He asked me the same question, but this time phrased a little differently. "Would your children really accept a black man for your husband?" OK, now the tone of this was changing a little bit. I said again, "The color of a man's skin is not important. There are many other things that are important, but not skin color." In my head I started thinking of the "Hey kids! Guess who's coming to dinner?" scenario, and was wishing I could make a joke about it, but he was so serious, it wasn't appropriate. Plus, I was sure he'd never seen the movie. The joke would have flopped. Then I wanted to say that it was a husband in general that the kids would most likely be opposed to, but that didn't seem right either. And then there was a thought floating around in there that I could blame everything on the kids, and made a mental note to remember that. Then he asked what qualities are important to me for a husband? Now, really, this was very touching, considering that the other marriage proposal I had went something like this:

Him: "What country are you from?"

Me: "The United States."

Him: "I would like to go to the United States. If I marry you, you could take me with you to the United States."

Me: "Well, I will be staying here until September, that's a long time. I will think about it."

Him: "OK. Thank you."

So part of me was very impressed with Mario's consideration, and part of me was thinking I just don't have a refined enough vocabulary in French to have this conversation. But he wanted me to give him a list of requirements, and I thought, "Oh, honey, if you only knew my requirements." But stupidly, I started listing them, or the ones I knew how to say in French (it didn't seem the right moment to pull out my dictionary): "honesty, intelligence . . ." and after each one he'd respond, "*Oui, oui, je suis tres honnête*" (Yes, yes, I am very honest) and then I realized this was dumb. I'm not going to make him answer to every character asset I can think of, so I just said, "There are many things that are important." And then he said that ever since I arrived in Shamwana he thought I would be a good wife and that he has been very attracted to me. I wanted to say I was flattered, but didn't know that word in French, either, so thought of saying, "Oh, that makes me happy." But I thought that would give him the wrong idea, so said, "That is very nice, but it is very difficult for us to be married. We are too different." He said, "*Non, non*! We are very similar!" (You can all see the similarities I'm sure, a Burundian Muslim and me.) And I said, "But I am only staying here for seven more months," and he said, "But you can stay here to live." And I said, "No, I can't leave my children, or my mother, or my job, or my friends, or my church." At this point he got distracted by the fact that my mother was still alive, so we talked about that for a few minutes and then he said that he could come to live with me in America, and I said the stupidest thing, "No, you would not like it, it is too cold." And he said, "No, that is no problem." And I thought of the evening before when I was comfortable in my T-shirt and he was wearing a jacket I would have worn skiing—no wait, I wouldn't have worn it skiing, I would have worn it to feed the chickens or light the winter solstice bonfire—and said, "You don't understand how cold." And then Margaret came over to us and told us that everyone was ready to go, so I jumped up and said, "We're coming!" I have a feeling there will be more to this story.

In the other local romance story, Bienvenu pressed Lucile again for an answer to his marriage proposal, saying he was very much in love with her. She told me she was very direct, and told him he had to respect her feelings too, that she was in love with someone else. So Bienvenu said OK, he would accept that. But his wife is pregnant and about to have the baby soon, and if it is a girl he would like to name her Lucile. Lucile told him she thought that was very nice.

See? So it's not all death and destruction. I thought I'd give you a break from those stories.

Thank you all so much for all the wonderful messages this week.

Love you all, Linda

Je suis flatté. *(I'm flattered.)*

February 7—I received a sweet proposal from Mario. I'm sure I am not the first expat to receive one from him, but still, it was very sweet. The sweetest part was that he asked me to stay here with him. I didn't feel like just a ticket out of here. I'm not sure I handled it very well. Lucile is much better at this than I am. I don't want to hurt his feelings. It certainly has brightened my mood.

February 10, 2008
Sunday morning, Shamwana

Hi Everyone!

Oh boy, big excitement this week. Don't worry, no one died, though I did have to restrain myself from strangling Carila a few times. We've had a visitor all week from Lubumbashi. Ursula, the big chief medical coordinator, has been here to see what's going on in the project, and to teach us all how to use this new data collection tool developed in Amsterdam. We have to count numbers of all TB cases, measles, births, etc. every month, and we've got a little system split between Margaret, Carila, and me. I don't think it's too hard or time consuming but they both complain about it a lot. Honestly, it just doesn't take that much time but they are on the computers for hours on end. Usually I enter all my data in an hour and am thinking, "What should I do *after* breakfast?" And that's coming from me, who hated doing charting at home, especially on the computer. But really, it's not that bad.

So there is this new, very complex tool that will be able to track all epidemiological trends, and does fancy graphs, and has the information broken down into very specific categories, and there are pages and pages, and folders and folders, and lots of cutting and pasting into different folders. Now, this would have been enough back home to make me, uh, run away to the third world where I thought I'd never have to do this! But, since I got my memory stick, I can cut and paste all by myself now, so was actually looking forward to a little data entry 101. I'm collecting new skills.

Ursula decided that the national staff should be involved in this, so they can enter the data when we are away. Away on vacation, that is. When MSF leaves the project they will, of course, take all the computers with them. I need to inform you that it was only two months ago that Benson, our medical doctor and surgeon, got his own stethoscope. We check for anemia by pulling down the lower eyelid and deciding how pale the conjunctiva is. We just sort of guess. That's how we decide who gets a blood transfusion and who doesn't, to illustrate the level of technology here. School kids write their math problems in the dirt because they don't have pencils or paper. And here we were, all set up in our mud brick office, with all the laptops connected to the generator, and Ursula even had one of those projectors that projected images on the whitewashed wall. The juxtaposition of the two scenes, the one outside the office and the one inside, was really a sight to behold. I couldn't stop laughing. Now I agree that this is the chance for the national staff to at least get exposed to what they are missing, but the idea that they are going to be able to do this on their own, my God, is just preposterous.

Ursula is from Belgium and speaks French at lightning speed. Oh yes, this course was given in French. Bear in mind that French is NOT the national staff's first language, either. There ensued complicated explanations of epidemiological trends, Excel spread sheets, moving data from one folder to another to be analyzed, info on how to figure out the beginning of an epidemiological week, which is different from a calendar week, etc. I mean, really. This to a group of people who, when Agna sent a box of felt-tipped markers, fell on them like dogs on a meat wagon. Now for me, it was great. I got to feel like the IT expert–a once-in-a-lifetime experience. I could even follow most of what Ursula was saying, because I could read it on the wall at the same time. And it was something to do and, frankly, I've been a bit bored the last couple of weeks. So after a couple of hours of instructions, we got to do practice exercises. This was great. She gave us sample sheets with data on them, and we were supposed to put all the data in on the new data tool. We were each paired with a national staff person (doctor, nurses, and the guy who is supposed to be our data-entry person. He is the one I was paired with, Raphael.)

Here's what the conversation in the room sounded like: "*Donc, clique ici ouvrir. Non, non, doubler clique gauch, non, non, plus vite, non non, regarde, tu as bougé la sourie, encore, garder la fleche ici ou la page n'ouvrir pas, trés bien! Voila, tu as ouvri la page!"* (OK, click here to open, no, no, double click on the left, no, no faster than that, no, no look, you have moved the mouse, try again, keep the arrow here or the page won't open, very good! There now, you have opened the page!) Oh. My. God. I could not stop laughing. I was hit by a monstrous lightning bolt of realization. So THIS is what my kids have felt like trying to teach me! I must say, I was a much more patient teacher than my own dear flesh and blood. I never grabbed the mouse out of his hand, never elbowed my way in front of him to do it myself (though I really, really wanted to), never insulted his intelligence or stomped away in disgust. During the seven or eight minutes it took Raphael to open the page, I busied myself by looking up words I didn't know in the dictionary. During the ten to fifteen minutes it took to drag the mouse to cut and paste, I daydreamed about this scene in a movie. It was very entertaining.

So that was Friday and Saturday. There were no movements this week to the villages or clinics, partly because the new drivers aren't ready to go out on their own, partly because we had to do all the end-of-the-month statistics and the pharmacy order, and partly because of Ursula's visit. One of our new drivers backed the vehicle into the wall of the lab while he was delivering the pharmacy order. I was in the pharmacy with Ursula showing her around, and heard this big crash. And we went out, and there was a big hole in the wall to the lab. Perrin had a fit, but by the end of the day it was all fixed. That's the beauty of having a single layer of mud bricks as the solitary structure. They are very easy to fix. I did feel badly for Freddy, the driver, though. He was sure he'd lose his job.

Mario, who told me on Monday he watched all weekend to see if I would walk by his house, left with the newly-fixed Unimog for Dubie to get cement and a thousand mosquito nets. He was supposed to drive there on Tuesday and come back on Wednesday, but he was stuck in the mud for four days, and just got back yesterday, so we haven't gotten our cement floor yet for the maternity tent. We did, however, get a door cut into the back wall of the maternity room, so now we can walk to the tent without tripping over tree roots and ditches in the middle of the night when we have a newborn in one arm, flashlight in the other, trying to hold up an anemic woman who just gave birth twenty minutes ago. The new door was my idea, and now Margaret's got her knickers in a twist because they fulfilled my request before one of hers. She just doesn't know how to ask, but I'm not going to tell her that. She should be able to figure it out since she supposedly knows everything.

Other than that, it's been sorta quiet. There have been several deliveries without problems, so they didn't even call me. Portefeille is doing a great job in the pharmacy, now that it's all set up, so I don't need to spend much time over there. We finally got the hang of ordering the right amount of supplies for the week, so my troubleshooting there has dropped way off. Like I said, there were no movements this week. Oh, except for one when we got a message from a guy on a bike that there was a pregnant woman in Monga bleeding heavily, so I went with one of the new drivers to collect her and bring her back here. We met her on the road, being transported by bush ambulance (the bike with the jury-rigged bamboo seat), got her here, and ended up doing a cesarean for a placenta previa. The baby had been dead for quite a while, but she survived, so that was good. It was the first time I have first-assisted at a C-section here, and that got Carila all in a twit because she wanted to do it to show off for Ursula. I had asked Benson to assist him when it wasn't an emergency, so when we did have an emergency and there was no one else to assist, I would at least be familiar with his surgical style. He was fine with that, and agreed, and since we knew the baby was not alive, I didn't need to be available for a resuscitation. Made sense to me. But this meant that Carila couldn't spend the rest of the day talking like she did the whole thing single-handedly. It messed up her whole day. Of course she didn't want to go with me to collect the woman who might be bleeding to death on the road. Sorry. I told myself I was not going to complain about the team anymore. It just slipped. I have been better about swearing, though.

Last night at our expat meeting, Ursula went on and on about the steps they are taking in Lubumbashi to get permission to vaccinate for measles. We just sat there nodding our little obedient heads, and I even gave a little show of being sooooo frustrated, but in reality we've been doing a good job of protecting the kids around here. I figure when they ever do get permission, we'll be way ahead of the game. What she doesn't know is not hurting her.

Tomorrow we go on another overnight. This time to Kampangwe, which does not have a little guesthouse, so I guess we'll be sleeping in the clinic again. I wish we had our own little tents. Margaret told me I had to take responsibility for my own cot and blanket this time, as I was going to have to "learn to do it myself anyway" after she leaves. Which, thank God, is in two weeks. This complicated task involves telling the driver to put six cots on the roof, instead of four. Let's see if I can handle that. I am being punished for getting the new door.

Lucile leaves for vacation next week. I can't believe she's been here long enough to take a vacation already, it seems like she just arrived. But she's meeting up with her boyfriend in Zanzibar for a week. Then he comes back here as Carila's replacement. She has asked her mother to send some kids' books so we can start a little story time for the kids at the hospital. As it is now, there are kids there for months being treated for TB or burns, and they have absolutely nothing to do. There are also lots of kids there who aren't sick, but are the children of patients, and they have nowhere else to stay, so they stay at the hospital. They are always just lying around in the dirt, and we thought in our soon-to-be new *tukul* we could have health education in the morning and a kids activity in the afternoon. I got this idea when Emmanuel started having me read stories out loud to him in French, that it would be good for me, too, to read to kids in French. They won't understand any of it, but it might give them a jump on the primary school years. If they live that long. We'll see how it goes. I'll let you know.

I guess that's about it for this week.

Sorry, sorry about the Patriots. Happy, happy about the Democrats.

Love you all,
Linda

⁂

Je n'a pas d'amant. J'ai l'amour. *(I have no lover. I have love.)* February 14, 2008–*Another Valentines Day comes and will go without a sweetheart. Being here clearly demonstrates how much advertising can manipulate your brain. The absence of reminders has been refreshing. I'm not nearly as anxious about it, or maybe it's because I'm not upset about not having anyone. Really—most of the time, after the rush of new love wears off, it's a bunch of work. I'm not sure I want that again. Yes, yes, yes, there are moments that are wonderful. But I have those moments now in a different way, without the anxiety or angst. (There's a little mouse in my tukul, sharing the space.) Bridgitte is going home. I'm sorry for her. No replacement yet for Margaret, and now Bridgitte will need one too. Lots of news from home last week . . . deepening ties, lives wiped out in an instant, new beginnings . . .*

February 17, 2008
Sunday morning, Shamwana

Hi Everyone,

Some changes are happening with the team here. Unfortunately, Bridgitte is returning to France after being unable to maintain her weight here. She's gotten dangerously thin, and it's at the point where if she got diarrhea, it'd be big trouble, with no quick or reliable way to get out of here. I am so bummed out about this. So is she. But we're hoping that within a few weeks she can regain the weight she's lost, and figure out a way to maintain it here, and come back in a month. She's already accomplished so much since arriving, and I know this might sound sexist, but I really like having a water/sanitation engineer who is female. She just added the woman's touch to the latrine/laundry/shower planning. Stefano was brilliant; he could figure out how to fix things quickly and was always tinkering with his new inventions. But he didn't notice things like the women washing bloody/shitty laundry right next to the well. It took a bit to convince him that a new laundry area away from the well was a high priority. But since December when Bridgitte arrived, we've got lots of brick latrines now, and nice bamboo fences around the refuse area, and a couple of brick bathing enclosures where people can do a bucket bath in private, and a nice cement circular area about two meters in diameter where the women can wash the laundry without disgusting mud puddles forming all around them. You know, it's just nicer. It's cleaner and easier to maintain some semblance of sanitation.

As much as we complain about how hard it is to live here, when it comes down to leaving early, it is harder to leave than stay. Bridgitte doesn't want to go, but the choice isn't hers anymore. If you don't like to eat starch, you'll starve to death here. We're cheering for her. I hope she comes back. She arrived back here yesterday after having spent the week in Lubumbashi where the decision was made. She got stuck in Dubie where the plane broke down on Friday, then finally made it by road late afternoon yesterday. She's only here to pack up her stuff and leave again on tomorrow's (hopefully fixed) plane. She's pretty upset about leaving. She brought back a bottle of some creamy liqueur made from Amarula (an African fruit), and we women sat in camaraderie drinking the entire bottle while the guys quickly disappeared, since there was emotion involved. Excellent: more for us. It was very high calorie, and we wanted to be supportive. I gave her a list of all the things I want her to bring back from France in a month (kids' books, dictionaries, blank DVDs) and we are trying to be optimistic. I'm not crazy about rice three times a day either, but if that's all there is, hey, eat it.

Margaret has one more week here, and so far a replacement has not been found. Apparently it's hard to recruit French-speaking nurses. So I'll be taking on some of her responsibilities, and I guess Carila will take on others. I'm not so worried about that as I am about having to orient a new person when she (or he) does arrive. An overlap is so much better. Carila will have a week here with Fabien (the new doctor) before she leaves. Lucile is really excited that it's finally time for him to come. She's leaving tomorrow for ten days in Zanzibar with him before he starts. I can't believe it's been almost three months since she arrived. Yikes! I 'm almost halfway through my contract. It's starting to feel like not much time. So we'll have a going away party next weekend for Margaret, and then I'll have my R&R the weekend after that, and then the weekend after that is Carila's party. Goodness, the social calendar is filling up. Bridgitte, bless her heart, emptied out her knapsack and left everything in Lubumbashi, and filled it with beer to bring back for Margaret's party. A party Bridgitte is now going to miss.

The party stress resumed this week with Margaret's imminent departure. I think I already explained that it is the responsibility of the departing person to buy a goat and drinks for the party. The goat costs about fifty dollars, and the drinks are whatever you can find. Beer is fairly expensive, about a dollar each. The national staff kills and cooks the goat and takes care of the dance music. The expat has to provide drinks for about forty people and there is nothing here! This is no easy task! I've seen the anxiety of departing Europeans soar to astronomical levels, trying to figure out how to get a couple of cases of beer here for their own good-bye party. I'm going to start hoarding months before I leave, though it'll be dry season then, and we can get the truck here more regularly.

Margaret was freaking out this week (and she never loses her composure) with the plane breaking down, food being a priority for freight on that, and this party the only thing for miles around to look forward to. It's terrible to disappoint the national staff. She got word from one of the drivers that there was someone in the village who brought back some whisky from Lubumbashi by bicycle and was selling it. She found him and bought all he had, ten 100 ml bottles. We tasted it. OK, now, I have never actually drunk paint thinner before, so I can't say for certain that's what it tasted like, but it's what I imagine paint thinner tastes like. It made my little plastic packets taste like single malt Scotch. It's made in Angola. I would not like to see people drunk on this stuff. Starting to get the picture of the desperation level? There was another guy who brought in some Bingwa, beer that is banned in Tanzania (though made there), and we bought some of that out of his mud hut. We literally had to wipe mud off the bottles. But since it came by bicycle, there wasn't a whole lot of it, and we drank it a few Saturdays ago. It wasn't bad. Of course, the wine we had in cartons was just above altar-grade, but after a while that didn't seem so bad, either. That's long gone, though. Then, enter Bridgitte, broken-hearted and sobbing, but still caring that she got beer here for Margaret's party. Her teeny frame could not lift the backpack with two cases of beer and one of soda inside. What a sweetie.

Let's see. Mario arrived with some of the cement and—hooray!—we have the cement floor done in the maternity tent. It is so much nicer! I'm going to plant some flowers around the outside, clear away all the rubble from cutting out the new door, make a little path from the delivery room, and—voila!—who wouldn't want to come here to have their baby? Now, before you all start making Martha Stewart jokes about me, the flowers will absorb the rain runoff and cut down on the mud around the tent. It has a purpose other than aesthetics, thank you very much, and has helped a lot around the *tukuls*. (No, I won't be stenciling the inside of the tent.)

The other huge addition to the maternity service here is the vacuum extractor that finally arrived from Amsterdam. I had been so frustrated having nothing to use to help a woman deliver if there was fetal distress or, more frequently, maternal exhaustion, or seizure. It has been really, really horrible. A month ago this vacuum, which had been in the pipeline for six months, arrived, and it is such a relief. I haven't used it too often, even with these long pushing stages, because I don't want people to think that everyone is going to deliver with this now, and never have to push, but let me tell you, it has come in very handy on several occasions. This is not the plastic model we use at home with the soft cap. This is an industrial strength, sterilizable metal cap, jar-on-the-floor number, and I was initially scared to death of it. But we've bonded.

We had a woman last week who arrived by bicycle, fully dilated for seven hours and in labor for God knows how long before that, and I could actually do something! Prior to this the only other option was pushing on her uterus physically, and that is just so miserable and dangerous. Last Sunday night it came in handy when, during an incredible deluge of rain, I got called over to the hospital to find a young girl had just arrived by bike from Kisele (eighteen kilometers away). She was drenched, along with the people who had accompanied her, two of them with babies on their backs. She had taken traditional medicine two days before and was unable to deliver. The baby was dead, and there was such a foul odor emanating from her that I gagged when I examined her, and almost threw up. If I couldn't get it out with the vacuum, the only other option was a C-section, and that would have been ghastly considering how infected she already was. So I put the vacuum on, and it took a while, but finally delivered what was (sorry about this) a rotting corpse. My God, it was awful. But then, what was even worse was that Gerardine and Benson started yelling at this woman—really, she was just a kid—for not coming sooner and for taking traditional medicine. The scene was so bizarre and, well, ghastly. Lying next to your dead, rotting baby was not punishment enough? Now we had to scold her? Then the whole family got marched in to look at the scene, and the scolding got turned on them. Drenched, tired, bone thin, in this eerie light and revolting smell, and being lectured on the evils of traditional medicine. This was not the way I wanted to go about it. I still haven't figured out how much is cultural, and how much is the national staff wanting to please us by driving home the western-medicine-is-better point, but there have been a few scenes like this one when I've felt like the suffering they have endured has brought them to a point of no return and there just isn't any compassion left. It's very upsetting. I could be kind to the young mother, say "I'm sorry" in French (which she probably didn't understand), help her to the maternity tent (after her sister had to take off one of her own wet *pagnes* to give her to cover herself), but I couldn't stop the onslaught of criticism as she was cowering and crying. I just stood between her and them, touching her head and wishing I had the language skills to explain in Kiluba what was happening. I had to be content with the fact that she hadn't had surgery, that Benson and Gerardine, who are really very good people, knew what they were doing, and that it was something I could never understand. And that's pretty much it. I don't know. I was glad for that vacuum, though.

I got back over to the base and finished cooking the supper I had started, now in complete darkness. Those kerosene lanterns are quaint to eat by, but hard to cook by. The last thing I felt like doing was eating, but the rest of the team was waiting, and we had made an agreement not to tell grotesque stories over dinner, so I just sulked.

The next day we were leaving for Kampangwe for the overnight. I didn't need to go until Tuesday but to be more efficient with the vehicles we went along with the outreach team. I was able to spend some time on Monday going over the new data collection tool, which is utterly confusing for the *accoucheuses* who don't speak French. I think I may have Gerardine translate it into Kiluba. I haven't decided which is better, to give them the credit of being able to learn this in French, or just make their lives easier and do it in Kiluba. In a way, I feel like translating it is insulting them. It's like saying I don't believe you can learn French. I'm going to have all of the *accoucheuses* come to Shamwana in March for a little two-day class to go over this stuff and give them a chance to talk to each other. That will be a test of my French skills.

I got a chance in Kampangwe to see first-hand the breast cutting, and I could not believe it. Sweet Mother of God. I mean, just about the only thing in life these women DON'T have to suffer from is sore nipples, and then to see nipples cut open, and have too much pain to feed the baby. OK, I can see after a while you might start scolding. I don't know. It's just overwhelming.

I had a lot of hanging around to do that day, and pulled out the *Bao* board I bought in Zanzibar. It's an African game that we played in Malawi, but I've never seen anyone play it here. Choco had never heard of it, but I taught him to play, and that passed some of the time. Then I played with Michel, the other driver. It wasn't long before we had a huge crowd of kids around watching. As it was starting to get dark and we were waiting for the village woman to bring our supper,

Margaret took my place and started another game with Choco. This was making me happy. I never see anyone playing anything here, and have been hoping we could get some kind of pleasant activity going. I started walking around in front of the health center, and the kids were all hanging on me wanting me to take their pictures. I told them it was too dark, and then one of them started making fun of me, dancing in a crazy way, blocking my path. I started mimicking him, mirror-like, and he kept it up, and then a few other kids started dancing, so I turned to them and did the same thing. Some of the kids started making synchronized music with their mouths, then one started calling out a song and the others echoed back his line, and the bipping and bopping was getting more like a variety of different instruments. I made a motion with my hands like playing a drum, and another kid started on a drumbeat with his mouth, and we were all dancing like it had been rehearsed. I wanted to call to Margaret to take a picture, but didn't want to break the spell. The contrast between dancing with laughing, singing children in the moonlight under a huge, starry sky and the scene in that delivery room the night before, well, it's almost a full-time job just to take it all in. The supper was fabulous that night, too. Manioc *fufu*, wild mushrooms which are being harvested now, and chicken! Yes, recognizable animal flesh!

I was telling Lucile about it when I got back, and we were saying how great it would be if we could dance with the kids at the hospital. We'll see if we can add it to our afternoon story time. Just dance with them and let them sing. It would be a little diversion from lying around in the dirt. Lucile is a professional dancer as well as psychiatrist, so she was all over it. They are supposed to start building the *tukul* this week. I have high hopes, which is always dangerous, but I'll never stop being thankful for that night in Kampangwe.

Oh, for those of you who've asked, manioc *fufu* is a starchy food made from cassava and water, which is served in a big mound, and you break off bits of it and make an indentation with your thumb to hold little bits of whatever food is being served with it. It has the consistency of gnocchi. Maybe a little gummier.

Love you all!
Linda

J'ai dansé. Nous avons dansé ensemble. *(I danced. We danced together)* *February 23, 2008–Saturday morning, light rain, sitting on the little step outside the dining tukul, just to have enough light to read by. Cat's on my lap, purring. Margaret left yesterday. Teary good-bye at the airport, telling me to feed the cat. I was struck by how (temporarily) sad her departure was. She was supposed to leave this Monday, but no plane is coming, so a hurried good-bye party Thursday, amid the most violent deluge of rain, then she left yesterday. News from home has been scattered this week. Only Perrin, Carila, and me here this weekend.*

February 24, 2008
Sunday morning, Shamwana

Hi Everyone,

I can't believe it's the end of another month. That means pharmacy inventory this week. Gee, they seem to come along fast. I've been trying to think what to write about this week. I used to have no trouble storing up stories for Sunday, but I have gotten used to so much of what happens here, it doesn't seem like news anymore. I guess that's a good thing for me. Maybe I'll just run down the week and see what comes up.

Monday was a very teary good-bye to Bridgitte, all 88 pounds of her. The plane made it here, despite some questions about the weather, but Bruce, our little twenty-three-year-old pilot had no problem except a bit of a bumpy landing. We got that on film. There was a guy on the plane whom we had sent to Lubumbashi to see if anything could be done for the huge cancer he has growing out of his eye. This poor guy– we don't see much cancer here, they die of something else long before cancer could kill them, but I guess he was just lucky. Nothing could be done, so he was sent back here to wait for the inevitable. In just one week, his bandage had doubled in size (nice clean bandage, though.) Lucile left on the plane also; off to meet her sweetheart in Zanzibar for a ten-day vacation before they both come back here to Shamwana. Nothing much else happened that day, I think I finished reading *The Mission Song*, a spy novel about the Congo. It was OK. Not Le Carré's best book. There were three cucumbers, a cabbage, and six tomatoes on the plane for us. That's our fresh food for the week.

Tuesday was immunization day in Kisele. Carila came along, not to help with the immunizations, but to teach the nurse there the new TB protocol. Since the roads have gotten so bad with the rain, we now have to go everywhere with two vehicles. If one gets stuck, the other can help pull it out. It's more of an adventure now. Add to that all the new drivers we have, and most of the day gets taken up with just getting there. While we were in Kisele, an incredible storm blew in. We had finished all the immunizations, but we still had to get back here. We started out with the pickup truck, which was our second vehicle. They were cutting wood for tables and shelves, and the biggest downpour was finished by the time we started on our way. The pickup was really loaded down with wood, and we had to keep stopping because it was getting caught on the overhead tree branches. Then we got to one spot where the pickup went into the water and stayed there. Stuck in the mud. *Embourbement*. It's a word we use a lot now. It was pouring rain and I had no desire at all to get out and help, so didn't. Gerardine and Carila felt the same way, so we sat like little princesses in the vehicle, while the guys worked a long time getting us out. First they tied the pickup to the Land Cruiser, and tried to back up. That didn't work. Then they cut down trees off to the right of the road (with axes) so we could drive around in front of the pickup and try to pull them out that way, but then we got stuck trying to do that. I was starting to think it was going to be a long night there, but then they got the winch off the roof, tied it to a tree, and winched us out first, then used it to winch the pickup out of the water. It was rather remarkable, I thought. We got lots of great pictures and videos of this (it was the least we could do). The guys all love telling an *embourmement* story to the others, and they don't usually have pictures to go along with it, so this was actually a great service. We got back here too late for me to go running, which is always frustrating. I know this seems so silly after watching the guys exert that amount of energy to free the vehicles, but it is the only exercise I get, and I feel awful if I don't go. I did get to make Emmanuel laugh a lot though, when I told him the story in French.

Let's see. Wednesday. Boring. Except that we got the news that the Monday plane was cancelled, so Margaret would have to leave on the Friday plane. This meant moving up her good-bye party to Thursday night. This also meant that the cabbage and cucumbers would have to last two weeks. I ran three laps on the runway. Read the entire book *Freakonomics*.

Thursday. After the morning routine, rounds, etc., we had to listen to the goat being slaughtered for the party. That was unpleasant. Perrin said, "I don't get this, in Pakistan they killed goats all the time. I never had to listen to the howling like this. What are they doing here?" I didn't watch, so I have no idea how they do it. It was very noisy, though. Just when I was considering taking a nap so I'd be rested up for the party (after all, I had that one beer to look forward to), I got called over to the hospital. A woman arrived here by bicycle from Kishale, in labor for days, baby already dead, in shock and bleeding. We took her straight over to the operating room. I haven't seen too many ruptured uteri, but this was bad. Benson couldn't repair it at all and had to do a hysterectomy. What a mess. Boy, is he good. And hardly anything to work with, it's amazing. We had a few units of blood in our fridge, luckily, and the woman is doing well. I was just circulating (Carila assisted with the surgery), so I left after about three hours and came over to see what was happening with the party. It was about six o'clock. No run again, but dancing is pretty good exercise here. I had that to look forward to.

Margaret was in a panic. It was so refreshing. I know I have described these parties already, but can't remember if I told you that the one departing has to give a speech. The project coordinator also gives a speech (which in this case was Perrin, since Anders is away), then the *chef du village* gives a speech, then the *chef du groupment* gives a speech, then someone from your department gives a speech, it goes on and on. No wonder everyone gets drunk as quickly as possible. Well, Margaret, despite her ice-maiden persona, is a very shy, insecure person. She had written her speech in English and had Perrin translate it, and was now panicking because she wasn't sure if she could read it. Now, she makes fun of me relentlessly for reading my little seventh grade French stories out loud to myself in my *tukul*. She calls me "teachers pet" because I keep continuing with the French lessons. Except for that one night when I was throwing up, she's really not very nice to me. So I was rather enjoying this. I got back over to the base at the time the party was supposed to start, soaking wet with sweat, and was heading to the shower when she saw me and said, pleading and panicked, "WHERE HAVE YOU BEEN? I NEED YOU!!!!" Ohhhh, words I've longed to hear. "HURRY UP AND TAKE A SHOWER AND GET OUT HERE WITH ME!!!!!" Oh, so sweet. What a relief to see her be real. I smiled. I quickly showered and dressed, and very, very generously shared my last packet of whiskey with her (and since there is only one shot of whiskey in each packet, this was extremely kind of me) and started helping her with some of the pronunciation of the words in her speech. Oh, this was so satisfying. She said, "I CAN'T DO THIS WITHOUT A BEER!"

Now, the drinks don't get served until after all the speeches, and remember, there is only enough for one beer each, and the whisky she had bought was just not drinkable, even in this emergency. So we made this plan to go confiscate two of the beers out of the cool box in the radio room. (I figured, I was helping, I get one too.) She's a large woman and could block the view of all the future partiers sitting in the prescribed circle waiting for the actual party. The party is really for the national staff, and to take some beer away from them is poor form, but we were in high school mode, and figured that since it was Thursday, some people might not show up. We just had to hope that Oscar was not in the radio room. I wish I could say that I was planning on just drinking my one beer early, but in all honesty, I had every intention of having a second. We got there and, good, Oscar was not there. So she blocked the doorway, and I had to move a bunch of stuff off the cool box, which was a giveaway. I lifted the lid just a smidge, only to find the stupid Cokes were on top of the beers, but I had already gotten this far, so I took out a few Cokes so I could reach the beer, got one and handed it to her, which she deftly hid under her shirt (I could tell she's done this before). I reached in and got a second, and replaced the Cokes just as Oscar came back into the room. (I had just finished a spy novel, so the logistics were fresh in my mind.) We did a quick and friendly, *"Bon soir Oscar! Es tu prêt pour la fete?"* (Good evening Oscar! Are you ready for the party?), turned and ran back to the kitchen to guzzle and laugh. It was really ridiculous. I haven't done something like that since a church supper when I was in ninth grade. While we were laughing and drinking, Perrin came over to get us, and we felt like we had to hide the beer from him too, but he didn't care what we were doing. He was just annoyed that he was the only expat over at the party, so we finished up and went.

I really like these parties, but there is rarely a party anywhere that

I don't like. Papa Gregoire, who is our stockman at the base stock pharmacy, showed up in a bright yellow print shirt with matching capri pants, which also happened to be the same fabric of my skirt. His outfit was enhanced with aqua socks and running shoes, whereas I went with the simple white tank top and flip-flops. But oh, the exclamations when everyone saw that we matched! Hundreds of pictures had to be taken! It was hilarious. Since dark, ominous clouds were rolling in, the speeches commenced quickly, and progressed at a reasonable rate. I was taking pictures and enjoying myself. Perrin decided that the drinks should be served early since rain was on its way (I'm sure because we had already had one and he hadn't), and it was all quite entertaining. Just as the dancing was about to start, the first big plops of rain started as well, so we picked up all the benches and tables and crammed them into the *tukul* where the national staff eats. Just as we got under the thatch, the biggest storm I have seen yet hit. Huge thunder and lightning, huge wind (that took down some trees), and rain that could barely be called rain it was so heavy. Margaret and Perrin got caught over at the office, and Carila wasn't back from the hospital yet, so I was the only expat at the displaced party. No problem. Dancing started in the little space we had, and I had a ball. Mario missed the party since it had been moved to Thursday. He was away with the Unimog picking up more cement. He was very disappointed.

Friday morning was taken up with getting some last-minute instructions from Margaret about the tasks I'm going to assume until her replacement comes, and after seeing a few problem patients over at the prenatal clinic, I went out to the airstrip to say good-bye. It made me dread my day of departure. I am getting more and more comfortable here, and saying good-bye to national staff is going to be very difficult. Just watching Margaret do it was hard. Carila leaves in less than two weeks so these good-byes are condensed, and it seems harder for the national staff. They continually have to adjust to new people.

It's so quiet at the base now with just me, Perrin, and Carila, and it will be like this all week. I don't even have to fight for computer time. I do, however, have to assume the role of sole audience for Carila. Perrin will have nothing to do with her.

Saturday, just as I was settling it with my next book, *In the Footsteps of Mr. Kurtz*, we got a message that there was a patient with obstructed labor out at Kisele and they needed a vehicle to go get her.

So I put the book down and went off. Perrin came along, since we only had one driver available, and a second vehicle couldn't come. Perrin hardly ever gets to leave the base, and he didn't want to stay there alone with Carila. We found the entourage on the road, having already started out by bush ambulance. I didn't think she was really an urgent case since she had only been in labor since six a.m. so was a little confused. Then I thought it was odd that the staff from the clinic were the ones transporting her. It's usually the family who does that. About halfway back to the base, it dawned on me that the staff probably thought the party was still on for Saturday and figured they might get to the base in time for that. They did seem awfully disappointed when we told them that Margaret had already left. Anyway, it wasn't an obstructed labor; she was fine. I hung out all day with Beatrice and Generose (our new *accoucheuse*) over in our newly improved maternity room, and by six that night with them all delivered and settled into the tent, I came back here for a dull Saturday night of reading. Good book, though. And the evenings have cooled off to the most glorious temperature.

I guess that's it. Next weekend I will be going on R&R in Lubumbashi, so won't write until the following weekend.

Love you all!
Linda

Je dis au revoir. *(I say good-bye.)*

February 26, 2008–It's morning around seven-ish. Going to Monga today. Rained all day and all night, which was unusual. Bright morning. I got way too much sleep the last two nights. Nothing else to do! It's been quiet. I'm going to Lubumbashi this weekend for R&R. I'm so looking forward to a break from Carila. She's exhausting. Bridgitte sent a note saying I'd LOVE Fabien. Things are looking up!

February 29, 2008

I signed up for an extra day apparently.

On ne sait jamais. *(One never knows.) That gets said a lot around here. It's Friday afternoon, and I should be sipping a cool beer in Lubumbashi, but instead I am sitting in the dingy office in Shamwana, not nearly as upset as I was an hour ago. The plane: it's coming, it's not. It's coming, it's not. It's not. This had been going on for three days, and this morning when we got word it was all set to go, I started looking forward to a change of scenery and conversation. Perrin has a flight tomorrow scheduled for Nairobi then Zanzibar with his girlfriend. He's been counting the minutes all week. Carila has been driving us both up a wall, and I was just keeping my eye on Friday morning, and a reprieve from her incessant self-worship blather. Her end of contract was supposed to be a week from Monday. She was nearly expelled five weeks ago, and fought hard to return here. But then when an opportunity came up to go to Zambia, she decided to just end her contract five days early, and expected everyone to fall into line with this change of venue. This involved switching her party three times to different nights to accommodate flights and her vacation plans, and the latest schedule put it tomorrow night. She's mad that I wasn't canceling my R&R to be at her party.*

SUNDAY MORNING, SHAMWANA

March 9, 2008
Sunday morning, Shamwana

Hi Everyone,

   Didn't do R&R last week. Not rested and refreshed. Or rested and recuperated, or whatever that stands for.

   On the Friday I was to get away, Mario was getting the Unimog ready for a trip to Dubie to collect food for the hospital. He was supposedly leaving that Friday as well, but his trip got delayed a day because of some minor maintenance. Early that morning, I walked by him and we did the usual greeting (which I must say I have been avoiding, having not figured out yet what to say to him about his marriage proposal) and I said, "So you are leaving for Dubie. Too bad you'll miss the party for Carila tomorrow night." Oh, he told me, he's not sorry to be missing the party because he knows I will not be there either. I'll be in Lubumbashi. I told him that was a very sweet thing to say, and then he took my hand and kissed it. Carila overheard this and sniped, "I don't think that was sweet. I think it was creepy." Now, I know I should not have responded to this, but I couldn't resist. Regressing to age thirteen I said sarcastically, "Why, because he didn't say it to you?" Ugh! Horrors! She said, "I'd be totally creeped out if he said that to me! It's so *creepy*! I would find it totally *creepy* if he flirted with me!" She was mad at me for not canceling my R&R to attend her party. She had vacillated between the whiny "Pleeeeze stay and come to my party!" to the snooty "creepy" exchange noted here. I decide to adopt the cold-shoulder treatment. She had really gotten on my nerves. (And it *was* a sweet thing for Mario to say!)

   It was Friday. Perrin was doing a million things preparing to leave for two weeks. I was finishing up things I needed to do, packing for the weekend, and collecting shopping lists, etc. We got radio word that the plane was going to be an hour late, then two hours, but I didn't care. I decided to organize my pictures on the computer. It was nearing one p.m. and we still hadn't heard that the plane had left Lubumbashi yet, when I heard yelps of excited laughter coming from the radio room and moving toward the office. Juvenile laughter. Spoiled-brat laughter. Carila bounded into the office "Ha hah! You'll

- 165 -

be at my party! The plane isn't coming!" Gales of laughter. Then came a stream of "Ha ha's" sung to the tune of "Nanny Nanny Boo Boo." She leaped at Choco singing, "You'll be at my party. You'll be at my party" (same tune). This was to Choco, who has been trying to get to Lubumbashi for months. He's been patiently sticking it out in this Congolese equivalent of Siberia, to help us. The inappropriateness of this behavior was beyond description. When she stopped to catch her breath, I glared at her and said flatly, "Glad you think it's funny." I am ashamed at my lack of creativity, but that was all I could come up with at the time. I wasn't so much disappointed about missing a weekend in Lubumbashi as I was that she was getting her way. I immediately started thinking of reasons not to go the party. The bubonic plague has resurfaced in Congo (this is actually true). Maybe it would choose this weekend to come to Shamwana! That would be preferable to listening to this for another four days. And poor Perrin was supposed to leave for a two-week vacation with his girlfriend and he'd been working his butt off, counting the minutes to get away. But, being the total brick that he is, just set about, step-by-step, dealing with the situation we now had. The plane was broken down and they didn't know when it would be fixed. We had no control over it. So Carila went out to gloat to whomever she could corner to hear the good news! The plane was broken down, ha ha! Everyone could come to her party!

Perrin got on the SAT phone to Francine in Lubumbasi to ask what we should do. We hadn't had a plane for twelve days. We were out of therapeutic milk and flour for the hospital. Our project coordinator, new doctor, and psychiatrist were all in Lubumbashi trying to get back to Shamwana. It wasn't just our plans that were a problem. I heard him responding, *"Oui, ça va, OK, oui, oui, ça va, ça va."* (Yes, OK, yes, OK.) He hung up and said, "The three of us need to meet right now with Benson and Raphael and all key national staff at five p.m." He was very serious. It scared me a little bit. I didn't like the way he said that. The guard went to get Benson and Carila, and Perrin got Raphael. I turned back to the computer and continued sorting my pictures, and braced myself for another dose of Miss Sunshine. The others entered. We were all seated in a circle, Carila still wearing the big, bright smile of the victorious, and Perrin started explaining the plan. "OK. Tomorrow all the expats and Choco are leaving here at seven a.m. exactly, by road, toward Dubie. We will be taking two vehicles and the Unimog, and meet the kiss from Dubie.

The team in Lubumbashi will leave by road on Sunday and arrive in Dubie on Monday night. Sunday, Choco and I will leave Dubie and meet the team in Kilwa (another kiss), then Linda, Carila, Lucile, Fabien, and Anders will return to Shamwana on Tuesday." I had to concentrate to get all this because he said it all in French, so I looked to Carila's face for confirmation that she was now going to miss her party too! The smile was gone. She was staring at Perrin with that there-must-be-some-mistake expression and said, "But I can't leave here! What about my party?" Perrin continued as if she hadn't spoken, "So we'll meet at five p.m. with key national staff. They will be in charge while we are not here." And then he got up and walked out. I would have done the same, but I wanted to enjoy seeing that fucking smile wiped off her face. Then she started in on me. "Do you think I should call Francine about this? I mean, why can't we stay here alone?" I silently turned back to my pictures, and, as if I had agreed with her, she said, "Well it's worth a try. I mean, the national staff has been planning this big party for me!" in that whiny-adolescent-girl tone. As if she were the only one that had a going-away party here. I was biting the inside of my lips to keep from smiling. I honestly had no idea why we couldn't stay here without Perrin, but the thought of being there alone with her, listening to this all weekend . . . uh, no. No. I heard her on the SAT phone whining and pleading, then switching to the I'm-a-doctor-and-you-have-to-do-what-I-say voice. It was quite pathetic to watch a grown woman behave this way. I smiled and looked at the computer screen. Some of my pictures are really quite good. She lost. We all had to leave.

I quite like Dubie, so started looking forward to spending the weekend there, and was already all packed. However I could not, under any circumstances, tolerate an eight-hour bumpy ride listening to Carila. Just couldn't do it. After we met with the staff and Perrin briefed everyone, I followed him back to the office (Carila went off to hold court with the staff to arrange another date for the party), and quietly said, "Perrin, if I have to listen to her all the way to Dubie I will slit my wrists. Can I ride in the Unimog?" He started laughing, and said, "I know, I've already planned on wearing my MP3 player the whole way. But sure, you can go in the Unimog." Oh, thank God. I knew Mario would love showing off his driving skills, and it would give me a chance to talk to him without it having to be too serious.

Perrin and I had supper together, venting, which felt good. I asked him what the real story was, why we were not allowed to stay here alone. Was it just my sanity they were worried about? Is there some security issue? He said, "Security issue. We're not allowed to leave two women alone in such an isolated place." Hmm, OK, fine by me. I was going to get a weekend in Dubie, *and* an R&R later. I told him about Mario's proposal. He cracked up. He said, "One of his wives must have died. He's got four, the most allowed by Muslim law, so I guess there's an opening." It was quite pleasant, making the most out of a disappointing situation.

Saturday morning I heard the Unimog start up and was afraid Mario was leaving without me, as he didn't know yet I was coming along. I jumped out of bed, ran over there, and told him that I wanted to ride in the truck, that Perrin said it was OK. He lit up like a Christmas tree, and I thought he might be taking this the wrong way, but figured I had plenty of time to explain. He walked to the truck saying, *"Ah, je suis trés content!"* (I am very happy!) We got packed up with a big flurry of activity, and said our good-byes. The convoy started out like a big parade, Unimog in front. The entire village was waking up, coming out of their huts and waving as we went by. The morning was spectacularly beautiful; these cloud formations are just breathtaking. It was so much fun riding up high in that truck. It's a truck designed for the military, I think, a Mercedes and some kind of hybrid of truck and tractor, and man, is that thing a beast. It can go anywhere. I took a bunch of videos through the windshield en route. I'm hoping to be able to give you a little bit of an idea of what it's like to travel here. It was Mario, me, and a *convoyeur* (a guy who gets paid just to ride along and help if there is an *embourbement), riding* in the truck. The other two vehicles were *derriere* and I noticed that Perrin and Carila were in separate vehicles (apparently the MP3 was not quite enough insulation).

It didn't take too long before one of the Land Cruisers was stuck, but getting it unstuck was fairly quick with the Unimog: just attach a cable and move forward. It's pretty cool. We were going along and chatting. He asked when my end of contract was, and I told him not until September, I have another six months, and he did the thumbs up. He asked if I will do another contract somewhere, and I told him no, I'd be going home to a job I love. This was a one-year thing only; I won't be staying in Africa. And then he asked if he could get a job driving a Unimog in the US and I said no, getting a visa to live there would be very difficult, and the work was very different, and there was just no possibility of it happening. It was all light and not awkward, and I was feeling good that this was finally clear. I was having fun. There was lots of good conversation about driving, what it was like in the US, family, and life in general. He wanted to know if I was very disappointed that I couldn't go to Lubumbashi that weekend. I told him that I wasn't really, except that I wanted to call my mother, and that is much easier and cheaper from the city, but otherwise, I don't really like it there. He told me my French was much, much better, and that made me happy.

We had three *embourbements*, but none that took longer than a half-hour to get unstuck. We met the kiss, switched vehicles, and made it to Dubie by four p.m. It was so beautiful. There was the gorgeous sky, orchids blooming everywhere in the thick jungle, good conversation in a foreign language, and adventure. As far as I was concerned, this was a perfect start to the weekend. I was looking forward to going to the market (where they actually have some food), and to church on Sunday, and running along a nice stretch of road toward the river. Life was good. I was smiling.

We got to the base in Dubie to discover that we were on a level-two security alert, which meant we were not allowed to leave the base. This was after a small military incident at the airstrip, where a drunk Air Force (as if there is a Congolese plane that can fly) officer decided to lock up some MSF national staff in a makeshift jail because he was having some tantrum about something or other. There had been a power struggle there with this guy, and he decided to use the week when all the project coordinators were in Lubumbashi to cause a little incident. Philip, a Kenyan MSF nurse in Dubie, was acting project coordinator. Given the recent violence in his home country, he was understandably a little jumpy. The whole incident was over in a couple of hours of negotiations with this guy, who wanted money to release his "prisoners," but we were still not allowed to go anywhere until it was clear there would be no more problem with him. So that kinda sucked. It was like being under house arrest, but at least we had some new faces, and there's more to do at the base in Dubie. They have a TV, movies, volleyball net, and a lot of books. We got settled in and visited with everyone. They have some new team members that I hadn't met yet, who are all young and lively and seemed fun to be with. We got a volleyball game organized, and that shows you how desperate I am for exercise, as I haven't played that since seventh grade gym class. I always hated volleyball. I could never get the ball over the net, and it hurt my arm to serve. But it was really fun! I am astounded! And they had beer for afterward! After we played, I was lying on some pillows reading, Perrin and Kristoff were bent over a chess game, and we heard Carila outside whining to someone, "My party was supposed to be tonight!" and without turning his head from the chess board, Perrin rolled his eyes toward mine, shook his head ever so slightly, and mumbled to the board, "Still at it." I looked back at my book and smiled. All it takes is one person who understands.

I had to get Philip's permission to go to church on Sunday. He said I could go if I took a vehicle and my handset, and then called when mass was over for the vehicle to pick me up. The church is literally across the street. My driveway at home is longer than this walk to church. I agreed to it, but on Sunday morning, there was no driver there at the base. They would have had to go get him from home. I looked out the fence, and there was a huge swarm of people walking down the road to the church. The thought of an MSF vehicle edging into the crowd to drive me thirty yards was just too absurd. So (shhhh) I asked the guard to walk with me to the front of the church and told him I'd call with the radio when I was done. I felt like a little baby, but was hoping people would think he was going to church, too. After the mass, I couldn't hang around, so went right back, but one of the sisters came over to the base to see who I was and introduce herself. (Wasn't too hard to notice a new white face there. Or the only white face there.) She asked why I had left so quickly, and I explained about the current security rules, and she burst out laughing. Believe me, no one in the village was worried about this airport incident, but still, there was nothing I could do. Breach of security rules is an instant ticket home. She asked me to come over to the convent, and offered to walk with me, but I had to wait to get permission for that, too. Philip did agree to let me go later in the afternoon, so she came back for me at four o'clock.

This was a group of Franciscan nuns who started the hospital and school fifty years ago. There are only five sisters there now, four of them Congolese and one sister from Poland who has been there for twenty-five years. There is a big primary and secondary school, a huge hospital, and there used to be a technical school where the MSF base is now. Sister Agnes is the one who came to get me, and she gave me the tour of the school and the convent. It is really impressive. The sister from Poland (I forget her name) is an agronomist and has the most beautiful garden full of fruit trees, a huge avocado tree, vegetables, peanuts, and flowers. The students help in the garden and sell the produce. I sat with them while they told me stories about how the place was started and how it had functioned until the series of back-to-back wars happened. It's in incredible disrepair now. I could just imagine it in its heyday, though. And it was so interesting to talk to people who had actually stuck it out there during the fighting. In the ten years of war, they only left for three months when the front line was very close. But they had stories of transporting wounded people with borrowed military vehicles, the Polish sister in her habit driving, and the soldiers at the roadblocks being so startled to see a nun driving that they just let her pass. Sister Agnes leaned over to me at this point of the story and said, *"Elle est trés forte"* (she is very strong), as if I couldn't tell. This is the place where the priest didn't evacuate in time and had to spend three days hiding in the water tank. It was just incredible. And the whole time I was listening to these stories, with these incredibly strong, dedicated women, we were sitting in the shade eating clementines picked off their trees. I asked what kind of damage happened to the buildings during the war, and they said that the military was using the place, as the sisters decided not to lock it. They said they knew that whoever wanted to steal stuff would, so they preferred not to have the doors and windows broken. And when they came back after three months, not one thing was taken. They told me they had always been kind to the military, feeding them when they needed food, and the soldiers took good care of their place in return.

The problem wasn't destruction of the buildings during the war, like it was in Shamwana, the problem is now all the roads have been destroyed and it's so difficult to get supplies in and out. So MSF came in and is supporting the hospital now in conjunction with the sisters, which I imagine must be hard for them, though they didn't say that. After all the work of building a hospital and administering it for fifty years, to be at the mercy of an NGO, it must be hard. They told me that there used to be regular trucks coming in with supplies, and a steady stock of medicines and school supplies, but that all stopped ten years ago. The school still has three hundred students, but it's very, very basic. They do have walls and a roof, and blackboards and some desks, which is way more than we have in Shamwana, but it's still very basic. Anyway, it was a nice visit and I really enjoyed it. I want to go back again and try to get more stories from them. I asked if they ever considered writing them down, but they just laughed. It seems tragic to me that all these stories could be lost. No one from the MSF base had ever been over there. Everyone at the base was interested when I talked about it, but honestly, it is just across the street.

Monday I hung around the hospital getting ideas for Shamwana. It is a large, sprawling campus with approximately thirty buildings, similar to other hospital campuses I've seen in other African countries. I doubt Shamwana will ever be like that, but you never know. They've got a great health education system set up, where one person goes around to all the different sites where people are waiting and gives a health talk. They gather all the children in the therapeutic feeding building to sing songs and tell stories. It's exactly what I want to get started in Shamwana. Their health educator, Jacques, is the uncle of one of our guards, and I am going to see if I can get him to come to Shamwana for a week or two to help me get a program going.

The group coming from Lubumbashi was supposed to arrive that afternoon, but they didn't make the six p.m. time cutoff so had to spend another night at the project in Kilwa. This meant another day for us under house arrest in Dubie. I got a lot of information and ideas from Sarah, the midwife there, so it was a productive visit for me. I didn't mind it. And she gave me some Delee suctions, which will be great for the babies with meconium. We don't have anything at our outer clinics to suction them with. The *accoucheuses* will be very happy when I present them with this little gift when they come for our workshop.

By Tuesday at four o'clock when the group arrived from Kilwa they were in rough shape. They tumbled out of the Land Cruiser, and weren't in very good humor. God, was Lucile a sight for sore eyes. She gave me a knowing look when she asked, "So. How are you holding up?" and I told her, "Yeah, I'm ready for a psychiatrist. Glad you're back. I'm sure you heard *the party* was postponed." She said, "Yeah, even though we hated being three days on these bumpy roads with no food, I still would not have wanted to be you." Fabien, her fiancé (they got engaged on Zanzibar), is a sweetheart, as we all knew he would be, having gotten to know Lucile. Though when I was telling Mario that I expected Fabien to be nice, because Lucile was, he said, "*Non, non!* One cannot assume that, because opposites attract!" (Fairly insightful, I thought.) I related this to her as we were gabbing a mile a minute behind a bush, catching up on the most critical gossip, making note where we would fill in the details. She wanted to know if I had "the talk" with Mario, and I said, "Well, not exactly, but while riding with him in the Unimog, I was very clear that I wouldn't be staying here, and that it was impossible for him to come to the States, so I feel like he got the message. I don't think I need to do the sit-down-and-reject-him thing." And then we moved on to the myriad of other topics to laugh about. Team living is a fertile breeding ground for gossip. I've got enough stories for years to come if I ever decide to write cheap romance novels.

Next morning we started off on the last leg back to Shamwana, and as we headed out of Dubie, Mario asked if I was able to call my mother, and I told him I was. I used the SAT phone because I don't know now when I will be going for my R&R, and he asked, "Did you tell her you have an African fiancé?" (Hmm, guess I wasn't as clear as I thought.) I laughed and said, "No I did not, because I don't have an African fiancé. For me to have a fiancé of any kind, all five of my children would have to approve, and that is not possible. They will never come here to meet you. This is not possible." It was not an untruth exactly, but with my French I think it sounded like this is a strictly adhered-to American custom, rather than a personal requirement. He nodded as if in complete understanding, and said, *"Ah oui, ça va. Je comprend."* (Ah yes. I understand.) He did come by with orchids he picked for me this week, though, and he sent someone to build us a chicken coop, and he's got chickens for us. I have no idea what this means.

All was well here when we got back, but I feel bad that we didn't meet with the *chef du village* before we left. The national staff understood that it was just against MSF policy to leave two women here alone with a plane broken down and no way to leave, but the villagers saw it as an evacuation, and they were scared that there was a possibility of another Mai Mai incident. Lesson learned. I came back here realizing how comfortable I've become, and full of new ideas and energy for the next six months. I'm not wishing it away. The logistics team couldn't wait to show me that they had finished the *tukul* where I want to do the health education. They call it the *"Mama Linda tukul."* They were beaming like little kids who cleaned the house while mom was away. I was very sincere when I said excitedly, *Je l'aime! C'est parfait!* (I love it! It's perfect!), and they were just busting with pride.

At the morning meeting on Thursday, Fabien was introduced to the thirty or so MSF staff. We all stand around in a big circle each morning at eight o'clock to give a little department report and relay any pertinent information. When there is someone new, they have to present themselves, and then we all go around the circle and introduce ourselves, give our *état civil* (civil state, i.e., marital status) and number of children. It's very simple and culturally expected. You can't get away without doing it. I'm used to it now, but initially it made me very uncomfortable to have to say "*Je suis célibataire et la mere de cinq enfants.*" (I am single and the mother of five children.) Everyone always bursts out laughing when I say that, it's a real crowd pleaser. When we got around to Mario—everyone knows he has four wives in Burundi—he said he was "*célibataire geographique.*" Oh, that was beautiful. "Geographically single." Beautiful.

The plane, which is now fixed, brought Dennis, the financial officer from Lubumbashi, on Friday. He's here for the weekend, having brought the boxes and boxes of cash needed to pay the national staff. He also wanted a field trip and has never been here. He's a very funny guy; I think I've described him before. He was all impressed with the remoteness of Shamwana (even after it's been described, you really have to see it to believe it), and after a long day of travel, touring the hospital, and going over the accounting with Gericose in the stifling office, he said, "Right! Well then. Jolly good. Time for a cool beer." We just looked at him and said, "So, did you bring some? We don't have any beer here. Oh my God, the look on his face was priceless. "What? Bloody hell! No beer? Well, I'll certainly have a word about that when I get back!" I said, "Well, it's six o'clock on Friday evening. Can I interest you in a cup of filtered river water?"

Last night was *the party*. The usual. Listening to the goat being slaughtered all afternoon, speeches, dancing, *c'est la routine*.

Love you all,
Linda

※※※≪○≫※※※

Quelques jours les heures passes très lentement. *(Some days time passes very slowly.)*

March 10—Carila's party was less fun than the others. I wonder if that was just my perception because of how depressed I am. I couldn't tell if people were having fun or not. There was a plethora of very drunk national staff. They must be finding something to drink somewhere. It seemed a bit of a chore to go to it. The rain held off, which Carila took as a sign that she is the chosen one. She leaves today. Thank God.

March 16, 2008
Sunday morning, Shamwana

Hi Everyone,

We got some sort of new satellite connection and now we can do downloads more frequently than twice a day. Progress.

It's been quiet here. The team is so small with Perrin away, Bridgitte still unsure about returning, and still no replacement for Margaret. We heard yesterday that there is a nurse who might be joining us at the end of April, but still a long time to go without an outreach nurse. I've been a bit frustrated this week trying to pick up some of what Margaret was doing. It seems to me that the planning could have been much better. It's not like they didn't know when Margaret was leaving. Yesterday Anders received the CV of the nurse considered for here. It didn't say what country she was from, but she has worked with MSF in Burundi, so presumably speaks French, and her first nursing job was in 1965 so unless she started work when she was nine, she might be older than me!

I passed a big milestone this past week. I did a two-day class for all the *accoucheuses* here in Shamwana. It was the first time they had all gotten together since September when Nina did this, and I was quite nervous about it. The *accoucheuses* at the outer clinics are isolated and never get to leave their villages, so they wanted me to do it again. Shamwana, laughingly, is a happening place compared to where they are. Plus they get a per diem and two free meals, and that's a biggie. I set the dates a month ago, and as I visited each clinic during the month, let them know. They don't have to do much planning, it's amazing how people can just pick up and leave for days and weeks at a time, but it's difficult to get messages to everyone, and I hadn't been to Kishale yet. I missed the trip there because we had to spend that extra day in Dubie, and Deo forgot to give Mama Marie the message. I was really upset about that; I had no way to let her know, and I knew she'd be upset if she missed this. I won't be doing it again until just before I leave In August. In the days leading up to it, I was fretting and fretting, kept asking at the hospital if there was anyone from Kishale who could bring a message to her, but had no idea how she would get here. It's thirty-five miles away, and she's not young. On Tuesday I gave up. I just figured I'd do it again sooner than August if I had to, and I'd buy her a little gift in Lubumbashi to make it up to her. But on Wednesday when the guard opened the gate for me to go over to the hospital, there she was, completely decked out in pink satin (or the cheap synthetic equivalent), smile bigger than life. Some guard from Monga had gotten on a bike and ridden over the mountain on Tuesday to let her know, at which point she packed up her best outfit and got on a bike to get here. I just love it.

It was so fun to see them all together talking a mile a minute and laughing. We gave them a tour of the new maternity tent. There were many exclamations of wonder at the new cement floor. But oh! When they saw the new delivery room and I turned on the solar light over the bed! I felt like Thomas Edison. I wish I had taken a video of that! The whooping and clapping carried on as if electricity had just been invented.

I had been dreading trying to explain this new data collection form to them, but I was under orders to do it, so gave it my best shot, in French, to women who can't read or write, and who don't speak French. Climbing Kilimanjaro was not this exhausting. Gerardine, Beatrice, and Generose took turns translating and explaining in Kiluba, but God only knows what they were saying. I tried. I kept saying to them that they didn't need to do anything different from what they were doing now. We just count it differently, so recording it now will be different. I tell you, I no longer have any confidence in statistics that come out of third world countries. While I was in Dubie, I went to an outer clinic with Sarah, and the *accoucheuse* there was the same level as Gerardine and very good. She's had one year of formal training and her French is excellent. The women who work in the Shamwana health zone have no formal training at all. Not even primary school. I'm at a slight disadvantage when it comes to epidemiological data collection. Just keeping a chart is ridiculous. For example, the Apgar score (standard in western obstetrics) is an evaluation of the newborn taken at one minute and five minutes after birth. I am supposed to teach them how to do an Apgar score when they don't have a clock! It's so stupid. This idea of having a western standard is ludicrous. I am all for believing that everyone in the world deserves the same quality of care, but who decides what that is? Part of my job here is to "supervise" the quality of the charting. I must admit that I just haven't been doing it. Charting at home was one of my peeves about the medical system, overdone and given way more importance than the actual patient. Here it is absurd. I mean really. Mama Marie has figured out how to get around this requirement. She can't read or write, so she tells the delivery story to the nurse at the clinic, and he writes the chart later. They sort of make it up together. I think this is brilliant. I couldn't care less what the Apgars are for a baby we are never going to see again, written on a chart that is going to be eaten by mice unless the leaking roof makes it too soggy even for them. The ants eat those.

So I spent Wednesday morning going over the charting requirements, trying to convey the message that it is not so important to be able to write it down as it is to be able to find out from the mother what she is going through, and help her cope, and try to refer her before there is a huge crisis. When you have to transport a bleeding woman by bike twenty miles over a mountain, and some *mzungu* is worried about whether it is written in the right place . . . good God, I just can't do it.

Wednesday afternoon I decided to just forget the charting stuff, and asked them what they thought I could help them with. I thought maybe they'd like another person to work with. They are out there all alone, day and night, never a day off. I thought another *accoucheuse* at each clinic was something I could work toward. No, No! They all said they prefer to work alone. If there was a second person she would want to "dominate" them, and it would cause all kinds of problems. I found that interesting. They all asked for more money, though, and a clock, and a new lantern, and new towels to dry the babies, and a scale, and a water filter, and their own small pharmacy, and . . . Thomas Edison and Santa Claus. And they wanted to be sure that they got a copy of the picture I took of the group, and a certificate for finishing the workshop would be nice, too.

Next afternoon when I was telling them about my idea to record the birthdates of the babies on a card for the mother so when they come for immunizations we have an idea of how old they are, I said that maybe we could do a postpartum visit when the mother brings the baby for the first vaccination. This stimulated about fifteen minutes of chatter in Kiluba, and when I asked Gerardine what they said, she said in French, "Mama Linda, a small preoccupation. We were told to teach women to wait three months before resuming relations with her husband. Do you agree with this?" All eyes were intently on me. I told them that while it would be a nice way to space the pregnancies out a little bit, I understand that if women have to wait three months for sex, they will have a lot of anxiety that their husbands will find another woman. So no. It's not realistic. She busted up laughing. "Ah, Mama Linda! You understand!" And then she translated it into Kiluba and there was much cheering and shaking of my hand. I felt like I was finally part of the club. It was a high note to end on, but I didn't feel like I accomplished much. Now I have to try and get some of the things they asked for. The lanterns we have in stock, but the other stuff will take forever to get. I am tempted to just buy it all myself when I go to Lubumbashi and consider it a donation even though we're not supposed to do it that way. I'm still thinking on that one.

We finally got permission to do the measles vaccination, and that will commence in the next couple of weeks. Too little, too late as far as I'm concerned, but it's better than never. We will do kids up to fifteen years old, so it's a huge number. People are coming from Lubumbashi to help with it–the target is eight thousand kids. They are even getting us an efficient freezer temporarily for all the ice packs we'll need. I'll let you know how that goes. Considering how much time we spent stuck in the mud this past week, this campaign could go on forever, but we'll see.

Let's see, what else? The chicken coop is finished, and—I am not kidding here—is nicer than most of the houses in the village. I can't wait to start getting some eggs.

We've got a little alpha dog thing going between Bienvenu and Fabien. Fabien is into gardening, too, and he's been making new beds and planting seeds that he brought from Belgium. Bienvenu, who has never lifted a finger to help me with the garden, has now decided that he could cultivate a section of land behind the *tukuls* for fresh vegetables. He told Lucile that my way of making disorderly beds was incorrect, and he would make rows similar to Fabien's.

I started making a volleyball net with some Chinese fishing line I found in Dubie. I tied two short pieces of bamboo to trees about eight meters apart. Fabien pointed out that an official volleyball net is nine meters, so I guess our team won't be heading for Beijing this year. I spent yesterday tying knots, and though it looks more like a spider's web right now, I think I can make it something usable. I want it to be portable, so we can put it out on the football field and play with the national staff. So all we have to do is put two long pieces of bamboo in the ground then tie the net to those somehow. I haven't figured that part out yet, but I'm sure someone can help with that. A couple of the new drivers were watching me yesterday and are very excited about it. The women who bring our water in from the river thought I was making a fishing net, and were laughing at how large the holes were.

And just when things seemed light and fun, a woman came in by bike from Kishale. She was the wife of the guard there, and had had a premature delivery and retained placenta. The placenta delivered on the way here, but she was in shock from losing so much blood. Fabien gave her the one unit we had in our fridge, but she died two hours later, twenty years old.

So I'll finish writing this, send it, and go back to tying knots and try not to think too much.

Love you all,
Linda

Je suis si triste. *(I am so sad.)*

March 18, Tuesday early morning

The horrors always blindside me. I can't stop thinking about a woman who died on the way here by bike. I could have helped her. I wonder if she knew she would die. I wonder if her baby will die now, too. They usually do when there is no one to feed them. I am so sorry. I want to cry, but feel sometimes that if I start I'll never stop.

March 23, 2008
Sunday morning, Shamwana

Hi Everyone,

This week's letter was supposed to have some pictures sent from my Hotmail account from Lubumbashi. But again, I am not in Lubumbashi, I'm still in Shamwana, starting to feel like this R&R

was not meant to be. Not a plane problem this time. Air Serv has acquired a new plane since the other one kept breaking down, and hired another pilot who's not afraid to land in Shamwana. So we have been getting regular flights now every Monday and Friday. But Friday as I was saying good-bye at the hospital an hour before I was supposed to leave, Beatrice came to me and told me Gerardine was having contractions. I went into the maternity room, and she was huddled in a corner crying, and I couldn't tell why. I thought maybe she was scared because the pregnancy was a little early, or she just didn't want me to leave now that she was in labor, I couldn't figure out what. I checked her, and told her she was four centimeters, but the head was very low, and the frightened look on her face made me say, "Forget it. I'm not going to Lubumbashi. I'll stay here." At which point she stopped crying, said a quiet *"Ça va,"* (OK) got off the bed and went back to the corner.

It had been a really crappy week, starting Sunday with that twenty-year-old woman who bled to death, something so preventable, and it really upset me. Then we had a baby born full-term weighing one kilo, to a mother who was so malnourished she couldn't walk. She had to be carried into the hospital, gave birth, and then couldn't roll over, she was in so much pain. I suspect her bones were fractured; maybe she had AIDS, I don't know. We can't test for it here. She took no interest in the baby, refused to feed her, and the prognosis was not good. We tried to express milk from her breasts to put into a syringe to give the baby and it was surreal trying to get milk from the breasts of a woman who looked nearly dead. We couldn't get any, gave up and put in a naso-gastric tube and fed her therapeutic milk. The baby was so thin I could see the tube in the stomach. I really wanted that baby to live. I had some bizarre association with this baby and the twenty-year-old who died, as if she was some sort of replacement for that lost life. The baby was jaundiced and I sat with her in the sun for a while every day, but Tuesday night she died, just when I thought she was perking up a little. I'm afraid she might have aspirated the milk I had tried to give her. I had a flashback to the tiny baby rabbits we found in the meadow when I was little. We couldn't find the mother and figured a weasel had gotten her. We fed them with an eyedropper, and I remember having that same feeling–oh, c'mon, live!– but they died one by one and I sat with this two pound human baby in my hands and felt the same little-kid helplessness.

The following day, a woman with a history of two prior C-sections came in, bleeding heavily, and we assumed she'd ruptured her uterus, so rushed over to the operating room. But it turned out that she had a placenta previa and the baby was breech, so every time it kicked, she bled. The baby was born very depressed from the ketamine, like they all are. She did come around, and I thought she was doing well, but she also died during the night.

Three kids came in with burns after falling into a fire. That happens a lot with epileptic kids. The fire stimulates a seizure and they fall face first into it. It's horrible.

And, there is a village north of Kishale where there is a huge measles outbreak with several deaths from the pneumonia it causes. I am so disgusted about this I don't even know what to say. I should have fought harder, maybe called Amsterdam. The small-scale stuff we were doing here didn't make any difference at all. So given all that, I just couldn't see myself flying off to Lubumbashi to shop and drink beer, leaving Gerardine huddled in a corner crying.

I'm glad I stayed. Gerardine had a healthy baby girl (her third girl—she was a little disappointed) a little after three in the afternoon on my son Jake's birthday. I took a bunch of pictures which, if I ever get to Lubumbashi, I'll get printed and give to her. It was interesting to see the difference between a birth to someone who is well off, and everyone else. MSF employees, of whom Gerardine is one, are millionaires compared to everyone else here. I am not sure how I feel about this. I understand the philosophy of equal pay for everyone who works for the organization, but it is such a disruption of the local economic balance that I am not sure if it's a good thing or not. And the jealousy it creates is actually dangerous, in my opinion. MSF national staff get $450 a month, which is what we get for our food and expenses, but for them it is more than villagers make in a lifetime. Most of our $450 gets eaten up (no pun intended) with the so-called food that gets flown in from South Africa. But the national staff doesn't buy that expensive food. They live pretty much the same as villagers, i.e., manioc *fufu* every day of their lives, cooked outside on an open fire. The rich ones buy their manioc flour instead of pounding it. They have chickens and goats, but live in grass or mud houses with no windows, used only to sleep, which they do on a mat on the dirt floor. They do have nice new clothes, that's the big difference–that and the prestige. We are not sure what they do with all their money, but it results in a lot of relatives hanging around, which is often a big problem. So it was interesting for me to see Gerardine come in laboring, wearing the same outfit she had on the day before, using her *pagne* as a sanitary pad after delivery, though she did have a pair of underwear to hold it on instead of the dirty string. And her *pagne* was clean, in one solid piece, not torn and filthy. In her purse she had crammed little baby clothes. Only the wealthy dress their babies. We usually wrap them in a towel the first day, then wrap them naked in a *pagne* on the second. That's it. So it was an interesting ritual to see Gerardine digging out red socks with the sticky treads on the bottom (way too big), a pink tank top (way too big), a used cotton frilly dress (the right size), and a pink and white hat with little ears on it, to dress her minutes-old baby. She also had small pieces of *pagnes* cut up for diapers which were held in place by a piece of thin plastic with little wings to be tied at the waist like rubber pants. I was fascinated by this display. The baby looked so uncomfortable. Benson transformed his office into a private room for her to stay postpartum. This involved turning the table up on its side and cramming a bed in there next to the exam table. If she rolls over in bed she'll get poked in the eye by one of the legs. It was a sweet gesture. She's miles away from a nurse, but whatever. She's doing fine. She named the baby after me.

Yesterday a MONUC helicopter was flying around about forty feet off the ground all day. I don't know exactly what that acronym stands for, but it's a UN peacekeeping helicopter. There are UN peacekeeping troops in Lubumbashi and Pweto, and the Kivus, but I've never seen them here before. We heard that they were looking around the area for planning purposes for other NGOs that won't come in unless the area is more accessible by road. That was the word we got from our capital team in Lubumbashi. One local person here said they were patrolling because it was Easter, whatever that meant, but Beatrice told me last night that villagers were scared they were looking for Mai Mai. These poor people are so fragile with post-traumatic stress. They are ready to flee at a moment's notice. Not that they have much to take with them, but every week we can see the difference in how settled they are becoming again. There are many more animals around now: goats, chickens, guinea fowl, and some ducks. Kids are playing more and people smile now when they greet you. It is a remarkable difference in the six months that I've been here. Plus there is more food now that the peanuts are being harvested, and there is plenty of manioc and greens and tomatoes. If there could just be peace long enough to get through the next rainy season, I can see how their lives could be more stable. But they have been at this point before, and then just as they started getting re-established, they have had to flee.

Last night, in pouring rain, a woman had her seventh baby on the road on the way to the hospital. Plopped out into the mud. She wasn't far away, and the family ran to get help at the hospital. They put her on the stretcher to carry her the rest of the way, and in the meantime the guard came to get me. They never tell me the story before I go, the guard just says, *"Mama Linda, ils vous veulent á l'hopital"* (Mama Linda, they want you at the hospital) so I never know what to expect. It was pouring. The road was a river to cross. I got there just as they were lugging in this woman with her newborn still attached, placenta still inside, drenched and shivering. Beatrice and Generose were bickering about how to get her from the stretcher to the bed (big jealousies between those two), while I cut the cord and took the baby to warm him up. Tough little thing. Gerardine came in from her private room to see what was happening (she's amazing), and I felt good. Everyone was fine. Cold but fine. I felt like part of a team that is working together, and doing something good. I needed that. It was nice getting everyone dried and warm, and walking into the lamp-lit maternity tent, and hearing the familiar greetings, and getting them tucked in. There was such good female energy in there, I almost felt like pulling in a mattress and joining the pajama party. And when I was leaving and one of the young girls tugged on my polar fleece shirt and motioned for me to give it to her, I almost took it off and handed it to her. But I knew if I did that there would have been a fight for it and it would spoil the balance, so I laughed and said, *"Oui, en Septembre."* She collapsed on the bed laughing.

Tomorrow I am going back to Dubie for a two-day midwives meeting. I'll take the plane there, and come back by road on Thursday. Then I'll try to do my R&R the weekend after next. Then it will only be five or six weeks until my next two-week vacation. I've got to start planning that. I can't believe how fast the time is going by. Perrin got back Friday from his two-week vacation on Zanzibar, and he looks great, happy, and rested. It's only four weeks until he goes to London for a course, then will only be back here one week before he leaves for good. That will be sad. He is so good at what he does. I asked Mario if it was hard for the national staff to have us all coming and going in such short intervals. I asked if the national staff were sad when an expat leaves. He said sometimes it's sad; sometimes it's a celebration. Same for us.

Mario brought over his gift of one chicken for the new coop, Beatrice gave us another one, and I bought another chicken and a rooster in the village. Anders told me I couldn't get a rooster because it was "too noisy," but all the national staff couldn't believe we would have females and no male. No, no, no, that would never work. I agreed, and wouldn't mind having young chickens for meat, so got the rooster hoping Anders wouldn't know the difference. And there are a hundred roosters now crowing on the other side of the fence, for Pete's sake! His face is always in the computer, he'll never know. We've already gotten a few eggs, but Bienvenu told me I have to leave them in there so the females aren't upset. When there are more than five we can start taking a few out. So, there'll be no Easter omelet today, but soon, I hope.

Love you all,
Bon Pâques!
Linda

Je manque aller à l'église. *(I miss going to church.)*
March 24–Easter Sunday was yesterday. No bonnets, no lamb with asparagus, no crocuses or eggs or mass at seven a.m. The "churches" here were singing as they always do–just another Sunday. I wonder if they even knew it was Easter. It's not like Christmas after all, same day every year. It was hot. I wrote, dealt with a couple of obstetrical complications, read. Nothing special. I missed my kids.

March 30, 2008
Sunday morning, Shamwana

Hi Everyone,

About a minute after I sent last Sunday's letter, three women arrived in labor including a woman transferred from Monga who arrived by bike. She had left Monga at two in the morning and I think it was around nine o'clock when she got here. That was after being in labor for two days. There is only one bed in the delivery room, so one woman was on the narrow examination table (her twelfth baby) and one was on the floor. And with Beatrice, Generose, and me in there, too, it was crowded and hot. All went rather smoothly, and though we spent the whole day in there, it wasn't traumatic. We chatting during the times we waited for labor to take its course. I asked how the women felt about polygamy. Just watching the jealousy between Beatrice and Generose, fighting for my approval, I can NOT imagine how multiple wives tolerate each other. OH! They told me there was *beaucoup, beaucoup* jealousy! Oh yes, much fighting and jealousy. The wives don't like at all when their husbands take a second or third wife. I asked where everyone lives. All in the same house? Different houses in a compound? Different villages? How do they do this? They explained that it's always different, but usually the wives all have their own houses close together. Generose described some situations she knew of where it was all one house with a different bedroom for each of the four wives, and the husband spent three nights, three nights, three nights, three nights (pointing to different spots in the room). Beatrice exclaimed in horror at this, like she'd never heard of such a thing! She said, *"Non, jamais,"* pointing at the ground, indicating that she would never allow that. I said, *"D'accord,"* indicating that I agreed with her. I mean really. It's not like these houses have long corridors and separate wings. We're talking bamboo walls between the rooms. They asked me if this happens in America and I told them it is against the law to have more than one wife. Men sometimes have another woman but it's a hidden thing. Most women in America don't accept this very well. Ah, *oui,* they nodded in understanding.

We finished up over there before dark, and Lucile and I went over to visit Gerardine, who had taken her baby home. That was fun, sitting on little stools outside her mud house with many village women sitting around talking. Little Lindarobinson Kilumba was bundled up as if for a snowstorm and I took photos, which they all loved. A few of the hospital nurses were hanging around shit-faced drunk. Hopefully they weren't on call for surgery. After leaving there we stopped to watch the football game going on between MSF staff and a village team. This was more opportunity for the men to show off for the women of their desires. Fabien and Bienvenu were trying to outrun each other, and Fabien scored the only goal after Bienvenu passed him the ball right in front of the net. Then Bienvenu sulked instead of congratulating him. Mario was the only MSF player who played the entire game. And I mean the entire game. He refused to go out and rest. He is the oldest player by about thirty years, and I was like, "Oh God, he's going to have a heart attack, and that would be one more death and I can't handle that. And he's my ride back from Dubie on Thursday! I felt like running out there and saying, 'OK! I'll marry you! Now sit down and rest!' "

Monday started at four a.m. with a woman having her first baby. She came in from home, had been fully dilated for five hours, water broke two days ago, and refused to push anymore. She was exhausted. I could see the head, it was so low, so used the vacuum and the delivery was easy. After about fifteen minutes of working on getting the meconium out of him, he took a good breath and gave a lusty cry. When I was sure he was doing well, I came back to the base to get ready to go to Dubie. Monday mornings are always a frig, because it's when I have to put in the stock request and I always have a million people asking me for things. Some of it is legitimate, but a lot of it is bogus. I've gotten tougher about it: "No. Sorry. I just gave you ten pens last week. They can't all be out of ink in one week." This kind of crap. I'm thinking back to how eager I was to help when I first arrived, and was so enthusiastic: "Sure! I'll do the stock! Whatever you need!" They must have been laughing their asses off. It's a pain in the butt. But anyway, I had to do that before I left, and then with all the vehicles that went out to set up new measles tents, three were stuck in the mud really badly. One was underwater. The one vehicle that was left at the base had to go help pull it out, so there was no car here to take us to the airport. We walked. It was no big deal, but it's against MSF rules to have no car at the base. Anders was leaving for his vacation to visit his fiancée (after not coming home Saturday night, I noticed), and Edgardo was coming in for the week, so Anders was all stressed. It's my personal opinion that he was feeling guilty and taking it out on us, but that's only MY opinion. MONUC has set up camp at the airport, and are looking rather settled. We had heard they would be here for a few days to check out the roads. When we got there, though, there were several big green canvas tents, a huge water tank, two big vehicles that came on the helicopter, and about thirty soldiers from Benin looking pretty comfortable. One was standing guard with the whole get-up on, gun and everything, and the others were all lounging around on cots, wearing an assortment of colorful shorts and shirts, which offset their stupendously gorgeous bodies beautifully. It was nine o'clock on Monday morning, and no one seemed like they were heading to work to check out the roads. I think there's more to it, but haven't figured out what yet. They are spoiling my nice picturesque running spot, though I was told I could still run there. I just have to wear an MSF shirt, and can't talk to the soldiers.

The plane landed, and little Bruce (the pilot) jumped out and pointed at the camp saying, "What the hell is this?" Edgardo (the fiery Spanish guy, head of logistics in Lubumbashi) got out and started going crazy, smoking and pacing while on his handset talking to the project coordinator in Dubie, because the Air Force dude there had just made another scene and arrested more staff. They wouldn't let us take off from Shamwana until we knew what was happening there. Bruce told us that when he landed in Dubie, this crazy guy came running up to him yelling at him about not having permission to land on his airstrip, he's the head of the Air Force and Bruce needed his permission. Bruce said, "I asked him 'What Air Force? You don't even have a plane!' and the guy tells me yes, he does, and points to this plane, and I'm like, 'That's not your plane! That's my plane!' " (I recall hearing this same conversation in a sandbox somewhere.)

I got on the plane, out of the sun, and sat to wait. They give out bottled water (my old water bottle was getting a little grungy. I haven't flown for almost twelve weeks). I sipped my water from my nice new bottle and watched the soldiers out the window. Those guys really have nothing to do. Two were playing cards, but the others looked bored out of their skulls. I was wondering if there was a gym in one of those tents. Those bodies were truly a feast for the eyes. And there was something about the way they carried themselves that was . . . riveting. Beautiful. Stunning. Anatomically perfect. Walking Michaelangelo sculptures.

We finally got to Dubie, and there I was again, under house arrest because of the airport incident. This was getting ridiculous. None of us could leave the base at all. The midwives meeting, which had been put off since November, was going to take up most of the time anyway but I really wanted to go walk around and go to the market. One of the German team members there said, "There's nothing at the market anyway." And I was like, "What? Your market is like frikkin' Zabar's compared to Shamwana!" He didn't get the joke, never having been to New York, and I didn't know of any famous markets in Germany. In the end, I gave their cook money, and he went for me to buy avocados, huge cucumbers, and passion fruit to take back. Thursday morning as I was bringing the bags of food out to the Unimog I saw that their damn cat ate one of my precious avocados— well, half of it—and left the mess.

The meeting was good. It was good to be together and learn about the different projects and to share ideas. I had thought the meeting would be in English (the expat meetings usually are), but there was national staff there, too, so it was all in French. At first I panicked, I hadn't really thought of how I would do my Shamwana presentation in French, but I considered it like a French immersion weekend (which I'd paid good money for at home), and it was fine. I'd also lowered everyone's expectations of my language skills because of my first three months here, so it was fun to see Ursula's face when I did my talk. She didn't think I had it in me.

The Unimog was supposed to show up on Tuesday, load up the two big freezers and food that we will need for this huge belated measles campaign, and go back to Shamwana on Thursday. I worried when it didn't show up Tuesday. There wasn't another flight until Sunday and I could not bear to be cooped up for that long with nothing to do. Turns out the Unimog had to help pull out the other stuck vehicles. The one that was underwater had to be towed back to the base, so they couldn't leave Shamwana until Wednesday. Mario showed up late afternoon, looking completely exhausted. He helped load the truck, which took until dark. He said the roads were really bad. He looked like he didn't care whether I was coming with him or not, but the next morning at six a.m. he looked rested and strong enough to make the trip. It's a lot of work to drive that thing.

The first half of the trip back wasn't bad. There had been no rain in Dubie for two days and the mud had turned to hard clay. It was rough and bumpy, but the road was firm for a good four hours. We got talking again about relationships, and Mario said that he knew of many expats in Burundi who married national staff and stayed in Burundi, and it was all working out very nicely. I said that it was against the rules of MSF to have relationships with national staff. He didn't believe that. Well, actually, I told him it's not really a rule, more like advice. (Not really the right word either, but it was the best I could do in French, couldn't quite figure out how to explain the power imbalance without wounding his male pride. Not something I wanted to do while he was driving this huge rig.)

"Anyway," I said, "You would not like a western woman. We are too independent."

"Not so!" He took my hand as he said this. "I like that you are independent and strong!"

I said, "But you are only saying that now. If I were married to you, you would hate me. You wouldn't like that I would not be a servant to you."

"Not true," he said.

I said, "Oh really? If I told you to give up your other wives, would you do it? Because I would never allow another woman." Here he just sort of looked out his window, smiling, and I said, "Aha! See! Men are always saying what women want to hear until she is caught. Then they can't remember what they said." Here, he and the *convoyeur* both started laughing like I figured out some big secret. I took this opportunity to get the male perspective on polygamy. I asked, "Don't the women get upset when you have more than one wife?"

"No! Not at all," he replied, the *convoyeur* nodding his head in agreement. "Everyone lives together very well."

I asked, "The women aren't jealous of each other at all?"

This time they both answered simultaneously, "*Non! Pas de tout!*" (No! Not at all!)

I said, "I don't believe that." but didn't add that the women actually confirmed the contrary. I didn't want to betray any confidences, if they actually were confidences; I'm not sure.

The *convoyeur,* Jack, said, "But men have more than one woman in Europe, also."

I said, "Yes, sometimes, but it's a hidden thing, the women don't accept it."

He said, "That's worse." (He had a point there.)

I asked them the same question I had asked Beatrice and Generose, "How does everyone live together? One house? Many houses? Different villages?"

They said it varies, but Mario grew up in a Muslim house with a father who had four wives all in the same house, four different bedrooms.

"And where did he sleep?" I asked.

He said that his father did the three nights, three nights, three nights, but others do one week, one week, one week. And Jack chimed in that sometimes it was two weeks, two weeks, two weeks, "whatever he decides." I did my Oh-my-God head-in-my-hands expression of utter incomprehension, and Jack asked, "This couldn't work in America?"

I said, "If a man did that in America, he would be dead in the morning." Or I think I actually said, "He *is* dead in the morning" (I'm still having a little trouble with the conditional tense of irregular verbs.) Here, I was going to launch into the Lorena Bobbitt story, but we were heading for a particularly bad stretch of road, and I wanted Mario to concentrate on the driving. Then when we were through that stretch, I had thought better of it. Dismemberment is a little too close to home around here.

Then the road got really bad. I have a new respect for mudslides. It was the first time I was actually scared we might tip over. We were going through a patch of bamboo blocking the road, which usually parts as we drive through it, but one clump had a huge tree branch in it, and it broke the antenna. This was bad—very bad—not to have radio contact. We were still four hours from the base and I knew they would start to worry if they didn't hear from us after two hours. But there was nothing to do but keep going. Then the truck started lurching and died.

Now, I have worried about getting stuck, but I've never been worried about breaking down before. They keep these vehicles in perfect condition. We have a mechanic here who cares for them like new babies. Mario went into this long explanation about air in some tubes, motioning with his hands how the tubes are connected, and I thought I heard the word carburetor, but I didn't think cars had those anymore, so maybe he was saying this would not be a problem if cars still had carburetors, I don't know. Mind you this explanation would have been a stretch for me in English, and all I was thinking was "Holy crap. We are in trouble. No radio. We're on the outskirts of nowhere. Perrin is going to kill us. They are going to send a vehicle looking for us, and we'll never hear the end of it. And how would we spend the night here?" So all this was going through my head while I was feigning interest in the mechanical explanation for our trouble, then Mario and Jack got out, pulled out a set of tools, and opened up the hood. Oh! It's fixable! This never occurred to me. I should have figured that someone who was capable of explaining the problem in that kind of detail was capable of fixing it. What was I thinking? We were going to call AAA?

All repaired and we started on our way again, and it was a rough ride. It was like driving down a river, and the hills were like driving down a waterfall. I was scared. There was no conversation. At one point, the road was like a pond and Jack had to walk through it so Mario could tell where the actual road was. About five miles from the base we saw a vehicle coming toward us, the search party. When we got to them I was like the bouncy teenager, "Hey Perrin! Aren't these roads something?" I thought he'd be happy we were almost home. He was not. With the menacing Edgardo in the back, they started on the inquisition: "Why no radio contact? How did the antenna break? Were you speeding? Why is the *convoyeur* out of the vehicle?" I answered them all, and was like, "So no 'Gee, glad you're all OK? Glad the branch only broke the antenna and didn't kill the three of you?'" I felt really bad for Mario, but he just rolled is eyes like he knew this was coming. He was totally exhausted and then got treated like a little kid not being careful with his toys. When we got back to the base, Edgardo pointed his cigarette at the antenna and said to me with his thick Spanish accent, "You see that? That gives my heart go—how you say in English? Very fast. That an expensive antenna!"

I said, "I think the word you want is palpitations, but keep smoking like that and pretty soon your heart won't be going at all. It won't be a problem. Hahaha." I thought I was being very funny. He just turned around and looked for someone else to harass. I went to put the vegetables in the kitchen, while Mario had to unload the truck and clean it before he could go home. God.

I learned that everyone here is stressed to the max and on edge. Measles has gone crazy, probably because we've had long, rainy days and kids are staying closed up in the little houses, buckets of snot running down their noses. The team came back from the field completely exhausted and discouraged. They have reports of thirty and forty sick kids in one tent, only one nurse, and hardly any supplies. Edgardo, who I don't think really believed what we had been telling him about the situation here, started overcompensating with concern, barking orders at everyone. (Suddenly the antenna wasn't such a big deal.) He said, "OK. Linda. You are now the outreach nurse. You no longer have time to work at the hospital. You go to Kyango on Monday to evaluate the situation," with the ever-present cigarette pointing at me. Oh, did I mention that we still didn't have an outreach nurse? Did he forget that Gerardine was now on maternity leave, and I had two fairly unskilled people dealing with all the complications that get referred here? And then we got a desperate message from Kishale, delivered by a guy on a bike, that they were swarmed with measles cases. They couldn't handle it. So I was told I was going there on Saturday to evaluate that situation.

While I was making plans to do that, and cleaning out the huge box with all our medical supplies that was sitting under water in the submerged vehicle, the president of the CODESA and Vindicien, the nursing supervisor, came to talk to me. I had heard the baby I delivered on that Monday morning had died. All had been fine for two days, then he started seizing and no one knew why, and he died on Friday morning. I had only seen him quickly when I got back from Dubie on Thursday night, and he looked like he wasn't going to make it, but I didn't know if it was herpes, or meconium aspiration, or what. Vindicien told me the family was very upset; they believe the bandage around the umbilical cord was too tight, and that's what killed him. They wanted to know if I would go to the house of the family and explain that this is not true. I didn't know what to do. I had no idea why the baby died. It could have been tetanus or meconium aspiration, I just didn't know. Vindicien said he would translate. I knew I should go, but I was scared to death. I didn't know if they were blaming me for the death, and with the way they all talk in circles, it's hard to figure out what the message is.

I didn't have time to think, though. I followed them through the village to the house, where all the men were sitting under a tree, and all the women were inside with the dead baby. They invited us in, and the three of us sat on a bamboo bed. The president of the CODESA started on a lengthy oration; I haven't a clue what he said. I did hear my name though. Then Vindicien talked for a long time, and there was the holding up of the dead baby pointing to the waist where the bandage was, and much nodding and "Ahhing," and then Vindicien asked me if there was anything I wanted to add, and since I had no idea what had already been said, I was at a bit of a loss. I have learned that it's not so much what you say here, it's more how much you say that's important. To say nothing would be not good. I started explaining that we don't have enough tests in the laboratory to tell us exactly why the baby died. He didn't breathe right away because there was a lot of meconium in his throat and it took me some time to get it all out. But once it was out, he breathed fine, so it is probably some infection that caused this. After Vindicien translated all this, they all nodded and thanked us, and we said we were sorry. A few moments later, we stood and bent at the waist to get out of the low doorway and crouched out of the house. It was very sad, but somehow made sense to me. My initial fear and paranoia about talking with them stemmed from my experience in western medicine that there must be blame laid somewhere. I have been wondering what they do when they walk home wailing with their dead baby in their arms. It was a privilege for me to see this gathering, this attempt at understanding, the acceptance of their situation, and the sincere efforts of the community to help them.

Saturday I set off for Kishale with Deo, Raphael, and Lucile. We carried more mattresses, some medicines, and some Plumpy'nut–the food that is given out to sick and malnourished kids. It is a paste, like peanut butter that comes in a foil packet. You cut the corner and the kids squeeze it into their mouths. It's easy to distribute, all calculated to have a taste they are familiar with, and all the right nutrients.

I know I keep saying it's overwhelming here, but, good God, the scene upon arrival. I looked in the tent. Bodies were everywhere. I went in and, my God, what a mess. Forty-six sick kids like piles of puppies strewn around the tent, vomiting, peeing, most of them too weak to move, all burning up with fever, mouths full of ulcers, eyes oozing. Oh my God. And there was a line of kids waiting to be evaluated who had just gotten there. Some of the fathers were carrying three kids. One nurse. He'd been there day and night for a week. I looked at him squeezing tetracycline ointment into the eyes of one of the new kids, and I thought, if I were him I think I'd just walk away and not come back. Deo set up a table to start checking kids for malaria. I didn't know where to start. There was no more room for the six mattresses we'd brought. The nurse asked if we could move some kids to the guesthouse, the mud house that we sleep in when we spend the night there. I went to the vehicle to call Perrin on the radio and tell him what a mess we had. He told me the plane had come a day early with two new tents and a big load of food and supplies (this never would have happened if Edgardo wasn't here), so I should reassure the staff that we would send supplies soon. In the meantime he told me move some kids to the guesthouse but, he added, make sure the guard there is on top of the hygiene. So Lucile and I set up the room at the guesthouse like a little intensive care for the sickest kids. We moved twelve kids and their mothers into a ten by ten foot room. Believe it or not, this was an improvement. Not three minutes later, one of the stronger kids stood up and peed. I said to Lucile, "Uh, I think this is why Perrin mentioned the hygiene." But then I thought, well, at least she's hydrated. What a sickening, horrible mess. I went to get the guard (the guy whose wife had just bled to death) to explain to the mothers to take the kids to the latrine, and we went back to the tent to pass out the Plumpy'nut.

Now, the Plumpy'nut (which is salty) is great if they know how to eat it, aren't vomiting, and don't have a mouthful of ulcers. We got in there and started passing it out. Half the kids were too weak to get it to their mouths, some were too sick to eat anything. A couple of the stronger kids were scoffing it down, then taking another from the hands of the weaker kids and eating it themselves. God, I can't even describe this scene. One thing I will say, though, it didn't smell all that bad in there. I don't know if I'm just getting used to it or what, but that did strike me. Lucile and I showed the mothers and fathers how to squeeze the paste up from the bottom, never having seen a tube of toothpaste, they thought it was empty when it was half full. This was stuff we didn't need language for. For the kids who couldn't get it to their mouths we squeezed a little in, but they couldn't take much, so we had to go get Deo to explain to the parents to keep putting a little in at a time. He was totally overwhelmed, and looked at me like he couldn't believe I was bothering him with this, but what was I supposed to do?

It was a nightmare. We had room in the car to transport two kids. I was supposed to decide which two kids were the sickest. Couldn't do it. Most of the families there had more than one sick kid; we just left them all. I felt like crying all day. Because of the distance, we only had three hours to spend there, which was nothing, but we told them a tent was coming Sunday. Deo was going to stay until another nurse could come from Lubumbashi, and we left. On the way back, we got waved down in a village where there was a pregnant woman bleeding and in pain. We packed her into the vehicle with her husband, and came back to Shamwana.

On the way back I was thinking about the volleyball game we were supposed to have that afternoon, and it seemed more important than ever. Denial, I guess. We got back here too late, and still had to take care of the bleeding woman. Amazingly, Lucile and I recounted the story to Perrin and Fabien with humor, which seems incomprehensible, but necessary, especially since I'm leaving tomorrow for Kyango without Lucile. I guess the gallows humor keeps the spirits up. It all seems so sick. I'm bringing vaccines with me tomorrow and will be in a village, not at a health center, so I'm not sure if I'll be sleeping in the tent with the sick kids or not. I'll be back here Tuesday night, and then we'll see what other disasters are cropping up before it's decided where I spend the rest of the week. I'm still scheduled to go on R&R next weekend, but oh, have you heard that before? I have picked out some pictures to try to send, so again, if all goes well and I get to Lubumbashi, I'll send them from my Hotmail account, but don't reply to that account. Reply to this one. Please. I still like hearing from you! In fact, my life depends on it.

OK, I've got to end this, though I don't want to. I can't believe it's the end of another month. I knew a year would fly.

Love,
Linda

Je pense trop et qui blesse. *(I think too much and it hurts.)*
April 4ᵗʰ or 5ᵗʰ 2008, not sure which day. It's Friday

It's early morning, after six-ish. It's been thirteen weeks since I've been back from Tanzania and I still haven't had my R&R. I'm going tomorrow (latest plan) and coming back Wednesday. I guess it's time for a break, but I'm not in love with Lubumbashi so it doesn't seem like something to look forward to. Perrin only has a few more weeks left. Bridgitte is not coming back and we still have no outreach nurse. Mario is away moving drilling equipment, and I rather miss having him around. I hope he comes back. Dubie's Unimog is broken down, so ours is going there. Only five more months left for me. I have two weeks vacation in there too, which I've got to start planning. I was supposed to be going in a few weeks, but I'm going to wait until June because Benson will be on vacation in May. It's a bit dangerous emotionally to wait that long (I can feel the burnout) but we can't leave the maternity uncovered. No one else wants to come here. I want to get Jacques here to set up the health education, possibly the first week of May.

A rooster is crowing behind me. We're not getting many eggs yet— don't know why. I don't hear from many people anymore, not like at the beginning. It freaks me out when I write home and don't hear back from anyone. I get irrational thoughts of having no friends anymore. It makes me wonder where my place is in the world. Is God telling me to stay here? Maybe there's nothing at home for me anymore? Maybe I'm cracking up? Maybe I shouldn't wait for that vacation?

I haven't taken French lessons for a while. Often Emmanuel doesn't show up. I can see why he lost his job as a nurse. Drinking has wrecked his life. But when he does show up, I'm still enjoying having structured lessons. It's good to force me to write stories. The evenings are so much more pleasant now, though. The French lessons used to be an escape. They got me away from that team that was driving me crazy, but now it's pleasant in the evenings and I don't feel the need to run away. The e-mail is more flexible and we can send and receive any old time we want! What a difference that makes.

Poker tonight, everyone is hyped for it. First time in a long time for that, too. It feels so good to watch these words form across the page. My journal is always there when I need it. A friend.

April 7, 2008–I made it to Lubumbashi, but I'm leaving a day early. Spent most of yesterday trudging through the market. Some guys circled and tried to mug me. Scared the crap out of me; they looked deranged. A very nice bank employee walked with me to the photo shop where I called a car. Then I came back here and just sat around depressed and shaken and read all afternoon. This sucks. I'm going back to my little world in Shamwana and totally ignoring all the Lubumbashi people. I hate it here.

I just had a protein-packed breakfast, two eggs, two slices of salami, and two pieces of cheese. At least there is food here.

I'm lonely. I started thinking again of relationships and some kind of romantic stability. More and more I don't think that's going to happen to me. I'm going to stay open to it, but I don't feel like it's out there for me. I hear from fewer and fewer people, and it makes me wonder who my close, dear friends really are. I was struck Sunday night by how little I want to be back home. I hope by September I'll be more excited about it. But I feel like it's going to be a big let down. I can see myself writing (I don't know what) and renovating the cabin. OK, I've got a plan. I'm worried about the dark side of going home. House issues, same old work issues, our stupid health care system. Oh well, it's still a ways off.

April 13, 2008
Sunday morning, Shamwana

Hi Everyone,

Yes, I did make it on my R&R last weekend, but it wasn't all that restful. Sometimes I think the purpose of R&R is to make you appreciate being in the field. Lubumbshi is noisy and polluted and hardly what I'd call restful. It was nice to take a warm shower, though, and eat fresh avocados. I wonder why there are no avocado trees in Shamwana or the neighboring villages.

The week leading up to R&R was intense, to say the least. I think the last time I wrote, I told you I was going to Kyango as the outreach nurse. We STILL have no outreach nurse, and little by little it seems like that job is being added to mine. I was afraid this was going to happen. The assignment was to go out to the temporary camp and assess the situation. We had previously sent two nurses, two tents, and some supplies for the measles cases that had originated in this very remote area. Monday I went with the two community organizers, Willy and Joseph, and another nurse to spend the night at the camp in Kyango. The nurse was to be dropped off in Kishale the following day to relieve Deo who had stayed in Kishale to help. Tuesday was our regularly scheduled day for vaccinations, so I had packed up all the routine vaccines, and I tossed in 1,000 doses of measles vaccine. This big campaign is taking fucking forever to get going. Nurses are being flown in from all over the world; we received two big iceliner fridges that only need eight hours a day of electricity (so can run off our generator), and great fanfare is being made of taking care of the crisis that we created by not vaccinating sooner. It is totally pissing me off. So, even though we have permission to vaccinate, I'm not supposed to do so yet, because the special "vaccination team" hasn't finished making their big elaborate plans. Meanwhile the measles cases keep pouring in. This makes sense, huh? I had had enough. I decided that since we had the government's permission, if I had the chance to protect the kids around Kyango, I was going to do it. I didn't have an exact plan. I figured I'd get there and figure it out. I also had no one breathing down my neck threatening to tattle, so I went ahead. I knew it wouldn't hurt anyone if they got two doses, so if the measles campaign got to some kids twice it was not a problem. I left not knowing for sure what I was going to do.

The road to Kyango was reasonably passable, and when we got

there I realized it was the same village where we had found the original cholera case. That was back in the days when I couldn't remember any of the names of the villages. Perrin had gone out with the logistics team the week before and set up a temporary facility consisting of two big tents, two latrines, two bathing enclosures, and a little two-room guesthouse. Except for the tents, these structures were made out of grass, but they were very functional and even cute, I thought. Two excellent nurses were there, and despite the fact that they had forty-eight sick kids in one tent, it was functioning fairly smoothly. Again, this is all relative, but it was nothing like the horror show I found in Kishale the previous Saturday (God, had it really only been two days?). When they set up this camp, there were fifteen sick kids. A week later, there were forty-eight. Wilfred, an awesome nurse, said, "Mama Linda, we need another tent." I told him that was not possible. We only had one other tent and that had to go to Kisele where there was a new outbreak. I stood there thinking of the irony of all this. I was the one who was jumping up and down arguing about preventing this very scene, and then I was the one who got sent out to deal with it. Margaret, who didn't want to do anything without the blessing of our (misguided, in my opinion) medical director, is gone. Carila, who didn't want to be involved if we immunized without permission, is gone. Edgardo, who decided I should now be outreach nurse, left for Lubumbashi to make other big decisions. I felt abandoned and alone, but then realized I didn't have to answer to anyone (technically, not exactly true), so decided to head to the chief's house to immunize this entire village. I told Wilfred it's our only choice to prevent more cases. There is not going to be another tent–or another nurse, for that matter. He agreed, smiling his beautiful smile. Willy and Joseph looked at me, agreed silently, and we all nodded and started out to do what we all knew was the right thing.

It was awesome. Willy, Joseph, and I walked into the village and talked with the chief. We set up a table and the word spread like wildfire. People were scared. There had been deaths from measles there, and they were scared. We immunized almost 200 kids within an hour. We moved down the road to the next village and did the same thing. Another 150 kids. Then it was getting dark and rainy, so we went back to the camp. I called Perrin on the radio and told him what the situation was and what I was doing. He was also disgusted with the handling of this, and he told me I had his full support, but I had to leave to get to Kishale in the morning. I wanted to stop in every village along the way, but time wouldn't allow for that. I had to get to Kishale; we were carrying lots of supplies for them, not to mention a nurse. We had to be there in time to do vaccinations, and be on the road back to Shamwana by 1:30 p.m. We were still a two-hour ride from Kishale.

I had just replaced the radio when Wilfred said he had a case he wanted me to see. An older woman, maybe in her forties (old for here), was in terrible pain, barely able to walk. The only place to examine her was on Wilfred's cot in the little grass house, so we went in there. I thought she might have an ectopic pregnancy. She was bleeding and in agony when I did the exam. It could have been appendicitis but she was really sick. We had room for two people in the car and could take her to Shamwana, but she wouldn't get there until late the next day. She and her husband said they would wait and come with us; they had no other choice. But if it was an acute appendicitis or ectopic pregnancy, I knew she would be dead before we could get her to surgery. In the meantime, Wilfred brought a little two-year-old over to me with an awful cellulitis she had gotten from a dirty injection from a local healer. She needed IV antibiotics, and with the other critically ill woman, we wouldn't be able to fit this child in the car the next day. I told Wilfred to tell the parents to start out immediately and take her by bike. It would take most of the night traveling, but it would be quicker than she'd get there with us. He translated this to the parents, and they looked at me with a combination of disappointment, acceptance, resilience, and fear, all mélange in one glance. *"Je regrette"* (I'm sorry) was all I said, hoping that all I wanted to communicate to them was expressed in those two words, knowing it wasn't. My frustration was bordering on despair. I knew very well that she might die, too.

By then, it was dark, and someone brought us some *fufu* and gorgeous fresh fish from the nearby river. We ate standing around the plastic table that we'd used for the immunizations, and went to bed. I was exhausted. There were six of us in this tiny space; my cot was tucked into a corner between stacks of supplies, but I didn't care. The rain had stopped and I fell asleep quickly. I was having a weird dream that had to do with a strange noise, and then woke to realize that the noise was right next to me. I opened my eyes to see a guard standing two inches from my cot, his face illuminated by the lantern he was holding, and knocking on a box of Plumpy'nut. I startle easily, but this just about gave me a heart attack. I caught my breath and, as I came out of my fog, could hear someone screaming. He said there was an urgent case for me to see. I got up, put on my boots (I slept in my clothes), and went out to see what was happening.

It seemed like there were hundreds of people around, but I was still half asleep, and everything seems magnified at night, so there may have only been about fifty. There was a young girl, who'd been in labor for two days, being transported by bike toward Mpiana where there is a government health center. They saw our camp and stopped for help. Oh my God. She was screaming, and when I examined her I could feel some limb, but I wasn't sure which one, jammed in the vagina. I was hoping it was a leg, and I could pull the baby out breech, but after feeling for a bit I felt fingers not toes. This was a totally impacted shoulder. Oh, my God. Middle of nowhere. Huge night sky full of stars. Screaming woman about to rupture her uterus. If they continued on to Mpiana they couldn't do surgery there. They'd have to cross a big river and go to Kiambi another seventy kilometers away. Wilfred just shook his head. I thought, well, we can take her instead of the other woman with us in the morning, or maybe get all the supplies on the roof, and have room for both of them, but even with transporting her in the morning, there was no way we could let her go on like this all night. By flashlight we were rummaging through our big emergency box and I decided to give her two doses of Buscopan (which I'd never used in the States, but it's a relaxant, similar to Vistaril), hoping to stop the contractions. It did nothing to help; she was screaming and flailing all over the place. Gave her 10 mg of Valium, thinking that there was a good chance the baby was already dead, and was just hoping she didn't die, too. No effect, she was still screaming. I called Perrin on the radio and asked what to do. He said he would send another vehicle first thing in the morning to get these critical cases, and that I needed to continue with my original plan. This was good, because they both would get to Shamwana much sooner that way. Then Wilfred handed me a huge list of supplies he needed, since another vehicle was coming. So for the next fifteen minutes or so, it was a conversation like this:

"Ampicillin 1 gram, over."

"*Oui*, ampicillin 1 gram, good copy, next."

"Metroclopramide, over."

"*Oui*, metroclopramide, good copy, over."

"Plumpy'nut, over."

"*Oui*, Plumpy'nut, good copy, next . . ." It took forever.

When I was done, the girl was still screaming. There was nothing else I could do. I tried to go back to sleep, but that was impossible, listening to her. Then Wilfred came to tell me that the family wanted to take her to a traditional healer in the village while they were waiting for the vehicle. I went out again, and they were loading her back on the bike, and took her away, screaming. I hate to admit this, but I was glad. I couldn't stand it anymore. They brought her back a few hours later in a deep sleep, so I don't know what he gave her, but it was a relief. I went back to bed, and a little while later, they came to get me again. This time it was about a man in his mid-thirties, who had been unconscious for twenty-four hours. Vital signs were all normal, he was breathing, but he was in a coma. I didn't know what was wrong with him. Could have been meningitis or cerebral malaria. It was weird he had no fever, but we started an IV and just waited for the car to come. I started thinking about friends at home asking me if I was scared about getting hurt. And I truly have never been scared of being hurt. I was, however, scared of this. I was scared that I'd have to watch people suffer, and not be able to do anything to help them. We set up this camp in the middle of nowhere, and people come here thinking we can do something to help, and then we look at them with dying family members in their arms and say, "Sorry, nothing we can do." And yet, I had a strange feeling of contentment. I don't know where that came from. I don't know if it was because the scene was such a fantasy of raw humanitarian drama, or if it was divine intervention. All I know is that I didn't want to be anywhere else that night.

At six a.m. Willy and I walked back to the village to immunize a few more kids that we missed the day before, and then we headed toward Kishale. When I called on the radio to say we were leaving, I told the night operator (a nice, but strange guy) that I needed to talk to Fabien so he'd be prepared for the cases on their way. But the connection was bad and it was too hard to get the message across, so just decided to wait until after eight when Oscar was there. We stopped in the first village and immunized another 100 kids, then feeling pretty good that we'd covered a good portion of the surrounding area, continued toward Kishale. We passed one big village but didn't have time to stop there. Then we got to a bridge that had been taken apart and was being rebuilt. We couldn't cross; there were four or five guys hauling huge logs to rebuild it. They said it would be at least three hours before they could put up something temporary for us to cross. So, I said, "Right then, let's turn around and hit that last village while we wait." It was fantastic. We went back and immunized another 150 kids. I was feeling great! I realized we wouldn't make it back to Shamwana that day, but could stay in Kishale for the night. I thought it was a good plan, and we didn't have much choice. We got back to the bridge after three hours and it was nowhere near ready for us to cross. So all the guys in our car got out to help, and I took pictures. During this time, I had talked to Perrin a few times on the radio. Fabien was at the hospital, so I left the message for him to call me when he got back, but in the meantime the second vehicle had radioed that the unconscious man had died in the car shortly after they left Kyango. The driver had to stop and leave him in the nearest village to be buried. That was not completely unexpected, but still, I felt awful. There was no medical person to help in the vehicle.

We finally got across the bridge and got to Kishale at 1:15 p.m. Everyone at the clinic was very upset because a lot of people had come for immunizations and, thinking we weren't coming, had left. There had been no way to communicate with them, so they didn't know why we were so late. I called the base and asked Perrin if we could spend the night so we could do the vaccinations. He said, "I figured you were going to ask that. Sure, go ahead." Then I gave Fabien the report of what was coming, and told him they had to be ready for surgery right away if the laboring woman was still alive when they got there.

We sent two people into the village with the megaphone to say we were there. Well, it was as if they were yelling, "FREE MONEY! FREE FOOD!" People came running—I mean running—from everywhere. It was a stampede! I was drawing up syringes so fast I got a blister on my thumb. It was a madhouse. A couple of times I thought, if someone falls forward we are all going to be crushed. I periodically glanced up to look around and saw five-year-olds carrying one-year-old siblings, holding up the baby for their shot, and then offering their own arm to get immunized. Many of the kids were scared to death being dragged into this scene by scared parents. Parents scared for a different reason. The kids were screaming, and Marcelain, who was helping us, pretty much just put them in a headlock while they got their shot, and when he let them go, the kids ran away like little captured animals set free. I have never seen anything like this. Fathers showed up with four kids on a bike, put them down, and then left to go get others. We did 366 kids. In the middle of this frenzy (it was now about four p.m.) the guard came to tell me that Perrin wanted to talk to me. I told him to tell Perrin I'd call him later, I couldn't leave, but he came back a few minutes later, and said, "No, he wants to talk to you now." So Deo took over for me, and I went over to the radio in the car where Perrin asked if I had remembered to bring the SAT phone with me from Kyango. It's against security rules for an expat to spend the night without the SAT phone. (This rule always makes me feel like we are saying that expats are more important than Africans. National staff doesn't need the SAT phone.) Well, I had forgotten to bring it, with everything that was going on when we left that morning. So there I was, too late to go back, and no SAT phone, and he started in on me, and I just said, "Perrin, before you say another word, I have not even had a cup of tea yet today. I got no sleep last night. I have about two hundred people in near-riot stage waiting for vaccination. Now. Can we talk about this later? I'm sorry. I forgot the SAT phone." He backed off, and just said, "Well, I guess there's nothing to be done, then. Just come back as early as you can tomorrow." He was just doing his job; I didn't think he would be too mad at me (I was wrong on that one). I found out later that all the other vehicles were stuck in the mud somewhere. One of them was underwater. He was stressed.

We finished vaccinating all the kids that came, and I was so happy. I felt so good. I was exhausted, but really happy. I could not believe how much we accomplished with just a few people and our own cool boxes. I know we could have immunized every kid in this entire district ourselves if we had started in October. We packed up, and I went over to the little mud guesthouse where we had put all the measles cases the Saturday before. They had been moved into the second tent so the hut was vacant. The guard brought me a bucket of water to bathe with, and I took a bucket bath in the grass enclosure that serves as a "shower," ate the *fufu* and dried fish that one of the village women brought, and crashed. Next morning we were up and packed and ready to go at six o'clock. We stopped in one more village and immunized until we ran out of syringes. In total we got to 900 kids. It was awesome.

We got back to the base late in the afternoon, and I bounded into the office bubbling over with news of how many kids we had immunized (well, OK, I was bragging), but no one seemed all that excited. Perrin said he had been really mad at me for forgetting the

SAT phone, but he wasn't so much anymore. That was supposed to be a compliment, I think. Fabien was mad at me because I should not have sent the guy in a coma here, because there was nothing they could do for him (and deaths look bad on our statistics). Lucile was mad at me because Fabien was. She told me it was very inappropriate to send such critical people in a car with no medical personnel. It wasn't fair to the driver. OK, she had a point on that one. But then I got really upset. I said, "OK, everyone. Let me get this straight. I am supposed to tell a woman whose husband is unconscious in her lap, that we have a car going to a hospital, but he can't go because HE'S TOO SICK? How was I supposed to know he couldn't be helped here? OK, so he died on the way. How was I supposed to know that was going to happen? He'd been in a coma for twenty-four hours. I couldn't say he wouldn't live another twenty-four. And I had tried to talk to Fabien earlier, but probably should have tried a little harder to get through before I made the decision about who to put in the vehicle. OK, I could see he did have a point, too. Though at the time it seemed reasonable to send the three sickest, and Fabien wasn't the one who was going to have to tell the family we couldn't take them. But the good news was . . . the mother and baby lived! I am so happy about that. They did the C-section as soon as she arrived, and though Benson broke the arm of the baby pulling her out (he just grabs a limb and pulls) , they are both alive and doing well. And the other woman *did* have an ectopic, and she had surgery and is doing well too. Ahhhh. I was glad. We did make a difference for them.

I went over to the hospital and found two fighting *accoucheuses*. There is this huge power struggle going on between them now that Gerardine is not there. It's a pain in the ass. Add to that that our deliveries have quadrupled. In the past week we've had sixteen deliveries; five were in one day. We only had seven the whole month of September. I was nervous about leaving again for the weekend, but gave them a little talking-to about fighting in front of the patients, and got the ball rolling for finding another nurse-midwife to work here. We really need someone who is a nurse also. It's just gotten too busy. And if Mama Generose complains one more time about missing a meal or staying up at night I'm going to fire her. Until now I've been making a light comment like *"C'est la vie de la sage-femme!"* (That's the life of a midwife!), but I'm ready to say, "Look, all of us missed lunch, not just you. Go work at a bank," or words to that effect.

Lubumbashi was the usual; people in the office chasing their tails, barely having time to say hello. I didn't have much desire to hang out there, anyway, so I went to the house with Betts, who was the outreach nurse in Kilwa. It was the first time I met her, and the last. She broke security rules on Friday, and they sent her home on the next flight Monday. They take these rules very seriously. She was so stupid. She sent the vehicle away while she was alone in a village without her handset, and then called Lubumbashi on the SAT phone to tell them to have the car come back because she forgot something in it. I said, "What, do you have a death wish or something? Or were you just flaunting that you were breaking the rules?" It's one thing to not have the SAT phone, but NEVER can we be without a vehicle. She said she never was very good at following rules she disagreed with–definitely the wrong organization to be working with. So, it was a lot of listening to that, and shopping for everyone in Shamwana.

When I was leaving the big market laden with heavy bags, I got circled by a group of thieves, one of whom managed to unzip the pocket of my backpack. A very nice man saw this, acted like he knew me, and walked me to a store where I went inside and called the base to send a car. The thief didn't get anything—I don't keep anything in that pocket in a crowded area—but it was still upsetting. Then the next day I was walking back to the base to get the plane back to Shamwana, and I heard a guy yell, "*Muzungu! Attend*!" (White person! Wait!) People are always yelling at *mzungus* here, and usually I ignore them, but something about the way he said it made me stop and turn around. He motioned for me to come, and pointed to a man looking deranged hiding behind a tree. I realized that someone had been following me. I had no idea he was there, and I usually have a good sense of what's around me. The guy who warned me was an off-duty security guard, and he walked with me to the base. He said it was unusual to see *mzungus* walking in Lubumbashi, and now I know why. That sucks. So now it's even more like prison. I don't think I was in danger of being hurt, just of having my pack stolen. And this was broad daylight on a busy street. I was glad to get back to Shamwana.

I have lots more stories, but I've been up all night, and I can't think straight anymore, so I'll save them for a slow week.

Love to all,
Linda

Je déteste la fumée de cigarette! *(I hate cigarette smoke!)*
April 19, 2008–Saturday morning, I sit here near my garden, the scene now profaned by cigarette smoke. I've been trying to be polite but that courtesy has not been reciprocated. Now I'm annoyed, which might make for good writing.

April 20, 2008
Sunday morning, Shamwana

Hi Everyone,

Perhaps it's because the rainy season is winding down, or the full moon was approaching, but we had a continual stream of laboring women last week. It was busy enough that Generose and Beatrice stopped bickering.

There was a baby born with major birth defects last Sunday. It was something I had never seen, no recognizable syndrome, but I have never seen a woman here so upset. The mother was way more upset than women are when their babies die. This baby was alive, but the head was misshapen, and the eyes were tiny and set very close together, and the mouth was tiny as well. I'm not even sure there was a tongue in there. But the strangest thing was the nose. It was a tubular protrusion with only one nostril, and didn't seem to have any bone in there. The mother was terrified. It was her sixth baby, and as soon as she saw her she tried to get up and run out of the delivery room. She said it was sorcery. We called Benson to help explain to her and to her family some possible causes. He took one look and then ran home to get his camera. I already had mine, but was waiting for a more appropriate time to take a picture, like when we took the baby to weigh her or something. But Benson didn't think it was inappropriate at all, and came back and just started snapping. Strangely, taking pictures of the baby seemed to calm the mother down. It wasn't quite as frightening somehow knowing that someone wanted pictures of her. She was an older woman, maybe late thirties. Old for the maternity crowd here. She had no idea what genetics meant, maybe could understand what a virus was with extended explanations in Kiluba, but couldn't associate this with what happened to her baby. There are no words in Kiluba for medicine or health, so the explanations take a very long time. Benson spent an hour with the husband explaining that this was not the fault of his wife, but the husband didn't seem to believe him. The next day at the morning meeting Benson spent twenty minutes in French explaining to the national staff that this was not sorcery but either a genetic problem or a virus during pregnancy. Still, one of the nurses asked me later that day if I really believed that it wasn't sorcery.

We had another woman from Kabala, forty-three years old (very rare that someone knows their age), having her eighteenth baby. She came in bleeding, with no fetal heart, and it turned out to be a placental abruption. I have never seen this much blood coming from one person. I do not know how she lived through that, but she did. Then arrived another woman with a cervical laceration who had delivered in the village, and was brought in by bicycle, pouring blood from her vagina. It took both Benson and me two hours to get her sutured and the bleeding controlled. I staggered back to the base, trying to get those sights and smells out of my mind. I have seen quite as much blood as I want to see for the very distant future.

It's crowded in Shamwana this week. We've got extra drivers sent from MSF-Spain to help with the measles campaign, nurses from Lubumbashi, and two vehicles sent from Dubie. There is also a very sweet nurse from Madrid coordinating this whole thing. All of our regular movements have come to a giant pause, so when I haven't been in the delivery room, there's been a lot of hanging-around going on this week. It should be more restful than it is when there's nothing to do, but I find it quite tiring. The idea of sending other people here to do the vaccinations is a bit misguided, if you ask me. No one has; that's why this campaign has been so bloody inefficient. The idea was to send another team, so the Shamwana team could continue on with their regular work, but the measles campaign needs all the vehicles and all the computers and all the meeting space and all of everything. All of a sudden, it's HOLD EVERYTHING, WE'VE GOT MEASLES GOING ON HERE! I've had to remove myself physically or I fear I'll say something I regret.

We've also got a photographer here from Holland with Edwin, a Public Relations guy from Geneva. Edwin is very peppy, positive, energetic, and enthusiastic about a photo exhibit that will display images of women working in various capacities from four different countries where MSF works. This photographer is a sports photographer who's never been to Africa. They wanted someone with a fresh eye, and one who was used to shooting action. It's been interesting. They go out and shoot photos with a camera that looks more like a cannon than a Canon, then come back to the base and play around with Photoshop. At first I found it very entertaining, and the pictures are really incredible, but after awhile I had to stop myself from screaming, "The color is fine! Leave it alone!" Then I got bored with the anal-retentive nature of the project and Edwin's use of the word "brilliant!" This photographer, Sam, spends way more time in front of his Mac than in front of the people here. Oblivious to the most beautiful sunset I have ever seen, he focused on the contrast of colors on his computer, but he *is* a professional. That said, his photos are amazing. It's interesting, though, to watch someone spend one week here trying to capture everything about the women's lives in thirty photos. He has taken about thirty thousand. Then he goes through and has to pick out the one that captures it all. And then Edwin interviews the women through whoever is nearby to translate, and will write their stories to go with the pictures. It's going to be a huge exhibit in Holland, but I don't know if it will travel at all. Edwin is repeatedly bounding into the dining area, "We've had a brilliant morning! Absolutely brilliant! I got some fantastic stories from some incredible women!" It's as if he found the key to unlock all their personal horror. I don't know why it's annoying me so much.

Friday morning they wanted to walk to some fields where they could photograph women working. I told them I knew where some rice fields were near the river, but I hadn't been there for a while since it got so wet. The last time I was there in December I fell in the mud and haven't gone back. There is a lot more water there now, but I offered to show them where it was. They wanted to go really early to get the best light, so we agreed to meet at six o'clock. At six I was pacing around outside the office waiting for them. At six fifteen Edwin got up and was having his first cigarette of the day. He said he didn't have any boots, and then what about a translator so he can get these women's stories, and what if we can't make it to the river, and would we get back in time for the morning meeting? These guys make such a project out of everything. I don't mind caretaking when I am in the mood, but I think it was the cigarette. I said, "What, you want me to carry you?" I just look at these people and wonder how the hell they got in the position they are in. It's like Anders being worried about a rooster. If you worked in public relations, and were supposedly well-informed, would you come to deepest Africa at the height of the rainy season without boots? I was low on exciting stories this week, and thought a fatal snakebite might add color, so I said, "Don't worry, you don't need boots, as long as you don't mind your feet getting muddy." Idiot. Then I had to wait and wait and wait while they got all the lenses ready and whatever, and the sun was well up by the time we set off, and I thought we missed the best light, but then I live here and can go get pictures whenever I want. I purposely didn't bring my camera, but I wish I had. Taking pictures of him taking pictures would have been excellent. I'm kicking myself for being intimidated by those lenses and thinking my little camera looked anemic and underfed. Especially when, just outside the base, a man on a bicycle was coming toward us wearing dark torn pants, a green jacket, and (I swear to God) a white Easter hat with a big brim and pink ribbon and fake flower on the side. It was the hat of my dreams when I was six. That was a classic shot. Sam was wearing the whole photographer outfit, the vest with all the little pockets, and the brimmed safari hat, balancing that huge lens taking a picture of this guy riding by. Damn! It was an award winner.

We got soaked walking through the tall grass that was hanging across the path. I was getting a little nervous that I'd get lost, as nothing was recognizable with the grass so high. What a contrast from the dry season. We got to a place that was a muddy gully last time I had been there, but now it's another river. I told them I wasn't crossing it. It was way over my boots, and it was hard enough when it was just mud. They considered going on without me, but Sam was worried he'd get his equipment wet, so we turned around, and didn't make it to the rice fields.

Later that day they came to maternity and took pictures of Beatrice and Generose doing a health talk. Beatrice was really hamming it up; she was hysterical. The pictures are beautiful, and Sam very, very generously left copies of his photos here so we could have them as long as they are just for personal use. That was extremely nice of him. These are magnificent photos. He left yesterday, but Edwin is staying for another week to collect more stories.

Perrin has gone to London for a course. He plans to work with MSF long term, at least for the next several years, so he's enhancing his career options. He comes back in two weeks, is here for a week, and then leaves for good. I cannot imagine who could possibly replace him. I'm dreading not having him here. He is tough and has high standards, but he's like one of those teachers who are a little too strict, but who everyone respects because he is so good and dedicated. He was a fireman in France and he is so steady even when everything is falling apart. He can do Anders's job when he's not here, but Anders can't do Perrin's job. It's going to be a big adjustment. Plus he's funny. I am really going to miss him.

Mario is back after two weeks of moving drilling equipment in Dubie, and three days stuck in the mud on the way back. It was rather sweet when he drove in like a hero yesterday. I waved to him, and he hopped out of the truck and as he was shaking my hand he kissed it and said, "*Je vous ai pensé toujours.*" (I thought of you always.) It was very charming. No other romance to report. That was the extent of it. And he's still using the formal *vous* and not the familiar *tu*, so you can see it's not going anywhere.

The truck with all our international order and food for the next month and beer for Perrin's party is stuck in Dubie. The driver is refusing to travel to Shamwana because the road is so bad. Can't say that I blame him. Another few weeks and the roads will dry out and life will be very different. I am looking forward to dryer roads and easier travel, but I am truly going to miss these cloud formations and clean drinking water. The replacement for Bridgitte is arriving May second, and the replacement for Margaret is coming on the fifth. That will change the dynamic again. We are hoping to finally get a volleyball game going today, now that the crises have subsided for the moment.

The chickens have laid some eggs but only one or two here and there. I just had to plead a case to let them free-range to see if the girls would be happier and lay more. They don't like being locked up. That was a big deal at our expat meeting yesterday, but Anders finally agreed, as long as they don't go into the kitchen. I explained this to the chickens this morning as I let them out, and hopefully they'll obey the rules. Like there's any food for them in the kitchen. Good luck opening those cans of peas.

The garden is a colossal joke, though the basil is still edible. When it rains, it pours down so hard that everything gets beaten into the ground. I did see that the eggplant, which I planted in October, has a few blossoms, so maybe by the time I leave we'll get an eggplant. It's fine. The food doesn't bother me anymore. I've given up.

That's about all I can come up with this week.

Love to all,
Linda

⟫⟫⟪⟪⟨⟩⟫⟫⟪⟪

Je veux quelques oeufs. *(I want some eggs.)*

April 20–Sunday morning. It's early and I've already written and sent my e-mail, so that frees up this whole day. The air is so clear. It hasn't rained since Thursday, and the change in the air is remarkable. The temperature is glorious. The chickens are milling about. It's pleasant. I feel content and pleased. Happy, even. It feels like a summer morning with the whole day stretched out in front of me. Though obviously I won't be going on an outing. I still feel like the day is loaded with possibilities. The air is so nice.

I feel like I look old. I feel fat and saggy and am trying not to dwell on it. Looking at pictures of myself (which I've done a lot the past few days with the picture/photo mania going on around here) I think I look older. I have definitely aged here. I read somewhere, "She was the kind of fifty that makes getting older look like a reward." I love that line. I spent yesterday thinking a lot about whether I'd ever find a life-long love again. Right now, though, life is all the romance I need. I'm reading Sartre. I feel so smart.

April 21, 2008–No e-mails this morning. None! Not even one. OK. The weather is getting nicer at home, and maybe people aren't checking their e-mails on Sunday anymore. I thought maybe one, since I sent it so early. Jeeze. More visitors come today. This should be interesting since we have hardly any food left. This afternoon Andrea and I will visit Mario. Also have to write a good French story today for Emmanuel. Sartre is going well.

April 23, 2008–Wednesday afternoon. It's raining lightly after a five-day pause, (maybe six). Very clearly see that the rainy season is winding down. It seems a bit cooler, the air is clear and the stars are out at night. The moonlight has been spectacular.

Timeline:

Amsterdam changes data collection system from simple and basic to detailed, complicated, and capable of providing fancy graphics.

Ursula is pressured from Amsterdam to implement this system. She is overwhelmed with micromanaging unnecessary things, tries to start implementation, doesn't work, stops, gets more pressure from Amsterdam.

Ursula does two-day workshop with two people who are about to end their mission, only one of whom is computer-savvy. They have both been treated badly, are unmotivated, and really don't care because they are leaving.

The one who stays (me) knows nothing about computers, is trying to learn this along with national staff who have never used or seen a computer before.

This person (me), whose French is very basic, is now supposed to teach the field staff who don't speak French, and who just finally got used to the other system, how to do the new one. She tries. Then all movements stop because of the measles campaign. No follow-up is done with the new forms, etc. Nightmare.

She sticks head in sand. New pressure from LBB now that the international order is done.

April 26, 2008 –Saturday morning. It's crowded here. Ten expats now with our limited food. Our new head of mission is here touring all the projects. Like the majority of capital team members, sure of himself. I don't know how these egos all fit in one country. He's just stepped into the shower and I always notice that when someone here takes two showers a day, they are a tad odd.

No rain for over a week except for one small light shower. It's a big difference. My sneakers get filled with sand now walking back from the airstrip. The air is lighter and cooler. And it's two more months before the cool season. I'm a bit chilly now. Wonder how cold it will be in two more months. I'm down to four months left to go. Seems long some days, like nothing on others. Throw my two-week vacation in there and it's a flash.

People are waking up and moving around. Really nowhere to hide anymore.

April 27, 2008
Sunday morning, Shamwana

Hi Everyone,

It's six a.m. and the wailing in the village has been going on for four hours now. It's the signal that someone has died, and it continues for twenty-four hours. Loud wailing moves around the village. Yesterday afternoon I went over to visit Gerardine and her baby, as I'd heard that the baby had been sick with diarrhea. Gerardine was very upset and crying when Beatrice saw them at the health center. When I got there the baby was much better, and Gerardine was calm, but when I heard the wailing I panicked because it came from the direction of her house. I was lying awake not quite knowing what to do, when they came to get me for a problem around four. While at the hospital I learned that it was not Gerardine's baby who died (Beatrice had been lying awake worried about that, too), but a child of ten months who had malaria. I felt relieved that it wasn't Gerardine's baby, but then thought, well, it was somebody's baby.

I considered going back to bed, but now with the roosters joining the wailing, I'm not going to sleep. It's a rare quiet moment in the office. Well, quiet for the office. It's very noisy on the other side of the fence.

There are ten expats here now, and after several weeks of only having four people, it's an adjustment. The food runs out, the shower water runs out, the clean dishes run out, and time on the computer is back to catch-as-catch-can. I'm incredibly frustrated and angry, not because of all the people here, I can deal with that, but because of the way this measles campaign is being run.

So as not to "disrupt" our normal operations, the great makers of decisions in Lubumbashi hired and moved staff around to pretty much invade Shamwana and immunize the area in a span of two weeks. Remember, we've had measles here since October. Andrea arrived from Madrid, to plan and execute this great campaign. She has no idea why we're all pissed off, and isn't making enough of an effort to find out. She spent the first week planning, the second week training staff and "sensitizing" the population, and the third week doing the vaccinations. Well, she doesn't go out to do them; the army of transplanted employees go do that. All unfamiliar with the area and roads, all unknown to the villagers and chiefs, and all getting paid more than our local national staff. This has not gone over well with either our national staff or the expat team who had no say in how this would proceed. Add Edwin, who was here to tell the world what a great job we were doing of vaccinating all these kids against measles, and who was annoyingly chipper and short-sighted.

The area where we had the highest concentration of cases was Kyango and Kishale, the area where I went with Willy and Joseph and immunized 900 kids in three days. Three of us. Oh, and surprise! The cases went from forty-eight in Kyango that week to twelve the next. Fifty-five cases in Kishale that week went to thirteen the next. There is a saying I learned in French, *"Je me jete les fleures"* (I throw flowers at myself), which means I'm bragging or flattering myself, and I know I'm doing that now. I don't want to sound like I know everything, even though that *is* how it sounds, but shit, we did a good job! People responded!

Well, people are not responding well to the teams that are out there now, and the response from Lubumbashi has been to send even more people. I'm furious. First of all, the timing for Shamwana was last on the list of the three projects. This coincided with when Perrin would be away. A logistician is a key ingredient when cooking up a campaign like this. In fact, it's paramount. Not to worry! They send someone else who doesn't know the place or the base, the goal being apparently to have many bodies here. Kristoff is a good guy, and learned quickly, so that hasn't been a huge problem. It was just unnecessary in my opinion (and remember, this is all my opinion).

I put off my vacation, which was originally planned for these two weeks, because of the campaign, thinking I'd be out every day doing what I'd been waiting to do since October. Oh no. I'm not allowed to go help. I'm supposed to stay here and pretend that everything is continuing along normally. But because all our vehicles are being used for the campaign, our regular activity has ceased, so I've been sitting around this week, pretty much fuming. Well, that's not entirely true. I only started fuming when I heard that the teams aren't achieving the numbers predicted. These numbers were obtained from a census that was done during a food distribution, where families jacked up the number of people in their families to get more food. OK. Good for them. I think that demonstrates good survival skills myself. But now it looks like we are not reaching our goals! And no, this is not what angered me. I don't care that we have gobs of extra vaccine. I don't care what the projected numbers were, and what the actual numbers are. What angered me was the discussion about local people screwing up our campaign. When the team went to a village where they predicted they'd vaccinate 500 kids and only did thirty-nine, they blamed the local traditional healer for telling the villagers not to bring their kids. Then the discussion revolved around how to remove the traditional healer so we could reach our goal! Excuse me, what happened to Cultural Sensitivity 101?

I can see why this organization has the reputation for being arrogant. I wasn't included in the discussion about how to go about solving the problem (neither was Lucile or Fabien), but I butted in anyway. I said to Anders, "Why do you think this guy has to conform to our schedule? For a population that's been traumatized by war, we show up in the village with strangers on motorcycles and tell everyone to show up on one day to receive a shot of something they have no idea about, and then get angry when they don't conform? They are scared! I think the guys on motorcycles look scary. The villagers don't give a shit about the expiration dates on the vaccines. The *guerisseur* (traditional healer) didn't run away when the Mai Mai came. He stayed, and the people trust him." Now, I agree that he doesn't always use safe methods, but he is not forcing people to come to him. They do have a choice. This is a village where there wasn't a lot of measles, so there isn't a correlation with the illness and death yet. Nor is there a correlation with the vaccine preventing kids from becoming sick. And so when I suggested we could follow up there over the next few weeks, and spend time every day talking to the chief and some of the other leaders in the village with the *mosos* who are already known there, that wasn't good enough. Because then that would mean the campaign doesn't get the credit for those numbers. I wish Perrin were here. In the end, most of the kids aged six months to fifteen years will be immunized, and that is a good thing. So I'm just trying to stay out of the way and shut my mouth until the heroes have had their day in the limelight and leave. Lucile and Fabien are doing the same. (Uh, they are doing a better job of shutting their mouths than I am.) It's just been a waste of resources and a source of aggravation for those of us who've been dealing with the acute cases, but right now we'll just have to accept what we've got.

It has been impetus for some reflection, though. After Sam, the photographer, left, Edwin went along with one of the teams to take photos of the projected hoards of people lining up to get their kids immunized. He just happened to go with a team that went to a village where the people trickled in tentatively and it wasn't the turnout they had anticipated. There shouldn't be anything wrong with that; we should just keep going back until we've reached every vulnerable child. But Edwin had an image in his mind of what the event should look like and wanted to get pictures of what he had in his head. I had told him about the day we were in Kishale, and I think that's what he had in mind, and was all bummed out that what he'd seen wasn't similar. This brought up an issue I have with journalism. I asked him why he was intent on getting pictures of what he thought it should be like, instead of what it really was like? And why does he get to come for two weeks and get to tell the story of Shamwana to the world? Thirty pictures to tell the story of women's lives in the entire Katanga district? He interviewed women through an interpreter, and gets to tell their story. He's Swiss and speaks French. The translator is Congolese and speaks pretty good French but uses different vocabulary. The women being interviewed speak Kiluba or Bembwe, which have very small vocabularies. So when he comes bounding in with "fantastic" stories, I asked him, "How do you know they are accurate? I mean, really, do you know that the translation was accurate?" And for a language that has no medical vocabulary, to get a description of a lifetime of trauma in a fifteen-minute interview, it seems a huge responsibility. It's like sound bite third world. Maybe the stories are accurate, I don't know. But the women aren't going to be able to proofread it before it gets printed to check for accuracy. Maybe I've got the story all wrong myself. Maybe this was the best way to immunize everyone, though I would have believed that more if this had transpired the week after we found the first cases. Then I could understand doing a blitz. But not when we've been here for months with the capacity to systematically cover the same area with the people who already live and work here. I think it was Edwin's assumption that he had uncovered long lost secrets and wouldn't shut up about it that made me confront him. That and there had been too many frustrations back to back. I had too much time to think this week that this is all a castle in the sand. The pictures are great and Sam will get a lot of recognition for that. Edwin will write the story and get recognition for that. Donors will hear about this great campaign and MSF will get recognition for that. And nothing will ever change here. Edwin didn't go into the tents where the acute cases were and take pictures of that. I asked him why not? Why not tell the story of the suffering we could have prevented? There are many aspects of this organization that I admire, but this, in my opinion, has been a major fuck-up. I know there are many layers to an organization like this one. I know there are touchy political issues, and logistics, and financial considerations. But kids have died because people higher up were looking out for themselves and didn't have the balls to stand up to a corrupt political system. So what does that makes us? And if I hear the argument one more time that "you can't save everyone" I am going to puke. The fact is that we could have saved some of them. I think to humor me Edwin interviewed me and taped it, about what it was like to see the tent full of acute cases. I wasn't very articulate; I had too many thoughts in my head, and was angry, so I gave him the description I wrote, and if nothing else, he read it. I was bracing myself for another "Brilliant!" but he said quietly, "Your description was mind blowing." He did say after reading it that he would think long and hard about how he wrote about his two weeks here. That was after I unleashed all my frustration about all the suffering we'd seen, all the arguing we'd done to try and get permission to vaccinate, and now to have this bouncy, well-fed team here, and a photographer and writer to put it all in a good light . . . well, I am sorry. That was just too much to take.

Fabien was writing a letter this week to Sheila in Lubumbashi about the possibility of transferring three suspected AIDS cases to Dubie for diagnosis and treatment. He asked me to proofread it because English is his third and weakest language (but it's still better than my French). The first line he wrote was "Now that Ursula is on holiday I suppose I have to deal with you." I read it and couldn't stop laughing. He kept saying, "What? What is so funny?" When I could talk, I said, "That just sounds so rude." And he said, "But it's true, I have to deal with Sheila now." And I told him that yes, it is technically a correct sentence, but to a native English speaker, this would sound rude. We played around with it, and then he did the same for me when I had to write the schedule for the week of health education in French. But it was another example of how easily we can be misunderstood when we are weaving in and out of all these different languages. It's made me think so much about the difference between language and communication, and the power they both possess. Like I said, I've had a lot of time to think this week.

It's been a week now without rain. The air is much clearer, though it is still hot during the day. The evenings are getting cooler and now that the clouds are gone, the stars are magnificent. We are surrounded by stars. All around, down to the ground. It's spectacular.

It's late afternoon now. There's a football game going on, MSF against the secondary school students. Last Sunday the school-boys whipped our butts and all week long Fabien and the national staff have been whining about it. I was surprised at what sore losers they were.

The woman I saw this morning had a nice vaginal delivery with no problem. Beatrice and Generose are getting along much better now. Less bickering. That's a relief.

I can't believe it's the end of another month. Days are getting shorter. Here near the equator it's dark at 6:30 now instead of 6:45.

It's late evening now, and once again, *je me jete les fleures*. I outdid myself for supper. There is hardly any food left, and if the plane doesn't bring some tomorrow, there will be a mutiny. I found a half a cup of flour in the metal supply box, two eggs in the chicken coop, a handful of basil from the garden, an onion, and some canned milk. Oh, and a pumpkin that had been in the kitchen for six weeks. The skin was so hard I could have built something with it. And there was some cheese that one of our visitors brought. I made pumpkin-filled crépes with cheese and basil sauce for ten people! This was no easy feat on a charcoal fire and no light. Fabien had to crank a flashlight for a half hour straight while I made the crépes. Then Jurgen, our new head of mission who is here touring the projects, pulled out a bottle of Famous Grouse that he brought, and the evening wasn't all that bad.

I forgot what else I was going to write, and having sat on this all day wondering if I should send it or write something more politically correct, the Famous Grouse is saying send it. I'm not going back to re-read it, so if doesn't make sense, I'll do better next week.

Love you all,
Linda

꧁❀꧂

Je pense, j'écris, je parle et je me sens mieux. *(I think, I write, I talk and I feel better.)*

April 28, 2008–Monday afternoon. It's hot and dry. I'm sitting in the hammock between the tukuls. It's the best place I can find to hide. Despite the crowded atmosphere and the measles frustrations, I am feeling better. I think writing home helped and talking to Jurgen today helped. Yesterday's e-mail must have struck a chord with people. I got several e-mails today saying I should write a book. Yeah everyone should write a book. I think we all have a story to tell. I also got a nice e-mail from an old friend. Short, to the point, but considerate and caring, and I truly appreciated it. It was well placed. It made me less afraid of going home.

SUNDAY MORNING, SHAMWANA

CHAPTER 10 ~ MAY

May 4, 2008
Sunday morning, Shamwana

Hi everyone,

It's quiet here this week. Five of the visiting expats left, food arrived on both the plane and the Unimog, beer for Perrin's going away party arrived, as well as huge amounts of medications and supplies. This is the final week of the measles campaign, which is winding down. They are only doing small catch-up areas now. Our movements can resume and the mood is a bit lighter. Mine is, anyway.

Our guests the past two weeks included Antoine, a psychologist from Holland, here for two weeks doing training for all the mental health counselors. Jurgen, our new head of mission, also from Holland, toured the projects, and spent four days in Shamwana. Oscar, a doctor from Burundi, was here for a week because the measles campaign in Kilwa ended abruptly and prematurely when the Ministry of Health officials there decided they were sick of MSF making such a fuss and stopped the campaign. Then Sheila didn't know what to do with all the people she imported for the show, so she sent them to Shamwana, but didn't think of sending extra food with them. This resulted in loud outcries to Lubumbashi from the team, which did nothing, and from the guests, which did a lot. We received lots of food.

Antoine is a guy in his late sixties, who retired from teaching psychology at university level and started his own consulting business. His specialty is war trauma, and he works for various humanitarian organizations for two weeks at a time doing trainings. He's been a breath of fresh air. It's been nice to see Lucile able to speak her native tongue and I realize how much effort she puts into talking to me in English all the time. Her English is excellent, but seeing these two together it's obvious how much more relaxed she is talking to him, and it makes me feel happy for her. Antoine goes running with us in the afternoons and has an air of comfortable confidence that makes him delightful to be around. He has skill and experience to offer, but doesn't need to prove anything, nor does he look for approval. It's lovely. In the evenings after he showers he wears a long white cotton sarong. He looks like Socrates.

Jurgen is our new head of mission, Francine's replacement who's leaving Lubumbashi in three weeks. This is his first time as head of mission, but he's been project coordinator in several hot spots including Mogadishu and Pakistan. He's quite sure of himself, but I like him, except for when he kept referring to himself as "old" at thirty-seven, and for one night at dinner when he said I was proof that it's never too late to do this. A little over-sensitive to the age thing I said, "You're only thirty-seven? I thought we were the same age!" Shut him up on that issue. He spent a good portion of time talking with us individually and, I felt, really listened to our concerns and frustrations. He knows way more about me now than Francine ever did. She has never asked me anything about myself. I got out all my frustrations with the measles mess, and, while I know that there's nothing to be done about it now, he acknowledged that it could (should) have been done differently and it did make me feel better. He also wanted to make sure I understood that not all MSF missions were run this way. It all depends on the capital team, and this capital team has provoked a lot of complaints. It's obvious that he will have a very different style of managing this project. It's not going to make a huge difference in the time I have left here, except that I feel better about what's possible to accomplish and what isn't.

Oscar was quiet and diplomatic and very polite. He is the tallest, thinnest man I've ever met. I thought his bones would snap at any moment. He looked a bit like a Masai, but didn't have the same facial features, and I never asked him what tribe he was from. I'm pretty sure he's a Tutsi. I was hoping he could stay here to cover for Benson while he's gone for his month's vacation, but apparently he's got another assignment in Burma.

There isn't anyone right now to do surgery while Benson is away, and that is a big concern. Fabien isn't a surgeon, though he said that in an all-out emergency he could probably do it. Well, I suppose I could, too, but that isn't the kind of stress we need here right now. Last week when I assisted Benson with a caesarean, the woman's intestines came pouring out around the uterus, and at first I gasped thinking it was a giant tapeworm. I have never seen that before. Benson just shoved them all back in, and I refrained from saying yet again, "Oh my God!" (I wish I had a nickel for every time I've said that since I've been here.) At any rate, I think we need a real surgeon.

My friends the clouds are gone. There are a few wispy high clouds, but the layers and layers of varying colors that made a different landscape every day are gone for the season. Two weeks without rain now and the dust is already insidious. I can't imagine what it's going to be like in another two months. We're back to drinking river water and, though it's filtered, it's still brown and tastes terrible after having had rainwater to drink. Supposedly a drilling team is coming at the end of May to drill for water that's potable (that is, without uranium or manganese), but it's already May and I haven't heard any more about it, so we'll see. I started making cold tea with lime from our lime tree. That way I don't mind if the water is brown.

Fabien hates the brown shower water. The water we shower with is not filtered and is in a white translucent barrel that does not conceal its abundant impurities. I guess I've just gotten used to it, but I'm not covered in bites like he and Lucile are. First they thought their mattress had bed bugs, and asked Jean Pierre to put that out in the sun every day, but now they are focused on the shower water as the source of their dermatologic stress. James, the lab tech who comes every once in a while to get our lab running, told us he's seeing schistosomiasis everywhere now, which doesn't surprise me, but I thought you had to be standing in the water for that to be a problem. (Schisto is a parasite found in standing water that bores into your skin then travels to either your urinary or gastrointestinal tract. Resourceful little bug, but quite disgusting.) Anyway, Fabien wanted to drop a chorine tablet in the shower water. I thought that was a good idea (we have big plastic containers of them), but in true MSF-Katanga fashion it had to be way more complicated than just tossing in a tablet. He and Andrea had to research on the computer (of course) what MSF standards are, how much chlorine for how many liters of water for each individual circumstance, who would be in charge of it, and on and on. I was watching them in the office, and wondered how these people get through life. I asked Andrea, "What could you possibly be looking for?" She was clicking on this file and that file, and opening pages of documents from cholera protocols, and getting more and more frustrated with the process, saying "I know I have the protocols on this computer. I recently did an inservice on how to clean the water with the *chlore* tablets!" I walked over to the container of *chlore*, opened it, pulled out the paper inside with all the instructions on it, and asked, "Is this what you're looking for?" Oh! Well, yes, that was it, but it was also on the computer somewhere.

Then it was how many liters of water in the barrel that holds the shower water? Hmmmm, Andrea said she'd go into the logistics stock report on the computer, look up that barrel (What was it called? We have many different types of barrels,) and see how many liters it contained. I walked over to the stock room and said, *"Bonjour Martin! Combien de litres dans un seau comme ça?"* (Hello Martin! How many liters in a barrel like that?) I pointed to one of the barrels. *"Cent vingt,"* he replied without a second's hesitation. I walked back to the office and said, "A hundred and twenty liters." This entire process took me roughly seventeen seconds. That included walking to the stock room and back. And Andrea said, "Oh, I almost had it here." Then started clicking and closing, and clicking and closing. But computers save so much time! OK, yes, the sun was scorchingly hot for my ten-meter walk, but the activity in the office was so much more uncomfortable. See why this measles campaign has been such a frig?

Speaking of hot. It is bloody hot. Really, bloody hot. I thought after the rains it would cool down a bit, but people say not until June and July do the days cool off a little. The clouds made a huge difference in the temperature, and while it's always been hot here, there's hot and there's *hot*. And this is *hot*. The evenings and nights are nice. Very early morning is lovely. But from nine a.m. until five p.m. oh my God, all I want to do is lie in the hammock. We've all been falling asleep after lunch, waking up in a pool of sweat, and slogging through the afternoon in a haze. The maternity room, with its brick structure and tin roof, is back to oven temperatures. I put on a pair of examination gloves the other day, and the gloves were hot. I got called over to maternity at nine p.m. this week, and arrived to find Beatrice and Generose in a bra and gym shorts, caring for a laboring woman. I had on a tank top and *pagne*, and felt overdressed. And the operating room! The room itself is a little cooler because it has an inside ceiling under the tin roof, but having to wear the surgical gowns and double gloves, it's like a sweat lodge. One of the nurses is continually wiping our faces because the sweat keeps dripping onto the patient.

The big new activity this week is starting the syphilis testing for pregnant women. Our lab is finally capable of doing it, but I knew the actual procedure of carrying it off would be very complicated. Explaining the disease and how it's transmitted, explaining the test and what it means if it's positive, explaining what the treatment will be for the women, their husbands, and all his other wives: it's all very complex given the population. In theory, it should be simple. The women go over to the lab, have their blood drawn, go back over to maternity, the lab tech brings over the result, then we counsel and treat. Then they get another appointment to bring in their husbands and the other wives. (THAT should be a fun clinic; I'm looking forward to that!) We've been trying to get this going since December, and Friday was the big day. The lab forms were all ready, and when all the women were seated in the *tukul* waiting for the health talk, I had Beatrice hand out the lab forms and tell the women to go over, have their blood drawn, then come back for the health talk. That way, by the time they have their consultation the results would be ready. I had made sure we had lots of the appropriate penicillin ready (after Portefeille realized that my two "ones" side by side was an eleven, not two slashes for two). I hoped we wouldn't have too many positives, but really had no idea what the incidence was. The big, BIG benefit for maternity is we get to have our own stapler to staple the result in the chart. Wooohoo! That was good news! Better than Christmas! Our own stapler! *"Merci! Merci, Mama Linda!"*

I'm not going to get into too much detail about the lab, or our local lab tech, but they have only a few patients a day that come in for some kind of test (usually a sputum for TB, which they can do very well), and aren't accustomed to lines of people waiting for blood draws. James told me it works very well in Dubie. They draw a batch, spin it (manually, in a sort of hybrid salad spinner on a c-clamp) then the women go back to the clinic while waiting for the results. Our lab tech, while a very sweet man, is legally blind and has been waiting for glasses since September. He couldn't figure out how to get the cap off the needle. He had no idea what to do with the line of waiting women. I was really annoyed with James, because he should have been over there walking them through this for the first day, so I ran over to the base where I found him (surprise!) doing something on the computer. He didn't seem to be stopping some nuclear attack, because he was able to shut it down immediately and come back to the lab with me. I left him there to sort out the lab end of it, and went back to maternity to make sure that the health education was happening. That is something I am very pleased with. We have a long way to go, but they are starting to do a health talk, sing some songs, and ask women if they have any questions. I know it must sound ridiculous, but really these are huge steps.

Then we started the consultations. The first two tests came back positive. Beatrice and Generose read the women's names and collapsed into fits of laughter. The laughter was only subdued when they got to do the very serious chore of stapling the result into the chart. To avoid jealousy, Beatrice got to staple the first one, and Generose got to staple the second one. We started the consultations, and normally there are two women in there at the same time, one getting weighed and having vital signs taken, and one having the obstetrical exam, but I told Beatrice and Generose that today I wanted the women to come in individually because we had to give them their syphilis results and that should be confidential. Oh yes, yes, right, of course. (More laughter at the thought of bringing in the first woman and telling her the result.) They called her name and I went to sit in the corner to watch how this was to proceed. They did the usual stuff: weighed her, took her blood pressure, asked about complaints, checked the baby's position and heartbeat. Then the woman got up and they started giving her some iron pills and turned to me and told me she has no complaints, and they were finished! I said, "*Attendez! La syphilise!*" (Wait! The syphilis!) Oh! That's right! *La syphilise!* They sat her back down, and explained in Kiluba, which I am sure wasn't adequate because it wasn't long enough. It takes a long time to explain anything medical in Kiluba because they have no vocabulary for medical terms. The woman didn't seem upset in the least, in fact she seemed rather happy that she got an injection. She wasn't overly excited about the second injection (that shit is nasty), but it all seemed like no big deal. She agreed to bring her husband on Monday; she doesn't know of any other wives. She's nineteen. This same scenario was repeated with every consultation. They'd do the routine exam, and then start to send her off. And I had to say "*Attendez! La syphilise!*" WITH EVERY SINGLE WOMAN. OH MY GOD! A third were positive. Half of the positives were one of several wives, the other half didn't know of any other women. The youngest was fifteen, the oldest was twenty-three. Oh my God. It was a zillion degrees. I had to run back and forth between the lab and maternity a hundred times. I got back over to the base at three p.m., got in the hammock, and didn't budge for hours.

My back started hurting, and I thought I had pulled something playing badminton with Antoine on Thursday (I set up the net I had made), but as the night went on I started feeling worse and worse, and yesterday was worried I might have malaria. Anders did a malaria test on me last night, and it was negative, so I stopped worrying about that, and today I feel much better. I have no appetite, but I'm not achy anymore. I went over to the hospital this morning for a delivery and Beatrice told me she had the same thing yesterday, so it must have been something viral. There is a party tonight for all the people who worked on the measles campaign, and listening to Mario kill the goats this morning got the stomach churning again, but I do think I'm getting over whatever I had. I won't be eating or drinking at the party, though. Figures. We finally get some beer and I don't feel like drinking any of it.

OK. Time to do the Sunday ritual of nails and facial. It's important to look good around here. Never know when a professional photographer is going to show up.

Love to all,
Linda

Je manquerai mon ami. *(I will miss my friend.)*

May 8–Perrin's party is tonight. I don't want him to leave. He is in such a good mood, though, it is a little infectious. I wonder if I will be that way when I leave. He can't stop smiling. He is looking forward to three months of visiting and partying with friends, then will go off to another exotic and dangerous place and offer his many gifts. Would I like that life? Could I make a career out of this? Not sure.

May 11, 2008
Sunday morning, Shamwana

Hi Everyone,

I remember thinking when I first arrived here, when Perrin leaves, I'll be the most senior person here, and my time will almost be finished. That was when I thought that day was a lifetime away. After being away at a course in London for two weeks, Perrin came back here on Tuesday, grinning from ear-to-ear non-stop until he left on Friday. Every question we hounded him with was answered with a good-natured smile and calm demeanor. There was none of the curt, efficient, you-should-already-know-that response that we've come to know and love. He was so glad to be moving on. It was hard not to be happy for him, though I wanted to throw my arms around his ankles and wail until he agreed to stay until September. I thought I'd be bawling when he took off. Lucile ran to get her sunglasses, in case she needed to hide her tears. He did a good job (as always) in the short time he had, to make sure someone knew how to take care of all the things he does. His replacement, a woman from Germany, won't be here until next month. His speech at his going away party was wonderful. It was funny and light, and he ended by breaking into a Congolese song and dance, and it was fabulous. Only he could have pulled it off the way he did. It made everyone a little less depressed. He's someone I know I'll see again—that's not the reason for the difficulty saying good-bye. It's that he's been so good at coordinating all the activity that has gone on here, which has been considerable, from building a hospital, to getting food and supplies for patients, as well as all the vehicle maintenance, and cold chain, it goes on and on. And he's been such a Papa to the national staff. He's only twenty-six, but is just a remarkable person. I am so going to miss him.

When an expat leaves, a group of us go out to the airstrip to say good-bye. The group usually consists of a few expats and the national staff closest to the departing. Well, you should have seen the procession on Friday. It was impressive. Every vehicle was filled with national staff, and the drivers and logistical team had decorated the cars with balloons and flowers. We slowly drove through the village like a funeral procession, and when we got to the airfield, the national staff all surrounded Perrin and sang and danced until the plane landed and the engines were shut down. Arriving were the two new team members, and they were quite impressed with their welcoming committee. We looked at each other, not sure whether to tell them, that um, actually, it wasn't, um, for them, but then I guess all thought simultaneously, "Ahh, let them think it was," because we all did a "Welcome to Shamwana!" After unloading the cargo, loading the cargo, and saying the last good-byes, Bruce said he'd circle the airstrip after he took off, and off they went. As soon as the plane was in the air, we went to the middle of the field and made a huge circle and some of the little kids that were there joined, too. Oscar arranged the kids so that our circle became a heart, and we all waved madly as the plane circled and passed over us, as Perrin left Shamwana for the last time.

I don't know what's come over me the past week. I know a lot has to do with Perrin leaving, and the new people coming, and feeling like the remainder of my time here is short, but I have had major emotional swings and feelings of being completely overwhelmed. Not overwhelmed in a bad way, but not in a good way either. Just sort of in an overwhelmed way. I can't really figure out how to define it.

On Tuesday I finally got to go on an outreach trip again, and it was just Willy and I heading out to Kishale. At some point during the drive there, passing one of the radio checkpoints, I casually took the radio, called the base, and when I couldn't get through to Shamwana, tried Dubie, and Lubumbashi, finally talking to the radio operator in Lubumbashi to explain our position. He then informed Shamwana. I replaced the handset, glanced at Willy smiling, and couldn't contain my emotions. I had come so far from where I started here. When I arrived I would do anything to avoid sitting in the front, so terrified was I of using that radio. I couldn't understand a word they were saying. I could barely understand the driver, never mind the static coming over the radio. It was so much work for everyone to tutor me along, and they were all so good-natured about it. And now, two-thirds through my stay here, I've finally become comfortable. Willy and I worked well together. The system I'd been trying (in my pidgin French) to establish for the routine immunizations is finally coming together. There were people waiting for us. Willy set up our station while I paid the staff their monthly wages, and we started. There was shade under the new *tukul* for people to sit. Willy did a health talk. We had an orderly system for recording the vaccinations for each child. I could talk comfortably, in French, with Willy and the health center staff. The women brought their cards we had given out in the previous months. We had a tiny semblance of efficiency.

I had brought a certificate for Mama Marie for attending my little two-day course. You'd have thought I gave her a million dollars. She danced around the *tukul*, doing that beautiful throaty yodel they do, and everyone was congratulating her. It was a little printout on plain paper with the MSF logo, and a border that I had colored with colored markers. It broke my heart; it takes so little to make them happy. She ran into the village to get three eggs to give me. That broke my heart even more. I couldn't figure out how I could be so happy and so sad at the same time. It was overwhelming.

Every philosophical question I've had since arriving seemed to be highlighted this week. I don't have any more clear sense of whether what I am doing is right than when I arrived. I can speak French better. I know the security rules better. I know how to get supplies out of the stock and deliver them to where they need to go. I can use the radio without having a panic attack. OK, yay for me. Papa Abel, who was a teacher before the war, still works as one of our guards and spends his days and nights opening and closing the gate for me. And he's happy and privileged to have that job. He always seems so happy to see me. Always thanks me for my work every time I pass through that gate. The fact that he can smile at all is amazing to me. It overwhelms me.

As I sit here in the office, writing on a laptop that wields all the strength of the powerful, I can look out the window and see Jean Pierre ironing our clothes with a charcoal iron. I wonder if he ever gets sick of us. I wonder if he thinks we are spoiled brats who can't do anything for ourselves. I wonder how in awe he is of *mzungus* who know how to use the computer, the tool that makes us powerful. We are able to get airplanes to come with supplies, petrol for the vehicles, the vehicles themselves! Just like magic, by clicking and typing. Friday everyone clamored to get into the Land Cruisers to say good-bye to Perrin, and Jean Pierre didn't know how to open the door. Mama Nasila, who washes our clothes, tried to tie the seatbelt in a knot around herself. Over and over this week I have sat wondering why I was born into my life, and they into theirs.

I don't know why having a good week should make me so sad. The day at Kishale was evidence of progress. The measles cases have dwindled down to single numbers, and are fewer every day. The woman who was sent by bicycle for obstructed labor arrived safely, Benson and I worked really well together during the surgery, and I felt like we were such a good team. And that made me happy, really happy. The woman (who was four feet tall) and her baby were fine. Benson and I joked around during the surgery. We chatted! Chatted! In French, with surgical masks on! Three months ago the thought of being able to do that was beyond the realm of possibility.

But for some reason this week, every time I got filled with that sense of satisfaction and happiness, the flip side would surface vividly, and I'd think, "My God, Benson. You are never going anywhere. I am so sorry. I'm so sorry that I get to travel and you don't. I get flown out of here to relax for a weekend, and you will continue to walk across that sandy path, day and night, forever and ever, every time they call you, and still you show up smiling." And of course, I keep all these thoughts to myself, because I don't want Benson to know how miserable he has the right to be. And if I did tell him, he'd have some perfectly placed piece of wisdom that he'd share. Not in a condescending way, though I think he has every right to be condescending. After all, we come in and tell him how to do it all, and go back to our comfortable lives and, really, we couldn't survive what they have survived, so what right do we have to tell them anything? None of them would ever jeopardize their jobs by not agreeing with everything we say. They agree with every expat who comes in, one after the other, all with different styles and recommendations, and I just don't know how they stand us. Oh, that's right. The alternative is starvation, disease, and death. How, how, how can this still be happening?

So this week, I've spent time thinking and thinking about all this, then will get jolted into the other world when Lucile and I start talking about her wedding plans, and we'll go on and on about the meal, the dress, the music, the rings, and I don't have the slightest feeling that it's inappropriate. It's like walking out of a sauna into the Maine winter night, and having both temperature extremes feel really good.

The new people. I am not the oldest anymore! Cindy is the new outreach nurse. She's American and has ten years on me at least. (If she doesn't, she looks really, really bad.) She's already done a nine-month stint in Burundi and worked in Australia with the Aborigines for several years. She makes me feel young, fluent in French, and healthy. She chain smokes. This is a problem. Loenis, a young, cute guy from Holland, with a name I CANNOT pronounce, is Bridgitte's replacement, doing water/sanitation. He smokes. A lot. This is a problem. I feel like I have been exceedingly tolerant of the smokers, but now we're outnumbered. The smokers who've visited here for a week or two at a time I've somehow managed to abide, but I am not going to be able to live with this amount of cigarette smoke day after day. It doesn't help that they go outside our screened eating area to smoke. I can still smell it, and now that it's starting at six a.m. (before breakfast!) we are going to have to set up a specific area away from the dining area and my *tukul*. Otherwise, I'll just be a bitch until September.

Cindy said this was the most remote, primitive place she's ever been. More remote than the Australian outback, that's saying something. I explained to her that the difference in Shamwana between now and last September is remarkable. I'm feeling like it's rather lively and built-up around here now. It's amazing how many people are building houses, putting up fences, and getting goats and chickens. You can buy a bike at the market now! It feels as if the population is finally feeling safe enough to settle again, and now that the rains have stopped and they've harvested some food, they can begin to live. It has been an amazing transition to witness, and I feel very privileged to have had this experience. I just hope it sticks. If they can have peace through another rainy season, then survival might not be their only goal.

I asked Beatrice and Generose how people store the groundnuts for the season. They have harvested lots and lots of groundnuts. They told me that people put them in sectioned-off areas of their houses, made from the bark of a tree. It takes up half of the house. I asked if they have a problem with mice getting into the groundnuts, and Generose said, *"Oui! Nous les mangeons."* (Yes! We eat them.) Oh. Pest or perk? It's all how you look at it, and all who's telling the story.

Two days in a row we've had a big volleyball game. The net I made (which was perfect for badminton, but really was too small for volleyball) was moved over to a section of the football field, a pickup game was started, and I was very happy. Pasquale, who does all the construction, did a beautiful job of rigging it up with strips of torn *pagnes*, and made it appear much bigger than it was. People were playing a game and laughing. Kids were watching and laughing. I was overwhelmingly happy.

Next weekend I'll be on R&R, so I won't write. I can't believe it's already been six weeks. My next vacation is planned and I've got my ticket to Lusaka booked for the fifteenth of June. From there I'll take a bus to Malawi, and then figure out what I'll do. Two weeks there doesn't seem like enough, but I'll just take it as it comes. Scary to think that it was twenty-eight years ago that Matt was born there. I wish he were going to meet me there.

Happy Mother's Day!

Love,

Linda

＊＊＊＊＊＊＊＊

Je suis effrayé. *(I'm scared.)*

May 13, Tuesday Something bad happened today. I'm scared and I don't know what to do. I stupidly, so stupidly, got a needle stick today. A bad one. Deep with a hollow needle. Damn! I had been so careful. Even when we were crazily immunizing hoards of kids with sharps everywhere being thrown in open basins, I was so careful. This was so stupid and preventable. It wasn't that busy. There is no excuse for this. There were too many of us trying to help, and arms were crossed and it was so fucking stupid. I feel like crying but I am scared to. I'm still out in the field, shaking, trying to act like this is no big deal. When I first realized it happened my initial reaction was to ignore it. Not mention it. Hide it. I was trying to hide the blood dripping down my hand. I didn't even feel it when it happened! Deo saw it. He said, "Oh, Mama Linda. You got a stick!" I had no idea which kid it was. Who even knows what the HIV incidence is around here? Calm down. Calm down. There are very good treatments nowadays. I can still live a good long time. Calm down. Don't go there. It's dark and you are spinning out of control here. You'll be more rational in the morning.

May 14

I told Benson. I asked him if he'd ever gotten a needle stick. He replied "Bien sur!" Of course he has. I've wondered several times how he manages to protect his fingers during surgery. He's always grabbing the needle with his fingers. He told me every time it happens he tests the patient for HIV status. Aha. He always knows from whom it came. I don't. A bit of a problem here. I asked him if he thought I should do the month of antiretrovirals. He said it was up to me, but he didn't like the side effects; that's why he's never taken them. Yeah, well, he doesn't use a mosquito net either. What should I do? What should I do? I can't write home about this. My mother will freak. My kids will freak. Should I tell Fabien? I should.

＊＊＊＊＊＊＊＊

May 18, 2008
Sunday morning, Shamwana

Hi Everyone,

I must have bad R&R karma. No room on the plane this week, so I got cancelled again. Francine (departing head of mission) is having a big good-bye party in Lubumbashi, and she thought it would be great if two local staff from each project attended. So that filled up the plane, and I got put off until next weekend. Anders spent hours fretting about which of the national staff should be the lucky ones to get an airplane ride and a party. After listening to our suggestions and rejecting each one, I asked why he doesn't just put the names in a hat and let them draw two random names. Hmmm, he reluctantly admitted that was a good idea. The only problem was he didn't think of it, so it had to be discussed for another while. I am really fed up this week and am having a hard time with how frigging long it takes him to make a simple decision. That, and all this fucking cigarette smoke.

Anders is very sensitive to the R&R problem, since it was so long between my last two, so on Wednesday morning as I was planning the health education with Jacques, who came here special from Dubie for the week, Anders called on the radio from Lubumbashi where he was attending meetings for the coordination team. (That was one less smoker for the week.) He wanted to know if I could be ready in fifteen minutes to leave on the extra flight that was coming with supplies. They were willing to let me spend Wednesday until Monday in Lubumbashi for an R&R. I told him I couldn't go, I had this whole week planned with Jacques, and said I'd just go the following weekend, which will then screw up Lucile and Fabien's R&R. But then I started thinking that it would be really dumb to go on R&R and then two weeks later go on my vacation, so I asked if I could combine them and leave here on Monday the ninth of June, and get five extra days in Malawi. Ohhhhh, big request, and against policy to combine R&R and vacation. That might be efficient or fun or something. Very much against the rules. So we had to sit through a frikkin' two-hour meeting last night to figure out how to do the R&Rs, which won't work now. After *beaucoup de temps*, Anders reluctantly agreed to at least ask them in Lubumbashi if I can combine mine with my vacation. I sat there thinking I will never work for this organization again. The longer I'm here, the more I see how militaristic it is. At

least this project is. We'll see what happens with the new head of
mission. Fabien keeps telling me not to judge the organization by this
mission. He's been in both Chad and Sierra Leone and said the
coordination was completely different and much more satisfying to
work with. In Sierra Leone, they went to an unspoiled beach for four
days every six weeks for R&R. Cindy said the same thing about
Burundi; it was very different from this. They had a great
coordination team and R&Rs on a lakefront beach house. I know they
are right; it is unfair to judge based on one experience, but I'm just
being cranky right now. So I'll wait and see what the big decision is
higher up. With that, and finding out my bank back home has been
sold so that now my ATM card won't work, this vacation planning is
getting complicated. I've got to figure out how to get money for
traveling. I'm in a bad mood. It's hot. Waaa.

The week started out good. I did have high hopes last Monday. I
had arranged for Jacques, the health educator in Dubie, to come to
Shamwana for the week to give us ideas on how to get a similar
system going here. I met him while stuck in Dubie, and followed him
around and observed. He's great: a short, feisty, dynamic guy who
spends his day going from department to department doing health
talks. He starts at the prenatal clinic and talks about some topic, then
moves to the people waiting in the outpatient where they sit for hours,
and does a talk there, then to the therapeutic feeding center, then to
the kids in pediatrics, etc. He's fantastic. And it's a captive audience
who otherwise sits staring blankly for half the day. With the kids he
sings songs and tells stories. It's what I had envisioned in the *tukul*
that was built at the hospital, but I couldn't quite figure out how to get
started with it. Perrin was the one who agreed to put Jacques on the
plane on Monday, and send him back on Friday. I was thinking it was
perfect; all would take care of itself.

I had made out a rudimentary schedule, but wasn't exactly sure
what I was doing. Writing in French is difficult for me, so I tend to
keep it very simple. Then I had a period of panic and self-
admonishment for not planning better when he hopped off the plane
and wanted to know what I wanted him to do. I did a, "Why, why,
why do I always do this to myself?" I thought a week was a long time
to fill up, but that's what the plane schedule was, so I winged it the
best I could. Shamwana is very, very different from Dubie. It is much
smaller. The hospital is just being established, and is still a series of
tents, whereas Dubie has been there for a long time and is a campus

of single story brick buildings. They have a huge kitchen where they prepare food for the patients. Here, we dole out flour and beans under a tree, and the *garde de malade* takes it and goes and cooks the *fufu* for the patient on a small fire in a grass shelter with all the other *gardes des malades*. The fact that it hasn't burned to the ground is miraculous to me.

So I spent Monday afternoon working out some kind of plan with Jacques, alone, since all the people I had invited to come and help plan ended up being busy with one thing or another. I was thinking that it was too small here to have a position like his and that the nurses could all take turns doing it, but as the week went on, I could see that was unrealistic. They are all too overwhelmed with working in a hospital that was projected to have twenty inpatients at a time, and now regularly has fifty or more. In September we had seven deliveries at the hospital, in April we had thirty-four. Everyone is pushing the limits of what they can physically do. But I think that over the week we did a good job convincing everyone that it's an important job and we can request the funding to hire someone specifically for that role. Now I have to go through that process of getting approval and, again, I thought, "Why did I do this to myself? I could have just hopped on the plane Wednesday and gone and had salad for lunch!" But I did do it to myself, so I'll follow through. At the weekly nurses' meeting I had asked him to give a presentation, and he was great. He pointed to one of the little kids who just happened to be squatting and shitting in the middle of the compound, and said, *"Voila! Regardez ça!"* (Look at that!), and explained that it was his job to take a situation like that and go offer some education to all the people around there about sanitation and use of the latrines and hygiene. It's terrible to say, but we've all gotten so used to scenes like that that most of us don't even comment on it anymore. I can see why it's important to have new people coming in continually. I was utterly horrified at the sanitation when I first arrived, and though it is way, way, way better than it was, there are still lots of improvements to be made (obviously, if kids are still shitting next to the latrines instead of in them). But because I am gauging it from what it was before, I've grown complacent–and tired. Loenis, on the other hand, is walking around saying, "Oh my God!" at regular intervals. It's good. When I first arrived, there was only one shallow latrine with a grass enclosure. Now we have ten brick latrines. On one of my first days here, I watched a caretaker drag an unconscious woman to the opening of the tent, where she peed next to someone's cooking pot. Then the caretaker wiped the snot running out of this woman's nose with her hand, and wiped this handful of snot on one of the tent poles. That was back in my "Oh my God!" days. See? We've come a long way. We hired someone to wash the tent poles several months ago. Now I'd like someone to teach people not to pee at the door of the tent and maybe use a cloth to wipe their noses. It's not as if every other person doesn't have TB around here.

Vindicien, the nursing director, was the likely person to help with the health education planning. He, however, couldn't come meet with us on Monday because it was International Nurses Day, and the nurses were planning a little celebration and a presentation for the community. We were told that at four o'clock they would march from the hospital down to one end of the village, then turn around and march to the other end, a distance of about 500 meters. A little before four we all grabbed our cameras and went to watch. I was remembering the same march for World AIDS Day, and figured it would be fairly entertaining. I was not disappointed.

The nurses, and all the other hospital employees, were dressed in a hodge-podge of white coats and smocks, and the two in front carried a banner. I can't remember what it said, but it was handwritten on piece of a flip chart attached to a piece of bamboo with surgical tape. Many of them wore latex exam gloves, and carried our lone stretcher and other assorted medical supplies. One carried the sole wooden IV pole with little pegs sticking out of the top. A few wore surgical masks. Benjamin, our *steralisateur* (the guy who sterilizes all our surgical instruments over an open fire in a pressure cooker) carried the big metal thing that we use to measure someone's height, slung over his shoulder like an automatic weapon. He wore one of the surgical masks, and took up the rear of the assembly and kept swiveling around like he was going to shoot someone with it. He is a sweet man, a mild-mannered stutterer, but looked incredibly menacing and evil in this get-up. It was so out of character. It was also pretty frikkin' funny. So they all marched out of the hospital, singing *"Infirmieres jusque la mort, Infirmieres jusque la mort!"* (Nurses to the death!) over and over and over, in the way armies sing a battle cry. This, coupled with Benjamin at the rear ready to take down anyone who challenged them, was something to see. Emmanuel (my French teacher, who is also a nurse) had the megaphone and was leading the battle cry. We're talking a four-double-D-battery megaphone here, with a siren. Serious stuff. He was marching along side with the megaphone, singing away, when—Oh!—one of them fell sick! One of the marchers fell to the ground, and instantly the others descended upon the stricken, taking the blood pressure! Starting an IV! Getting him onto the stretcher! The whole time Emmanuel is calling the play-by-play over the megaphone, "He's down! The Congolese nurses! They are starting an IV! Yes! The nurses of Congo! They have started the IV! Oh, voila! The IV is started!" Here, they hung the IV, which was now actually running into this guy's arm, on the IV pole and picked up the stretcher and started walking with the fallen comrade. Benjamin the whole time swiveling around making sure no one attacked from the rear.

They resumed the song as they marched back toward the center of the village, carrying the unconscious patient on the stretcher with an IV running, when—Oh!—he starts to sit up! And Emmanuel over the megaphone shouts, *"Il se léve! Il se lève!"* (He's getting up! He's getting up!) As if it was a miracle right before our very eyes! He sounded exactly like Johnny Most on WHDH (or was it WBZ?) screaming, "He stole the ball! He stole the ball!" Then after repeating this fifteen or twenty times, as the stricken patient rose from the dead and brushed off the sand from the road and pulled out his own IV, so cured is he now, Emmanuel started repeating, *"Les infirmieres de Congo! Les infirmieres de Congo! Les Infirmiers de Congo!"* (The nurses of Congo!) as if only they could have cured a patient as sick as this. And all I could hear was, "Petrocelli's back, and he's got it! The Red Sox win! The Red Sox win! The Red Sox win!"

Oh my God, it was hilarious.

This entire scene got repeated twice more. Once at the other end of the village with a different patient and once more when they ended the parade at the base, again, with a different patient. All three "patients" had real IV's. All were cured in the same fashion and all had the same enthusiastic commentary. Blew us away. The expat team members were like paparazzi with our cameras fighting for the one photo that would make our entire career.

A little later, when everyone had regained their composure, there were speeches and more songs and Benson and the village chief spoke, and it was very sweet–a classic. And what do nurses get at home, a boring cake or something?

Later in the week I got invited over to Geradine's where she and her husband had a little naming ceremony for the baby. There were no other people there, and the ceremony consisted of the father of the baby saying something in Kiluba I could not understand. I just sat there smiling; I had no idea what was going on. Benson told me later that it is traditional for the one the baby is named for to be at the small ceremony where they give the baby its chosen name. It was an honor. They gave me a gift of a live chicken, a pot of rice, and a small can of tomato paste. It was wonderful and I felt honored and blessed. They said they wanted me to stay for two years. I don't know why they picked two years and not five or ten. Maybe that's as far ahead as anyone can think around here. Other people have said that to me too. "No, no, you can't leave in September. You must stay for two years." I always respond that I must leave because otherwise my mother will be too sad. *"Ah, oui."* They nod, agreeing. Everyone seems to understand the universal language of mothers.

Hmm, that would have been a better ending for last week's letter. Oh well.

If you don't hear from me next week it's because my request to attach my R&R to my vacation was denied, and I am in Lubumbashi being bitchy.

Love,
Linda

Je me sens malade et nauséeux. *(I feel sick and nauseated.)*

May 23, 2008

Lubumbashi—These antiretrovirals are making me sick. I decided it would be very foolish and irresponsible if I did not take them for four weeks. I feel terrible. The ride on the airplane today was ridiculously bumpy. Jesus, it was bumpy. If anyone lights up a cigarette near me this weekend I will stab them.

May 24, 2008

I think it's Memorial Day weekend at home. I'm sitting on the porch of Maison 3 watching the colors change on the high clouds. It's what will have to settle for a sunrise. The barbed wired wall blocks any type of horizon. I'm really getting a feel for what prison must be like, though I do have a nice pot of tea. The air is perfect temperature. It's almost June. Another month gone by. I've only three months left in this country, and I'll be out of it for three weeks of those months. God, I can't wait for that. I'll be done taking this medication and will feel more like my old self I hope. Still have a bit of a sick headache.

May 25, 2008 Sunday morning–It's cool. I have on a polar fleece shirt and it's still chilly. It's early morning, and I have decided to go to the French mass at nine a.m. instead of Swahili at seven. There is a Catholic church close to Maison 3, so I'll walk over there. Later I'll go to the market, the zoo, and botanical garden. Those are my Sunday plans. I've been so tired. I took a long bath, read, watched a movie, and went to bed. I feel a little better today. Thinking about going back to Shamwana. When I'm there I think I can't leave, but as soon as I'm away, I don't want to go back. There's not much time left. I can stick it out. It would have been so wonderful to travel for three months, and I am kicking myself for signing up for a year. I'd be leaving now, to start in Malawi, and then would have gone to Mozambique. Oh well, that's not what happened. I'll have something to dream about for the future. I feel like Africa is in my blood. It always has been, really, or for as long as I can remember. People at home don't understand this. I don't understand this either. This continent, the people, the landscape, the clouds, it all has a constant pull in my gut. I feel so alive here.

May 26, 2008 Monday morning. I'm having my tea in bed waiting for ham to fry so I can cook some eggs. That electric burner is really unsafe. I swear I'll be electrocuted with it; I got a shock when I placed a piece of ham in the pan! And it takes longer than starting a charcoal fire in Shamwana. I'm craving protein, though, and will take the risk. Going back to Shamwana today. Called home last night; couldn't get through to Mom.

May 29, 2008 Back in Shamwana. Mom is in the hospital with congestive heart failure. I just got the e-mail. I am so tired and feel like shit. I should be there. I should be with her. I feel terrible.

CHAPTER 11 ~ JUNE

Je me sens très vieux. *(I feel very old.)*

June 1, 2008–My babies are 22 today. That's an entire lifetime around here.

It's Sunday morning, another six days of the ARVs and then I hope I'll have more energy. It's another week after that before I go on vacation, so I am hoping to liven up a bit. I slept a bunch yesterday. Wrote a lot. I'm thinking more and more about going home. Can't quite imagine, though, being done yet.

June 1, 2008
Sunday morning, Shamwana

Hi Everyone,

As if life in this country wasn't depressing enough, I decided to go to the zoo in Lubumbashi. I thought maybe the city would grow on me if I became a little more familiar with it and saw the tourist attractions, which include the museum, zoo, and botanical gardens. The zoo and botanical gardens are one and the same. Good idea, bad execution.

The day started out nice. It was Sunday, and I decided to try a different church for mass. There is a Catholic church near *Maison 3* (House 3, where we stay when we go for R&R), and that meant I could walk without calling a car. It just happened to be First Communion Sunday. It was fabulous. I was covered in goose bumps the entire three hours. I counted fourteen altar boys, and the procession alone was worth the Sunday morning. The first kid had the incense, and though I thought he should have shortened the chain a bit lest he knock someone in the head, he danced down the aisle to the beat of the choir singing a song that sounded like the theme song to one of those teenybopper shows. Same tinny electronic keyboard, but they had some drums, and of course the voices, to smother it. The music built and got more complex, and then came the kids with the

- 243 -

candles, all doing the same dance, step forward, bop, backward, bop, swivel right, bop, swivel left, bop. I'm sure at home this would have been against fire code with lighted candles, but it was gorgeous. Huge procession, glorious music that made you forget you were in a structure that could have doubled as an airplane hangar (Just remove the benches and the hanging Jesus, the green Christmas stockings strung behind the altar, and there you go. Oh, and I forgot the confessional made from rebar draped with *pagnes*.) There were at least a hundred kids making their first communion. The ushers wore satin banners (Miss America-style) that had *Sainte Elizabeth* scrawled across them with that puffy fabric paint, and the four guys with cameras wore plastic press badges that had *Sainte Elizabeth, photo* printed in black block letters. I was thinking it was a good thing my kids weren't there. One well-placed comment from Jordan and we would have had holes in our tongues from biting them. The church was so packed it was hard to even turn sideways. During the procession, which took a full fifteen minutes, I felt huge drops of water plunking on my head, and looked up to see if the tin roof was leaking. Turns out it was the priest blessing us with holy water, but I couldn't see him coming through the crowd. Buckets of water were used, and I mean buckets–my hair was wet, my clothes were wet. It felt good in the hot, crowded church. In fact, after the first two hours, I was wishing they'd do it again.

After mass, I went back to the house to eat, and planned my afternoon. I had a driver take me to the market to buy vegetables for Shamwana, and then asked him to drop me at the zoo, which made him very nervous. This in turn, made me a little nervous. I told him I'd walk back. Just the parking lot was enough to depress me; the trash was unbelievable. Rotten trash. Revolting trash. It only got worse. After paying my 1500 Congolese francs (three dollars), I began by visiting the monkeys. Solitary monkeys were in tiny cages, with peeling green paint on the bars. Trash was inside the cages, and scattered everywhere. There were four of those small cages, and I'm not sure why those particular four monkeys got chosen for solitary confinement, but it was very sad. Then came the crocodile. It was a small one, sitting on a rock near a pool of green slimy water, with crushed plastic bottles and candy wrappers floating on it. There were lids from paint cans lying around on the paths. I almost turned around and left, but then I figured there was nothing else to do, and I'd already paid my three dollars. There were a couple of larger cages that had monkeys in them, and I was entertained for a while watching three of them fight over a torn pink plastic makeup case. In what looked like an abandoned weed and trash covered inner city lot, were three huge ostriches. An enterprising young man with a camera took my picture near the ostriches and wanted me to pay him to send me the picture when he got it developed. Bless his heart. I gave him a few francs and a *"Bon chance"* with a heart swollen with admiration. There was a lion in a very large enclosed area that had the ever-popular razor wire coiled at the perimeter. I actually wasn't sure if he was dead or alive. He never moved, and he was too far away to tell if he was breathing. The parakeets were probably the healthiest looking things there and one of them said, *"Bonjour!"* as I approached. There were three of those in a cage bigger than the ones the monkeys were in. They still had the peeling paint, though. Egad. It was awful. When I saw the eagle, looking embarrassed, in a cage smaller than the one the parakeets were in, I decided I'd had enough. The most exciting moment was when I was close to the monkey cage, sort of apologizing to him, and he reached out and grabbed the strap of my backpack, and yanked me toward the cage. That little thing was strong! I screamed, and fell backwards, which gave the group of kids behind me a full five minutes of backslapping hysterics. So I suppose it wasn't a complete waste of time.

I finally found what they call the botanical garden, and it's just more of the same: dusty banana trees, a few mostly-dead poinsettias, and a hibiscus struggling to stay alive. There isn't much left post-war. The jungle around Shamwana is much more beautiful. As I was walking out, I saw the remains of what was a terraced garden with a series of pools that connected to each other, but these now had small amounts of standing water with floating trash in them. I could see, though, that it was probably a very beautiful place in colonial times.

The museum I had tried to visit the day before, but missed the opening hours, which are just nine to twelve on Saturdays. It does look like it would be interesting, though, and I will make a point to get there when I go back in two weeks. The building itself looks sound, and the grounds were fairly clean by Lumbumbshi standards. The entryway to the museum was pretty ratty, but way, way, way better than the zoo.

The city is back to being very, very dusty, now that the rains have stopped. It was cooler there than in Shamwana, though, and the nights were very pleasant. I didn't do much besides read and sleep and eat salad. Saturday I went to the market and bought lots of fresh vegetables for salad, and made one big enough to feed five people and ate it all myself. It had been seven weeks without a fresh vegetable other than cabbage, and my gut sort of said, "What the hell is this?" but I couldn't stop eating it.

This weekend Lucile and Fabien are on R&R, and I gave Fabien some pictures on a memory stick and the password to my Hotmail so he could send them to you. I couldn't do it last week. I've already heard from some of you, so it looks like they went through. Yeah! The people here always look very serious in photos. They can be laughing hysterically and as soon as you pull out a camera, they stop dead in their tracks and put on this very serious face. It's hard to catch them smiling. Sometimes the kids will smile, but the adults, never. They love having their pictures taken, though. When I go to Lusaka I am going to print out a bunch of them to give as gifts. It's a big deal. I tried to do it last weekend, but the photo shop in Lubumbashi had no electricity.

I cannot wait for this vacation. I can feel myself losing steam. Two more weeks. Benson is away for the month and I hate not having him here. They sent another doctor from Lubumbashi to cover for surgery while he's away, and I realize how lucky we are to have Benson. I watched this guy do one cesarean, and I was horrified. First of all he started sorting the surgical instruments before putting on sterile gloves, then he made an incision so huge he could've done a friggin' heart transplant along with the cesarean. It started at her breastbone and went down to her pubic bone. I could have crawled in there to get the baby. She got a post-op infection, which I am surprised was her only problem, given how her intestines were pouring out all over the place. My God, it was barbaric.

I am conflicted with equally strong feelings of needing to get out of here, and needing to stay to protect these women. While I was gone last weekend he did two cesareans on women who, Beatrice told me, had the heads way down into the pelvis, practically crowning. I know I could have delivered them with the vacuum. These babies are all five pounds or less, but still the women just won't push them out. Sarah, the nurse-midwife in Dubie, just sent me an e-mail saying that while she was on vacation the C-section rate doubled there. We are in the process now of getting a position approved for a Congolese midwife who can use the vacuum. Right now the *accoucheuses* here don't have the skill level, and aren't nurses. I'm just hoping we can find someone who is willing to live in Shamwana.

I hope I come back from vacation with some new energy for the last seven weeks.

Loenis and Cindy are settling in, and have adjusted to our grumbly, burned out attitudes. I remember thinking when I first arrived that everyone was so negative, and I was all bubbling over with excitement for working here. They are doing the same thing, and it's both incredibly annoying, and a godsend. I see now why you can't do more than short contracts. The burnout is just too high and you start becoming ineffective. Or *are* ineffective, not sure where I fall now.

The really cool thing for me, though, is I get to translate for them. I'd dreamed about this day. I shock myself when I can take a conversation and translate it from French to English or vice versa. I love it. I'm still not fluent like the people who forget which language they are speaking, but I can translate for someone now, and that is very exciting for me.

It's incredibly hot, and I'm heading to the hammock to sleep. Cindy found a goat leg at the market, and she's planning on cooking today so I can relax until another obstetrical catastrophe strikes.

Love you all,
Linda

⚜

June 7, 2008–Saturday morning

Autant d'inconnu. Qui peut savoir l'avenir? *(So much unknown. Who can know the future?)*

Next weekend I'll be packing to go. I'm worried about getting money. This bank card thing is such a pain.

I am feeling so much better off the ARVs. More energy. I've been running, and don't feel so depressed. That's all good. Anders is on R&R so the weekend promises to be pleasant.

The nights are cool. Lots of intense stuff going on at the hospital. I felt unsafe for the first time among the staff. There seems to be a shift in attitudes. I feel like this doctor who's replacing Benson for the month, is turning the nurses against us. It's unsettling. Mai Mai are moving back to Kabala. That's scary. A house next to Beatrice's burned down yesterday. There is so much burning going on that the air is filled with smoke in the mornings.

Morning sun feels good. My feet are cold, that's a feeling I am going to have to get used to again. Lord only knows if I'll be able to heat the house! I heard this week that Obama is our candidate. I'll look forward to listening to him: inspiring, intelligent, and the election might not be so painful. Funny—same feeling coming back from Samoa in 1992. Driving across the country, listening to Clinton at the National Convention, full of hope for the future. Life was so perfect and complete back then. How different my life is now.

June 8, 2008
Sunday morning, Shamwana

Hi Everyone,

Ah, it's so satisfying to hear the new kids on the block complaining already. As always, the first thing to whine about is the food. At first when they heard us scowling at yet another can of mushy green beans, they responded with, "Oh, they're not so bad!" in that chipper, positive tone that implies that our scowls were uncalled for. And most of us muttered something like, "Just wait." Well, the plane that brings the food is on Friday, and if there is a problem with weight excess, the first thing that gets taken off, by people who eat elsewhere, is our food. It is dry season now, and we should be having a truck once a month, which brings the heavy staples. But since the capital team was less than efficient at replacing our logistician—who is responsible for, um, logistics—we haven't had a truck since Perrin left. Let's see, that would be five weeks now. Supplies are running low. The "fresh" food supposedly sent on the Friday plane is purchased by someone on Thursday. They only buy food that will not perish over the weekend, in case the Friday plane gets cancelled, because then the food will rot, and that will be a waste of donors' money. A chunk of cheese, a head of cabbage, and a bag of old green apples flown in from South Africa is what we usually get. We used to get carrots sometimes, but those seem to have stopped, for some reason. Mind you, this is for a week, for six to eight people. It's all gone by Tuesday, and then we complain until Friday. It's our weekly routine. We have been labeled as whiners in Lubumbashi, and Edgardo (who has clearly never missed a meal in his life) gets furious with us for sending e-mails saying, "We have no coffee, milk, or flour. Please put some on the next plane." Because then that implies that he's not doing his job. He acts like we are making this up. He's obviously never done the grocery shopping for his family either.

So, after a week of meals that consisted of: rice, a can of green beans, a can of mushrooms, cut up oranges, bananas, and papaya (which currently are fresh, local, and delicious), we were looking forward to Friday's plane, and our head of cabbage. Anders left Friday for R&R and will be back Monday with six visitors. In the fresh food box this past Friday was a large chunk of cheese, one bag of apples, and two heads of garlic. I've stopped expecting anything else, so wasn't surprised. Plus, I'm leaving next week for vacation. But, there was a fair amount of snickering by Fabien, Lucile, and me Friday night as we heard Loenis in the kitchen yell, "They didn't send any beer!" Cindy said with a sinking voice, "I actually think I might lose weight on this mission." Let's see, they've been here five weeks. The reality shock is right on schedule. Everyone but me has lost weight; I move so much more at home and I never eat this much starch. Sometimes we have a package of white macaroni to go with the rice. If we had butter it would be a four-year-old's dream menu. I can't wait until tomorrow when the others arrive. There's not even any tuna or sardines left. And we are going to eat every scrap of that cheese before that plane arrives on Monday. It's almost gone already. If there's any left by tonight, I'll use it for supper, as our sole objective this week is for the capital team to share in our culinary misery, though since it's only for a week they won't care.

Let's see. What to tell you about this week? I came close to complete burnout after going to Kishale on Tuesday, when we had to end the vaccinations quickly because a woman was hemorrhaging with a placenta previa, and we were three hours on a dirt track away from surgery. We threw a tarp in the back of the Land Cruiser, started an IV, and poured her, unconscious, into the back. I thought, "If she bleeds to death and we have to dump her in some village on our way back, I am leaving here. I can't take this anymore." God must not want me to leave yet, because the woman was still alive when we got back to the base (after stopping to throw another woman, who was being transported by bike, in the vehicle). Since I had radioed ahead and told them to have the operating room ready, it was all fairly efficient when we finally got back. We had some blood in the fridge to give her, and she is doing quite well, actually, and so is the baby. Again I marvel and rejoice at their fortitude. I see her alive and smiling and I am happy.

Then on Thursday, just as I was sitting down to talk with Anders we got a call on the radio that the team in Kishale that was taking down one of the tents (because the measles cases have diminished to almost none after vaccinating–funny how that works) was transporting another urgent maternity case here. Since the pickup can only take the driver and one other person, we didn't want him to go the whole three hours alone with her, so I jumped in another vehicle, and we did a kiss. We met them just about halfway; she had delivered a stillborn baby the evening before but the placenta was still inside. This was about noon. She wasn't bleeding very much, and was conscious and lucid, so we bundled her into our vehicle and headed back here.

When we got her onto the maternity bed and unwrapped from the *pagne*, it was clear she was not more than twelve or thirteen years old, barely through puberty. Here she was alone, her baby dead, with a group of total strangers, and a manual removal of the placenta is not pleasant. This doctor who is replacing Benson is always hovering around, and I don't trust him. He doesn't like letting me make medical decisions, and it's a bit tense. He was in there, ordering Beatrice to put in a catheter, and started getting ready to do this by himself (Benson wouldn't have even been in there unless I asked him to be), when I said, "Wait! We aren't doing anything until she is asleep." He looked at me sharply, like he's not used to being usurped, as all the nurses jump as soon as the doctor says something. No matter how stupid or inappropriate, they never question him. But I just stared at him, and said we are not doing one thing to her until she has some ketamine. He backed off (white nurse trumps black doctor– terrible, I know), and went to sit and write orders as a way of saving face. We sent for the nurse who does anesthesia.

Wilfred arrived and put her to sleep. She hadn't said one word, but stared at us with her eyes darting around like a trapped animal. It was so sad. She must have been terrified. As soon as she was asleep,

Wilfred said, "She's ready for you doctor." I looked at him in shock. He knows I do this myself! As soon as this doctor was there, though, he deferred to him. I then acted like I didn't know what he said, and just proceeded to put on gloves and get the placenta. The doctor, who got up from the desk and importantly turned back to the patient, saw that I was already getting the placenta out (it was easy) and just turned back to the desk and started writing something else. After it was all done and I had sutured the laceration (another thing this guy was surprised to see me do), I realized part of the problem was that he just doesn't know what my skills are and how I am accustomed to working. We haven't developed any kind of trust. So I could understand his behavior a bit. My back started coming down a little. Then, as we were cleaning her (she was caked in mud and blood), Generose made a comment that this was no more than a girl, and she had been violated. This doctor said (as if not inappropriate in the least), "If a girl this age has sex, it's because she tempted the man into it. It's her own fault." Well. I turned around slowly. Glared at him in horror and said, "If. The man. Who did this. Was more. Than. Fourteen Years old. This. Was. A. Rape." He looked confused, as if it was just sinking in that maybe I thought what he said wasn't completely appropriate. He turned and left. After he left, Mama Generose said sadly, "A Congolese woman cannot refuse a man. She is always afraid." I just said, "I know." And we finished cleaning the girl up, and carried her over to the maternity tent.

Now I am extremely proud of the stance that MSF takes against sexual violence. It is not tolerated whatsoever. So to hear someone who is employed by this organization (a plum job), and a doctor, talk like that, was unbelievable. The Congolese usually have more self-preservation instincts. Even if a man were thinking the same thing, the ones that work for us know better than to say it. The day before this incident he and I had another disagreement about a seven-year-old girl who was brought in when her four-year-old brother tried to put a stick into her vagina. He didn't succeed, but she was bleeding, and I could see the blood was coming from two cuts on her labia. I could see that her hymen was intact, but this guy wanted to put a speculum in "to make sure there were no lacerations inside." I'm like, "Over my dead body are you putting anything into her!" I carried her into the ward, and ran to get Fabien to tell this guy not to touch this girl, and that I would take care of her. He won't touch her if Fabien tells him not to, I hope. He gives me the creeps; I can't wait until

Benson is back here. Beatrice and Generose know to come and get me if he starts doing anything to one of the women in the hospital, but it's adding to the already high level of stress here. The awful thing is, we have to keep him here until Benson gets back, because he's the only one that can do surgery. Such as he does it. Julian from the capital team will be here tomorrow, though, and he's a surgeon, so hopefully he'll be on top of this. God. It's not like the women here haven't suffered enough.

With the dry season well under way, the local people have started burning everything in sight. I don't get this. On the way to Kishale on Tuesday we passed hundreds of acres on fire. If that much land were burning at home, it'd be on the national news. I asked the driver why they do this and he said, "To make it easier to hunt. They are burning the animals out of their homes to hunt them. Then they take the trees for firewood. They are easier to cut down." Sometimes I think there's just no hope here. I had to roll up my window in the Land Cruiser because the flames were so close to the road they were licking the vehicle. The road traversed this fire and we just drove through it. I've never seen any animals, so it beats me what they are hunting. The driver told me antelope, but I have been told before that there aren't any left.

ONE MORE WEEK UNTIL VACATION! I can't wait. Right now I don't care what I do as long as I am out of here.
It has gotten quite cold at night. The days are incredibly hot, but the evenings cool off to the point of being chilly, and last night my feet were cold. I had to go over to the hospital early this morning, and I swear I could see my breath. That might have been smoke from all the fires, though.

More next week ~

Love,
Linda

J'aime voyager. *(I love to travel.)*
June 14—Saturday morning. I'm getting closer! Just the weekend to get through. Then Monday to Lubumbashi, Tuesday to Lusaka and I'm on my way! Got that giddy, pre-vacation feeling. Can do anything! Mario got back yesterday after six weeks. I'm going to visit him later today. In my

head, I'm already on vacation. Only doing the basics now. Maybe I'll run this morning. Lord knows, it's cool enough. I'm a little nervous about going to visit Mario, but also a little excited. I feel a little superior having someone to visit. I get to leave the base and for once it's not to go to the hospital.

June 15, 2008
Sunday morning, Shamwana

Hi Everyone!

Twenty-nine more hours! Not that I am counting or anything, but this week was never ending. In fact, right now it seems painful to recall for you. Plus, I was up during the night with a premature birth, so my head is a little fuzzy.

I had a date last night. Ha hah! Betcha didn't see that one coming! It lasted one hour and ten minutes, and I ate fried manioc and roasted groundnuts at Mario's and I was so thirsty I thought I would die, but was afraid to drink the water he put out. It was probably fine, but I didn't want to take any chances two days before my vacation, especially if I plan to hitchhike.

Mario's been gone for six weeks with the Unimog, moving drilling equipment around near Dubie and Kilwa. The drilling team is coming here now; there's a plan to put in four deep wells closer to the river and see if we can find some water without uranium in it. Boris, a guy from France, a bit strange, arrived Friday by plane to lead the drilling. Late that afternoon Mario rode in like a hero with this huge rig in the back of the truck. It's adorable to watch them return here. The other national staff come running out of every corner, and there's hugging, hand shaking, head butting, and general whooping that goes on for a long time. I love watching it. I've gotta say, I missed having Mario here. He's such a character, and I was rather enjoying his attention. Cindy worked with him in Burundi, and when they closed that project last October, he was offered a position here. I was telling Cindy about the little marriage proposal, and she said, "Oh, yeah, he's quite the ladies' man. There was a French nurse he was after in Burundi." Her comment was a bit of a dis, but not malicious. Mario's got four wives, and I know his attention is not all that flattering. I was not under the impression that he thinks he finally met his soul mate.

I was watching the homecoming, wishing I had my camera in my hand so I could video it, and Mario turned and saw me, spread his arms out wide, walked toward me with his hands over his heart, saying "Ah, Mama Linda," and gave me a hug, which I realized was the first hug I've had since Bridgitte left in February. I miss hugging. It was a revelation. The Europeans don't hug. It must be an American thing. They do this little triple kiss-the-air-next-to-the-cheek thing, which isn't as satisfying as a hug. And since the men only shave once a week, it's a little painful too.

Mario is leaving on his four-week vacation tomorrow. We will be on the same plane. He left this morning for Dubie again to leave the Unimog there, and when the plane stops in Dubie, we'll pick him up. When he found out I was leaving on the same day, he asked where I was going for my holiday, and I told him Malawi. Oh! He could change his plans and go to Malawi instead of Burundi! We could have a holiday together!

I said, "Mario. Your wives are waiting for you in Burundi. You can't go with me." He said this was no problem. He was just there a year ago. It wasn't essential that he go back to Burundi. I laughed as if the idea of traveling together was just a funny joke (which it is).

I was bopping around yesterday morning, near giddy, packing and organizing my stuff. It was a nice, quiet Saturday morning, and I had slept well the night before, so I had all this energy to prepare for the trip. That usually never happens. I usually work until the last second, throw a bunch of things into my pack, and just figure I'll do without whatever I forgot, or buy new stuff when I get where I'm going. Yesterday I had four whole hours, and even copied all those numbers I have on scraps of paper into my address book to tidy that up. Then I made plans to walk to the river with Loenis to check out the new sites for the wells. I was going to go for a run, then go over to visit Mario, since he keeps asking me to come over and I keep making excuses not to go. I decided since I wasn't letting him come on vacation with me the least I could do was go chat for an hour. His invitation was actually to come spend the night, to which I responded with a belly laugh, as if he meant it as a joke (which he didn't). I said I'd come at six p.m. and would have the guard walk me over because of security rules. Spend the night. Good lord.

The walk and the run never happened, because just as I was settled in the hammock to take a nap, I had to go over to the hospital for a labor with another five hours of pushing, and we finally ended up in the operating room. I was near tears thinking over and over, *I don't want to do this anymore.* I got back to the base at six, showered, and left for Mario's amid jeering from the entire team, who told me I had to be back by midnight. They were in the process of drinking as much of the beer that arrived this week as possible. It was irritating, as I knew there wouldn't be any at Mario's, and he's Muslim, so I couldn't bring any. Because I am leaving tomorrow, I was merely irritated. If I weren't leaving tomorrow, I would have been infuriated. It's not like more beer is coming this week. But I don't care because I won't be here.

Papa Abel walked me over there (it's like fifty yards away) and Mario was out in the road waiting for me, worried that I wasn't coming. I was late, but he knew I was working. There were big formal introductions; the people living there with him were sitting around a charcoal fire and they all got up to greet me. They were an assortment of relatives and I don't know who else— no wives, so he claims. Then he ushered me into one of the rooms of his house, which is quite a nice house for these parts. It's made of mud bricks, but the walls are a decent height and the thatched roof is quite high. It's possible to stand up in there comfortably. I didn't have to crouch to get in the doorway. This is remarkable. When I visit Gerardine, I have to crouch to even sit outside next to the door. And I'm short. Anyway, there were two woven chairs in there, and a small table. One of the girls brought in a plate of manioc and one of groundnuts, and a pitcher of water and one cup. Then a young boy brought in a little battery-operated light, like a small reading light you'd use in bed so as not to wake your partner. It was pitch-dark in there, so this lit up about four square inches of the table. Then as the kid was leaving, Mario told him to close the curtain, which he has hanging as an outside door. That was a little awkward, but it was just a curtain, and there had to be fifteen people sitting outside. I shrugged. We chatted pleasantly; I told him I'd been hearing from our new logistician who comes next week, and she seems really nice. He perked up at this news, because the logistician is in charge of the drivers and can make their lives miserable. He was interested that it was a woman, wanted to know which country. I told him she was German, and he did this "Ohhhh, geeze, just my luck" type of response, which made me laugh. I asked him what was the matter with Germans? He said in his experience they weren't very nice. Other national staff would never say something like that. I don't know if it's because he's from a different tribe, or just because he's older, but he is so much more outspoken than any of the others. They might think that, but they'd never say it. I told him she seems really nice by e-mail, and in my experience, Germans are organized and efficient and that's what we need here. Plus they built the truck he drives, and doesn't he think they did a good job with that? "Yes, yes, yes," he said, "but it's different to work for them."

After some chit-chat about the well drilling, Mario got right to the point. He thinks a marriage between us would be perfect. Doesn't understand why I am so reluctant to agree to this. I seem quite comfortable here in Shamwana, my French is better, his heart is full of love for me, what's the problem? "Well, just for starters," I said (actually, I think I said, "Well, first." My French isn't *that* good.), "you have four other wives! You have no idea how this doesn't work for me. My culture is very different. I see men and women as equal, and African men see women as beneath them. I don't like that." Then he made a feeble attempt at denying this fact, as if I fell off the turnip truck yesterday. Then he said that he only has one wife! *Bien sur! Oui Oui!* Yes, he's been married four times, but the first wife died in an accident, the second died in childbirth, the third died of diabetes, and now he has the fourth but that's all! He thinks I would be a good friend with her! This résumé could have been scary for a potential bride, but I decided not to point that out. It was one of those moments when I was outside myself watching the scene. I was thinking, "Wow, this is me. I am sitting in a mud house, in the deepest heart of Africa, in a village that hardly any westerners are ever going to see, eating manioc root, explaining in French why I cannot accept the marriage proposal of a Burundian tribal chief truck driver, and I feel totally comfortable! This is crazy!" I was so thirsty I wanted to leave, so told him I would think about his proposal while I was traveling ALONE in Malawi, and we'd talk again when I get back. I brought up my children and mother waiting for me again, but he seemed to have already thought of a response to that. He said rather curtly, "Your children are grown, and you have other family to take care of your mother." Wooo. He's getting bold.

I was supposed to call the guard on the handset to come and get me, but Mario offered to walk me back, and I accepted. I feel like such an idiot calling the guard to walk me home past little kids playing in the road. I figured Anders was well on his way to being smashed when I left; he was not going to notice. I got back and sucked down two beers while there were still some left. The only one coherent enough to talk when I got back was James, who wanted to watch season one of "Grey's Anatomy," so after the national staff were finished watching their movie, we watched two episodes which made me oddly miss our screwed-up health care system at home. Not that the show was in any way realistic, but I kept looking at the clean sheets and sterile operating room, and got all nostalgic. Then an hour after I went to bed, Papa Abel came to get me, and I had to go over for a woman who was bleeding heavily, and delivered a little premature boy, who only lived for a few minutes. The mother was working in the fields that afternoon when she started bleeding. Turns out she had raging malaria. There was no bicycle, so she had walked five kilometers, bleeding, to get here.

Twenty-six more hours.

I had a whole bunch of stories to tell you this week, but I'm running out of steam. Monday I did an overnight at Kampangwe, where we watched, in the dark, a huge bush fire work it's way toward us. I was sure we'd be cooked in our cots, but no one seemed the least concerned about it. It was blowing a gale, and everything is dry as a bone, so I could not see how it could possibly put itself out, but sure enough, it did. The rest of the night I was kept awake by the wind lifting the tin roof and slamming it back down on the health center where we were sleeping. Then at two a.m. a woman came in in labor, so I got up with the *accoucheuse* for that delivery, and the baby howled the rest of the night, so I didn't sleep at all. Plus I was cold, and I was worried that the baby was, too. The village there is high in the hills, and it has suddenly turned cool. Just like the rains come all of a sudden, the cool nights did the same. Even back in Shamwana we need a fleece at night.

Then we had Ursula here for the week. Ugh. It is so much extra work. It was like having the state come for inspection. Thank God the beer arrived. I had to sit for hours and get coached on the new data tool, which I had apparently been doing wrong. We all had been doing it wrong. It's so confusing. So what I want to know is, who is doing it right? I got grilled on how I was obtaining the vaccines from the Ministry of Health, which I must admit, has been a bit fly-by-night, but it's worked, and I've always managed to get them. When someone is going by bicycle to Kiambi, I send a message, and then somehow they either come here or we go to Mpiana to pick them up. I would like to go all the way to Kiambi to get them (after all, we are the ones with the vehicles, not them), but every time I suggest that, the response I get is, "What will they do when we're not here? They have to participate in this as well." Which, as I pointed out finally, is bullshit. In my escalating voice I asked, "How are they going to do anything when we're not here? You think they are going to have the means to do surgery? Two hours after we leave there isn't going to be a single Tylenol left in that hospital. Or a bed. Or a mattress. Or a tent! They don't have transportation and we do, so why don't we just go get the frigging vaccines?" And then my outburst made everyone awkward and no one had anything to say. God, I hate this power-trip bullshit.

Thirteen hours to go.

…Got called away. Two more babies. Two more women who wouldn't push. Fully dilated since eight this morning, they called me at two this afternoon, and the babies were out by six thirty. This is obstetrical hell.

I've got to go. Fabien and Loenis want haircuts before I leave.

It'll be the 13th of July before I write again, but it'll be a long one.

Love to all,
Linda

CHAPTER 12 ~ MALAWI

July 13, 2008
Sunday morning, Shamwana

Hi Everyone,

Ever have a vacation so good that you are actually happy to get back to work? Feel like it was such a gift that you can do anything afterward, it was just that good? Or maybe it's that now I can write about it that is making me so happy. Or maybe it was the contrast between life there and life here. Not sure, but I'm back and happy and am trying to figure out where to start.

I left here feeling like I really didn't care if I came back or not. The cigarette smoke and the hopeless feeling I had about the future for this place made me think I might just go AWOL. Cindy, even though she'd been here almost six weeks and was ready for her first R&R, was still stuck to me like glue and that got worse during the twenty-four hours before I left. She was doing what I did with Nina, having me translate everything, and wouldn't go anywhere without me. At first I was flattered, and so proud that I was even capable of doing it, but being tired and burned out, it was starting to bug me. And it was six weeks! Her French is very bad, so very bad. I don't know how she got by in Burundi. She says she didn't need it that much, she mostly worked in the office, but that's not the case here. None of the national staff speak English except for Oscar, the radio operator. You can't function if you don't speak French. But she was letting me do it for her, and I was getting very full of myself doing it for her, so she had a panicky meltdown when I was leaving. I told her I felt the same way when Nina left, and there is no way to move forward but be on your own. She was literally hanging on my arm when I was getting in the vehicle to go, like my kids used to when I left for work when they were three years old. I gave her a hug, said "*Bonne chance!*" (Good luck!) and left. I never once thought about her again.

I was dancing a jig getting on that plane. Since I didn't have any set plans, I didn't care what got delayed when or where; it was just so nice to not be working. All the little scraps of paper with lists of things to buy for people I had tucked in one spot, and planned to give them all to Justin, the radio operator in Lubumbashi to deal with while I was gone. I decided not to spend any of my time running around for other people. Selfish of me, but I was over an edge. I was in a say-yes-to-anything mode, as long as it was recreational. As I was getting on the plane, Lucile got off, having spent the weekend in Dubie giving a course to the mental health team there. She said, "Wait until you see Mario. He's all dressed in white, pacing around waiting for you."

I boarded, beaming. The plane left Shamwana and went to Dubie, where we picked up a few more people including Mario, then went to Kilwa where everyone except Mario and me debarked. It was like our own private little flight from there to Lubumbashi. He pleaded his case again, though it was very loud on the plane and difficult to talk.

He said, "If I can't go to Malawi with you, you can come to Burundi with me!"

I said, "Oh I'm sure your wife would be really happy if you brought me home after you've been away a year. That'll be fun." I shook my head *no*. (Though I must say, I have always wanted to go to Burundi, and it might have made for a very interesting story. Maybe another time.)

We usually get to Lubumbashi and go to the office for a while, but this time the driver drove directly to *Maison* 2 saying that's where the expats were having lunch. We were suddenly at the house and our discussion about a vacation together ended abruptly. I jumped out and yelled, "*Bon Congé!*" (Have a good vacation!). When I saw the desperate, disappointed look on Mario's face I felt awful for a moment, but then decided not to think about that again.

Thomas is the one in charge of IT and when he was visiting Shamwana to set up the new satellite system, I told him how I didn't like going to Lubumbashi because I don't know anyone there, and it's boring. He promised the next time I was in Lubumbashi he would take me out to a local place where we could dance, and he made good on the promise the night before I left. He told me to meet him at five thirty at a local restaurant. It seemed odd that he didn't want to have the driver take us together. Wanting to meet there seemed a bit cryptic. I know there is a policy against expat staff dating national staff, but I didn't think there was a problem with socializing. He acted like this was a secret rendezvous. I didn't understand why until later when I was appalled to learn of the rule that national staff isn't allowed in our vehicles after five p.m. if it's for social purposes. The rationale is ostensibly that there was great potential for abuse, but it was incredibly embarrassing for me. I arrived at the restaurant before him and was getting uncomfortable sitting alone there. It was a relief when he arrived. We ordered drinks and spent an hour having lively conversation with many people stopping to talk to Thomas. His father was some big guy in the government. He had a decent education, speaks four or five languages, and his English is very good. He's one of twelve children–all still alive. Father is still alive. Mother died of cancer a few years ago. Eight of the twelve kids live in Canada. His oldest brother had been a political refugee, then other kids followed. They all work in IT. He's married, with three little girls. His wife wants to start a small grocery store near their house. He's setting that up—took some calls on his cell phone from the guy painting the sign for the place. He told me he called his wife to let her know he'd be late, but didn't say he was out with me. "No need to cause problems," he said. When we were ready to leave there, I had to call for a car to come get me, because I was not allowed to walk the two blocks (well, there is nothing like *a block* in Lubumbashi; it was about a hundred meters) to the next place we were going, even with an escort. He wouldn't get in when I slid into the middle of the front seat. Shook his head *no* then closed the door. He had to walk behind the vehicle. I got driven the hundred meters, then sat in the car waiting for him to get there, and felt like the biggest fool. I spent the next half hour apologizing, but it was putting a damper on the evening and, as he said, the rules are the rules, so I dropped it. This local place was small, had no sign, and was behind a cement wall with old razor wire along the top. It seemed like a private club. I don't even know if the place had a name. It was a little enclosed courtyard with white plastic tables and chairs. The moon was nearly full, the temperature was pleasant, and we drank more beer and kept up the talk. I had had enough to drink, and when I didn't want anymore, he said, "Let's dance one dance before we go." We danced to some music coming from a boom box and in my tipsy brain I was thinking "This is special. Appreciate this." We didn't talk after that. We went outside, called a car, I got in, and he took a taxi home.

Next day, freedom. I took all the money in American dollars out of my per diem account, which ended up being $800. Not too bad! One of the perks of having nothing to buy in Shamwana was my per diem accumulated and I could use it for the trip. That money had to last until I found the guy I was meeting in Malawi who had my bank

card, which would be eleven days later, but I figured I could get by on
$70 a day. By a huge stroke of luck a friend in California had a friend
going to Malawi the same time as me. I had the bank send my new
card to him. Pretty good! (As long as I could find him.)

I took the forty-five-minute flight to Lusaka, and discovered I had
to pay $135 dollars for a visa!

I said, "But I'm only staying here one day!"

Didn't matter, the visa is good for three years and I had no choice
but to pay it. I started trying to redo the math in my head of how
much per day that leaves me, and someone told me the cab ride from
the airport was going to be thirty dollars. That was really cutting into
my cash, and I hadn't even started yet. I turned to the two men behind
me and asked if they knew of a bus that went from the airport. They
said it would be no problem to drive me into town, and I thought,
"Ahhh, perfect, my first ride." OK, so they were two men speaking
Arabic, or what I thought was Arabic. It turned out to be Lebanese.
They seemed nice enough, and the thought of saving thirty dollars
was overriding any anxiety I might have fostered about getting into a
vehicle with two strange men from the Middle East. I was chuckling
to myself about my luck. I waltzed out of the incredibly clean airport
with two very attractive guys. An expensive car with tinted windows
pulled up, the driver quickly opened the doors for us, we hopped in,
and went off in utter comfort! They were two businessmen but were a
little vague about what the business actually was. If they went
between Lubumbashi and Lusaka it's probably gems or minerals.

I asked, "Where on earth do you stay when you go to
Lubumbashi?" It's not like they have any nice hotel there.

Ahmed said, "I own a house there." He only goes for an overnight
once a month or so. They were Ahmed and Ahman. Both gave me
their cell phone numbers and told me to call them right away if I had
any problems while I was in Lusaka. I hopped out near the Chinese
embassy. From there I had directions to walk to Maureen's house.
Maureen is one of the women I climbed Kili with. I stood in front of
the Chinese embassy, wearing my L.L. Bean backpack, leaning
toward the car gushing thanks. Ahmed and Ahman stuck their heads
out and said, "Remember. You call us." They drove away and as I
watched the dark windows of the car slowly rise I thought, "This
vacation is off to a perfect start."

Lusaka reminds me of a city in the midwest United States. It's
sprawling, there isn't a real downtown, and there are lots of new

shopping centers already, with more being built. It's clean, though I am comparing it with Lubumbashi, and that doesn't take much. I found Maureen's place well before dark, and it was so good to see her again. She lives in an adorable little guesthouse behind a bigger house in a residential neighborhood. The gardens were gorgeous, and the guesthouse looked like something out of Beatrix Potter. We visited for a bit, then went out and had a great meal at an Indian restaurant a short walk from her house. It was so nice to be able to go out and walk. I felt like a dog being let off her leash. The next day she had taken off from work, so we went running together (I was very relieved to see I could keep up since she's half my age), had breakfast, and then walked all over the city. It was just a nice, relaxing day getting a feel for the surroundings and sharing our experiences. She's going into her extension year as a Peace Corps volunteer, and as with all PCVs, there's just no end to talking about our experiences. We bought food and a bottle of wine and went back to the cottage and made dinner. I was leaving the next day early to catch a bus to Chipata on the boarder of Malawi, so we just had a mellow evening. It was really nice.

The "express" buses supposedly leave at six a.m. so I had a taxi pick me up at five to be able to get there and get a seat. Getting to the bus station was no problem, but God, trying to get from the taxi to the bus, a distance of ten feet, was a huge problem. Before I even got out of the car, it was swarmed with guys trying to get me to buy a ticket for the bus they worked for. There are several competing bus companies, and even though Maureen had warned me about it, it was very disturbing and disorienting. They were all yelling lies like, "No, no, that bus is already full!" "No, no they won't take you to Chipata!" "That bus is no good! Use this one!" They were SWARMING, and it was hard to even take one step. I was trying to plow through them to get the bus that Maureen said was the best one, but in the dark it was hard to figure out. At one point I got back in the taxi just to get my bearings. They easily could have stolen everything I had; there had to be at least twenty of them. I finally got out and plowed my way through the crowd to one of the good buses. I got on and was relieved to see that there were plenty of seats. Silly me. That's not something to be relieved about. The bus would not leave until it was full. The correct way to take the bus, I learned, is to look and see which is the most full and get on that one. This was what the hawkers were trying to prevent me from doing. My six a.m. bus left at 10:45 a.m. It took that long to fill up. I was getting so frustrated trying to figure out what the problem was. And I was afraid to get off the bus to pee because no one would say when it was leaving, so it was a very uncomfortable first half of the ride. On the express buses everyone has a seat, but they are narrow seats and we were crammed in like sardines. And there is no limit to the stuff you can bring on. It's just unbelievable, the amount of cargo people cram on the bus. It finally filled up and we left. By then I was starving and had to pee really badly and there was a Christian fundamentalist walking up and down the aisle preaching at the top of his lungs, repeating the same thing over and over and telling us to bow our heads in prayer. The difference between the $30 bus ride and the $600 flight was starting to feel like less of a bargain. That guy finally got off the bus when we were just outside the city, but then they turned on the video player and it was loud rap Christian music and prayer for the first five hours and then a video of wrestling for the second five hours. I was reading *The Dharma Bums* about a Buddhist experience hitchhiking around the country in the sixties, and I felt like this was the balance to my cushy ride two days before. I felt like my trip would bounce back and forth between these two extremes and I was in the mood to just go with it. That wrestling was getting to me, though.

I had thought that we'd make the 700-kilometer trip in about eight hours, and if we left at six, I would have been there with plenty of daylight to find a place to stay. Chipata is still twenty-five kilometers from the border of Malawi, but the bus doesn't go all the way to the border. You have to take a cab. There is a big Catholic mission near Chipata, and my plan was to stop there and see if anyone knew where Richard and Fiacra were. They are two priests who I know who I thought were still in Malawi; I wanted to look them up. They had both lived in Karonga when we were there, and we were good friends at the time. Richard is the one who baptized Matt, and we took several little trips with him. Fiacra is an Irish priest, and I hadn't been in touch with him since I left there. I wasn't quite sure if he'd remember me, but I thought it would be fun to look him up. Well, it was getting later and later, and then the guy next to me told me that the mission, St. Francis, was way before Chipata, and if I got off there, there was no way to get to Chipata. It was already very dark before we passed St. Francis, so I had to scrap that plan. We didn't arrive in Chipata until nine p.m. Similar buzzards were outside the bus and I had no idea where there was a place to stay (Chipata is not a big city), but I was so relieved to get away from that horrid wrestling video that I rushed off the bus and then got very nervous about what to do. I didn't want to just start walking (we weren't in a very nice part of town), and I was famished and couldn't think straight. I was getting swarmed again and didn't like that, so I quickly turned to the guy who had been sitting next to me on the bus and asked him if he would accompany me while I found a place for the night. (Having just written that I could see how you might think that this guy would get the wrong idea, but believe me, the tone of my voice was not seductive.) He had already told me he was from Chipata, and he actually bowed his head and prayed when that Christian kook on the bus told us to, so he seemed safe enough.

I said, "Excuse me, I hate to bother you, but I'm really uncomfortable here, and I need a place to stay until the morning. I have no idea where to go; could you help me?"

He was very nice and said, "Follow me." We walked past loud local bars with drunken people pouring out into the street to a taxi, we got in together, and he told the taxi driver where to go. They dropped me at a little guesthouse just out of town a bit. I paid the taxi driver five dollars, which was probably ten times the going rate, but I didn't care. I was so relieved. Shelter. The place was simple, but nice enough. No hot water and a shared bathroom, but since I was the only one there, it didn't matter. I dropped my stuff and went into the kitchen and asked if there was some way to get some food. No problem! The cook in there told me he'd make me some supper while I showered. I didn't care one whit what it was, I was just so glad I could eat there. So I got cleaned up and went into the living room where the manager was watching some European football match and I chatted with him, ate my sausage and fries and coleslaw, and was quite content. He gave me some tips about getting across the border, told me how much was reasonable to pay for a taxi, etc. It was lovely, and at thirty dollars for supper, sleep, and breakfast, right in my budget.

⸎⸎⸎⸎❋⸎⸎⸎⸎

Je me réveille de bon matin. *(I wake early in the morning.)*
June 20, 2008–It's earlier than I thought. Had to wash with cold water and had to use my bottled water to brush my teeth, but didn't care. At least

there was water to flush with today. Slept like a rock—I was so tired. I am famished again, sipping my tea with white bread and margarine . . .

❈❈❈

The next morning I ate breakfast, packed up, and walked to town, which didn't seem nearly as dangerous in the daylight. I had to change some money into Zambian *kwacha* and find a taxi, but both those things found me first. A swarm of taxi drivers surrounded me, and their group included street-urchins with wads of Zambian and Malawian cash. I started trying to figure out the exchange with them, but there were too many of them hounding me, so I said screw it and went to the bank. A taxi driver had two people in the cab waiting to go to the border, and I thought it would be great to share the cab, five dollars instead of fifteen, so I told him to wait for me while I went to change some money. Brand-spanking-new bank, just opened the week before. Beautiful, sparkling new. I went in and went to the teller where it says "Currency Exchange" and told him I wanted to change some dollars.

He said, "Ah, sorry sister, I don't have today's exchange rate yet. Maybe you could come back in one or two hours, sure, sure."

I said, "One or two hours? I've got a taxi waiting for me now! Can't you use yesterday's exchange rate?"

He said, "No, sorry, that's not possible. Come back in one or two hours."

I said, "You've got a computer right in front of you; isn't the exchange rate on there?" No, apparently it wasn't. I started to remember all the frustrations of living and traveling on this continent. I am so insulated from all this working for MSF. When I want my money, I walk in the office and tell Dennis to give it to me, and he walks over to the safe, opens it, and hands me money. Come back in one or two hours? I said, forget it and went back to the kids on the street but then they knew they had me and were jerking around the exchange.

I said, "Forget this." and I handed the driver five dollars in American money and said, "Here, you can come back and exchange it yourself. Let's go."

It's twenty-five kilometers to the boarder. The cab was a little car that seats four. There was a nun in the front seat, and a young man in the back. I got in the back with my pack because I didn't want to put it in the trunk. I figured it would be a half-hour at the most and I didn't mind being a little crowded with the pack for a short time. We pulled out and drove about fifty feet and stopped and three more people got in the car. The poor nun was sitting on the stick shift. We now had four in the back, which was already crowded with two of us, and my pack was like another person. Then we stopped thirty feet later and another guy got in the back. At five dollars each, this guy was making a decent wage here. I couldn't believe the trunk wasn't scraping the ground. Fortunately all the people were not going all the way, but even when two people got out, it was still ridiculous. He drove too fast, but there weren't any other cars on the road, so I just decided not to think about the safety aspect of this leg of the journey. In a way, it was like driving with the airbag already inflated.

At the border everyone had to get out and walk across, and then find a Malawian cab on the other side. That cab does the same thing, takes you twenty kilometers to Mchinje, the nearest village, then you can get a bus to go the 100 kilometers to Lilongwe. On the Malawi side of the border I saw a group of nuns from Canada (I could tell by their accents), and I asked them if they were going to Lilongwe. Well, yes they were, and if I was alone, sure they had room for me! Perfect. Not only was it a ride all the way to Lilongwe, they also knew all the people I was looking for and where they were living! They filled me in on all the ones who had died or retired. It was fabulous! I learned that Richard was in Mzuzu and Fiacra was in Chilumba. They told me that Michel Van deWynckele had died, and I told them I knew that; I had seen him in France just three months before he died. It was so pleasant to be with them. They were returning to Lilongwe after a meeting at the mission in Zambia. They told me the sisters who were in Mzuzu who took care of me when I was pregnant and stranded there twenty-eight years ago were no longer there. Just on and on. It was great. They had all been in Malawi since the sixties, and were teachers, not medical people, so I hadn't met them when I was there, but we knew many of the same people.

Sister Noella, who was sitting next to me, asked softly, "So, your husband is gone?" with a little lilt to the "gone" in a way that implied that he had died. And then I was faced with a small emotional crisis that I hadn't really expected. I was going to have to explain all over again, and start pulling that scab off the wound. But the way she said it made me think to myself, "I could lie! I could just say he died! Because, in a way, he sort-of did. Well, the man I married did anyway. And they'll never know the truth." In the second that this all went through my head, out of my mouth came, "Yes, he's gone." With the same "gone" that she used. There, I thought. That wasn't really a lie, though I know how it sounded when I said it.

And she said, "Cancer?" Now thinking I was into a lie, I just tapped the side of my head, which, again, wasn't technically a lie, and she said very sympathetically, "Oh, brain tumor?" and I realized I couldn't keep this up with this sweet sympathetic old woman.

I said, "No. I wish that's what it was, but he just went crazy and left six years ago after twenty-five years together."

She chuckled and shook her head and patted my leg, and said, "Yes, the same thing happened to my niece. I'm so sorry. I don't know what happens to these guys." And I sat there thinking, "How can you not love nuns? How have they gotten the reputation of all being mean, ruler-slapping ogres? Every one of them that I've known—and that is a considerable number—have been warm, helpful, sympathetic, strong, spiritual women." I was happy to be in their presence. I felt cared for. They dropped me off in front of the Lilongwe hotel (which I barely recognized) with information about cheap hotels, best deals on foreign exchange, e-mail addresses to stay in touch, and good wishes for a safe journey. The bus-ride balances out.

Lilongwe. Wow. It's taken some steroids since I'd left in 1981. There are shopping centers and hotels and big grocery stores and banks all over the place. The Lilongwe hotel—where we first stayed when we arrived in Malawi, all twelve of us new volunteers, getting to know each other and our new surroundings, where I stayed for two weeks waiting to go into labor, where I knew every waiter and cleaning person—has gone corporate! Big circular drive with a big awning, long corridor down to the reception desk, meeting rooms, little side restaurants, it was all disorienting and I didn't like it. It was so impersonal. Plus it was expensive. I decided to walk around and find the new Peace Corps office and look into one of the other hotels that the nuns had recommended.

The Peace Corps office used to be just a block away from the hotel, with not too much in between. Now there are restaurants and stores and banks all in that short distance. I wasn't sure if I'd recognize it, but there it was, the Bata shoe store! Just the same, where it always was. Where the office used to be, just above the store, is now a communications office, and I didn't go up there, but it brought back lots of good memories. I felt all warm and fuzzy just seeing it. Across the street is a huge supermarket with a big parking lot (there are a zillion cars in the city now) and a huge line of mini buses, all a confusing mess. I asked a few people where the Peace Corps office was, and finally found it a five-minute disorienting walk away. It's huge! It's behind a big wrought iron fence with guards sitting out in a little gatehouse. I went up to them and asked if I could go in and visit, and they wanted to know if I had an appointment with someone in there, and wanted to know who I was. I started gushing with excitement, "I used to be a volunteer here, many years ago! The office used to be over the Bata shoe store! It was tiny! I lived in Karonga! Now I live in DRC and I wanted to come back and visit here!" (Like they give a shit about any of this, but I couldn't stop myself.) It all seemed to satisfy them (or maybe just to shut me up), and they let me in. Nice office, friendly smiling people with American accents. I went up to the desk and did a replay of what I did with the guards, and felt welcome. A tall, grey-haired guy (I forgot his name two seconds after I heard it) was walking by, and the secretary introduced me to him. He turned out to be the country director, and I did another rendition of my story, and we talked for a long time. He was very interested in what it was like back then (we were twelve volunteers, now there are 150), what life was like in DRC, and what it was like working for MSF. He told me about the Crisis Corps program they have now with Peace Corps (very interesting), and about what big changes have occurred in the twenty-seven years since I left. It was a wonderful visit. He introduced me to a few volunteers who happened to be in the office. In the major cities they now have a Peace Corps house where volunteers can stay when they are passing through and need a place to stay. We were always freeloading off the other volunteers in our day. I felt so happy. I was just so glad to be there and to have been part of this organization. It made me want to sign up again on the spot. The volunteers I met were all interested to hear what it was like years ago, eager to share tips about where to stay, and were full of good wishes. They asked me what my plans were, and I said, "I don't really have any. I want to go north first having found out that an old friend is in Mzuzu, so I'll head there tomorrow and then figure it out." The director laughed and said, "Yup, typical Peace Corps volunteer. Never changes."

I found a cheap room in a small hotel (twenty-five dollars with breakfast), dropped my big sack, and then went to walk around the old city. The route to Old Town started coming back to me, though there are so many more new buildings. I walked along and looked for things I recognized. I saw an old building tucked in between a bunch of new ones, and thought, "That looks familiar; it looks like Jeff's old office." Then I saw the sign that said, Department of Agriculture, and said, "It *is* Jeff's old office!" It felt good to recognize old landmarks.

I thought the development would bother me, but it didn't really. Coming from DRC obviously made me look at things differently, but I wasn't expecting a walk down memory lane that hadn't changed. I was happy to see development, and didn't find it too obnoxious. The traffic was a bit of a problem, and EVERYONE is talking on a cell phone, but in general I was happy to see progress. Old Town has changed a lot. The shops were still there, but Indians who had been forced from the rural areas into the cities no longer run them. The restaurants are mostly gone, and the market is huge. There is an enormous mosque right in the center of Old Town, which looked a little incongruous, but it was pretty. There is a huge and chaotic bus station that is right across from the old government rest house. The rest house is exactly the same, except now it's called "Crystal Lodge Luxury Accommodation." I cracked up! It was EXACTLY the same building in exactly the same condition, and it was pretty grubby thirty years ago, so I thought "Luxury" was a bit of a stretch. There are still poor people washing their clothes in the river; still beggars on the street. There is a ton of trash around. That was depressing. Everything is put in plastic bags now, and they are everywhere on the streets and along the river. That was very depressing. In our day, if there ever was a plastic bag around, kids grabbed it to make into a ball. Nothing was ever wasted. I just meandered around and didn't feel the need to do anything else. I ate in a local restaurant in Old Town, went to check out the buses to Mzuzu and bought two Greens (Malawian beer) and went back to the hotel when it got dark.

The next day I packed up, ate a huge English breakfast and walked back to the bus station to catch a bus to Mzuzu. Same deal, it won't leave until it's full, but this time I was smarter, and got on one with only two empty seats. I sat, and a few minutes later someone else got on, and we were off. It took a half-hour to get out of Old Town the traffic was so bad. Then when we got just outside Old Town where things start to sprawl, the bus pulled into a gas station, and everyone had to get off while they filled the tank. I couldn't believe it! It is so hard to pack everyone and everything on these buses; it was such a pain for everyone to get off. But with gas at eleven a gallon— yes, that would be eleven dollars a gallon—I understood that they don't want to fill it up until the last second. My stomach was full, I had my book, and no one was expecting me at any time, so it didn't matter. Once we were on our way and out of the city, things looked remarkably the same as they were thirty years ago. I was chatting with people on the bus, everyone a little curious about a *mzungu* taking local transportation. I gushed to everyone, "I used to live in Karonga! Many years ago! I came back to visit! My baby was born in Lilongwe!" I was saying all these things like they somehow legitimized my being there. I couldn't stop myself. I didn't want to seem like JUST a tourist. I somehow felt like I was special. Some Chichewa words started coming back to me, and everyone on the bus loved that. I was just having a ball. It used to take days to get from Lilongwe to Mzuzu. It's five hours on the bus now. Seemed like a breeze. As we climbed higher with the elevation I started realizing that I had never traveled between Kasungu and Mzuzu by road. We always flew to Karonga, because the road wasn't completed then. The scenery is spectacular! Climbing up the plateau into the mountains, I found myself wondering if I appreciated back then how beautiful the country is. I'm anxious to reread my letters home to see what I found important to write about back then. It was just so pretty.

We pulled into Mzuzu around four p.m. and I did not even recognize that city. There used to be just one place to stay in Mzuzu, and that was the government rest house. Now there are at least five hotels and one big conference center, and they seemed to have moved the entire city. I couldn't get my bearings or figure out where the Catholic mission was. I know I'd stayed there plenty of times; I figured it'd come back to me, but I was completely lost. The bus station is huge and the streets crowded (the population of the country has grown from five million when we were there to thirteen million now). I had been getting so excited as we approached the city, thinking of how surprised Richard was going to be to see me. We hadn't communicated for years. Somewhere along the line we lost touch, and I only heard about his whereabouts through Michel, whom I did stay in touch with and visited every year in France.

I walked into the town, stopped on a corner, and asked where the Catholic church was, and a man told me it was five kilometers out of town, up the hill. OK, so that's only three miles, I figured I'd get there before dark, but then I started thinking, hmm, just what everyone loves, an uninvited, unexpected guest showing up at dinnertime. I was also expecting to stay there for the night, and realized the timing wasn't great. A street kid standing there asked who I was looking for and I told him, "Father Dechénes," and he said, "Oh, I know him well. He is very good to me. Come, I'll show you." So this kid named Peter walked with me all the way to the Father's house, chatting away the whole time. His parents had died when he was little; he lives with different relatives, etc. I told him how I knew Richard.

He said, "I wonder if you will recognize him. He's very fat now. He will be so happy to see you."

I said, "I know, I can't wait to see his face when he sees me." I was thinking I don't look THAT much different. I look older, sure, but about the same size and everything. So we trudged along, and it was getting to be dusk, and I was looking around at the setting sun, and just kept repeating, "It is so gorgeous here."

When we arrived at the driveway to the house Peter said, "Here it is, but first I was wondering if I could show you some of the things I sell." I figured this was coming. He sells stuff out of his knapsack, just like all the other street kids. They are not supposed to be doing that, but I wanted to give him something for walking me all the way there. He was asking too much money, though, and I was still worried about having enough cash, and as I was making this feeble excuse about not having enough money, which sounded ridiculous compared to his circumstances, a pickup truck approached, and he said, "Here comes Dechénes now!" So as the truck slowed down, I stood up and walked toward the driver's window, and thought, "Yes! He looks just the same!"

I said, "Richard! Hi! It's Linda, remember me?"

He looked at me like I was out of my mind, shook his head no, and said gruffly to Peter, "Hey, what are you doing here?"

I said, "Richard! Remember? I lived in Karonga when you were there." He looked at me blankly, and shook his head no again. I had a George Bailey moment and then started a desperate routine, saying, "Richard! You must remember me, you took us to the Misuku hills!" Shook his head no again. "I had a baby!" No, shook his head no again, doesn't ring a bell. "You baptized him! We had a big party at your house!"

He shook his head no again, and said, "Are you coming here?" pointing to the house.

I said, "Well, yes, I was."

He said, "OK, come and we'll talk." And he drove up the driveway.

I turned then to Peter who had his little paintings spread all over the ground, and I thought he must think I am a big fat liar! I said, "I don't have time to look at these now. Here." And I handed him 500 kwacha (about $3.50).

He said, "No, I don't want to take your money. You never asked me to come with you." Which I thought was rather kind.

I said, "Just take this. When I come back through maybe I'll buy something. I have to go talk to Richard; it's an emergency. He doesn't remember me." And I grabbed my stuff and started running up the driveway.

Now, I had prepared myself for him being ill, being dead, being lost, but never had it crossed my mind that he wouldn't remember me. How presumptuous of me. I was only there for two years; he's been there for forty. Why should he remember me? What an idiot I had been. As I was walking up the driveway, I was thinking, great, now I'll have to find a place to stay and it's almost dark, and, and, and... And then he got out of the truck and turned to me and said, "LINDA!!!! Yes! Now I remember! The bees! You were the one with the bees!"

I jumped up and down, and said, "Yes! Yes! That was me!" He was referring to a time twenty-eight years ago when Joe and I were at the mission and Matt was only a few weeks old. We started getting swarmed by bees, and I was scared out of my mind that if the baby cried we would be attacked and killed. Richard took both of us by the hands and whispered, "Silence," and we slowly walked to the house where I fainted.

He said, "Oh my God! It's you! But, you were two, where is your husband?"

I said, "Long story."

He smiled and hugged me and said, "OK, we'll talk later, for now let's put your things in a room, you'll be staying here, yes?"

I said, "Well, I was hoping to, if you have room."

He said, "Of course, of course, come now, have a shower and then we'll have a drink and dinner and then we will talk." Ah, I felt like I'd gone home.

I settled into my room, took a warm shower (it's cold in Mzuzu; it's high up on a plateau) and went into the common room where I met the other guests who were staying there. We had some wine and caught up a bit and then had dinner together. Richard and I were reminiscing and telling one story after another, and it felt like no time had passed at all since I'd seen him. After dinner, we went into another room where we could talk privately, and he wanted to hear the whole marriage story, which I ended up sobbing through. I knew it was going to be a little hard to explain to him, someone who hadn't seen us since we left there, about all we'd been through and done together, and then how it all ended. It's hard to summarize in a short visit, and I got more upset than I thought I would. I felt like I was somehow disappointing him, though he was incredibly supportive and wonderful. I was revisited by that feeling of failure, which I hadn't been haunted with for a while. But then it was done, and I felt much better. It was all out on the table, where I like it.

Je suis content. *(I am content.)*

June 22, 2008 – Sunday morning—Mzuzu. I sit in a grotto with the Virgin Mary. She is standing in a tukul, built around a huge tree that was struck by lightning. She stands on a shelf in the V of the tree, looking like she's just being born. She makes me feel safe and content, always behind me with a word of encouragement. In a way I feel her with me when I'm watching the suffering of the women in Congo. It's the only way I can imagine that they can bear it. She's holding them in her arms, helping them. For some reason, they were chosen to have this trauma be their lives and she gets them through it. It's chilly this morning but I'm not cold. I sit and write and try to store this feeling of contentment.

The next day I went to two masses with Richard, one for kids and one high mass. They were nice, though nowhere near the extravaganzas that they are in DRC. When I was telling him about the masses I went to in Congo he said, very briskly, "It's a mass, not a concert. I don't like too much singing." I smiled. I spent the afternoon walking around Mzuzu, and passed another pleasant evening and night there, but was eager to keep going north the next day to Karonga.

The road passes Chilumba on the way to Karonga, and I planned to stop there to see if I could find Fiacra. The smaller buses are quite reliable as far as scheduling goes, but they look like death traps. I hadn't been in one, but hitching would have taken forever since there isn't a lot of traffic between Mzuzu and Karonga. Most people take these buses, which are Toyota minivans that seat eleven people. There were twenty-four passengers in mine. I thought, OK, I'll start out, and if I don't feel safe, I'll just get out. Not too far out of the bus station, a goat ran in front of the van, and the driver stopped short to avoid running him over. It seemed like a good enough test of the brakes for me, so decided to stick it out down the steep, winding road that goes down to the lakeshore. This is the part of the road that wasn't there before. It used to be the only way to get up or down was a dirt road similar to a mountain trail. (A group of us made that trip one Christmas on the back of a flat-bed truck with a motorcycle tied onto the back. When we got to the top the motorcycle was in pieces; that's how rough the ride was.) Now it is a beautiful paved road with winding hairpin turns that brings you from the pine forests of the plateau to the tropical heat of the lakeshore. It was spectacular. Groups of monkeys were playing on or near the road, around each corner was a gorgeous view of the lake, we were driving at a reasonable speed, and if I wasn't crammed in between six people with my pack on my lap I would have pulled out my camera and made a video of the ride. I was enjoying it. We reached the bottom where it's a clear flat road along the lake. We were heading for a police roadblock (these are set up at different places along the road) and, having too many people in the bus, we stopped about 200 meters before the barricade. The driver made four people get out, then paid four kids on bicycles to give them a ride to the other side of the barricade where we stopped so they could get back in the bus. It was hilarious. Not one of the inconvenienced passengers complained about this. I loved it. There is always a way to get around the rules. I could have used these guys as consultants during the measles epidemic.

I got off the bus at Chilumba where I was hoping to find Father Fiacra. I went into the beautiful new church that was there, made my way over to the house, and was completely prepared for him not to recognize me. It turns out he wasn't there. He was on home leave in

Ireland, and wouldn't be back until September. I asked the cook if there was anyone else I could talk to there, and he went to get the other priest, another Irish guy, who invited me in for a bit.

I was explaining who I was and how I knew Fiacra, and he said, "Ah, Fiacra tells this story of an American woman who was pregnant and Michel asked her if she was a virgin."

I jumped up and said, "Yes! That was me! I was very pregnant, I think it was around Easter time, and we were over at the Father's house and talking about birthdays and when I said my birthday was in September, Michel said, 'Oh, so you're a virgin?' and I know he meant to say "Virgo," but Fiacra thought it was the funniest thing he ever heard. Obviously, he's still telling the story." And then the afternoon turned into a wonderful visit of storytelling and philosophizing. We had tea and cheese sandwiches on the bougainvillea-covered porch looking out over the lake, and I thought life just doesn't get better than this.

He drove me to one of the clinics I used to visit on my motorcycle during my outreach days and after visiting the Catholic hospital he offered to drive me all the way to Karonga, another seventy kilometers. That was above and beyond the call of duty, but I accepted (my own seat—what a luxury). He said he wanted to see my reaction when I saw Karonga for the first time. As we drove along the lake we passed a village on the shore that looked exactly the same twenty-nine years ago. I made a comment about it, and he said in that beautiful Irish brogue I love so much, "Ah yes, if Adam and Eve came back today, they'd feel right at home." Driving into Karonga I was almost out of my seat. A rotary! They have a rotary in Karonga! I couldn't believe it! I kept saying, "Oh my God, is that . . . fill in the blank: the ball field, the agriculture office, the market?" He took me to Club Marina which is right on the lake, a very simple hotel with a restaurant and bar (VERY simple) and asked if I was all right there, and I thanked him a million times, and he was off. He said he felt better knowing I had a place to stay. This world is full of so many good, good people.

I was so happy. I dropped my stuff in my room, and then went to walk around. I wanted to see if my house was there, and if any of the nurses I knew were still around. It was a little disorienting, because the lake has receded so much. The water was right up to the road before, there was no beach at all. Now there is at least 100 meters of sand and marsh between the road and the water. It's beautiful. So beautiful. I walked over to where our house was, and found it. It is still there, though the bricks are painted white now. All the trees behind it are gone and the neighborhood has about eight satellite dishes, but it was otherwise remarkably the same. I walked toward the old hospital (they've built a new one out near the airport) and that was a depressing sight. My old office is there, but it's now the district health inspector's office. I stopped and talked with him for a while, and he told me that the old hospital is now an immigration office. It's a holding area for refugees, and it was disgusting. The structure is still recognizable, but the filth was overwhelming, and there were groups of men who looked desperate. They were from Somalia, Congo, and Zimbabwe. They were urinating and defecating right in front of me. That was a little upsetting. I didn't stay there too long. I walked on past Joe's old office, which looks like a private house now. The prison is still there next to the old hospital, and was by far cleaner and more welcoming than the hospital. The prisoners were all friendly and chatty, and they had a beautiful garden growing. I took pictures of some of them posing in front of one patch of vegetables, all smiles. I wanted to walk over to the Bongarette (the bottle store) where we used to go meet up with people in the afternoons. I was hoping that Mr. Mwenefumbo, who owned it, was still around. His wife was one of the nurses I worked with, and the woman who inspired me to become a midwife. As I headed over there I saw the path that cut across the field (which is not a field anymore but a neighborhood full of houses) and thought, that's the path I walked to go tell Gene that Mount St. Helen's had just erupted! The memories were tangible! I got to the bottle store, but it was deserted and obviously had been for many years. I asked a guy nearby if he knew if Mr. Mwenefumbo was still around, and he told me he was, that he now keeps his office at the Safari Lodge, which was a hotel I passed on the way into town. Karonga, little Karonga, has five hotels. But they are not big corporate hotels. They are small, locally-owned hotels, and it was good to see. I found his office, but he wasn't there. The secretary told me that his wife now owns a bakery, and gave me directions to get there, another half mile away. I quickly walked past several maize mills (no one was pounding maize anymore) and found the bakery. She wasn't there, but they said she'd be coming soon for closing, so I sat out front to wait.

A few minutes later I saw her coming. I ran to her, and said, "Mrs. Mwenefumbo! I don't know if you remember me, but I was a

Peace Corps volunteer here many years ago, and . . ."

Before I said any more she said, "Linda! Of course I remember you! I saw you sitting there and thought you looked familiar! You had the baby here!" and then she told me that her fifth child, Rueben, who was born just a couple of months after Matt, was killed in a car accident five years ago on his way home from engineering school. I have pictures of the two babies together. That news was tragic, but I was relieved to hear her other children are alive and doing very well. Two live in England, one lives in the States, and one still lives in Malawi. It was starting to get dark, and I had a long walk back to the hotel, so we made plans to meet the next day to talk and catch up.

I walked back toward the lake in the fading light, relishing the happiness of being there. I was thinking, "The only way this day could get any better would be if the man of my dreams were sitting at that bar when I arrive." I rounded the corner and headed to the outside tables facing the lake, ready for a Malawi gin and tonic, and . . . there . . . was Parker watching me. Oh, what great scene. Seeing this overweight, well-on-his-way-to-being-pickled guy wearing short-shorts with a gut so huge you couldn't even see the shorts, sitting in the corner watching, was just too funny, considering the George Clooney fantasy going through my head at the time. I just had to go over and talk to him. Plus I was bubbling over with excitement about being there, and needed to tell someone.

I asked if I could sit down, and he was all greetings and welcomes, and I ordered a gin and tonic. But oh no, they were out of tonic (it was so Africa) so I just said bring me a green, and Parker said he'd have another, too, which, judging from the number of bottle caps next to him, was about his seventh.

Parker is a white Zimbabwean, living in Karonga now, managing an Australian-owned coal mine, where they pay Malawians a dollar a day to do hard manual labor in the hot sun. Ooohh, I thought, this is my kinda guy. I decided not to ask him any more about himself, and then launched into MY story which, after downing the first green, I thought was much more interesting. So I started going on and on about living there years ago, and what I was doing now, and the greens kept coming, and then we got on to the trauma of turning fifty, and of being divorced (him twice), and when I asked him what happened, he said, "Well, I had an affair and she wouldn't forgive me."

I asked him if he had begged for forgiveness or just expected it?

And he said that, well, she forgave him the first time, but the second she wouldn't even consider it. I was well into my third beer at that point, so said something supportive like, "You lying, cheating piece of shit! Why on earth should she take you back? I'm sure she misses the fun of watching you drink like this every night." He laughed as if I were being charming.

※※※§◯◯§※※※

Je suis stupéfié. *(I am amazed.)*

June 24—Karonga—It's incredible, not so much that things are so good here, or so bad here. It's just incredible to be here. I'm sitting at a dirty breakfast table at club Marina, slightly hung over. The lake is in front of me, cold shower behind me, waiting for tea. I'm desperate for tea. Four beers last night with Parker, a fat Zimbabwean guy. I wanted to stop after three, but the Malawian guy behind us running for some position, MP, I think, bought us a round, so I had the fourth. Parker was well into his eighth or ninth when I left. I have this annoying cold, can't believe I caught a cold. Now I have a sinus/ hungover/forgot-to-eat-supper headache. The tea is helping, though it tastes like the inside of the thermos it's in. Oh well, it's liquid and it's hot. Unlike the shower.

The receptionist, dressed beautifully, is mopping the front entryway. Evangelist is on the television in the restaurant behind me. I'm eating outside; I couldn't stand listening to it. I scoffed down my omelet, sausage, fried potatoes, toast with margarine, and banana. The juice is undrinkable, some super-sweet flavored yellow colored drink. Awful. Second cup of tea isn't bad.

There's a monkey on the beach. I can see it from here.

※※※§◯◯§※※※

I saw Parker a few more times after that evening; he took me out to see the mine (which I had asked to see) and drove me out to see the border of Tanzania (which was a really pretty ride). My last evening there he was saying stuff like, "Yeah, I should start running again."

And "I'm not going to work at this job much longer." And, "I was thinking of buying a piece of property on the lake and building a little house, and I think you should just stay here and live with me." He wants me to go to his son's wedding with him in South Africa in September, because his wife is remarried and he doesn't want to have to go without a date. Tempting offer, but I just had to decline. Despite the differences between us, though, we did have some laughs, and I did have a couple of pleasant-enough evenings hanging out at the bar. It was more fun than sitting alone writing in my journal. He was a little like that guy Norm on *Cheers*. Same seat every night.

June 26, 2008 Thursday morning—

Je regarde le lever du soleil. *(I watch the sunrise.)*

Sunrise on the lake. I was locked into my room and took a while banging on the door for someone to come let me out. That was bloody weird and scary. It was for "security reasons" they told me. Apparently, me locking my door from the inside wasn't enough; they had to lock the outside door too. Jesus. Good thing there wasn't a fire. Parker is all over me. He's coming here for breakfast this morning. He was probably hoping I'd ask him to stay last night, but when I said goodnight and left for my room, he said he didn't want to say good-bye and never see me again, so he'd meet me for breakfast. It's rather ridiculous, but I've had an offer of moving to Karonga to be with him forever. He's planning on buying a piece of property on the lake and building a little house for us. If I ever get that desperate I will kill myself. I didn't sleep well. Drank too much, too noisy, didn't eat supper, I was starving during the night. Ate my four bananas and two tangerines and was able to get back to sleep, but I am tired now. Kids are watching me as I write; maybe I'll sketch them.

OK, enough of him. I spent an entire day with Mrs. Mwenefumbo at her house, the one they were building when we left twenty-seven years ago (her husband was not there, but I found him the following ·

day). It's a beautiful home, and it was great to visit with her and find out what happened to all the people I knew. All the people I worked with, except one, have died of AIDS. I was afraid of that. She has lost three siblings to the disease, and her husband has lost two. The resources that have poured into that country now for HIV prevention and treatment are impressive. The smallest health centers have counseling and treatment programs. She retired as head nurse at the hospital ten years ago, but the family has many businesses; she started a bakery and a clinic for contraception counseling. This was unheard of in my day. It was illegal to even mention birth control. Now there is a billboard near Karonga that says, "VASECTOMY, FOR MEN WHO LOVE THEIR SPOUSE." No lie. Another, less funny, says; "CHILDREN BY CHOICE, NOT BY CHANCE." It was progress, and I was glad to see it. We always knew we were living there under a ridiculously repressive dictatorship, but we somehow adapted. To see the difference now was quite remarkable and I was enjoying it. I was wishing my old buddies were there with me; we could have had so much fun.

Je me souviens de ceux-là de mon passé. *(I remember those from my past.)*

I talked with Mr. Mwenefumbo before leaving Karonga. He's an incredible man. His hair, moustache, and eyebrows are all white now. Still very handsome, still the dimples, still the eyes twinkling. We talked about the mines, how upset he is about them, how he tried to stop them. He's worried about the environmental effects, the way the displaced people around here are being treated. They've found uranium and the Australians are the ones benefiting. It's making me think I need to learn more. He was so gracious and friendly. I am so glad I stopped to see him.

I was bowled over to see that Karonga has a museum now! There have been two huge archeological discoveries there. They've built a museum with funds from several different donors, but a German archeologist was the catalyst. A huge dinosaur bone was found, and the upper jaw of what is thought to be the earliest human. Quite the find, eh? I spent a morning at the museum. It's simple, but very well done, and I learned that the archeologists come back to the dig site every year for a month or so, and it's possible to stay at their camp and explore. I decided to do that. The camp is set in the hills thirteen kilometers away, and I had the museum curator call and tell them I'd be there the following night. There is a caretaker staying there and will cook for you, but you have to bring your own food. Before leaving Karonga, I went and toured the new hospital, walked to the huge market with cascades of colorful foods, and shopped for my meals for the next day. I bought greens (vegetables, not beer), tomatoes, rice, dried beans, sweet potatoes, avocado, onions, and eggs, all for about three dollars. It was a bit to carry, but I was up to it. I decided to forgo the beer, though; that would have been a bit too heavy. I stopped to buy some *sousa*, the small pieces of spicy beef on bicycle spokes that the kids cook over coals with a roasted green banana, and headed toward the camp.

I started hitchhiking, hoping to get a ride the first ten kilometers, but nothing came, and when the third bicycle stopped to ask if I wanted a lift, I got on it. These guys use bicycles like a taxi; the back rack is padded and one can sit sideways on it. It's cheap and efficient, but not really intended for long distance travel. I think he expected to take me only a short distance. I told him I wanted to go very far, but he didn't speak much English and didn't understand. I told him to go to the roadblock, but he didn't get it.

He said, "Airport?"

I said, "No! ROADBLOCK!" He stared at me blankly. "Never mind, just go." I said, and got on, straddling the seat and holding on for dear life. The pack and all my groceries made me very unbalanced and I'm sure very heavy for him to transport.

After about a mile, he said, "Ah sister, I am tired." I got off, gave him 120 Kwacha (about seventy cents), and started walking again.

Twenty meters later, another bike stopped. "Where are you going, my mother?"

"Roadblock, very far."

"200 Kwacha, get on."

I sat sideways, and went the next five miles on the back of his bike, rather enjoying the ride seated like this. I was much more balanced. I gave him 300 Kwacha. That guy worked his ass off. From the roadblock I walked about a mile to the turnoff to the camp. From there it was a three-kilometer walk into the hills and I wasn't quite sure which path to take.

I asked a man where it was and he said, "Malema camp? Ah! Mother! It is very far, you cannot walk." (This was not good news.)

I walked a little further and a woman on her way to church fell into step with me and asked where I was going. She said, "You are going to Malema camp? Oh! That's good! It is just near. Just go direct, past the school, it is just there, you can walk, sure." (This was good news.)

It wasn't long before my food started getting extremely heavy, and the sun was hot. It was late in the afternoon, and I began to get a little nervous. Hoards of kids started following me; they were cute at first but then got irritating. They were asking for money and pulling on my pack, and it was getting more and more obnoxious. The concept of personal space is still a few light-years away here. They said they knew where the camp was, though, so I kept walking along. One of them spoke English well; he was probably about twelve years old and seemed to be the leader of the pack. When I'd turn and tell the kids to stop touching me, he'd reinforce it in Chitumbuka, and they seemed to listen to him. We came across some older boys, who were taunting him, and they made me more nervous, but by now I had no choice but to keep going. I started thinking, this was a mistake, why didn't I rent a car, I had no idea what I was getting into, there was nothing even remotely resembling civilization as far as the eye could see. The sun was getting lower and this pack of kids easily could have overwhelmed me if they wanted to. They kept asking if they could carry my pack, and I kept saying, "No, I'm fine."

The leader said, "You're face is red, and you look tired. Let us help." He was right, but I wasn't about to hand over all my stuff to kids who could have outrun me with all my belongings. I was being paranoid. I was hot and tired and thirsty, and they just wanted to make some money, but at the time I wasn't seeing it that way.

We finally approached the camp, and my anxiety drained into the baked earth. It was Oz. Gorgeous. Sampson was expecting me, and quickly took my pack and bags. He brought the pack to a *tukul*, and the food to the cooking area. He spoke to the kids in Chitumbuka and they all waved, turned, and ran away. He explained that the camp had been set up ten years ago to house archeologists when they came for their digs. He stays full-time as caretaker, and they rent out the *tukuls* to visitors in between the digs. There were three round *tukuls* for sleeping; each had two twin beds with mosquito nets. There was a large thatched roof between two huge mango trees over the dining tables, solar-powered showers with loofah vines climbing over them, beautiful gardens all around; it was perfect. I was the solitary guest, settled in, showered, and rested while Sampson cooked dinner with the food I brought. It was the best meal I had had all year. I was astonished at the transformation of ingredients. I decided to stay two nights. I wanted to stay forever.

June 27–Friday morning—Malema camp
J'ai trouvé le camp. *(I found the camp.)*
It's incredible here! Best night's sleep I've had in months! Dinner last night was magnificent—sautéed vegetables with rice and avocado that was seasoned to perfection and melted in my mouth.

The next morning after my breakfast of eggs, sweet potatoes, grapefruit, and tea, Sampson and I walked along some trails near the camp on our way to the dig site, and he pointed out all the plants and trees used for medicinal purposes in traditional medicine. I was madly taking notes and pictures, as I've been really curious about what the local healers use here, and no one in Congo seems willing to share that information with me. Then we got to the dig site, and I thought, I have to bring my daughter, Rachael, here. She's an archeologist. It's beautifully laid out and there were fossils lying all over the place. What an idyllic site to come and dig for a month every year. I'm sure funding prevents them from coming more often, but I could just imagine what a hot find those bones were. This was the jaw site, not the dinosaur site, but still pretty cool, especially when you've got an archeologist in the family.

We walked back to the camp for lunch (I read and sketched, he cooked). Sampson told me there was a traditional dance competition between the villages that afternoon, and invited me to go along. After lunch we walked about three kilometers through gorgeous fields and woodlands, and sat under a huge cashew tree in a village where he was one of the chiefs. Women from all the neighboring villages arrived with boys to do the drumming, and we watched the show. These are women who used to be called *Mbumba,* who danced only for the president, but now they are free to dance whenever they want, so they make these little local competitions. I just happened to be lucky enough to stumble on one. There were a lot of drunken men around. Very drunk. But Sampson was sober, and a wonderful escort. His three wives were there, dancing, and he introduced me to all of them who seemed like the best of friends. I sat there thinking maybe this was the image that Mario had in his mind, everyone having fun together and sharing the guy. It was interesting watching the three of them dance. They did show off a bit when passing by him, as if to appear the most attractive. It was very interesting. The drumming was incredible, and I thought, I have to bring Matt (a drummer) here. Before each of the groups of drummers started, they lit a little grass fire and laid the drums around it to tighten up the skins. Then some drunken guy would fall over on the drums and they'd push him off, and he'd stumble over to bother someone else. It was astonishing that no one got burned to death. We stayed there for three hours or so, and late in the afternoon, Sampson said we should probably start walking back. What a beautiful walk, with the sun getting lower and the mountains all around us, and occasional glimpses of the lake in the distance. We stopped to visit a traditional healer, because he knew I was interested in healing arts, and then made our way back to camp. It was Friday night, and I gave him money to send Michael (another guy who works there) on a bike to buy beer for all of us while I showered. Refreshed, I relaxed with a beer while they made another great meal. We sat around a fire talking into the evening, and then I went to my *tukul* to read and sleep. I was wrong in Chilumba. Life can keep getting better.

The next morning I was served another great breakfast, and then we walked to some plantations where I could see how much they have diversified their plantings. They now have a good supply of food year-round. Chinese workers had been there and did an impressive job of teaching about rice cultivation. Now they grow rice and maize during the wet season and cassava during the dry season, and have different types of vegetables growing in a variety of soils. I was so impressed. They showed me a treadle pump that they use for irrigation, very simple technology, but very effective. It was fantastic! This two-day stay there with food, beer, and lodging cost less than twenty-five dollars. My cash was holding up quite well!

I left there mid-morning to find a ride to the base of the escarpment (the road that goes from the lakeshore up into the mountains), where I wanted to spend a night on the lake. I wanted to walk up the escarpment the next day so I could enjoy the views and take it slow. Then I planned to hitch a ride back to Mzuzu where Richard was expecting me Sunday night. Michael insisted on accompanying me back to the main road, and carrying my pack. I felt like such a princess, but he insisted. When we got to the main road, he stayed with me until the first car came by, which he flagged down and made sure it was safe for me to go with them (so sweet). It was a pickup truck with the head of the forestry department in Mzuzu, and it was a pleasant but squished ride the 100 kilometers to Chiweta where I wanted to spend the night. It was so crowded because they wouldn't let me sit in the back of the truck, and I wouldn't put my pack back there without me, so I had it jammed between the dashboard and me. Even though I had had incredible luck and good interactions with people, I didn't want to leave my pack unattended because I knew he'd pick up other people who'd sit in the back. Even though stealing isn't a personal affront here, it's very common. We had pleasant conversation about people we both knew (he knew Richard very well), current American politics (which he knew more about than me), and the changes in Malawi since independence. I was also very interested to hear about what the forestry plans were, as I could see acres and acres and acres had been deforested near Mzuzu. Some of the mountains were bald.

They dropped me at a local hotel on the beach where the driver told me he'd spent his honeymoon and I spent a relaxing afternoon sitting on the beach watching the fisherman in their dugouts, and buying some fish for dinner. The girl at the bar kept coming down to the sand to ask if I wanted anything, and again, they had plenty of alcohol, but no mixers, so I stuck with the greens.

※※≪≈8○8≈≫※※

Je m'assieds sur la plage et regarde les pêcheurs. *(I sit on the beach and watch the fishermen.)*

June 28—I'm tired now as I sit on the beach at Chiweta. Beautiful spot. The sun is moving behind the tree. It's breezy cool. Kids with fish walk by. The cook came down to the beach to ask what I wanted for supper. I told him I want fish and vegetables. He said, "Thank you, mother."

June 29, 2008
Beach at Chiweta. Sunrise Sunday morning. Kids watching me sketch, trying to get the rocks in the sunlight. Failing miserably, but it feels good to have something to do while waiting for breakfast. A wave came up and soaked the page and actually improved it. I slept great again last night. Read on the porch by the solar light for a while then tucked in and read by candlelight. Dinner was mediocre. Too much rice, not enough meat on the fish, but chambo is scarce right now.

⁂

Sunday morning I happily began the fifteen-kilometer walk to the top of the escarpment. Occasionally cars stopped and their inhabitants asked what on earth I was doing. Two Irish guys who looked like they'd just washed up on shore reeked of alcohol at ten a.m. and said they were heading in the wrong direction to give me a lift, but would I like a beer? When I was nearing the top, and could feel the bottom of my feet starting to burn and blister, I waved down a local bus and wedged myself into the throngs already on board. As I got into the bus, I heard a guy in the back say, *"Wakazi!"* which means "woman."

I turned around and said, *"Aiye, wakazi."* And the bus exploded in laughter. They all thought I was a guy before I got on, and didn't think I'd understand what he said. It was a satisfying moment.

The bus ended up breaking down about twenty miles before Mzuzu and it took a long time for another to come and collect us. I was getting nervous because I knew Richard was expecting me for dinner. It was getting dark by the time I arrived in the city; I ran from the bus to the mission with my pack, and was dripping with sweat by the time I arrived. I collapsed into the room where they were all gathered for their pre-dinner cocktails. It was sweet as they all ran around getting me a drink, helping me off with my pack, pulling up the chair for me. Richard rushed me off to the shower, as dinner MUST NOT BE LATE, and I spent the evening regaling them with stories. I loved having someone to tell my stories to, in English, who understand.

⁂

Je voyage seul. *(I travel alone.)*

I think being with Richard has brought back feelings of wishing I had an intact family again. I've been thinking at night about whether I'm meant to be alone from here on out. I don't know. I'm fine during the day, but I find myself at night wondering if I'll ever hold someone in my arms again. I'm trying to accept my situation the way it is. Trying to channel the energy I put into the relationship in other ways. Give it to people who need and appreciate it more. It is early morning and I am sitting in the grotto again looking for some of Mary's grace.

⁂

The next morning Richard took me to the bus station, because that was the day I had to be in Lilongwe to meet the guy from California who (I'd hoped) had my bank card. That was an interesting visit. This is a doctor who works with a friend from my Peace Corps days in Malawi. Through her, I learned that he would be there during my trip participating in a workshop on HIV. I had arranged for my card to be sent to him in California, and to meet up with him to collect it. I planned to talk with him for a bit, get my card, then head south where I thought I'd visit Club Makokola where we had our annual Peace Corps meetings on the lake. It was a small, nice resort back then; I had good memories of the place and wanted to check it out.

I found the place where he was staying, and it turns out he was part of a group of fundamentalist Christians who come to Malawi and work for a few weeks a year at an orphanage, but it took me a while to figure that out. He wasn't there when I arrived, so I spent a pleasant afternoon with his wife and some of the other women, waiting for him to get back from town. It was just pleasant chat; they were all from the southern US and seemed interested in my stories of the Congo, and I was enjoying myself. But slowly I started getting that sheep-like feeling of being brought in. I had already been invited to have dinner there and spend the night, and had already accepted when I started getting uncomfortable, but figured what the heck. It was only a night, and it was getting to be too late to travel any further anyway.

The doctor arrived, gave me my card (hooray!), and then we started talking, and I was feeling reeled-in with him, also. He started telling me how Catholics are not accepting of any other religion, it's written right there in some document he claims to have read, and I was thinking, whoa, there's the pot calling the kettle black.

I said, "Hmmm, funny. I've been Catholic all my life and I've never heard anything like that." The look of horror on his face seemed not to come from the fact that he may have just insulted me, but that I was Catholic! Like I was some kind of antichrist witch. I swear these people don't believe in evolution, based on the awkward looks I received when describing the archeological finds in Karonga. My God, that was a strange night. I declined the invitation to go to the orphanage to do "evening devotionals," since the planning I watched going into it beforehand was orchestrated as to have the most "effect." I have nothing against prayer. But not when it's specifically designed to brainwash or control people.

They said over and over, "You are welcomed to come with us."

I said, "I know that, thank you. But I'll stay here." (I had a thought to go see what they did, but didn't want to be associated with them.) When they all came back, they reported to the leader of the group what they accomplished that day, and one woman said she spent the afternoon entertaining "angels unawares." Knowing she spent the afternoon with me, I thought, oh that's sweet; she was calling me an angel. But then people were sort of nodding to her in this secret code way, and I realized she meant that I was some sort of pagan that needed saving. All these squeaky clean, cheery, smiley, Stepford-wives types nodding in agreement about some secret meaning. Very creepy. So weird. The next morning I sat through the morning songs and prayers, and even sang along with "Amazing Grace," which I think got them thinking I was starting to see the light, but when one of them started to tell us all "What Jesus meant to say," I had to bite my tongue to keep from laughing. Having spent this year seeing all the problems with communication between Europeans of equal intelligence and intention, based on language differences, I found that comment utterly absurd! To claim to know what Jesus *meant* to say, after thousands of years and God-only-knows how many translations is downright comical. I had an image of a frustrated Jesus saying, "C'mon, that's not what I meant to say!" But they were sincere in their good wishes for me, and before I set off, three of them said a prayer over me and seemed quite nice, and I was appreciative. No lie, it took five full minutes of praying over me. I felt well blessed and spiritually endowed and off I went.

Next leg, Mangochi. Got into Lilongwe, tried out the bank card, and it worked! Yeah! I had money! But by this time, I was rather enjoying traveling frugally and didn't have the desire to do anything extravagant. It took three local buses to get to Mangochi, which was further away than I remembered, and then I had to take a *matolo*, a truck that functions as a bus with people stacked in the back like cordwood. Guys buy these trucks, just like the guys buy the vans that are used as buses, and then have a private business transporting people. The advantage of the *matolo* is that it can take cargo, as well. I got a seat in the cab and told the driver I wanted to get off at Club Makokola, which was well before Monkey Bay. He obviously didn't understand or hear me, because later, when I went to take a picture of the setting sun out the windshield and we started talking about my camera and where I was heading, he slammed on the brakes and said, "You wanted to go to Club Mak? That was ten kilometers ago! Why didn't you say something?" I freaked and yelled, "TEN KILOMETERS AGO? LOOK AT THE SUN! WHAT AM I GOING TO DO NOW?" He told me to take one of the bike taxis back, and dumped me on the side of this dirt road, while about a hundred people in the back of the truck waved good-bye as he pulled away. Oh shit. The sunset was beautiful, and ordinarily I love that time of day, but there is a visceral response when you're traveling and it's starting to get dark, that every fiber of your body starts screaming, "FIND SHELTER."

After leaving me, the truck had stopped to tell a guy on a bike to go get me and take me to Club Mak. So this kid cycled up to me, pointed to the back rack and I hopped on. In the darkening evening I had a hair-raising ride on a loose gravel road on the back of a bike in the middle of nowhere. I had forgotten how isolated Club Mak was. And why was there no sign? This kid was peddling like crazy, and I wanted to be enjoying the ride more but I was afraid we'd crash so I just held on for dear life. A half hour later we were at the driveway of the hotel. I paid this kid three times what he asked for, walked through the gate, and thought, none of this looks familiar. The driveway was overflowing with bougainvillea. I walked by a GOLF COURSE, followed by a huge parking lot full of white SUVs, then a conference center, and by then it was pitch dark, and I was thinking,

"I don't belong here." I couldn't even find the reception desk. I had to ask three people where it was. I finally found it down an incredibly slippery polished hallway. I was covered in dirt and sweat, and there were lots of well-dressed people with American accents milling around. I asked the receptionist for a room, thinking this is going to cost a fortune, but at that point I didn't care.

She said, "Oh, I am sorry, we are full."

Now mind you, at every place I had stayed thus far, I was the only guest in the hotel. It never crossed my mind that there would not be a room. There had to be 200 rooms in this place now, and where was the lake, anyway? How could you not see a lake the size of the entire country? What did they do with the lake? OK, another moment of panic.

I said, "I'm sorry, but I just took three local buses, a truck, and a bike to get here, and it's pitch dark, and I have no where else to go. There must be someplace I could sleep here for the night; I don't care if it's in a housekeeping closet." I said this as if it were her problem not mine.

She looked at me, as if she didn't care, and said again, "Sorry, we are full." I thought if I could just find the lake maybe I could sleep on the beach. Well. Standing next to me was an angel named Rob (I knew because he was wearing a name tag that said "Rob, Loma Linda"), and he asked me what was going on. I started pouring out my predicament, and he told me that the place is full because they are having a big conference on HIV with people from Loma Linda, John's Hopkins, and Chapel Hill.

I was looking at him incredulously and said, "And you have a meeting in MALAWI?" (Isn't that a little inefficient?) Well, behind him was a woman named Jennifer, a sweet Asian American woman, who was way down low on the academia food chain, and Rob was her department head. He turned to her and said, "You have two beds in your room, don't you Jennifer? Can this woman spend the night? She needs a room."

Sweet Jennifer, said, "Uh, well, yes, um, sure, I suppose that would be OK. Sure, I'll take you there right now." (Poor thing, I'm sure she couldn't say no because I doubt she was paying for the room.) And I followed her while gushing out thanks and apologies for crashing, and said I wouldn't make a single sound and she'd never even know I was there, and on and on, but she was acting like it was my room and she was in my way. She was moving all her stuff, and I told her to stop, I'd just put my stuff in one little corner, and we were having a little subservient competition.

The room was fabulous! It was one of those $250 a night, plush towels, porch out to the lake (I knew it was around somewhere), beautiful tiled bathroom, the works kind of rooms. She had to go the business center and I desperately needed a shower, but there was only one key and I didn't want to put her out at all, so told her I'd shower, then find her at the business center, give her the key, then just eat and sit at the bar until she was ready to come back to the room. They were having a big banquet for the last night of the conference and she wasn't sure what time it would end, but I told her I'd just sit and wait. I was sure this place would have tonic to go with the gin.

I got cleaned up, brought her the key, got myself a drink, and walked around the place. It was ridiculous! Huge pool, huge beach (because the lake has receded so much) dotted with lounge chairs and thatched umbrellas, building after building laid out in a confusing way. The intimate little resort was lost in the maze of new oversized buildings that had a corporate, sanitized feel to them. I knew I wasn't staying more than one night even though the conference was ending and everyone was leaving the next day. I was starving, but I couldn't find a restaurant, so asked the bartender where to eat. He told me the restaurant wasn't open that night because of the banquet, so I could just eat there, but I told him I wasn't part of that group. He got one of the waiters to come help, and the waiter told me to go ahead and eat, and not worry about it. So I helped myself to the extravagant buffet, ordered another gin and tonic, sat and wrote in my journal, and tried to recover from the shock of what they had done to the place.

Jennifer had traveled extensively around the world, as well, so was completely sympathetic to me, and we ended up chatting in our beds until very late, like old college roommates. What a sweetheart she was. She was leaving at five a.m. and before she left she gave me her little packs of Kleenex, wet wipes, rubber bands and a couple of granola bars that she didn't want to carry home. She also told me to go eat at the breakfast buffet, because it was already paid for and she wasn't going to be there. We exchanged e-mail addresses and she left, and I had the place to myself. The only thing I had to pay for was my two gin and tonics. And so the evening frenzy balanced out.

After stuffing myself at the breakfast buffet, I waltzed by the woman at the desk who'd told me the place was full, handed her the key, said, "Thanks, it was a great night!" and headed to Cape Maclear which I had never seen and had heard was very beautiful.

Cape Maclear is not easy to get to. It's at the very base of the lake on the Mozambique side, and you have to cross over the mountains to get there. No buses, so it's *matolo* all the way. I started walking and waved to the cars that passed to hitch a ride. Several SUVs with two *mzungus* each passed by, but none stopped to pick me up. Assholes. I took a *matolo* into Monkey Bay, and saw that the *matolo* going to go to Cape Maclear only had a few people in it. I knew it would be hours before it was full, so told the driver I'd come back, and went to find the fisheries office where I'd heard an old friend from Karonga was working. I found the office, but my friend had moved to South Africa ten years earlier. The staff at the office showed me around, though, and I talked to them for a while about what was happening with the fish population. The lake is being fished out, which is no surprise, but it was interesting to hear what they were doing to limit the environmental damage. All the workers in the office had their faces in a computer, which made me laugh. Same scene, different office.

As I was leaving there, the truck was coming toward the office looking for me. It was full, and they were going to leave, but didn't want to leave without me. How sweet! Then I learned that they don't leave without everybody and everything they can possible cram on that truck. I climbed in the back and had a comfy seat on a sack of maize, and then every twenty meters, it seemed, we picked up someone else and their load. It was starting to have a *Grapes of Wrath* feel to the trip. By the time we actually set off for Cape Maclear, I'd lost count of the people piled on top of me. There was sugar cane, chickens, tons of maize, milk, and God knows what else back there. I wanted to take a picture, but couldn't move my arms. I'm assuming it was a pretty ride, but I was buried and couldn't see much. I could tell we were going uphill as we all got thrown together toward the back of the truck, then the opposite coming down the mountain, when all the babies got passed back so they wouldn't get crushed. You had to see it to believe it. Everyone was laughing and joking, and loved it when I said anything in Chichewa. It was fun. I never felt unsafe, actually. It seemed like an efficient way to travel, and I started wondering if we are really any safer back home. OK, yes, I know the benefits of seat belts. But really the problem is that there are too many cars on the road, and if we all piled in together, how much less safe would it really be? I know this was taking carpooling to the extreme, but I thought it was great.

Cape Maclear is an idyllic little village where there is an underwater national park. However, every inch of lakeshore is being gobbled up by a foreigner building a hotel. I found it both gorgeous and depressing. I found a room at an Irish-owned place, very simple rooms with one common bathroom, right on the lake. There were plenty of other places to stay, South-African owned, German-owned, Australian-owned, but those places were bigger and had fences around them and I had no desire to be fenced off like I am in Shamwana. There were kayaking companies and safari companies interspersed with villagers washing their dishes, laundry, and bodies on the beach. There are attempts by tourism entrepreneurs to get the locals to stop using the lake for their every water need by installing taps in the middle of the village. And I did see them being used, but there was still no end to the housekeeping activity on the beach. I found it entertaining, seeing toothbrushes sticking up out of the sand, with buckets of laundry next to them and the dishes from last night's dinner just under the shallowest part of the lake. Women scrubbed the pots with sand, then scrubbed their feet on a smooth stone before collecting all the dishes, putting them in a big basin, placing it on their heads, and gracefully walking home. Next to them were men hollowing out new canoes, mending fishing nets, or boiling fish over open fires before placing them on long bamboo racks to dry. The mix of activities was fascinating. There were dozens of men selling the same old woodcarvings, trying to say they'd carved them themselves, which was a joke. I don't know where all this stuff comes from now, but it is definitely mass-manufactured somewhere. All the same stuff, all next to each other. I wanted to say, "C'mon people! Diversify!" They were all drunk by noon, and were obnoxiously following me around, hounding me to buy something or (get this) let them take me out in their boat—for a very good price—to see the fish that you can't see from the shore. Oh yeah, there was a trip I wanted to sign up for. I told one of them (who wasn't too drunk) that I'm not a water person. I don't like boats. I like to stand on land and look at the water only. "Ah," he said, "you are like the hyena." Not sure what that meant.

Je suis une hyène. *(I am a hyena.)*

July 3, 2008—Cape Maclear Sunrise. I'm facing west now, completely

turned around. Karonga was due east. Last night, sunset was right in front
of me. I'm hungry. I want tea and breakfast. A woman to my right washes
her face in the lake. She's doing her evening dishes, washing her face, blows
her nose in the sand, I see her toothbrush sticking up out of the sand where
she stuck it as she varies her morning activities, morning hygiene and last
night's washing up, as my British friends call doing the dishes. Takes beach
sand to rub on the pots and plastic basins. A woman to the left of me gives
herself a little pedicure on the rock rubbing her feet with sand then rubbing
them on the rocks. It's chilly. I'm wearing my pagne, long sleeve T, polar
fleece, and flip-flops. I'm chilly and hungry. She's got soap, her dishes are
all soapy. A kid to my left now has dived into the lake and is covering himself
with suds. Kids to my right help her with the dishes now, squatting,
scrubbing, rinsing. The only section of this beach not full of activity is the
thirty meters or so in front of our little guesthouse, where I sit writing. Little
colorful signs at each end say "No vendors here," though I noticed that
didn't stop a few yesterday when I was sitting and reading. It's getting
lighter, ducks are swimming by; a man walks behind me looking for cigarette
butts. Several dugout canoes have paddled by. There are mountains behind us,
and the sun isn't over them yet. Way to my left I can see sunlight shining
on the boats.

Still July 3, lunchtime

Strange place this village. Remote, but accessible to Mzungus with
vehicles—being developed for a clientele that I can't imagine coming.
Walking the village, fish markets, dishwater and laundry, nsima in the water,
plastic in the water, national park here, somewhere a clinic too, upscale bars
on the water, repugnant to me. Here at Thomas's restaurant, Grocery/
Restaurant/ Bottlestore 24 hours. Kuche Kuche Mowa Watu Watu.
Taking the matolo early tomorrow. The class distinction, us and them, is
everywhere. I found some lake glass. I'm going to make myself something
beautiful with it. Gifts from the lake, from this country that has given me so
much. Just took off my long sleeve T, it's hot. The women next to me have
strappy tanks on, so I guess I can go sleeveless. Guy in the bar just gave

me the thumbs up. Guy at the next table wants to sell me crocodile bracelets. I told him, please don't kill the crocodiles. He said, no, no, he'd never kill a crocodile. Then he showed me a hippo tooth. Don't know. He's sitting there polishing the hippo tooth with sandpaper. I'm starving, where's my fish and salad? OK, here we go. Two beers, delicious fried fish, cabbage and tomato salad all for 500 kwacha. What's that, $3.50? Maybe less. Toss in the tip, OK, 600 kwacha, that's exactly $4. In 1980 it would have been $600. Now I'll go relax on the beach for the hottest part of the day.

※※◎※※

I think the most beautiful thing I saw on this entire trip was a group of fisherman, young boys, hauling in a net as the sun set. There were five boys sitting on the beach, one behind the other, pulling on a line and coiling it. About fifty meters away was another group doing the same thing. It took me a few minutes to realize that they were pulling in the same net. A kid in a small boat was paddling around disentangling the net when it got caught on something. Slowly and methodically they pulled and coiled and moved closer to each other. It looked like a well-orchestrated dance. This scene, with the sun setting into the lake, was magnificent. As the net drew closer to the shore, more and more villagers came down to watch. It seemed like they were catching dinner for everyone. Some people had bowls and baskets. Finally, they pulled the huge net onto the shore, and the villagers descended on it as if it were a competition and the person who could pick up the most fish wins. The little kids were pulling the smallest fish through the net, and putting them into small bowls, the adults were taking the larger fish. It seemed like a village ritual— graceful, productive, respectful of the lake and each other. I sat there, thankful for all the incredible experiences of this year, and thought, again, life just doesn't get better than this.

※※◎※※

Je fais partie d'une plus grande famille. *(I am part of a bigger family.)*
The night watchman sat with me on the beach later in the evening. He asked where I was from, why I was there, about DRC. I told him I was

worried about missing the early truck because I didn't have a watch. He said he'd wake me at five and he'd be sure to tell his friend to stop the matolo for me at six. I gave him my empty green bottle to get the deposit back. He said he might just keep the bottle. I told him I would love to bring my kids back here someday. It was very dark by then and the lanterns of the fishermen's dugouts were all over the lake. Stars in the sky, and stars on the water.

I had to start making my way back to Lusaka. I knew it was going to take a bit to get back there with my choice of local transportation. Similar *matolo* ride out of the village to Monkey Bay, but it left at six a.m. and wasn't as crowded, so I got to enjoy the view, which was breathtaking. I am so fortunate to be able to do this. Then it was a series of dusty *matolo* rides and crowded local buses to Salima where I had spent three months in training when we first arrived as volunteers. Then it was another bus to Lilongwe.

Je reprends mon voyage. *(I resume my journey.)*

Someone told me there was a bus to Lilongwe via Salima along the lake. I don't even remember there being a road along the lake before. That ended up being erroneous. A matolo was leaving for Salima (so he said) and a big group of us piled on. Dirt road, under construction all the way. Clay dust covering us. Boiled maize at one village stop. Babies on my lap. Everyone smiled at my Chichewa. The women smiled as if they liked me. They nodded when I tied a scarf around my head—the dust was making my hair stick straight up like it was full of hairspray. They told me to wipe my face. Wanted to know how far I was going. Noticed and smiled when the kids wanted to hold my hand and I took their hand in mine. I felt good in the back of that truck.

I had planned to spend another night in Lilongwe, but as our bus pulled in another bus was leaving for Mchinje on the Zambian boarder, so I took that as a sign to keep going. On that bus I met a man who lives in Chipata; he's from Trinidad originally, is married to a Zambian woman, and writes schoolbooks for Africans on farming, entrepreneurial skills, and community development. We had a good discussion about what it will take for things to change on this continent, and he had some good insights and ideas. He was just returning from three months in the States meeting with publishers. We shared a taxi to the border, and another one on the other side into Chipata. We dropped him at his house, and he told the driver not to leave me until I had gotten some cash from the bank machine and found a place to stay. He said he would have offered me a room at his house, but didn't think it would look too good after being away for three months to come home with a *mzungu* woman. I understood completely, told him not to worry, I wanted to be closer to the bus station anyway. The taxi driver took me to the bank and waited until I was safely back in the car with my money, then ended up going to three different places to get a room. Since the early buses are the most popular, everyone wants to stay close. I finally found a room in a place that had a local restaurant.

I ate in the restaurant with a group of Zambian policemen who'd come the day before to accompany some cargo (specifics not disclosed). One likeable officer told me I look no older than seventeen, after I described my living in Malawi many years ago, five kids yadda, yadda, yadda. He asked where my husband was, and I told him in the States. "He has no problem with you traveling for a year alone?" he asked.

"Nope. None at all. He just stays home and waits for me." I replied. There. Not technically an untruth. He does just stay home. And who knows if he waits for me, maybe he does.

I asked the receptionist to bring me a bucket of hot water, because I wanted a warm bath and the rooms only had cold water. I was caked in clay with my hair standing on end.

She asked incredulously, "Hot water? You want hot water? OK, I bring you some." Moments later she arrived at the room with a large green bucket full of boiling water. I mixed it with the cold and took a bucket bath as the Malawian clay went down the drain. I laid on the plastic covered mattress, looking at the TV locked in a cage, listening to blaring music pouring out of all the local bars, and didn't sleep much.

I was nervous about getting to the bus on time, and I didn't have a watch or alarm clock. I kept getting up to check the sky to see if it was getting light. When I heard the first rooster crow (which seemed to be about an hour after the music stopped), I got up, dressed, walked to the bus station, and got on the fullest bus, which miraculously left at six thirty a.m. back to Lusaka. There was an evangelical preacher walking up and down the aisle going on and on and on as we sat waiting to leave. It was painful to listen to, and I sat praying my own prayer that this guy would shut the hell up and get off the bus. That prayer was answered as we pulled out of town. The bus stopped, and he got off. Praise the Lord.

Maureen was away, so I got a motel room and walked around. The next morning I took a cab to the airport and flew back to DRC.

I was actually happy to come back. That shows you what a good vacation it was. Everyone in Shamwana seemed happy to see me. Gerardine is back from maternity leave, and Benson is back from his vacation. Kim, our new logistician is here, and she seems great, so things are functioning fairly smoothly. No epidemic at the moment. I only have six more weeks here, then five days in Lubumbashi before heading home, and it feels a little bittersweet. My big worry for the week was how to find time to write all this. But with the handy dandy memory stick, I could just sneak in whenever I had the chance at night, lunchtime, and early morning to write. Believe it or not by the length of this, I left a bunch out, but it was getting ridiculous. Maybe someday I'll fill in the corners. Did I already write that? It sounds familiar.

OK, that's it for this week. I'll save the local news for next week.

Love,
Linda

CHAPTER 13 ~ JULY

July 20, 2008
Sunday morning, Shamwana

Hi Everyone,

It's been really quiet here this week. We've only had one visitor, a French guy who's here working with an organization with the acronym of MAG, which is a group that goes around post-war areas removing unexploded ammunition. They've been sweeping Katanga district, and this guy got really sick this week. Since they live in tents and abandoned structures while they are working, he asked if he could stay with us until he felt better. In order to maintain our neutral status we have no affiliations with other organizations, therefore, no one is allowed to stay with us other than MSF-associated persons, but for some reason this guy got a special dispensation. There was some kind of illness going around, causing fever and vomiting, and this is the only place with some clean drinking water and relatively comfortable shelter. So far I have managed to avoid catching it, but Cindy and Kim were also sick with it this week. They seem to be fine now so I guess it wasn't terribly serious. It is scary to get sick here because there is no immediate way out. I've often thought that maybe MSF should only accept workers who've already had their appendix removed.

It's been quiet in maternity, so it has an eerie, calm-before-the-storm feeling. Gerardine is back from her maternity leave so it seems like another vacation here. Loenis says that all creatures living close to the earth are calm and quiet in the dry season. Most of the activity here has been of the positive and productive sort. Everyone is building a house. There are people making mud bricks everywhere, and there are lots of big kilns being constructed to fire them. Most people don't use the fired bricks to build their houses, though; those are used to build the schools and hospital and are sold for a better price.

I love how they make these kilns. After the mud bricks are dried in the sun, they are stacked in a way that leaves a space at the bottom for building a fire in four or five places. Then the rounded pyramid, which is about ten feet high and wide and five feet deep, is covered with mud and the fires are lit and kept going for several days. It's so efficient and simple. I think they are works of art. When building with the bricks they use the soil from the huge termite hills for mortar, which dries almost as hard as cement. The roofs are thatch, of course, and there is plenty of dried grass around for that. The supports for the roof are branches lashed together with palm fronds. It's lovely to watch them take shape. It's so green, so simple, and so functional. I love seeing these houses being built. It makes me feel like the people are putting down some roots again, and feel safe enough to make a permanent home. The difference between now and last September is remarkable. Lucile and I were considering that maybe the real benefit of us being here has just been being here. Maybe we are giving them enough sense of security to feel like they could establish themselves again, and our whole western idea of listing accomplishments shouldn't be a measure of success or failure. I'm glad I stayed here long enough to see this for myself. I hope it stays calm and peaceful. There's never going to be a chicken in every pot, but maybe they'll be spared being uprooted and tortured again. I hope so.

I added on another outreach trip this week to give some support to the *accoucheuse* out in Kampangwe, Mama Lisette. We are doing an overnight every Monday now, to try to improve the turnout at our Tuesday immunization clinics. Gerardine—with baby Linda—and I leave on Monday morning for one of the outer clinics and spend the day in the surrounding villages meeting with the chiefs and spreading the word that the immunizations will be done the following morning. Then we go to the health center and set up camp and spend the night. It has doubled our turnout, and I love the camping trip feel to the outing.

Last week in Kampangwe, there was a perfect example of how one tiny little detail can change the whole dynamic of a situation. It was right out of *The Tipping Point*. Kampangwe is a clinic that was used as a military base during the Mai Mai war. There are munitions cases all over the place and lots of bullet holes in the walls of the clinic. When I first arrived the place didn't even have a roof. Over the year, we've gotten the place functional, built latrines and waste pits (that now have to be redone since they collapsed during the rainy season), put on a roof, built some desks and chairs, and, most recently, put doors on the rooms. Everyone seemed to get along fine here in the past, but when we arrived last week, Mama Lisette wanted me to settle an argument between her and the pharmacist.

There is one water filter in the center for drinking water, and it stays in the pharmacy because that's where the people take their medication and they need water to swallow it. Well, now that there's a door with a lock on the pharmacy, Mama Lisette can't get to the water filter after five p.m. to give a laboring woman a drink if she wants one. The pharmacist claims now that it's *his* water filter, *his* key to the door, and the women are just shit out of luck at night. A month ago there was no door, and this wasn't a problem. Two weeks ago there was no lock on the door, and this wasn't a problem. They were both standing there with their arms crossed, refusing to budge on their stance. I was really proud of Mama Lisette for holding her ground, but the only way it could be resolved was for the expat (the only reason there is a water filter, door, lock, or any medication to swallow) to settle it. It took an hour of explaining that it was EVERYBODY'S water filter, and we had to find a solution to the problem. Either Mama Lisette gets the key at night (horrors no! key=control=power) or the pharmacist gets woken up and comes to the health center every time a woman wants a sip of water (actually considered for a few moments) or the water filter gets moved into the maternity room every night when the pharmacy is locked. Finally, after much discussion the pharmacist reluctantly agreed to the third option. Mama Lisette did the little "Ha! So there! I told you so!" response, and I was afraid that she might pay for that later.

So even though this was our week to vaccinate in Kisele, which we did on our Monday overnight, I went along on a water/sanitation trip to Kampangwe on Thursday and Friday just to make sure things were calm there and that Mama Lisette wasn't being punished. It gave me something to do since it's so quiet here in Shamwana. It was Loenis's first overnight, and Fabien decided to come along too; he hardly gets out of here at all, and since he's leaving in four weeks, he took advantage of the opportunity to see another clinic. It was a fun little excursion. I felt like the old pro, and it gave me a chance to see the kids again whom I dance with every time I go there.

It's a unique group of kids in this village. They are more energetic and engaging than in other places and I have become very, very fond of them. It helps that they treat me like some visiting rock star. As soon as the vehicle drives into the village this huge group of kids starts cheering and running toward the health center yelling, "*Mama Linda! Mama Linda!*" (More flattering than the standard and impersonal "*Mzungu! Mzungu!*") It's a riot. I feel if they were given half a chance at an education or some kind of intellectual stimulation, they could run this country. They are so eager to learn. A few of them speak a little French, and I brought out a children's book this time to read to them. We ended up just looking at the pictures of animals and saying the names in four different languages, but they were captivated for a long time. There are many aspects of living here I will miss.

It turned out that everyone was getting along just fine at the center. It's been quiet there too; the water filter is being moved nightly into the maternity room, and my work consisted of about thirty minutes total for the two days we were there. So I danced with the kids, walked around the surrounding villages with Willy and Joseph doing a census and checking on mosquito net usage, spent two hours at a CODESA meeting held on a windy spot under a mango tree, and daydreaming. Loenis was supervising the construction of two new waste pits. They are putting in cement footings and bricking the walls this time to keep them from collapsing. It's a new design he's trying. So we stood around and watched that for a while, got the male side of wedding planning from Fabien, and shared thoughts about the future of this place. It was nice. It was the first time that Fabien and Loenis had *fufu*, but we had guinea fowl to go along with it, so it was hardly roughing it. It was fun. And it was progress! Measurable progress! Guinea fowl was poultry, after all, and we found them in the village, alive, healthy, and for sale. The rats are for when you can't find anything else. I felt like I belonged.

This week will be taken up with hiring a new nurse-midwife for the hospital. There is no replacement for me as of yet (apparently French-speaking midwives are hard to come by, not that I considered myself French-speaking when I arrived here) so I hope we can get a Congolese nurse-midwife who is willing to work in this setting for a while. I'm hoping to find someone who comes from near here, and not from Lubumbashi, because all the staff we've hired from Lubumbashi will leave as soon as MSF does. I'd like to think we could find someone who will stay, but we'll see. The job posting went up more than a week ago, and I only got four letters. Cindy and Loenis got thirty-four for the Health Educator position. One of those was from Bienvenu, our cook. As Loenis pointed out, at least that would get him out of the kitchen. I think Bienvenu has realized that Lucile is not leaving Fabien for him, and he's lost all motivation. Hard to believe the meals could get worse, but they have. On Wednesday the midwifery applicants will have to take a test. Those that pass will have an interview, and then we'll make a choice by Friday.

Lucile and Fabien only have a short time left here. There are replacements for both of them coming the first of August. Lucile's replacement is a psychologist from Canada, and Fabien's is a Congolese doctor from Congo-Brazzaville. I'm bummed that there is no replacement for me. I don't like the idea of leaving here without someone to hand-over to. I cannot imagine having started here without an overlap with my predecessor, but that's out of my hands. And it does eliminate the what-if-they-like-her-more-than-me worry when one leaves, or the flip side, what-if-the-national-staff-doesn't-like-them worry. But of course, all that ruminating is meaningless. They got along without us before, and they will again.

I'm starting to think about my good-bye party. It won't be hard to find a goat these days. There are plenty of those around now, but the beer is still hard to get. I'd better start working on that. I'll also have to obsess about my good-bye speech for a while. I want all the *accoucheuses* from the outer clinics to come; they never get to do anything fun. I've given them the date and they are all excited. And everyone is putting in requests for my stuff (this is standard practice). Patrice, a driver, wants my daypack, Generose wants the canvas bag and about a thousand people want my little yellow French/English pocket dictionary (that's gonna cause a fight). I'd say twenty people have asked for my camera, to which I always reply, *"Oh non, non, non, c'est un cadeau de mon fils!"* (It's a gift from my son!). And Jean-Pierre was trying to cram his feet into my hiking boots, wicked step-sister style, to show me that they would fit him. I'm full of mixed emotions about leaving. Excited to be going home and seeing everyone, but nervous about being cold and lonely. Looking forward to hot showers with clean water, but knowing I'll miss the exotic feel of showering in the moonlight and appreciating how much effort went into getting the water up into that barrel. Working with people who make me feel like I'm not at work but collaborating with friends, but missing the excitement of making a joke in a foreign language and having everyone get it, while making do with almost nothing. The food, I am not going to miss. Five more weeks of canned peas, and I never ever want to see another can of mushrooms as long as I live. I stopped eating the corned beef months ago, so that's not an issue for me anymore. Loenis complains about it, but he doesn't want to go without meat. I don't consider it meat myself, or food for that matter, but he *is* Dutch.

Well, I'm cooking today, so I think I'll go forage. The garden reality is sinking in to Fabien and Kim, who had the same high hopes I did when I arrived, but not much will grow here. There is a little lettuce coming up that is not completely dead yet; I think I can eke out a small salad with a tablespoon each for everyone. The papayas are ripening nicely, though. Beer's gone, wine never came, and the local rice wine is not drinkable, though Jimmy, one of our drivers, managed to choke it down this past week during working hours and got fired.

Hope everyone is enjoying the summer back home . . .

Love,
Linda

⊰⊱

Je prépare à partir. *(I prepare to leave.)*

July 23, 2008—Before noon. I'm hiding. A month from today is my good-bye party. I'm making plans for the weekend in New York when I get home, and that makes it seem very close. I am furious that Anders made an issue today about Gerardine taking her baby on our outreach trips. Now that is going to be forbidden and I am pissed off. It's quiet today. I have nothing to do and I hate trying to pretend I am busy when I am not. I want to avoid everyone, eat lunch early, and then read my French book. Mario is coming back with his wife! Juan comes next week, then Tony the week after that, so there will be diversion. No plane Friday, so no fresh food again.

A woman behind me is singing.

Lucile and Fabien only have two more weeks here. Cindy will be away then. Loenis leaves next week for his vacation.

I'm sitting here thinking how little I need to take home. I'm looking forward to leaving it all behind. Aside from my hiking boots that carried me up Kili, my GORE-TEX jacket and my jeans, I am going to give the rest of my stuff away. Why do we have so much stuff, anyway? A year of living with the utter basics has been refreshing. Stuff consumes us. At Kisele last *week when I used the latrine, I saw they had old prescriptions torn up and piled in a corner that they were using for toilet paper. Now there is recycling. I remember Margaret being worried about confidentiality because the prescriptions had people's names on them. Honestly, must have been a week lacking other worries. No one here can read anyway.*

July 27, 2008
Sunday morning, Shamwana

Hi Everyone,

I'm not sure where to start this week. I don't want to complain about the food anymore, I feel like I've beaten that dead horse as it is. But there was no plane on Monday or Friday; it's broken down and they are waiting for some part to get here from the US, so it might be a while before it gets back to Shamwana. So, again, nothing "fresh" arrived, and I won't get into the canned description, because it's getting rather repetitive, and since I've only got a few weeks left in the project, I don't care so much anymore. In fact I'm being a little anti-social and not showing up for meals. Except for Lucile and Fabien, the team is really bugging me again. It's like having college roommates again, leaving their dirty plates on the table, as well as their full ashtrays. Once the ashtrays are full, instead of emptying them, they put out their cigarettes in the gravel next to their chairs. It matters not whether it's outside under a tree, or in the nice little thatched-roof sitting area we had built adjacent to the eating area. In each of the camp chairs (the only place to sit other than the hammock), in the little pouch that is supposed to hold a drink, is now a crumpled cigarette pack and lighter, or a half-full cigarette pack and lighter, and since there is almost always a smoker sitting in one of the chairs, I've just given up. We (the three non-smokers) asked at the last expat meeting if the smokers would kindly clean up their butts, and of course they all agreed but don't do it. If someone is watching me, I take the cigarettes and lighters out of the pouches and throw them on the ground when I want to sit in one of the chairs. Then I snicker when I hear Cindy groping around in the dark saying, "Hey, what happened to my cigarettes?" (I actually saw Cindy light one cigarette from another one. I didn't think anyone had done that since the 1960s.) But if no one's around, I've started throwing all the half-full packs in the latrine, an activity I find immensely satisfying.

Cindy's not going on many of the outreach trips, because she can't smoke in the car, and sometimes we are in the car for over three hours at a time. Between that and the music they play (which doesn't bother me anymore), she hates going out. And she doesn't want to be forced to speak French, so she spends all her time in the office doing I don't know what. She won't go on an outreach trip without me. This annoys me. I was scolded for taking over the immunizations when it's supposedly an outreach job. I then told the outreach team they are more than welcome to have the job, so long as they actually DO it since I spent so much energy getting the program functioning, so I get annoyed when she makes up some excuse not to go. Really annoyed. Then when she comes along on the trips, she stays within six inches of me (except when she moves away to smoke her cigarette, knowing it would be her last one ever smoked if she lit it up near me) and fills syringes. Now during the measles crisis, when there were 300 people crowding the table, it was helpful to have a person sitting there, filling syringes. When we have forty kids over four hours, it's not a job requiring an extra person. But, whatever. She has, however, convinced Anders to get the vaccines here from Lubumbashi, and I do appreciate that. So there has been some good that has come out of her and Anders sitting and smoking together and drinking all of the beer and wine meant for everyone.

I'm stunned at the maturity level when it comes to moderation and restraint. I would rather have one beer a day for a month, than six beers a night for four days, knowing that no more is coming. I brought back a bottle of Malawi gin, fully planning to share it with everyone, but after watching the evening behavior for a couple of nights, I decided to keep it in my *tukul* and let them have the beer (which is now long gone). There's no tonic to mix with the gin, but each evening I squeeze two limes from our tree, add some water and a piece of sugar cane for a stirrer, add a little bit of gin, and sit by myself on the step of my *tukul* as the sun sets, and am quite content.

Everyone is commenting on my sudden change in social habits. Honestly, I tried. I tried to figure out which direction was downwind, tried finding a chair without a pack of cigarettes in the pouch, but I just wasn't enjoying myself, and the conversation wasn't so riveting that I was willing to put up with the smell, so I just have been avoiding the whole smoke-filled evening, and am either at the hospital, in my *tukul*, or in the office. I've been skipping what is laughingly called supper. Anders told Lucile that he thinks I'm suffering from "end of mission syndrome." That's when someone is conflicted about leaving, wants to go, but doesn't want to go. I asked Lucile, "Did you set him straight and say 'Actually it's because she hates your smoking'?"

Oh, which leads me to another story.

I told you how Gerardine brings baby Linda on the outreach trips with us, right? Well, Anders has decided that's not OK. "It's too dangerous." says he, with the same conviction one would use to describe playing with hand grenades. So, without discussing it with me, he told Gerardine she could no longer bring the baby when we do outreach. I was furious but didn't over-react. When I learned of this I quietly said to him that I appreciate his concern, but has he noticed that every African woman takes her breastfeeding baby with her wherever she goes? And it's not like there's a refrigerator for her to pump and store the milk, and I would have appreciated being consulted first before he made this decision, and I would like to ask Jurgen's opinion, etc, etc, etc. I was calm. I was proud of myself. Congratulated myself, even. This was when I was thinking that, of course, Jurgen would agree with me, that we can't expect Gerardine to leave her baby for two days at a time when she's only four months old! Jurgen is married to a Kenyan woman! Of course he would agree with me!

Well, he didn't. So that invoked a quick and quiet, "There's a response from Jurgen, you can read it" from Anders, as he ran by me out the door to smoke.

Jurgen's response was that it was MSF protocol not to allow family members in the vehicle (an insurance problem), so we had to be consistent and refuse to allow her to bring her baby. This illustrates a problem with having European standards in a third world setting. To me, anyway. Maybe I'm the only one who has a problem with this. So I wrote back to Jurgen with copies to the same people he copied the e-mail to me, which was a lot of people in Amsterdam. Anders was copied on this also, and I wrote that I was disappointed with the decision, but of course we would obey the rules. I added that I was not going to ask Gerardine to leave her baby, so she will not be coming on the outreach trips. This will then compromise the quality of the work we are doing, since the *accoucheuses* in the clinics don't even speak French. I continued, saying that at a time when we are trying to promote breastfeeding, and with the numbers of babies that die in Africa from diarrheal diseases from supplemental feedings, and with the lack of reliable potable water in Shamwana, and lack of refrigeration or any means to preserve breast milk, well, gee, I'm surprised that this decision wasn't made by Nestle. Then I added that I was surprised that Europeans were so much less progressive than Americans. They don't even want her bringing the baby to the hospital, but I'm not telling her she has to stop that, and I'll just be quiet about it. The baby sleeps in a little corner of the maternity room; and when she needs to eat she eats, and it's not a problem. But I can't hide her in the car. I never heard back from Jurgen, not that I expected to. Marie is the new nurse-midwife starting this week, and she will come along with me to the other clinics. "Too dangerous." Give me a break.

Well, it's a bit late. I ended up at the hospital all day. Juan, the Spanish surgeon who was here last November (or was it October?) arrived yesterday by road from Dubie. I am happy to have him here, especially since today we ended up in the operating room for a caesarean. Juan was great at showing Benson how to deliver the baby head-first instead of yanking on the arm or leg, something I had been trying to explain but, not being a surgeon, I really didn't have the clout. The woman had been in labor for two days, and the baby was quite compromised; we tried for two hours to resuscitate him, but he died, and I'm sort of down. Yesterday we picked up a woman traveling here by bike, in labor with her ninth baby (only two of them are still alive). It turned out she had twins; the first one was fine, but the second was born dead and that bummed me out too. So I guess I'll finish up and go to bed, and not subject you to more of my whining.

I need a haircut; my hair is driving me crazy. Cindy offered to cut it, but after watching her fill syringes I don't want her cutting my hair.

Oh, hey, Mario is coming back this week and rumor has it he's bringing his wife back with him—one of them, anyway. I wonder what this will mean. I can't wait to meet her. I'll let you know how that goes.

Love,
Linda

CHAPTER 14 ~ AUGUST

August 3, 2008
Sunday morning, Shamwana

Yikes, did I just write August?

I'm appreciating the party anxiety a little more these days. It's not easy to get drinks for seventy people to these parts. My idea of having Dennis put them little by little on the plane went down the tubes when the plane broke down. I even brought him back some Malawi gin from my vacation to grease the wheel a bit. That was a waste. They are adding an extra truck trip to bring supplies, but with the fuel diminishing, as well as food and supplies for the hospital, beer for a party is not a priority. Ugh. I hate lame parties. I may have to ask Mama Nasila to help me make some palm wine, though that's hardly a treat for the national staff. Another thought is hiring a guy to take a bike to the Tanzanian boarder to buy some Bingwa, the Tanzanian beer that I actually think is better than the watery stuff that comes in the cans here. And the bottles are recyclable. Hmm, I'll have to think about that. It'll cost a fortune, but it may be worth it. I'll have to see what the truck situation is this week and decide soon.

Lucile and Fabien are having the same problem, but I think they already got their beer approved for one of the trucks. Fabien made some wine from limes (I tasted it; it's disgusting). He's saving it for their party as well, so we're having a little competition. Oh, and get this. Gerardine and her husband told me they are having a traditional dress made for me to wear to my party. I AM DREADING THIS!!! God, I hope it's not one of the over-the-top shiny, polyester numbers with huge puffy sleeves. Because I am going to HAVE to wear it, you know. There is just not enough alcohol around here to get me through this. Between the dress and the speech, oh, I am so dreading this.

The dynamics of the team changed overnight. The replacement for Lucile, a Canadian guy named Tony, a psychologist in his fifties, is Mr. Super Healthy-runner, NON-SMOKER, intelligent, soft spoken, good listener, gift from the gods for my last few weeks. The new doctor is a guy from Congo-Brazzaville, sweet, soft-spoken, super athlete (he was amazing in the football game yesterday), NON-SMOKER, with surgical skills. His name is Noel. I love them both already. Loenis left yesterday for vacation, so that's one less chain smoker, and now Cindy and Anders look a little lonely and embarrassed over there smoking, away from the group who are sitting around the table, NOT SMOKING and having a good time. It's lovely. Just lovely. Instead of the conversation being centered on the group of smokers, the smokers go off by themselves, get their fix, and rejoin the social circle, as it should be. And that cigarette-pack-in-the-latrine trick has worked like a charm. I haven't seen a pack left around for days now. Don't know why it took so long to think of that.

Juan has been here the whole week and will go back to Dubie tomorrow. I adore him. He recently finished six months traveling in Africa, and is an amazing photographer as well as surgeon. He spent a month in Malawi and we had a good time talking about that country and comparing photos. His are way better than mine. He's back in Congo for six weeks and leaves soon to go back to his home in Spain. He's been busy all week doing surgical cases we've saved for him and we also had two obstetrical emergencies. It was a godsend to have him here to help with those. Great guy.

Two months ago, a woman came here complaining she had been pregnant for over a year, and the baby stopped growing but won't come out. Bizarre story. Fabien examined her and asked me to do a pelvic exam because he couldn't quite figure out what he was feeling. Ditto for Benson. I felt a mass in her abdomen, but could feel very well that her uterus was normal and empty. She didn't have any pain, but did have a weird abdominal mass. We knew at the time that Juan was coming, so decided to wait for him to open her up and see what was in there. The mass wasn't getting any bigger, so we waited. Well, Monday they opened her, and sure enough, there was an encapsulated fetal skeleton, which had been there for over a year. This was not your run-of-the-mill finding. None of us could believe it. There was a complete skeleton, surrounded by decomposing tissue, all in its own little pouch. The stench was overwhelming. No other organs were involved; it made nothing else necrotic. Juan left her abdomen open and packed it with gauze to make sure it stayed "clean." He sutured it closed on Thursday and she's recovering beautifully. Amazing.

Another woman in her forties (ancient for here) was complaining of being pregnant for two years and said that bones were coming out of her. Juan found a fetal skeleton in her, too. That one was embedded in her uterus, and was in fragments. Her body was trying to pass it, small pieces of bone at a time. Now honestly, how bizarre is this?

During the night Thursday they came to get me for an obstetrical emergency, a woman who had arrived here by bicycle from near Mitwaba, nearly 200 kilometers away. When I got over there and looked at the woman lying on the bed, I initially thought she had come in with a shoulder dystocia, and the head was delivered but the body wasn't. She was alive but unresponsive. As I approached the bed, I realized that it wasn't the head, it was her labia, so swollen they were unrecognizable. They were the size of a baby's head. Gerardine handed me the paper she arrived with. A local healer had written out a few details, saying he had given her oxytocin and an antispasmodic two days before. I did a vaginal exam, which, let me tell you, was not easy. I had no idea what I was feeling. Whatever part was presenting, I could barely reach it and it obviously wasn't coming out. She had no pulse, no blood pressure, obviously had a ruptured uterus, and didn't flinch when Diam, one of the nurses, miraculously got an IV in her. We sent for Benson and Juan, and carried her to the operating room.

During the day it's a huge project to do surgery here. At night it is infused with eeriness. The guard has to send someone running in the dark past the market to get the lab tech. Then he has to grope around with a flashlight to start the generator, while Benson fishes in the dark for keys to open the room. When there is no moon, getting a patient to the operating room is downright dangerous. We put her onto a stretcher, which two of us carry and maneuver through a narrow doorway, across the dirt path up the little cement ramp into the operating room, literally groping in the dark. Mama Generose tripped one night, and we actually dropped that woman. (Every time we do this I imagine OSHA watching us.) Now that most of the construction is finished it's a little less risky than it used to be, having the stones and bricks cleared away, but it's still dangerous. Just getting her onto the stretcher is hideous, trying to pick up a floppy pregnant woman in shock, whose limbs are so flaccid they sort of collapse away from you. Most of the time she's covered in blood and mud, or muddy blood. It's just hideous. Then we get into the operating room, put the stretcher down on the floor, and the nurse (in this case Diam) bends over and scoops her up by himself (like you'd carry a bride over the threshold) and plunks her on the operating table. You've got to see it to believe it. Then (I am still incredulous at this every time) they wash her abdomen with betadine, and she is lying in mud. Mud. Dirt mixed with betadine drips down the abdomen until she's lying in a pool of mud. I watch this and think every time, it's as if you dug her out of the earth. Then they drape her (and the mud) and start operating. Just ketamine for anesthesia, though I'm sure they could have done it this time without anything and she wouldn't have flinched. She was so close to being dead. Just as I was setting up stuff to receive the baby, bracing myself (I knew that it wasn't going to be pretty), Gerardine came running in to tell me that the heart rate of the baby of the other woman in labor was dropping, and the woman wouldn't push (surprise). This was a woman having her third baby, first two born dead. So I left the OR, groped my way back over to the maternity room, set up the vacuum extractor, and delivered a healthy, screaming baby. Yeah! I love that thing. While we were cleaning up from that, we could smell the other baby coming toward us. Benjamin (*steralizateur*) came in with the baby who had been dead for God knows how long, wrapped in a cloth. The smell was putrid. I uncovered him and could tell immediately what part of the baby was presenting. It was the face, impossible to deliver vaginally, and so horribly impacted into the pelvis that Juan put his finger through one of the eyes trying to get it out. That poor woman. Her previous two days must have been unimaginable. She was eighteen years old, now without a uterus, and it's still not certain if she'll survive. Juan said the uterus was so necrotic, he's afraid she'll die of sepsis.

Then, as word spread by bush telegraph that we've got a surgeon here, a nineteen-year-old woman arrived by bike with a huge bony tumor growing out of one of her knees. This thing is huge: an open, oozing tumor growing out of her knee. It's obviously been growing for a while, and she'd been lying on the ground just waiting to die when word got to her that maybe someone could help her here. Juan has to amputate the leg, but he doesn't want to do it here. The hospital in Dubie is bigger and they are better equipped to handle something like this, so yesterday she was loaded into one of our vehicles and sent to Dubie. It has been heart wrenching to see her lying on the ground in the tent, an enormous tumor consuming her, her toddler quietly sitting beside her, spending her days swatting the flies away.

Kim, our logistician, went with the vehicle to collect her for the trip to Dubie, and spent time later at the expat meeting crying and telling the medical team that we should have been doing more to help this woman. She kept repeating, "It was so awful to see her! She was in such pain! It was so hard to get her into the car! Why weren't any of you there?" I was trying to be sympathetic to Kim, but honestly, it irritated me. I felt like saying, "Well, welcome to our lives, honey" but that would have been crueler than necessary. She was traumatized. She's a logistician, not a medical person, and the boxes in the log stock don't groan when you move them. I guess I was expecting more of an empathetic, "God, I don't know how you guys do that all day," not a scolding. I thought back to Mario's comment.

Ah, Mario! He arrived this week with his wife! I haven't seen her yet, and probably won't unless I get invited over there again, since I doubt she'll be leaving the house. Word is she arrived in full burka, only her eyes showing, and it's just the talk of the village. I was at the hospital when they arrived in the Unimog, and we could hear everyone cheering. (Mario is a bit of a big man on campus; it's always an event when he shows up.) When Raphael was walking by a little while later, I asked if he had seen Mario's wife, and when he said he had, I asked *"Alors, elle est gentile? Elle est plus jeune que Mario, ou le même age?"* (And, is she nice? Is she younger than Mario or the same age?) I was a little surprised at my curiosity. I somehow saw her as some kind of commentary on me. Or competition? Or threat? What was the matter with me? I was trying to appear nonchalant even though I was dying to lay eyes on her.

Raphael said, (I'm only going to write this in English), "I don't know, I could only see her eyes because of her clothes, and she doesn't talk."

I'm like, "You are kidding me! She's in a burka?" Raphael had no idea what a burka was; there are no Muslim women around here. None. Zero. And I'm thinking, geez, talk about eclectic taste in women. She was quickly whisked away to his enclosure and has not emerged since.

Gerardine and Generose went over to greet her (curiosity was killing them, too), and it's like she is some kind of freak. They can't stop talking about it. When I went over to maternity last night for a problem, Generose was all wrapped up in her *pagne* with just her eyes showing, and when I walked in and said, *"Qu'est que c'est?"* (What is this?) she and Gerardine had to hold each other up they were laughing so hard. *"Vraiment! Les yeux! Seulement! C'est tout!"* (Truly! The eyes! Only! That's all!) They told me they had never seen a woman dressed like this, never. Not even in a picture. On one level I was thinking, "Boy, oh boy, are you guys un-PC" (although they were pretty funny), but when you think about how women here have their breasts out all over the place, how some older women in the villages don't wear tops at all, and how many of the women's heads are shaven as closely as the men's, it does seem utterly incomprehensible that someone in this heat would be so covered up. Hmm, I was planning to invite her to my party, but now I'm wondering if that would be inappropriate. Goodness, where's Emily Post when you need her? Does one invite the Muslim wife of one's suitor to an evening of drunken debauchery? Hmm. Thoughts anyone? Advice? Maybe I won't. I'm sure her French is better than mine, and I'm going to look like a complete clown in that dress. Plus I need a haircut. She'll look way better than me.

We've got some international visitors coming over the next couple of weeks. A couple of people from the the Canadian office are coming all the way to Shamwana to get an idea of what life is like in the field. They will be staying here from Friday afternoon until Monday morning. Seems a little inefficient to me. Do they not believe the reports we are forced to write? Have to come see if we are making all this up or something? Are they planning on helping over at the hospital to get a real feel for the place? Hopefully they talk to Kim first. I was telling Juan that this seemed a little wasteful to me. Why do people come to evaluate this place over a weekend? Why not come during the week so they can see the real work?

He said (imagine the Spanish accent), "I call them seagulls. You know seagulls? Yes. They come. They eat. They shit. They leave."

All the mango trees are in bloom. The trees are massive, and they are covered in blossoms that look like huge astilbes. A feast for the eyes.

I'm going to miss these Sunday musings.

Love you all,
Linda

Qui le l'un est choisi? *(Who is the one chosen?)*

August 8–I'm consumed by thoughts of survival. Are we just born more or less able to survive events? Why can people at home get septic from a splinter and women here have decomposing bodies contained within them for years and still survive? Darwinism is just so in your face here. It gives me hope that they will not be eliminated. They will continue on this earth as long as we will. There is a force bigger than humanity at work here. It is mind-

boggling and I must leave those thoughts alone and just look in front of me. It is the only way to get through a day here.

August 10, 2008
Sunday morning, Shamwana

Hi Everyone,

Oh, so much to tell this week. Last Sunday afternoon, Gerardine came to get me with the fabric for my dress, and it is beautiful. It's a black background with a floral print, almost like chintz, and I heaved a huge sigh of relief. I know it's expensive fabric and felt guilty about what they spent, but admit feeling more relieved than guilty. We walked together over to the grass house of a nurse who does sewing on the side. He took my measurements and said he'd take care of the rest, and in just two days, the finished dress (actually it's more like an ensemble) was delivered, and it's not bad! Simple lines, fits me perfectly, quite nice actually. I won't be wearing it to Lucile and Fabien's wedding, or fundraising galas in Bar Harbor, but it's not bad! Phew. I spent way too much energy worrying about that. When you see some of the pictures of the dresses around here, you'll understand.

Next on my list of anxieties is this marriage proposal that won't go away. Mario left last Saturday to move some drilling equipment to Dubie. I left on Monday for an overnight in Kishale, so I didn't get to talk to him until Wednesday. I asked him how his wife was getting along here, and he was so genuinely sad that I hadn't gone over to greet her that I felt terrible. I didn't know how this worked! I knew that Gerardine and Generose had gone over there, but I thought they had been invited. Well, it turns out that no, they were just doing the friendly woman thing as the local midwives and went to welcome the new woman to town. I was a huge disappointment in this respect, and he acted like I should have known better. And I should have. I should have asked what the polite thing to do was, but I was thinking that if it were me, I wouldn't want the woman my husband was chasing to come around being friendly. I would want to kill her. And him. I'm supposed to know how this polygamy thing works? So I told him I was sorry, I thought I needed to be invited. He told me that, no, she was waiting to meet me.

I said incredulously, "She knows about me?" I was still in the western mindset. The western monogamous mindset, that a man would never tell his wife that he was pursuing another woman, so this was shocking to me.

He said, "Yes, she knows about you, and she doesn't understand why you keep refusing me. She said, 'Mario, why would she not want you?' " And he said this with such sadness and such sincerity that I was stunned. I have completely insulted him. But he's not being cocky or obnoxious at all. He just doesn't understand it. And it makes him sad. He said every day that gets closer to my leaving, his heart is getting a little smaller.

I said, "But Mario, the same way you don't understand why I won't marry you, I can't understand how your wife can accept this. It's just a thing I cannot understand. Not at all." I said this shaking my head, walking around in little circles, while we were out behind the office where they were working on the Unimog, he in a grease monkey suit, covered in grease, still wearing the little hat that Muslims wear. But this made him laugh, and then I felt a little better.

We chatted about the upcoming outreach trips, and he said he'd be leaving for Dubie again for two weeks.

I said, "Oh, that's too bad, you'll miss my party." The shock on his face actually scared me a little bit.

He said, "Two weeks? You said you were leaving in September!" And I told him, well that's when my contract ends, but with the flights out of here (or lack thereof) and how long it takes to get home with all the debriefings in Lubumbashi, Amsterdam, and New York, it'll be well into September before I get home. I thought he was going to cry.

He started pacing around in circles, muttering, *"Deux semaine!"* (Two weeks!) shaking his head, like time was running out and he had to think of a new strategy.

Next day, after the morning meeting, he came over and invited me to come to his house for a meal that evening.

I said, "Of course, I'd love to!" and then proceeded to have a nervous breakdown. I eventually got distracted with whatever was going on that day. There was a fuel crisis (Kim thought that they sent us kerosene instead of diesel, which would mean that everything would have to stop, and there was much hoo-ha about that), so didn't think much more about it until late afternoon. I went for a run and thought to myself, "It's just one evening, just a couple of hours, maybe even less. You'll get through this, just sit and nod and smile, how bad can this be?" I came back to the base and begged Lucile to come with me.

She said, "Nope. Sorry. You're on your own." She was starting to feel like Bienvenu gave up too easily. She refused him once and he just accepted it. She said, "Boy, Bienvenu is rather lazy, isn't he? I think I am insulted."

Shower, dress, deep breath, and off I went. It was after six so had to have the guard walk me over there, the first humiliation. Technically he's supposed to wait outside for me, but I told him to leave and I'd call him on the radio when I wanted to go back.

Outside Mario's grass fence I said "*Odie!*" which is Swahili for "Can I come in?" or something like that. It's what you say when you approach to let the people know you are there. No doorbells (or doors for that matter), so this works well. You say it when you approach the river to warn people who are bathing that you are coming–very useful. And then from inside the fence they sang back, "*Karibu!*" which means, "You are welcome." And then it's OK to go in, which I did–so far, so good. Not bad at all. I entered and saw Mario sitting in one of his very nice wicker chairs wearing a white tank top and looking like a king on a throne. His little hat looked like a crown. There was an empty chair next to him and a little stool in between. Inside this enclosure, which I'd say is maybe sixty feet by eighty feet, are ducks, chickens, goats, cats, and people, all scurrying around seeming healthy and happy. It was quite nice.

Flowers were growing all around the perimeter of the fence; there are several small buildings in addition to the house, all nicely kept. One of them is a latrine, one a bathing area, it looks like one house for the servants, a nice house for the chickens, another one for the goats. It was wonderful. The last time I was over there it was dark and we were inside; this was the first time I'd sat outside and enjoyed the surroundings and taken it all in. The light was beautiful, just before sunset, a nice soft pink. It was rather enchanting. I was escorted to the empty chair next to Mario, and his wife came over to greet me. She was draped in an orange cloth and I couldn't even see her eyes. We're talking seriously draped. And she kept her face toward the ground. She greeted me, "*Karibu.*"

I said, "*Asanti sana.*" (Thank you very much.)

She laughed and said in French to Mario, "She can speak

Swahili?" and commenced scurrying around waiting on him hand and foot. I just sat there awkwardly watching her, as she poured him a cup of water from a thermos that was sitting right next to him, carefully placed it in his hand, and I thought she was going to feed it to him, but he managed to raise the cup to his lips on his own. Then she put some porridge-looking stuff in a cup and placed that carefully in his hands as well, and again, stopped just short of raising the spoon to his lips. These things had all been laid out on a little table that was right next to his chair. If he lowered his hand from the arm of the chair he would have knocked them off the table. It's as if they were placed there as props just waiting until I arrived so she could show me what wives do. It was fascinating.

I've got to explain a little bit about Mario. He is one of those people who have an aura about them that attracts people. Everyone respects him here. Other drivers come and go and, yes, people are happy to see them when they arrive, but there's something about Mario that when he shows up it's some sort of celebration. People come running from everywhere to greet him. And it's not that he is in any way cocky or conceited, but he has a charisma that commands respect that others don't seem to get around here. Even Benson, who has a much more prestigious job, doesn't have the kind of respect from the national staff that Mario does. Lucile said she overheard some of the national staff talking about his wife and how they would love to take the burka off to see what she looks like, and someone said, "But the person who did that would not have a life worth living if they did that to Mario." They didn't mean physical violence. It's his manner that makes people like and respect him. And he is very kind and helpful and generous to people. When I rode back from Dubie with him he was always stopping in the villages to give shoes and food and money to people he knew. So I've witnessed this over the past year, and I understand the allure, but this marital doting was something I have never, ever, ever seen before. I was starting to understand why he's so confused by my rejection. People just don't reject him and he doesn't understand what the problem is. And I have been expecting him to understand how absurd to me the thought of marrying him is, but these two mindsets are mutually exclusive.

So after feeding Mario his snack, she hurried over to the cooking area and brought over a plate of sugar cane that was peeled and cut into pieces. She placed it on a little stool in front of us, and then sat between us on another stool. She did all this activity bent over at the waist always facing the ground. Sitting on the stool, she was conspicuously lower than us. It made me feel extremely awkward.

The sugar cane was like an aperitif, and we took pieces and chewed on them and spit the pulp into a bowl she had placed on the ground for that purpose. This activity relieved some of the awkwardness and it became rather comfortable.

Mario said to her, "Linda thinks polygamy is a bad thing. She doesn't understand it."

Iyesha laughed and said, "Non, non, non, it's a very good thing!" And she was shaking her head and laughing, like how could anyone be so silly to not know this? And I was thinking, this is how we try to convince the village chiefs to encourage the people to vaccinate the kids! Then we started on an evening lesson on the virtues of polygamy.

I said, "But I'm Catholic and you are Muslim. Isn't that a problem? Catholics do not believe in polygamy." Mario scoffed like this was a minor detail to deal with.

He said, "That's not true! Abraham had two wives." (Not sure what his point was there.) They worked as a team, both in synch and agreement, and it was interesting to witness the love they clearly have for each other and how they wanted me to share it with them. Her French is very basic, so she was speaking mostly in Swahili and he was translating, but honestly, I liked her! I felt like we could be friends. Well, not like yuk-it-up friends on girls' night out, but friends. There was not even a hint of jealousy on her part. She wasn't threatened or intimidated. She was nothing but kind and welcoming and loving. It was fascinating. I actually had a tiny inkling of understanding how this works in their culture. And if marrying a Muslim tribal chief requires the kind of doting I was witnessing, I'm sure it's a relief to share the workload.

While the three of us were sitting together, there were several other people there (servants, younger brothers, etc.) a few meters away in the shadows watching us and listening to our conversation. It was like being in a play on stage. Iyesha cleared away the plate with the sugar cane and brought out a plate of sweet potatoes and a bowl of stewed duck (they eat way better than we do). We shared that between us, leaning forward, eating with our hands, and then got onto the subject of my departure.

Mario lamented about the fact that it was supposed to be September, and now it's August, and this is a big problem. He decided to let me know why (aside from the fact that he now has less time to change my mind). He told Iyesha to go get the gift she was making for me. She rose immediately, went into the house, and came back with a huge piece of yellow fabric folded up. As she unfolded it, two people come out of the shadows, as if on cue, to hold the edges. I nearly fell off my chair. I was praying that I had misunderstood.

I asked, "You didn't mean to say that this was a gift for me, did you? Did I get that wrong?" No, no, he reassured me that this was the gift he had asked her to make for me, and now she only had two weeks left to finish it. He had told her September, and he was looking at the ground, shaking his head, like a father trying to convince his son not to drop out of school. I was totally overwhelmed. My initial reaction was to exclaim, "I cannot accept a gift like this!" but I was too overwhelmed to know what to do. I just kept saying, "Oh my God, it's beautiful!" I almost started crying. It's probably a good thing that we have the language barrier because in English I think I would have said too much. Analyzed the situation too much. Explained too much. She was embroidering for me, in brightly colored threads, a huge bedspread. She was beaming with pride at the pattern she had drawn all over the cloth. (Well, I couldn't see her face actually beaming, but I could sense it). She had already finished the edges, but the whole center was drawn in pencil and still to finish. It was incredible. Incredible enough just as it is, but knowing how much I sew, and understanding the work that goes into something like this, and just the meaning of it, the symbolism (a bedspread?), just showed me how earnest he is about this. I am at a total loss. I just didn't know what to do. It was beautiful, and I want to accept it, but I didn't know what accepting it meant. Was I agreeing to something? I felt like I'd already offended them enough (now I felt like it was "them," not "him"), and I needed help here. I wanted to hug her, but do western women hug a Muslim woman so shielded from public her skin has never seen the light of day? I sat back down and put my face in my hands and said, "That is a very beautiful gift." Fortunately, Mario relieved the tension in the air by asking me if I sew like that, too? She put the work of art back in the house and sat between us again. By this time it was pitch dark and he had his (surprisingly bright) little light on the ground between them pointed at me so I could not see them and I felt I was on stage alone. The audience was in the background waiting to see the ending. Alas, sewing I can talk about! Anything done with a needle. I told them that, yes, I know how to sew like that, so I understand how much effort it takes, and appreciate it so much. I have sewing I am doing, too, and offered to bring it to show them. Mario brightened up considerably. It seemed like he was thinking, "Wow, maybe this will work!" The dynamic changed completely and everyone relaxed. It gave me an opening to leave, now that we had another date to exchange sewing ideas. I was about to call the guard, but Mario said, no, he and Iyesha would walk me back.

He said something to her in Swahili, and she jumped up and went into the house and brought out a shirt for him, which, she literally helped him don. I was biting my lip thinking, "Mother of God, could anyone see me doing that?" Or is it that I would be the head wife and she would be the servant wife? And what happens when he brings home a new playmate? Do I then drop to servant wife while new wife gets to sit in the throne? And is there some sort of schedule for who sleeps where and when? All questions I was dying to ask, but didn't want to appear too interested.

So the three of us left together, strolling along, me in the middle, and she told me how nice it is in Burundi, and I would really like it there. He said they have a house right on a lake and there is plenty of fish and I would never be hungry.

I thought, "Oh my God, this is so sweet. Talk about perseverance!" and said, "Oh, I am sure it is very nice there. Maybe someday I can come and visit." And instantly regretted saying that, because it was an expression that implied I might stay. (Though everything implies something, so who knows what's the right thing to say.) But the fact is I would love to go there and visit them. I'm not marrying him.

We arrived at the base, shook hands, made plans for me to visit the next day with my sewing, and I ran—ran!—to the computer to e-mail a friend traveling in Egypt to ask around for advice. I was at a total loss.

The last time I had Mario walk me home without a guard, Anders was drinking all the beer and didn't notice, but this time, being sober, he wasn't pleased with me that I didn't have the guard wait at Mario's. I played dumb and pretended I didn't know it was a rule. I said, "Oh, I'm sorry! I thought if the guard walked me over there, it was OK! Terribly sorry!" He bought it. Dipshit. I'm still mad at him about baby Linda. It is so ridiculous; Mario's house is not fifty yards away.

Friday, I was busy all day at the hospital, then when I was getting ready to visit Iyesha we got a problem patient in maternity and I couldn't leave. I ran to the base to tell Mario to explain why I couldn't make it, and to tell his wife I'd come Saturday morning.

I went on Saturday, and it was a very pleasant visit. She was really curious to learn how I was doing the appliqué on my quilt squares, and pulled out the bedspread to show me how she does the embroidery. I noticed she'd done a lot of work on it since Thursday. It was sweet, really. I thought she might let the scarf drop a bit with just me there, but no, I have not seen her face. When she moves her head, she holds the scarf over her face so it doesn't become displaced. It's amazing. I asked her if it was hard to leave her family to come here.

She said, "Oh yes, it was very difficult. Our house there is much nicer." She laughed at how primitive her living situation is now, though Mario did get a small generator, and they even have a small TV and can watch movies. I saw that, and pictured the three of us cuddled up in bed watching some movie dubbed in Swahili, and thought, I have GOT to make a movie out of this. She said it must be hard for me to only work on my sewing on the weekends because I have to work during the week. She wants to understand me too. This is a whole new realm of cultural awareness for me. I told her I'd try to come back this week sometime and we could sew together and talk and I sensed a smile under there somewhere. She must be lonely here. I felt badly that I didn't visit sooner. Fabien said to be careful, that now I am giving them hope (them!), but it felt right.

Last night was the party for Lucile and Fabien. It was a fun night. Mario came over to me to tell me he was very happy I had gone to visit his wife, and that she was happy too. She wasn't at the party. It was the usual celebration, but the mental health team made a dress for Lucile, and gave it to her AT the party and then she had to go change into it. She'd look good in a paper sack though, so she wasn't worried about it.

There was an argument before the party, because the mental health counselors wanted to give a speech, but the party committee wouldn't allow that, so there was some negotiating and bargaining going on. Fabien tried to intervene, but they all looked at him like he was insane so he removed himself and let them work it out. In the end, they did not gain approval, so they wrote a message and placed it on top of the gift they were giving Lucile. It was an awkward moment for her. There was plenty of drink for everyone, two goats (double party) and the usual dancing. I'm always on call so don't drink too much. Consequently I had the entire Sunday morning to myself while everyone else slept it off well into early afternoon. I usually leave the party when the drunkenness gets intolerable. At some point there's a line that gets crossed from funny drunk to obnoxious drunk. When people start dancing with lit cigarettes, I leave. Not sure what I'll do when it's my own party. Guess you'll find out in two weeks.

After finally having the airplane repaired, the country has run out of airplane fuel. The international flights had to leave luggage behind to be able to get here and back to Nairobi without refueling. That's reassuring, huh? There's some problem on the Tanzanian boarder with transporting the fuel. Hopefully that gets resolved soon. No plane again this week.

The new midwife started this week, and that's going well. I feel like I'm winding down.

Until the next time,

Love to all,
Linda

Mon coeur est lourd. *(My heart is heavy)*

I've gotten too involved. I didn't stay neutral and aloof and detached. I am terrified of leaving here. I don't want to say good-bye because I know there won't be a meet-again clause. Dear, sweet Mario. Strong man. Cares so much. I do wish there was a way to deepen the understanding of why I can't stay. And if I did stay, or could stay, how we might grow to be friends—man and woman—without being husband and wife. Is that possible here? Not sure. May be introducing a new concept, like running water.

August 17, 2008
Sunday morning, Shamwana

Hi Everyone,

This is not going to be an easy week. I am not looking forward to this week. There are the dreaded administrative chores, like evaluation of Gerardine and handover report to write, and writing in French takes me forever. I hate doing evaluations, and in this context, I hate it even more. Anders already did mine, and I gagged my way through that, so that's done. He leaves tomorrow for meetings in Lubumbashi, so there'll be one less smoker for my last week here. There's a check in the plus column. I've got to write a speech for the party next Saturday, and now that's stressing me. I usually just shoot from the hip when I do any public speaking, but I can't do that in French. So I have to write it all out and bring it over to Emmanuel. He will correct it and translate the beginning and ending into Kiluba. Then I have to plan for the little education session I am having for all the *accoucheuses* on Friday, to give them a legitimate reason to come to Shamwana so they can stay for the party on Saturday. I did this all to myself, as usual, only myself to blame for putting things off. Now it'll all have to be crammed into a day or two since I am out in the field for three of the days this week, and it will make the week go so fast. I am finding it really hard to think about not coming back here.

Then there are the sad puppy-dog faces everyone gives me and it's ripping my heart out. I am the only expat who has stayed in Shamwana for a year, and since they haven't found a replacement for me yet, everyone is begging me to stay (national staff, not the expat team, who I am sure will be happy to smoke in peace once I leave), until they find someone else. Papa Rigobert, a mental health counselor, told me this week he is now counting hours until I leave instead of days, because it's a bigger number and it makes it seem longer that way.

Mario was supposed to leave on Friday for Mutendeli where the drilling team is. He was hangdog all day Thursday muttering about missing the party. Thursday evening I went over to his house to say good-bye and give him and his wife a couple of gifts. I've been trying to figure out what to leave him with; nothing can compare with what Iyesha is making for me. When I got over there she was madly embroidering, sitting on a little stool with the bedspread in a large plastic basin on the ground to keep it out of the dirt. Mario wasn't there; he had gone to see what the wailing was about further off in the village. Other people sat around talking while she worked diligently sewing. Early evening in the village–I am going to miss it.

Guys from the market stopped in to say hi and chatted for a while. I love the stop-by visits. I love the outside life where people have time to stop and talk. I felt comfortable just sitting and visiting with everyone. A short time later Mario came back and told us a woman had died after giving birth in Kisele, and her family here had just gotten word of it. He didn't know the details. Everyone sat hushed for a few minutes, murmured words of grief and sadness for her family, and gradually moved on to other topics. It was getting dark, and Iyesha put the sewing in the house. Then she got busy preparing food for us. I felt like I should get up and help, and offered, but she laughed kindly like it was the most ridiculous thing she'd ever heard, which it was. *Mzungu* women sit with the men. I waited a while to give them the gifts I had brought.

She brought out a plate of bananas, one for each of us. There was a merchant from the market there, and Papa Rigobert, and it was just plain pleasant. Next came a plate of hard-boiled eggs, still warm, one for everyone. We peeled and ate those. Then she brought over a plate of sweet potatoes cooked with tomatoes. She put the plate on a little stool in the middle, and we all leaned forward and shared. I am going to miss this.

When we finished eating, and the bowl was passed for us to wash our hands, I pulled out the gifts I had brought. I gave Iyesha a jar of beads that Angelien had left with me. I thought maybe she could use them with some future embroidery project. Then I gave her some of the stationary I had brought (thinking erroneously that I would be able to handwrite letters). I had tied that up with a scarf to make it look like more of a gift than it was. Then I gave Mario one of the Swiss army knives I had brought, one that came in a case that he could attach to his belt. He loved it. We had an amusing fifteen minutes opening all the parts and explaining what they were used for. They loved those little hidden tweezers. The corkscrew was interesting to explain. I have no idea what they'll use that for, but I'm sure they'll find something to do with it. So that was nice; I felt good and happy. I gave them a postcard of Bar Harbor with my address on the back, and a photo of me on top of Kilimanjaro. This made the guy from the market jealous. I had tried waiting until he left to hand out the presents, but it was getting late and he was firmly planted, so I just went ahead with it.

Before I left to go back to the base, we talked about how nice it would be to start a school here for women to teach them how to sew and do some needlework they could sell. I told Iyesha she could easily have many women as students, and she should consider doing something like that. Then the guy from the market told me it would be better if I gave them money to build a proper school for women and girls (I knew that was coming). I told them that would be a really great thing, and I'd love to see that in Shamwana, and if they started something on their own, I would see about trying to send supplies. All that would be needed is a mail delivery system, and maybe a few roads.

On Friday Mario heard that the drill for the well had broken, so he won't go to Mutendeli until it's fixed. Don't know how long that will be, so maybe he'll be here for the party after all. We'll see. It's dragging out the good-bye process, but at least the talk of marriage has stopped.

Yesterday I was sitting in the shade picking the tiny hot peppers that grow by the zillions, thinking I could bring something home to share besides parasites. The bushes are dried up now, and I broke off some big branches and was sitting picking off the little peppers and putting them in a bowl, a fairly tedious job (I really don't want to write those evaluations). The women who fill the water barrels walked by me, put down their buckets, sat around me in a circle, and without a word, started helping pick the peppers and put them in the bowl. The one who was closest to me passed out branches to the others, and for the next fifteen minutes or so, we all silently sat picking *pili-pili*, and I thought, I am going to miss this.

The guard, whose job it is to supervise the water-filling process, saw the scene, picked up the buckets, filled the barrel himself, and then sat down to ask what I wanted all these peppers for. I told him I wanted to bring them back for my friends, a souvenir of Shamwana. He translated this to Kiluba for the women, and they wanted to know why I just don't pick them at home. This got translated. I told them, this kind doesn't grow where I live; it's too cold and the growing season is too short. Translation. They would have sat there captivated all day with stories about my home. I thought how great it would be to have a school for women here so they could have something else to do with their minds and hands besides filling up our shower water. For so long in this country the goal has just been survival. I wonder what it will take now to maybe move to a next step.

I've been thinking of what message I want to leave with the *accoucheuses*. I'll have two hours with them together, and I really don't care about how they do their charting, or if they know how to calculate an Apgar. I just don't care about that. I really just want them to stick up for the women. I'm afraid the C-section rate will skyrocket once I leave if there isn't an expat midwife to be a voice of reason when deciding when to do surgery. The Ministry of Health doctors love doing surgery. They can charge money for it, and it makes them seem very important. This is a huge problem. Juan spends most of his time explaining when surgery is necessary and when it's not. Teaching the surgical skills is only a small part of it. The midwives here don't stand up to the doctors. The women don't stand up to the men for one thing, but the hierarchical system is very well entrenched. And the way MSF functions, it reinforces that. There is very little, if any, critical thinking that goes on here. Everyone just follows orders.

I've tried to model that behavior, but who knows what sticks. I told them this week, "You know the women best. You have to be the ones to decide if you need the doctor here. Tell them not to come in unless you call them." And of course, they all agree with me, because that's what they do, they agree. But I doubt it will happen. This past week I was in the maternity room, and the MoH doctor, not knowing I was there, bounded in to get his hands in the laboring woman. He looked surprised when he saw me, and I said, "If we need you, we will call you. Thank you." And he turned and left, but I know that won't happen if I'm not there.

I said to Benson, "When I leave, you are going to protect the women from unnecessary surgery, right?"

He smiled, and said, "I am going to wait until you leave to tell you what your name means in Swahili."

I said, "OK." I am going to miss his gorgeous smile.

I've got everybody and his brother trying to sell me a goat this week. I need to buy two, to the tune of $140, and I have no idea how to judge what's a good goat. I asked Fugeance, a guy in the logistics department, to take care of it for me. There is no way I am adding goat negotiations to my list of things to do. This way when I am walking to the market and three guys start telling me about their goats I can just say, *"Parlez avec Fugeance."* (Speak with Fugeance.) I asked Fugeance to get a decent price and to ask Gericose to take the money out of my account and pay for them. Simple. I love it. Beer's still not here, though I did receive a promise from Lubumbashi that it would come somehow, so I'm going to trust it will.

OK. I've got to go write reports. My goal is to have it all done so next Sunday I can write to you for the last time, and then just hang out in the village.

Love, Linda

Je ne peux pas expliquer comment je me sens. *(I can't explain how I feel.)*

August 21–I'm paralyzed with anxiety and sadness. I can't even write.

August 24, 2008
Sunday morning, Shamwana

Hi Everyone,

Writing this letter is another in a long list of "lasts" this week. It's been a very emotional week. My party was last night and I can say with complete honesty that I am not hung over, and will be able to write in the cool morning hours like I have done every Sunday this year. I'm sure many people are, though, or will be when they emerge from their unconscious state many hours from now. Perfect.

I had intended to write every day this past week, because I knew it would be difficult to capture all the emotions in one sitting, but I just couldn't do it. It was a combination of exhaustion and anxiety and sadness. I was simply immobile in the evening and couldn't organize a thought.

The party was a complete and total blast. I'll run down the week first, and then get to the social column.

After I finished writing last Sunday, I wanted to spend the day walking around in the village and visiting. I tried to run, but it's so hot, and I felt like I was wasting time alone when I could be spending it with the people here. I decided to scrap the exercise for the week, and gave my running shoes to Mama Nasila so I wouldn't be tempted. The market has turned into an unpleasant place to go, because that guy who saw Mario's knife will not stop bugging me to give him one just like it. It's terrible, but I'm saying things like, "I don't have another one!" (Not true; I do and I am giving it to Papa Abel later today), and then he goes on and on like a little kid begging and begging, and the only way I can shut him up is to say something like, "OK, I will try (and I do emphasize the word try) to find one to send you." Which is a lie, and he knows it. I feel terrible, because there are plenty of other people I would rather give my stuff to, but it's the only way I can shake him.

Then, feeling terrible from that, I talk to another man who says, "You will forget all about us after you leave." Which I vehemently denied (obviously sincerely; I could never forget this place), and then he said, "But you will. Everybody does." And I knew exactly what he meant. The experience is so intense while we're here, but I know that once I am home, life will get in the way, and it's not the kind of remembering that he's talking about. So I walked to the river crying. I got distracted by the overwhelming beauty of the surroundings and, while wondering how to capture the scenery with words, I decided to walk with my camera on video, and felt like a two-year-old who stops crying when you give her a toy. I felt many times this week like I was cracking up.

Then I got a bunch of beautiful e-mails from home, and just felt so blessed to have all of you in my life, that I sat in front of the computer crying again, which made all the men on the team uncomfortable. They all scattered, and I had the office to myself, the realization of which made me stop crying. I am cracking up.

Sunday night I started thinking about how much more I could have done, how much more I could do if I stayed another year. Cindy and Noel keep asking me to tell them what I do so they'll have some idea when I leave since there is no replacement. Monday morning when I was packing up stuff for the overnight in Kisele, I panicked, thinking, oh shit, I have to do this and this and this and this and this, and it's a steady stream of "Mama Linda's!" asking for stuff. I grabbed Noel, whose English is about as good as my French, so we did a bit of "Franglais" as I was trying to explain how to do the weekly ordering for the drugs they have run out of in the pharmacy. It's a system that worked for me but I made it up, and explaining it to someone else made it seem unorganized. I felt guilty for not being more organized, and maybe some people aren't comfortable with my style. I felt like I was throwing him in the water and saying, "Just swim!" It's terrible. I feel awful.

Mama Marie, the new Congolese nurse-midwife we hired, is wonderful. She's coming on the outreach trips, since baby Linda has been banned, and she is really great. She is very organized and I feel good about leaving the immunization program with her. I spent the week repeating over and over to her and the outreach team, "Please make this a priority, no matter what. Do it for me. It's the only thing that will last." And they all reassured me that of course they will, and my mind went back to the guy at the market, and I thought it's not only me who just says what people want to hear. It's terrible, but I want to say something like, "I'll haunt you if you don't" (they are really superstitious). I stop short of being that inappropriate, though, when they do the sad face and say it's like a death that I am leaving, I have said jokingly, "I am leaving my spirit here, so I'll make sure you continue with the immunizations."

I'm so excited about how well it's working. We make two teams now, one stays at the clinic and one goes to an outer village as a mobile clinic. Monday we go to the surrounding villages, the chief collects the people and we sit under a tree on small pieces of wood while Willy and Joseph talk about the importance of immunization, and tell them to please bring the children and pregnant women the next day. I love it. I love arriving in the village, greeting the chief, and watching how, within twenty minutes or so, we've got a crowd surrounding us. I wanted to start meeting with the village matrons, the ones who do the homebirths, but they are afraid to identify themselves, as homebirths are technically illegal, so that will take more time. I put that in my hopes for the future here.

When we get back to the health center, we set up our cots before it gets dark, clean up, and sit around and talk (starving, waiting for one of the village women to kill and cook the chicken or guinea fowl we found somewhere). Oh, how a beer would fit into that scene, but I'm usually sipping the last of my filtered water that I stash in my daypack. Just doesn't cut it. This week while sitting around waiting for the evening meal, I wrote the introduction and ending of my speech in French, so Deo and Willy could translate it into Kiluba for me. That gave them a few laughs. It's not a written language, and trying to write it out phonetically was quite funny. That, and me trying to make my tongue do what it was supposed to do. I had second thoughts about the wisdom of trying to be this catchy (the French is hard enough), but I really wanted to do it. Then I started thinking, gee, this is a real act of faith. I have no idea if what they are telling me for a translation is accurate and conveys what I want to say. I could get up there and say something really stupid and insulting. Then I thought, no, Deo and Willy would never do that to me. And then I thought, hmmm, I've said those words before, and decided to recite the speech to Emmanuel later in the week and have him tell me what I said.

I repeated that speech at least a hundred times in my *tukul*. I visited Emmanuel and read it aloud to him. He was very impressed, and gave me back the exact translation that I wanted. I didn't once get through it without crying. I wrote e-mails to Angelien and Carila apologizing for not being more sympathetic when they were freaking out about their speeches, and about leaving, and about readjusting to life back home. At the time of their departures, I just wanted to get out of here and was kicking myself all over the place for signing up for a year. I remember thinking to myself, "What's the big deal? No one even listens to these things anyway; they just want to get drunk and dance." Oh, but now! Now that it's me! It's the State of the Union address. Terrible. At least I wrote and apologized. They both wrote back and said they didn't notice me being unsympathetic, but I'm still ashamed of myself.

The beer arrived, seventy-two large cans and thirty Cokes. I felt like that was a bit lame—there are so many people here—but that was all they could get on the plane because of the weight. Then, of course, it was talk all week of the party. One of the guards asked nervously how much beer was here, and I told him not too much, but I will *"augmenter un peu avec quel'que whisky"* (I'll add to it with a little whisky).

He said, *"Non! Pas un peu! Beaucoup!"* (NO! Not a little! A lot!) Fortunately someone came on a bike from Lubumbashi with a couple of cases of small bottles of whisky. I bought as many as I could (they sold out pretty quickly, let me tell you), kicking myself for not planning ahead and bringing back more myself last time I was there. Oh well. He gouged me, but he did spend five days with the bike getting it here, so whatever. He knew I was desperate.

And then there were the logistics of getting all the *accoucheuses* here for the little meeting I planned on Friday so they could stay over for the party. I felt like I had to have the little education session to validate the transportation, but don't think I wasn't kicking myself for adding that to my week of things to do. It's so stressful putting together something in French when half of them don't speak French and Gerardine has to translate. But I got through it, and told them how much I admired them, and how strong they were, and how I want them to be strong for other women, and make sure the immunization program continues. I told them that from the beginning of time it was the midwives who were the protectors of the children. It is even written in the bible. Mama Marie was crying so hard that I said I was going to find a way to come back here to see what progress has been made, so don't be too sad. I felt like total shit for saying that, because that is a ridiculous long shot, and she probably believes me and now I'll disappoint her. This is awful. I sat there and could think of a million things I could have done better if my French was better. Suddenly another year here didn't seem like such a bad idea.

Then I had to do Gerardine's evaluation, which took forever to write in French, and when I gave it to her I told her to feel free to correct the French. Completely ignoring the paper in her lap, she reached into her purse and pulled out a dress she had made for baby Linda to wear to the party that is exactly like mine. She held it up, beaming at me. Clearly this was *way* more important than the evaluation. It broke the tension, and we laughed hysterically. It really was a hoot. Nothing more was said about the evaluation, but we sat chatting like girlfriends about the party. I loved it.

Two visitors from Toronto arrived on Friday with Anders. They brought two bottles of vodka, a bottle of gin, and red wine. How lucky could I get? At least the expats didn't have to dip into the national staff's party stock. My stomach was so upset yesterday that I couldn't even finish drinking an ounce of the vodka mixed into some apple juice, but the others had no problem with the high-school-grade cocktails. There's nothing left this morning, so I don't expect to see people for a while. One of them said to me last night, "I've had more fun here in thirty-six hours than I've had for the last three years in Canada!" It WAS a great party, but I told her don't extrapolate this out to paint a picture of life here. You just hit it right.

When I first met them Friday afternoon, they were sitting with Anders, and I had just finished the meeting with the midwives. I started blubbering and crying and apologizing for being psychotic, and they were like, "No, no, no! This is just what we want to hear!" They asked me a million questions, but at the time I was thinking, I only have a few days left here; I don't want to start any new relationships. I was exhausted and nervous about the party and getting through the speech without crying, and at one point they asked me to describe something, and I said, "I am sorry. You are just going to have to buy the book."

Loenis is back from his vacation, so, together with Anders, the smoking resumed full force. It had been lovely this week sitting outside watching the moonrise without inhaling smoke, but Friday night I just didn't want to deal with it, so I went back to my little stoop and read over my speech and couldn't stop crying. Partly it was my own grieving process of saying good-bye, but when I would try to read the ending of my speech I would get overwhelmed by how utterly meager and basic my wishes for them were. In Kiluba I would say aloud to the walls of my *tukul –Nemusakila ndoe, kutupunzala, kutupuvita, bumibuyampe ne tukemone nenu, monka. Leza emwesele.* (My wish for you is to live without war, to live without hunger, and that someday we shall meet again. God bless you.) I always added silently to myself, "Please God, let this be true for them."

Tony came over to sit with me. He listened while I blubbered on about how much more I could have done, and how shitty I felt for telling people I would try to come back when I know the chance of that is close to zero, blah, blah, blah, waa, waa, waa. I appreciated his presence. I got some of it out of my system, and saying it out loud seemed to help. Then I woke up yesterday with such a terrible backache and upset stomach that I was too worried to be sad. (I swear I am buying one of those expensive memory foam mattresses the minute I get home.) I still had my end of mission report to write (in English, thank God), stuff to sort and pack, and of course the speech to practice. I started thinking I had malaria; I really felt like crap. I took a bunch of ibuprofen, which upset my stomach more, but at least the backache went away, and I slogged through the day. I know it was nerves, because today I feel fine, but yesterday was rough. When our guests cheerily came over to ask if I wanted to go for a walk, I told them, I am going to walk over to that hammock and sleep for a while, that's as far as I am going today. I got the report written. It's a lousy job; that's what I get for leaving it to the last minute, but to my knowledge, no one reads it anyway. Then I piled up all the stuff I want to give away, and decided to leave that activity for today.

I went to read the schedule for the party, which gets posted the morning of. It's hysterical. The party committee chooses a moderator, speaker, and a group of three to make sure the protocol is carried out and serves the food and drinks. It is such a hoot. Here it is:

1.. *De 17h30 á 18h00: Mise en place*
2.. *De 18h00 á 18h30: Installation de matériels*
3.. *De 19h00 á 19h15: Introduction par le modérateur*
4.. *De 19h15 á 19h30: Mots d'ouverture par le Coordinateur du projet,*
Anders
5.. *De 19h30 á 19h45: Sketch par les sage femmes de CS*

6.. *De 19h45 á 20h00: Lecture du mot d'au revoir par KISILE MIZOA Marie*
7.. *De 20h00 á 20h15: Remise du cadeau par KISIMBA Gerardine*
8.. *De 20h15 á 20h30: Mots de Maman LINDA ROBINSON*
9.. *De 20h30 á 20h40: Mots par le chef de groupement*
10.. *De 20h40 á 21h00: Musique par le discojocker MAYELE BADIMBANGA Oscar*
11.. *De 21h00 á 22h45: Repas et 1ére distribution de la boisson, Boissons*
12.. *De 22h45 á 23h30: Ambiance du staff MSF-H/Shamwana et autres et 2éme tour du boisson*
13.. *De 23h30 á 24h00: Prolongation!!!!!!!!vvvvwwwwwxxxxxyyyyy zzzheures*

I'll leave out the official stamps and approval signatures and other legal looking accoutrements, but this is the meat of the schedule. So I saw the midwives were planning a skit, and then realized why none of them had come around all day. They were practicing. I took a shower and ate some crackers and felt a little better; when I put on the dress, I actually felt pretty good. It didn't look bad. The other expats had settled into the new alcohol inventory, and I went to greet people. It calmed my nerves to walk around, and I couldn't put any alcohol into my stomach. I tried a little, but it didn't go down well. I was hoping that after I was done with the speech, I could get into it, but by then there was just too much going on, and I didn't want to stop dancing to drink.

I felt like the president. Everyone lined up to have a picture taken with me; it was a riot. (They do this with everyone who is leaving, not just me. I'm not that important.) Mario and his wife arrived; she had on a beautiful white embroidered burkha, and she danced! I was shocked! It was great! Oh my God, the speeches. They were beautiful. The skit. You had to see this. I was laughing too hard to take a video, but hopefully someone got some pictures.

The skit: Picture us all sitting in a huge circle in the dark with two fluorescent light bulbs hanging from wires across the circle. Beatrice was acting as a pregnant woman in labor at home in the village. She was sitting on vegetable oil containers in one corner. Her husband (our new health educator) had one leg bent up into his pant leg like an amputee, and he hobbled around with a stick. He was refusing to let her go to the hospital. Mama Joseline was yelling at him in Kiluba, scolding him for keeping his wife at home. Mama Astride joined her, as Beatrice gave birth and then collapsed in a dead faint. All the other midwives ran out, picked up Beatrice and carried her to the "hospital" where Gerardine was waiting, wearing a white lab coat and holding an IV. There were all sorts of flurries of activity, and then someone yelled, "HEMMORHAGIE POST PARTUM! APPELEZ MAMA LINDA!" Oh my God, it was so frikkin' hilarious. Joining the skit, I ran to the table, but I was laughing so hard I couldn't do anything. The whole point was to make it look like I run in and save the day. Jacques (the health educator from Dubie who's here for the week to train our new person, strategically planned to coincide with the party), was narrating this whole thing. It was performed in front of the two village chiefs as a little lesson for them to relay to the women of the village who dare to stay home to have their babies. Jacques is not one to miss an opportunity for health education. It was similar to the spectacle on nurses' day. I think they learn to do this in school or something.

Marie then read the speech that Benson wrote. She stood in the center of the circle, robed in a beautiful, colorful traditional dress. Oscar held a flashlight over her shoulder and shone it on the paper she held. In French she read:

Words of Good-bye, Linda Robinson
It is with joy and melancholy at this time that we find ourselves this evening at the grand event for the departure of "Mama Linda" as say all the children of the village when she passes through and also the staff of MSF Shamwana.
Her name "Linda" is a literal translation in our language of Swahili "Ku Linda" which means "to protect, to save, to secure, to defend, to support, to preserve, to safeguard."
For us it is very troubling that we are separated from this name that has such a huge significance. We have seen you protect our children at birth and our women during childbirth. We thank you, Mama Linda.
Unfortunately this loss in the midst of our project is felt all around the community of Shamwana, Kishale, Kisele, Monga, and Kampangwe. We are aware of your ability for work, your professional merits, your determination, and your devotion to others. This you have proven to us.

Linda, you have assisted the team with improving their knowledge with the classes for the midwives. With the same zeal you have enhanced the collaboration with the health centers that this collaboration will continue for the betterment of the project.

Linda, neither rain nor being stuck in the mud has prevented you from going to the different villages to help the health center teams with enlarging the vaccination program; for example Lenge and Kiango, where you were the first to organize strategies and move them forward in our health districts. For you, "It is better to prevent than cure." You never missed an opportunity to help the midwives with their work.

Linda, we have signs that you have contributed to install a reproductive health package in the health centers citing: Monga, Kishale, Kampangwe, Kisele, and especially Shamwana.

Linda, your theoretical knowledge and practical skills, together with your simplicity, will remain like a sign traced indelibly in our hearts. You have fully filled your role as the AFRICAN MOTHER!!!!

Maman Linda, with all your praiseworthy acts, the staff of MSF/Shamwana wishes you a good journey, a good future career with MSF and that All Powerful God bless you.

Safari njema Maman Linda Robinson
Good Journey

Tony, who was sitting beside me during the speech, said quietly, "Wow." Then Gerardine presented me with a huge piece of Malachite with a copper map of the Congo in relief on it. It's the standard gift for departing expats, but this one is slightly larger than the ones I've seen. In fact, it's huge. It weighs a ton. I stood in the small spotlight and received the gift. Next on the schedule was my speech, but Mario stopped that announcement by saying that his wife also had a gift to present to me. Iyesha then came forward and handed me their gift. I was completely overwhelmed. She couldn't finish what she was making for me, so they gave me the bedspread that she had embroidered for her and Mario. She took it off their bed. It is stunning. *Merci, Asanti Sana, Mwafuko,* none of the words of thanks could come close to what needed to be said for that. It is just amazing. I was at a loss to express what I wanted. I said the words of thanks in the three languages with the gift clutched to my chest and willed the message into their hearts. Then I did my speech. By this time I wasn't even worried about it anymore. I still felt like an observer watching outside myself. Oscar stood behind me with the flashlight, and I started:

Kekiolwai ne mwaiyai bonso. Welcome ladies and gentlemen. It gives me pleasure to have everyone gathered here this evening that we may celebrate together.

It is never easy to say good-bye when the distance between us will be so great. It is always easier when we know we will see each other again. For me, I would like to believe this is would be possible. Perhaps when I come back to see baby Linda receive her diploma as a midwife like her mother.

I would like to thank you for all the kind words you have given me during the last several weeks. It is difficult to leave, especially when I can finally understand everyone! When I arrived here, I could understand no one, not even the expats! Thank you for your patience with me and my struggles with the French.

To all the drivers and Oscar, I am sorry that it was so painful to listen to me on the radio. I know that your jobs were harder when I was speaking. For example, when during the cholera epidemic I announced "Mosquito" as "Mosquito net" and Choco laughed so hard he had to stop driving the vehicle.

I have said to you that I am leaving my spirit here. But in fact, I am taking your spirits with me. I have learned so much from you, and I believe that I am taking with me more than I am leaving behind.

At my home I will tell the story of the people of Congo who have a strength of body and spirit that I have never seen before.

For all the times when I have called you to help and you arrived with a big smile as if I was giving you a gift instead of more work, thank you.

For all the tender and compassionate care that I have seen you give to all who suffer, thank you.

For all the times you have listened to the ideas of others, and done your best to turn those ideas into a reality, even when the ideas change with each expat, thank you.

For the warm and friendly greetings that always made me so happy, even during the night, thank you.

You have shown that kindness and hard work can improve the lives of others. You have certainly improved mine by sharing yours with me. And for that, I thank you.

My wish for you is this: that you may live without war, that you

*may live without hunger, and that someday we shall meet again. God
bless you.*
God bless you.

I got through it, and delighted in hearing the gasps when I spoke
in Kiluba (quite flawlessly, I might add). It was great. Didn't cry. I
had done enough of that on Friday. Everyone clapped and I sat down
next to Mario and he said, "You did perfectly! I was frightened for
you! But you did perfectly!" Then the chief spoke, then the music,
then the dancing, and it was a blowout until I couldn't take anymore
at one a.m. and went to bed. The midwives were all still out there
dancing up a storm and passing around a whisky bottle that they kept
pulling out of one of their purses. I was so happy to see them having
fun. I didn't hear what time the music stopped, but it was still going
strong when I left.

Today I'm going around the village like Santa Claus passing out
all my stuff and, I'm sure, creating jealousy and hard feelings, but I'm
planning on being discreet. Before I went to bed last night, Gerardine
asked me if it would be easier if they all came to the base to get their
gifts. At first I said, sure, and then thought better of it, and said,
"Wait, no, I'll come to your houses."

She nodded and said, "Oh yes, agreed," knowing exactly what I
meant. This stuff cannot be divided up equally.

There is so much more, but I've got some processing to do. And I
still have people to visit, and a last walk to the river. I am realizing
that maybe I need to have an epilogue when I get back to Maine in
two weeks, because really, I'll have to tell you about what happens
tomorrow, and what the debriefings are like. It feels like another
good-bye to end the story here, and I'm not ready to let go yet. Thank
you all. Thank you for being so supportive to me over this year. There
is no way I could have done this without you. I love you all.

Linda

EPILOGUE

While writing my last letter home, the four *accoucheuses* from the outer clinics came to the base to say good-bye to me for the last time. I had prepared bags for each of them and had planned to visit them all later in the day, but they were leaving early—apparently walking home. Isaac, the guard, found me at my usual Sunday morning spot in the office and announced their arrival. I walked toward them with the leftover jovialness of a rowdy party–but they weren't smiling. They were so colorful. They sat side-by-side, like schoolgirls, in the guard's *tukul*. They were all crying. I told them I'd be right back and ran to get the bags I'd prepared for them. They were all labeled, one for each. I had divided up some of the stationary I'd brought, some beads, thread, needles, and some of my clothes: tank tops, T-shirts, and skirts. I knew they wouldn't wear the clothes, but knew they would either give them to other women or keep them for their own kids. I didn't care what happened to all this stuff, but I was careful to divide it up evenly. I thought they might compare it all and have it be a measure of my affection or respect for them. I loved them all though. I didn't know how to let them know that. I didn't think I could ask Isaac, the guard, to translate my thoughts into Kiluba, though I wasn't thinking of specifics about what to do. I merely felt my heart breaking. I felt like they really liked me. I felt like they really didn't want me to leave. Mama Marie cried the hardest. She clung to me. Then they all reached around and touched me as well. There was a huge bundle of words I wanted to say. They were wrapped in a *pagne*, tied together at the top, bulging out the sides, and jammed firmly in my chest.

We're all together in this! I am the same as you! I've only had more gifts in life, that's all. I've never gone without food. I've never had to watch anyone in my family die. I have had an education handed to me–handed to me! You've all done the same as I have, but with so many obstacles to surmount–mountains, canyons, floods, wars. Whatever made you survive this horror and continue to use the gifts you have in your hearts to save other women, I will never understand. Maybe it was the grace of God. I admire you so much! I couldn't do what you are doing! I love to see you so eager to learn. I wish I could give you everything you need to do your job with some small measure of comfort. A year of my life is nothing. And now that it is over, it seems less than nothing. This invisible cord that binds us together as midwives is permanently coiled around my heart and makes it stronger. I will find a way to come back. I feel now that I have to.

But all this was left unsaid. At the time I couldn't have found the words in English, never mind expressing these concepts in French. And Kiluba? Well, I don't even know if it is possible. I don't know if the words exist.

I felt so close to these women, this colorful pile that we then were. In reality, we'd hardly spoken to each other but there was a bond I couldn't explain. I was sad, but I didn't cry. I wanted to give them some of the strength that I had to spare, as if that was the only gift that really mattered. I didn't say this. I thought it hard. In my head I said, "Please be here when I come back. Keep going. You can, I know you can." I thought that hard. We all hugged one last time, then they filed away–a parade of color, bent at the shoulders, plastic grocery bags dangling. Papa Isaac opened the corrugated aluminum gate, and they filed out and didn't look back. I stood and watched them go, some piece of myself going with them, and I tried to grasp at some invisible trail of strength that they were leaving in their wake for me.

I went back to the office and wrote.

Later, I walked around the village doling out my belongings. It was tricky business. I had to pretend I was just on a stroll saying good-bye. I didn't want to be too obvious about the booty in my sack. I felt happiness and contentment. People were smiling and chatting. It had an air of Christmas afternoon when everyone is relaxing and is tiredly welcoming. The party had its lingering effects. I hadn't thought I'd brought that much stuff from home with me, but now passing it around, it seemed endless. Why had I brought so much stuff? Shirts here, pens there, my day-pack to Patrice, some postcards and a little visor to Freddy, toiletry bag and shoes to Beatrice, other clothes and toiletry bag to Gerardine, big canvas bag to Mama Generose with more sewing stuff. It was rather fun. Festive. And if it weren't for the hungover guest tagging along with me, would have been just as pleasant as could be. I tried to walk her to death in the heat and she finally gave up and went back to bed.

Late in the afternoon I was walking along a familiar path from the

airstrip and an old woman came out of her grass shelter and handed
me a pot she had made. She held it out with both her arms extended
and bowed her head a little. An amazing gift she had made for me
with gifts she had taken from the earth. She'd shaped the clay into a
smooth practical vessel, decorated the top with slashes made with a
knife created from old barrels, fired it in a hole in the ground, cooled
it until she could handle its strong, smooth shape, and handed it to
me. I looked at the pot with surprise and excitement. I loved it! I had
no idea how I was going to get it home, but I loved it! She smiled a
toothless smile when she saw my reaction. A gift for me from this
village elder: I accepted it and bowed a little. *"Mwafuko Mama.
Mwafuko."* I hugged the pot to my chest and rocked it a little–to show
her it was like a precious baby that I loved. *"Mwafuko Mama.
Mwafuko."* I said over and over. She smiled and waved as I turned to
walk back to the base just as the sun was setting behind me.

I spent the evening at Mario's. I had already given them the gifts I
had put aside for them a few days earlier, so just went to visit. Mario
wanted a family portrait with me included. It was pitch dark. No
moon dark. Pitch. They had little lanterns around the sitting area, but
when we all gathered to take the photo, nothing could be seen in the
viewer. Pitch. Gericose was there visiting with other men from the
village, and he tried to get us all in the shot. He'd snap, flash, and
look, and each time he'd cut someone out, or a head, or body. He kept
trying, we kept laughing and posing. Mario, Iyesha, me, his brother,
his brother's wife all posing in different styles and looking at the
pictures which were all a fraction of that whole. Heads cut off–oops!
Pose again, flash–oops! More amputations. More laughter, more
posing, more flashing. At some point, it seemed very late, I said my
good-byes and went back to the base. It didn't seem sad. It felt like
the good-byes at holidays when you know it will be at least a year
before the group gathers together again.

I was up very early on Monday. I started panicking about leaving.
The plane was coming for me at eleven. The outreach and the mental
health teams were leaving at seven a.m. Mario was leaving with them.
I had to say good-bye. I still had my gift to give Benson, who was
going out with the mental health team. I had chest pain. I couldn't
breathe. Panic ran through me.

I was in the office when I heard the Unimog start. I looked out the
office door and saw Mario across the field with the hood of the truck
open, checking the engine as he always does before a trip. In the

early, grey morning light his white cap stood out in the distance, like an accent in a watercolor painting. It was the coolest part of the day. The air is the cleanest. The village comes to life then. All of it was suddenly too much for me, and it came up–a big, fat fur ball of sadness, the scene before me an emotional Heimlich. It was the sadness of only knowing a tiny part of a cataclysmic situation, and accepting, despite my fantasy of retaining it somehow, that my lesson was done. Inadequate, incomplete, unexplainable, but done. Mario, who I believed really did love me, was leaving; I was leaving. When he returned to Shamwana from Dubie I would be gone. I wouldn't be back. How will I ever find him again? One more death to endure. One more sadness. When does it become too much, and you just give up?

I walked toward Mario to say good-bye and the tears started. It all bubbled up out of my chest and choking sobs poured out as I walked toward the truck getting ready for another day of work. I was crossing the thirty meters needed to say good-bye forever. Mario saw me and seemed horrified that I was crying. I gave him a hug. He hugged me quickly and said, "*Courage, Mama Linda.*" He told me to be strong. Be brave. I felt like he wanted to add, "Say good-bye like a grownup, for God's sake." This was not going well. My panic grew.

I walked back to the office (feeling a bit rebuffed) to say good-bye to the mental health team as they were getting ready to leave. I swallowed the sobs, but the tears kept running down my cheeks. This was a disaster. Benson arrived, and I ushered him into the office and handed him a little packet I had put together for him. Nothing really, just a token. I had so much I wanted to say to him. It was all stuck again in my chest.

He was terribly uncomfortable as I tried to talk with the tears pouring out. I didn't want to put him through this ridiculous exercise. I managed to say only, "I have so much respect for you."

He didn't look at me, but replied, "And I for you." And that was all. He took my little gift and walked out of the office. We didn't say good-bye.

I broke down again sobbing, pulled it together and said out loud, "My God! This is horrible!" and went outside to say good-bye to the outreach team and the drivers. There was one last anticlimactic good-bye to Mario as he got into the Unimog. He didn't seem sad; he seemed detached and distracted. His manner confused and scared me. It was seven a.m. and I said, "My God! I have four more hours of this. This is torture!" The Canadian visitors were leaving, as well. They left with promises of sending me all the pictures they took of the good-bye party. Somehow I didn't believe I'd ever see those.

I ran to my *tukul* to try to pull myself together.

At the last eight a.m. meeting before they leave, the departing expat usually says a few more words of good-bye. Anders looked at me and I just shook my head no. He didn't push it, but said a few more nice things about me in the way of thanks, I said feebly that I would write to everyone via Anders and he could read it to them later. I wasn't able to talk, and no one wanted to see me cry again, so it was just left awkwardly hanging. I thought, " OK, just three more hours."

I went over to the hospital. I took pictures of everyone at their respective posts: the guards, the sterilizers, receptionists, nurses, etc. It was a distraction and gave me something to do to fill the gap until the plane came. I was wearing my traveling clothes, my bags were packed and ready to load into the vehicle to go to the airfield, the good-byes were already said. It was just a matter of awkward waiting then to get on the plane for my last trip out. There is something very surreal and awkward about saying good-bye and then not leaving for a while. I felt like I wanted to just go hide in the hammock but didn't want to waste the last few minutes I would have with people I admired so much.

Then word came that the plane was going to be late. When I heard that I was horrified. I had all I could do to get through until eleven a.m. At this time it was about ten o'clock and I was thinking just one more hour and I could move on to the next phase of this drawn out good-bye. I had to meet in Lubumbashi with various people that afternoon as a debriefing, and that would be exhausting, as well. I wanted to get on with it.

Oscar came to give me the message that the plane was now scheduled for one o'clock. There was a problem with the fuel supply and they had to combine some flights. Oh, God.

I knew there weren't going to be many people at the airfield to see me off because so many of the teams were away for the day and wouldn't get back until at least four p.m. I felt a mixture of mild disappointment and relief about that. The huge good-byes at the plane are a bit dramatic and fun, but after being so emotional all day, I just wanted to slip away quietly and have this over with. Now I had two more hours to wait.

I went over to maternity and sat with the midwives and the other women. It was like a wake. We didn't talk much or laugh. Every once in a while we would say some small comment, but mostly we just looked at the floor and sat. There was no one in labor. They had finished their work for the day. We just sat. I felt drained. I had cried so much and there were still all these feelings I had wanted to share, but just couldn't get them out. So we just sat.

A while later, the guard came to tell us that the plane would be delayed even longer. No. This was not good. Even with the plane coming at one o'clock it was pushing it to get to Lubumbashi before five. It couldn't be delayed longer, I'd never get out. There was no other plane coming all week. I went back over to the base to find out what was going on. Oscar told me the plane would be coming at four. This had never happened before, not in my year there. The plane can't come at four; there is nowhere to go in one hour. He said we'd fly to Dubie for the night, and go to Lubumbashi very early in the morning. My eyes bugged out of my head. The night in Dubie? Where Mario is? After I just said my heart-wrenching good-bye to him?

I went into the office and sat down and cried again. Gericose said, "Mama Linda, why are you sad? You are leaving to go to your nice home and your children. We have to stay here."

I stopped dead in my tracks. How can I explain to him what I am feeling? How ridiculous I must look to be carrying on about leaving when, (sob) I have to go home to my comfortable job, (sniff) my SIX bedroom home, (sob) astronomical amounts of food, (waaaa) poor, poor me. This was my last chance to explain that I wanted to stay and try to help more, but I also needed to get home or I would go crazy. But then, I already appeared crazy. The comfort and abundance I had in store for me was part of my grief. I wanted to share that abundance, divide it all up evenly among them.

I don't need all that I have. No one at home will understand how I feel, either. I'll be stuck in this emotional limbo. I know how hard it will be to convey this experience to my friends and family even though they are intelligent, worldly people. It will be impossible to explain this love and affection I have for all of you here. I won't be able to fully describe your lives, your strengths, your sufferings, and your triumphs. Everyone at my comfortable home is busy. They won't sit for hours around a meager meal hanging on every word I say. They won't ask enough questions. Everyone is too busy doing . . . I don't know what! I can't help you the way I want to. This is frustrating me!

All this I wanted to say. All this I did not say. It was stuck like a huge glob of gum in my throat. I was choking on it, while appearing utterly ridiculous. What I managed to say was, "I wish I could take you all with me." Or more likely it came out as, "I wish you can all come, too." Gericose laughed and went back to his accounting book. I was nobody. I was a blip on the war-torn screen.

I went off to sit by myself for a while.

I tried to write and couldn't. I didn't want to unpack my journal that was tucked inside my pack. I was restless and spent. I tried to just sit with it and not fight the feelings. Not long afterward I felt like I was wasting precious time alone and went to walk around again. I talked with Jacques for a while. Took more pictures, tried to imagine a night in Dubie and what that was going to be like. Saw the irony in seeing Mario again after he had said to me that his dream was that he would one day see me again. Should I walk over to him and say, "Mario! Your dream has come true"? I don't think he was expecting the reunion to be twelve hours later. I think I may have chuckled.

As the hour of four approached and Oscar got word that the plane was indeed on its way, I saw that a few of the national staff started decorating the vehicles that were left at the base. There were only two there since all the outreach teams had gone off for the day. They had taken the windshield wipers and pulled them away from the windshield and placed little yellow wildflowers between the wiper blades. I cried again when I saw that. Palm fronds were attached to the antennae: marvelous works of art and ingenuity.

Then the other vehicles started returning. Oh Lord. I hadn't even thought of that! All the outreach teams were once again in front of me after the teary good-bye in the morning. I stood and waved, smiling this time, at the situation. *"Oui, c'est moi. Encore ici."* I said. (Yup, it's me. Still here.) At this point there was festivity in the air. The delayed plane meant that everyone got to go to the airstrip for the sendoff. I felt a sense of relief that they would be there. It is really very sweet when a lot of people are at the airfield, and after the plane takes off the pilot circles around and everyone rushes from the sidelines onto the field and waves as the plane passes overhead. I had been thinking I wouldn't get this sendoff, but here it was happening anyway.

As the plane sent word that it was leaving Dubie, a mere twenty minutes away, everyone clamored to get into the recently returned vehicles. I sat in the middle front seat of the most decorated Land

Cruiser. Freddy was the driver and was wearing the white sun visor I had given him. He handed me five letters in five envelopes, each with one of my children's names on it.

He said, "I wrote to your children."

I took the letters and tucked them in the bag on my lap, the bag that held the hand-made pot. *"Merci, Freddy. C'est trés gentile."* (Thank you Freddy. That is very nice.)

Oscar sat on the other side of me with a palm frond in his hand hanging out the window and slowly waving it up and down as we made a parade through the village. Villagers lined the dirt paths and waved good-bye. Little children did their familiar chant, *"Mama Linda!"* and I thought, good Lord, where else in the world can one feel so important after only one year? It was beautiful.

I was sobbing, waving, and muttering, "Oh dear, oh Lord." My cup was overflowing.

The airfield is a huge open landscape ringed with mountains in the far distance. It was a place where I had spent a good deal of time over the year, finding a bit of solitude, overwhelming beauty, and a release for frustrations and physical inertia. I had been there for welcoming and departing friends. Early on in my year there, though scared out of my mind, I was already dreading my day of departure.

There were hundreds of people there. Not only the national staff and the expat team (which would be about fifty people alone), but the plane's arrival is a weekly show for villagers, and since it was so late in the day the women were on their way for water and back from the fields. It was an unusually large crowd. The plane landed, which is always a rush laced with a tinge of danger and excitement. Being on the ground, watching the much-anticipated deliverer of necessities approach, feeling the ferocious wind it creates, seeing the dried grass flattened by it, well, it's a rush. Usually, I get a thrill when it arrives, a little jolt that makes me feel like I am living on the edge. This day as I saw the plane approaching, I thought, "No! Go back! Don't land here. I changed my mind! I'm staying!"

The plane landed and out hopped two pilots I had never seen before. This was unexpected. We all know the pilots quite well, and are familiar with their routine and personalities. And normally there is only one pilot. I was expecting Bruce. Rather, it was two young, tall strangers, one of them just learning the Air Serv routine. There was the usual unloading of supplies, the reloading of supplies and empty fuel barrels, the checking of passengers' names. I was the only one on the list. The only one getting on that plane with these two strangers who don't understand what it is like! This was all wrong! I expected sympathy and support, and now I just looked like a blubbering fool. I stalled, walking around saying good-bye to everyone again. I was avoiding the midwives; I didn't want it to be final. I wasn't crying; it was all too overwhelming. Sensory overload.

Au revoir, merci pour tout, au revoir! Merci, je vais vous manquer. (Good bye. Thank you for everything. I am going to miss you.) The pilots were getting impatient. They were standing by the open door of the plane waiting. We had to get going; we had to be on the ground by five p.m.

"I'm coming!" I called over to them. Just a few more good-byes as I walked closer to the plane. I felt a tap on my shoulder and turned around. It was Benson with his huge, gorgeous smile. I lost it. I leapt into his arms sobbing, saying over and over, *"Merci, Benson, merci."* I finally let go and turned, and there were Gerardine and Beatrice a step closer to the plane. I didn't move but just put my arms out and they both fell on me, crying. We didn't say anything at all, but stood locked together, the three of us crying. Hundreds of people were watching this. The pilots said something to Anders who then came to try to pry us apart. Somewhere in there I started to giggle at the absurdity of how we looked and what drama this departure was turning into. We separated without saying a word, and I got onto the plane and resumed crying my heart out. Anders said something to the pilot, and I assumed it was explaining the routine of circling over so the stay-behinds could make their circle on the airfield underneath the passing plane. The pilot nodded, and took his seat.

The co-pilot unwrapped a wad of toilet paper and turned around to hand it to me, and said, "You all set back there? Seat belt on?"

I said, "Yes. Sorry about all this. It's been a year here." I blew my nose, looked out the window, waved as the engine started and they did the checklist. I started crying again. I had chest pain. Chest pain! I thought I would die of all the emotion I couldn't express and thought, "My God, some people live their whole lives like this. How do they exist?"

The engines (are there more than one on that little plane?) revved and we turned and started moving. I do love takeoff, and was frantically waving as I zoomed by, everyone standing back now into the grass. We took off and started circling around to fly over the field again. I stopped crying and thought I might try to take a picture of them gathered in the shape of a heart underneath us waving up at me for one last time. But as we came back toward the field, the plane swooped down toward the ground and I thought we were going to crash. Moment of terror. I looked out the windshield and saw everyone arranging themselves on the field look over in horror at the plane that was now coming straight at them. They ran madly off the field as the pilot pulled up and dipped the wings of the plane to the left and then to the right, and then to the left again. I was about to scream, "What the hell are you doing?" when I realized he was making the plane wave good-bye. Jesus. He must have given them a freakin' heart attack. That's not how we usually do it! We were nearly to Dubie before I stopped shaking.

I thought to myself, how am I ever going to tell this story?

ACKNOWLEDGEMENTS

There are many people who encouraged me to make these letters into a book. I am eternally grateful to my readers and those who believed in this story and in me. It has been a long road of editing and refining and the end product would not be nearly as good without their input. My thanks go to Ron Beard, Tim Brooks, Colleen Conlan , Annie Dundon, Jane Dystel, John Gallagher, Barbara Gifford, Kathy Gilpatrick, Miriam Goderich, Judith Leipzig, Sandy Morse, John Overton, Steve Powell, Nina Ryan, Ruth Steinberg, Candice Stover, Jane Tawney and Anna Walker. Many others cheered me on and my heart is full of gratitude for you all.